HIPPOCRENE LANGUAGE STUDIES

D0555879

CANTONESE BASIC COURSE

HIPPOCRENE LANGUAGE STUDIES

CANTONESE BASIC COURSE

Elizabeth Boyle

HIPPOCRENE BOOKS
New York

First published in 1970 by Foreign Service Institute,
Washington, D.C.

Hippocrene paperback edition, 1995.

For information, address:
HIPPOCRENE BOOKS, INC.
171 Madison Avenue
New York, NY 10016

ISBN 0 7818 0289 X

Printed in the United States of America.

CANTONESE BASIC COURSE

TABLE OF CONTENTS

CANTONESE BASIC COURSE

INTRODUCTION

Scope of the text:

     This Cantonese Basic Course is a course in spoken Cantonese. It uses all the basic grammatical structures of the language and a vocabulary of approximately 950 words. The subject matter of the course deals with daily life in Hong Kong. The course was designed to be taught in an intensive language program of 25-30 class hours a week. Students are expected to spend additional time outside of class listening to tapes of the lessons. There are 30 lessons in the course, and the rate of progress in an intensive class is expected to be approximately 2 lessons per week, including time for review and testing. Each lesson contains five sections: I) a Basic Conversation to be memorized, II) Notes, III) Pattern Drills, structural drills of the type in which the teacher's cue is the stimulus for the students' response, IV) Conversations for Listening, a listening comprehension section, and V) Say it in Cantonese, English to Cantonese practice, much of it in conversational question-answer form, in which students activate what they have learned in the lesson. The early lessons in addition contain explanation and practice drills on pronunciation points, and some classroom phrases for the students to learn to respond to when used by the teacher.

Method of Instruction:

     Ideally, but perhaps not typically, instruction is by a team consisting of a native speaking Cantonese as instructor and a native speaking American as linguist, with the instructor teaching by voicing the Cantonese sentences of the text for the students to imitate and the linguist giving explanations in English when required. A good 80-90% of class time will then be spent with the native speaking instructor drilling the students in recitations, during which time the language in use is entirely Cantonese. Students will read the notes of each lesson outside of class, and questions they have on the text will be answered in English by the linguist during periods set aside for that purpose. Questions in English are not asked during drill sessions with the instructor. Psychologically this establishes the habit of using only Cantonese in classes with the instructor. Class time is concentrated on learning the language by imitation, repetition,

and transformation, according to spoken cues. The instructor speaks
at natural speed, and the students learn to comprehend and speak at
the same natural speed. If there is no linguist to explain students'
questions, special periods are set aside for students to ask questions
of the instructor. It is recommended that the rhythm of the drills not
be interrupted by questions in English.

ace:

    Although the course is projected as a 16 week course if studied
on an intensive program, the time plan is to be viewed as a rough
guide only. The number of students in the class, their language
learning aptitude, their amount of previous experience with related
languages, the amount of time available for outside study, the
excellence of the teacher--all these are variable factors which could
affect the pace of learning.

    An earlier version of the course was tested out on a pilot class
of five students during the summer of 1967, and the proposed pace of
two lessons a week seemed about right. However the students in that
course had been selected on the basis of a roughly the same language
aptitude score on the Modern Language Aptitude Test, and they had all
previously studied Mandarin Chinese, a closely related language.
Also, the present version incorporates pronunciation practices which
the earlier version did not have, and additional Conversations for
Listening and Say It in Cantonese sections.

    It is therefore suggested that the teacher rely on his own
judgment in regard to the pace of the lessons, rather than follow a
set pace rigidly. The text has been devised so that the crucial
grammatical structures are covered in the first 26 lessons. By
covering the first 26 lessons well students will gain a firm structural
control of the spoken language. We firmly feel that confident mastery
of the first 26 lessons is preferable to hesitant control of the entire
text, if a choice must be made between the two. The rule of thumb
should be that before going on to a new lesson students should be able
to recite the old lesson's Basic Conversation fluently and with
expression and should be able to do the Pattern Drills without looking
at the book and without marked hesitation.

CANTONESE BASIC COURSE

Objectives of the course:

The objectives of the course are to teach students to speak
Standard Cantonese in the locales where Cantonese is spoken, to speak
it fluently and grammatically, with acceptable pronunciation, within
the scope of topics of daily life. The course was not designed to
lay the groundwork for learning the written language. At the end
of the course students will be able to buy things; talk on the
telephone; ask and give directions; handle money; discuss events past,
present, and future; make comparisons; talk about themselves and their
families; tell time; order simple meals; talk with the landlord,
doctor, servant, bellboy, cabdriver, waiter, sales-clerk; discuss
what, when, where, why, who, how, how much. They will not be able
to discuss politics or their jobs or other topics of a specialized
nature.

Reliability of the material:

All the conversations and drills in this book were written by
native Cantonese speakers working under the direction of an American
linguist who specified which grammatical points to cover and what
situations were required. The design of the text--what to cover,
what sequence to use in introducing new material, what limits to set
on vocabulary--, the write-ups of structure notes, types and layouts
of pattern drills, and the contents of the English-to-Chinese
translation sections, were done by the American linguist.

What we have done to handle the problem of limited structures and
vocabulary is to plan the lessons so that certain topics and forms
don't come up until rather late in the course. The words 'yesterday,'
'today,' and 'tomorrow,' for example, don't occur until Lesson 16.
Meanwhile the student has built up the grammatical structure and
vocabulary to talk fluently on some subjects which don't involve
these expressions and the complexities of verb structures that are
involved with time-related sentences. For this reason the present
text is not appropriate for use of students whose needs are for just
a few phrases of Cantonese--it takes too long from that point of view
to get to some of the phrases which a tourist, for example, wants to
use right away. But the student who can study hard on an intensive
program for 4 months and cover at least 26 of the 30 lessons, will

then speak natural-sounding and grammatical Cantonese, and will be able
to cope with most daily life situations in the language.

ocedure:

Basic Conversation. Each lesson begins with a Basic Conversation
covering a daily life situation, organized around one or more grammatical points. The conversation is presented first in build-up form,
then in recapitulation.

The buildup is partly a device to isolate new words and phrases
for pronunciation and identification, partly a device to enable
students to gain smooth delivery and natural sentence rhythm by
starting with a small segment of a sentence then progressively adding
to it to build a full sentence.

The recommended procedure for the buildup is as follows: Students
open their books to the new lesson and look at the English equivalents
as the teacher voices the Cantonese. The teacher voices the first
item six times--three times for the students to listen only, three
times for them to repeat after the teacher. (The teacher may voice
the items more times, but it is recommended that he not do less.)
The teacher then moves on to the next item and repeats the same procedure. When the entire buildup has been performed this way, the
students close their books, and the teacher leads them through the
buildup again giving each item one time, the students this time
watching the teacher and imitating his behavior both vocal and
kinetic--his lip movements, facial expressions, and body gestures.
If the students have particular trouble with a portion of the buildup,
the teacher may give it a few more repetitions than the rest, but if
the difficulty persists, he drops it for the time being and marks
it to return to later. Repetitions under pressure are quite tension-
producing, and it works better to return to a difficult passage in a
more relaxed mood.

In the recapitulation section the conversation is repeated in
full sentence form. The teacher voices each sentence at least two
times, with pauses after each sentence for students to repeat. The
first goal is for the students to be able to say the conversation
after the teacher at natural speed and with natural sentence rhythm.

Details of pronunciation are spotlighted in another section--the first
goal for the conversation is sentence rhythm and natural speed.

The second goal is for the students to memorize the Basic Conversation, so they can say it independently without the teacher's
model to follow, maintaining natural speed and rhythm. Students will
find the tape recorder a valuable aid to memorizing. The tape recorder
is tireless in furnishing a model for students to imitate, and enables
them to procede at the pace best suited to their needs.

The purpose of memorizing the Basic Conversations is twofold.
Memorizing situational material gives students tip-of-the-tongue
command of useable Cantonese. Secondly, since the basic conversations
are organized on grammatical principles, students by memorizing the
conversations will be learning the grammatical framework of the
language, on which they can construct other sentences.

The second day on the lesson, when students have memorized the
conversation, it is recommended that the teacher have them act out the
conversational roles. Later, after moving on to a new lesson, the
teacher has them act out the Basic Conversation of an earlier lesson
as a form of review.

Pronunciation Practice:

In general, the Pronunciation Practices concentrate on giving
limited explanation and fuller practice drills on new sounds encountered in a lesson, plus comparison drills with sounds previously
learned and sometimes comparisons with American close counterparts.
Instead of giving many examples, using items unknown to the students
the pronunciation drills stick to examples from material they have
met in the Basic Conversation or Pattern Drills. The exception to
this is Lesson One, which presents an overview of all the tones,
consonant initials, and vocalic finals of the language, in addition
to giving an introduction to intonation and stress. Students who
absorb pronunciation best thouugh mimicking the model and who find
the linguistic description of sounds confusing or boring or both,
should concentrate on mimicking the model and skimp or skip the
explanations.

otes:

There are two kinds of Notes--Structure (grammar) Notes and
Culture Notes. These are to be read outside of class.

The structure notes summarize the structures used in the Basic
Conversations and practiced in the Pattern Drills, and are for those
students who want a general explanation of how the language works.
The students who absorb language structures better through learning
model sentences and drilling variations of the model can concentrate
on the Basic Conversations and Pattern Drills, and skimp on the
Structure Notes.

The Culture Notes comment on some Cantonese life patterns which
differ from our own.

attern Drills:

There are six kinds of Pattern Drills in <u>Cantonese Basic Course</u>.
The purpose of the drills is to make the vocabulary and sentence
structures sink in and become speech habits, so that the student
understands spoken Cantonese without having to translate mentally
and speaks fluently and grammatically at natural speed without awkward
hesitation and groping for words.

The Pattern Drills give students practice in structures and words
which have been introduced in the Basic Conversations. In addition,
there are other vocabulary items which appear first in the drill
sections. A plus sign marks each occurrence of a new word in this
section, and the English equivalent is given.

Each drill begins with an example giving a model of the teacher's
cue and the students' response. Then there follow 8 to 10 problems to
be done on this pattern. The teacher gives the cue, and the student
responds to the new cue following the pattern set in the example.
The response is thus predictable, controlled by the pattern and the
cue. In the book the cues are given in the left hand column and the
responses on the right, with the example above.

Students will find that going over the drills in a session with
the tape recorder before performing them in class with the teacher
aids their grasp of the material and smooths their delivery. In
class students look at their books to check the example for each drill,

to learn what their task is. Then they perform the drill with books
closed, relying on the pattern of the example sentence and the cues
provided to know what to say. A drill is mastered when the student
can respond to the cues promptly, smoothly, and without reference to
the book.

The types of drills follow:

1. Substitution Drills.

The teacher voices a pattern sentence, then voices a word or
phrase (called a cue) to be substituted in the original sentence. The
student notes the substitution cue and substitutes it in the appropriate
place to make a new sentence.

>   Example: T (for Teacher): Good morning, Mrs. Brown. /Jones/
>   S (for Student): Good morning, Mrs. Jones.

2. Expansion Drills.

There are two kinds of expansion drills. One could be called a
listen-and-add drill, using vocabulary and structures familiar to the
students. The teacher says a word or phrase and the students repeat
it. Then the teacher voices another word or phrase and the students
add that word to the original utterance, expanding it. The teacher
adds another cue, and the students incorporate it, and so on, making
each time a progressively longer utterance.

>   Example: T: Hat
>   S: Hat
>   T: Blue
>   S: Blue hat
>   T: Two
>   S: Two blue hats.
>   T: Buy
>   S: Buy two blue hats.

This type of expansion drill is handled a little differently if
it includes new vocabulary. In that case it is performed as a listen-
and-repeat drill, the students echoing the teacher.

>   Example: T: Hat
>   S: Hat
>   T: Blue hat

```
S:  Blue hat
T:  Two blue hats
S:  Two blue hats
```

In the second type of expansion drill the example sentence gives the model to follow and the students expand the subsequent cue sentences according to the pattern set by the example.

```
Example:  T:  I'm not Mrs. Lee.  /Chan/
          S:  I'm not Mrs. Lee--my name is Chan.
```

3. **Response Drills.**

The response drills involve 1) question stimulus and answer response, or 2) statement stimulus and statement response, or 3) statement stimulus and question response.

```
Ex. 1:  T:  Is your name Chan?  /Lee/
        S:  No, it's Lee.
Ex. 2:  T:  He speaks Cantonese.  /Mandarin/
        S:  He speaks Mandarin too.
Ex. 3:  T:  He speak Cantonese.  /Mandarin/
        S:  Does he speak Mandarin too?
```

4. **Transformation Drills.**

In transformation drills the students transform the grammatical form of the cue sentences from positive to negative to question, according to the pattern set in the example. A positive to negative transformation would be:

```
Ex:  T:  Her name is Lee.
     S:  Her name isn't Lee.
```

5. **Combining Drills.**

In combining drills the students make one long sentence from two short cue sentences, according to the pattern set in the example.

```
Ex:  T:  It's nine o'clock.
         We study Chinese.
     S:  We study Chinese at nine o'clock.
```

6. **Conversation Drills.**

In conversation drills students carry on a conversation following the pattern set by the example. The book or the teacher furnishes cues to vary the content while retaining the structure.

```
Ex:  A:  Good morning, Mrs. Lee.
     B:  Excuse me, I'm not Mrs. Lee.  My name is Chan.
     A:  Oh, excuse me, Miss Chan.
     B:  That's all right.
A.........Miss Smith.        A.  Good morning, Miss Smith.
B............Brown.          B.  Excuse me, I'm not Miss
                                 Smith, My name is Brown.

A..................          A:  Oh, excuse me, Miss Brown.
B..................          B:  That's all right.
```

Conversations for Listening.

The Conversations for Listening, recorded on tapes, give the students a chance to listen to further conversations using the vocabulary and sentence patterns of the lesson under study. These can be listened to outside of class and replayed in class, with the teacher then asking questions (in Cantonese of course) on the selections and the students answering. Usually several replays are needed before the students' comprehension of the conversation is complete. After they understand a conversation in its entirety, it is recommended that they play it through two or three more times, listening especially for the expressive elements of intonation and final particles, as these occur primarily in conversation and not as natural features of pattern sentences which the students practice in the drill sections.

After Lesson 10, there will be new vocabulary in the Conversations for Listening, to help the story along. These words and phrases are glossed in Cantonese and English at the foot of each conversation in the printed text, but students will not be held responsible for learning them.

Say It in Cantonese.

The Say It in Cantonese section gives situations and sentences in English, and students are to give Cantonese equivalents. This section is to be performed in class for the linguist or the teacher, though the students may prepare it beforehand if they like. Students should recognize that there is often more than one acceptable way to 'say it in Cantonese.'

Vocabulary Checklist.

At the end of each lesson is a vocabulary checklist, giving the new vocabulary for that lesson, the part of speech for each entry (noun, verb, etc.), and the English translation.

Suggestions for Further Practice.

The Say it in Cantonese section is the final working section of each lesson. After doing that section the teacher is encouraged to allow time for the students to carry on conversation practice using the material in the lesson. The teacher should be referee for this part, and make sure all students get a chance to participate. Some students are by nature more talkative than others, and the teacher must see to it, by asking a few questions of the more retiring students, that participation in free conversation is fairly evenly distributed and that the naturally talkative students don't do all the talking.

Repeating the dialogue of the Basic Conversations of earlier lessons is a good way to keep those vocabularies and sentences fresh in the students' minds. Also, selections from earlier dialogues can often be used during free conversation practice of the lesson under study.

System of Romanization Used.

The system of romanization used in the text is a modification of the Huang-Kok Yale romanization. It is described in detail in Lesson 1. In comparing Cantonese and Mandarin sentence structures the system of romanization used for the Mandarin is Yale romanization.

SYMBOLS USED IN THIS TEXT

adjective	QV	quod vide (Latin for 'which see')
adjective suffix	QW	question word
adverb	S	subject
auxiliary verb	sp	specifier
boundform, boundword	SPr	sentence prefix
conjunction	SP	subject-predicate sentence
co-verb	SVO	subject-verb-object sentence
exclamation; example	ss	sentence suffix
literally	sen.suf.	sentence suffix
Measure	sur	surname
moveable adverb	t	title
noun	TA	term of address
noun phrase	TW	timeword
number	v,V	verb
predicate	VO	verb-object construction
paired adverb	VP	verb phrase
paired conjunction	Vsuf	verb suffix
phrase	var	variant
phrase frame	(-)	= doesn't occur
placeword	[ ]	▪ 1. re pronunciation ▪ phonetic transcription.
preposition		2. in cumulative vocabulary list, following noun entries ▪ M for the N
pronoun		3. within the text of English gloss ▪ literal translation of the Cantonese term.

CLASSROOM PHRASES

The instructor will address you in Cantonese from the first day of
class. The following are some instructions which you should learn to
respond to. Look at your books while the instructor reads the phrases
the first time. Then close your books, and the teacher will give the
phrases several more times, using gestures to help you understand. Repeat
the phrases after him, mimicking his movements as well as his voice, to
help you absorb the rhythm and meaning.

1. Yìhgā néihdeih tèngjyuh ngóh
   góng.

   Now you (plu.) listen while I
   speak. (i.e., listen, but don't
   repeat.)

2. Yìhgā ngóh góng, néihdeih
   gànjyuh ngóh góng.

   Now I'll speak and you repeat
   after me.

3. Kámmàaih bún syù. or
   Kámmàaih dī syù.

   Close the book. or
   Close the books.

4. Dáhòi bún syù. or
   Dáhòi dī syù.

   Open the book. or
   Open the books.

5. Yìhgā yāt go yāt go góng.

   Now recite one by one.

6. Yātchàih góng.

   Recite all together. (i.e., in
   chorus)

7. Yìhgā yātchàih gànjyuh
   ngóh góng.

   Now all together repeat after me.

8. Joi góng yāt chi.

   Say it again.

9. Mhhóu tái syù.

   Don't look at your book(s).

1

I.   BASIC CONVERSATION

   A.   <u>Buildup</u>:

(At the beginning of class in the morning)

hohksāang	student

Hohksāang

Hòh	Ho, surname
Sàang	Mr.
Hòh Sàang	Mr. Ho
jóusàhn	"good morning"
Hòh Sàang, jóusàhn.	Good morning, Mr. Ho.
sīnsàang	teacher

Sīnsàang

Léih	Lee, surname
Táai	Mrs.
Léih Táai	Mrs. Lee
Léih Táai, jóusàhn.	Good morning, Mrs. Lee.

Hohksāang

deuimhjyuh	excuse me
ngóh	I
haih	am, is, are
mh-	not
mhhaih	am not, is not, are not
Ngóh mhhaih Léih Táai.	I'm not Mrs. Lee.
Deuimhjyuh, ngóh mhhaih Léih Táai.	Excuse me, I'm not Mrs. Lee.
sing	have the surname
Chàhn	Chan
Ngóh sing Chàhn.	My name is Chan.

Sīnsàang

síujé	Miss; unmarried woman
Chàhn Síujé	Miss Chan
A	Oh, Ah, a mild exclamation
A, deuimhjyuh, Chàhn Síujé.	Oh, excuse me, Miss Chan.

Hohksāang

Mhgányiu.	That's all right. <u>OR</u> It doesn't matter.

2

(At the end of the day, the students are leaving class.)

Hohksāang

Joigin.   Goodbye.

Sīnsàang

Joigin.   Goodbye.

B. Recapitulation:

(At the beginning of class in the morning:)

Hohksāang

Hòh Sàang, jóusàhn.   Good morning, Mr. Ho.

Sīnsàang

Lèih Táai, jóusàhn.   Good morning, Mrs. Lee.

Hohksāang

Deuimhjyuh, ngóh mhhaih Lèih Táai.   Excuse me, I'm not Mrs. Lee.
  Ngóh sing Chàhn.   My name is Chan.

Sīnsàang

A, deuimhjyuh Chàhn Síujé.   Oh, excuse me, Miss Chan.

Hohksāang

Mhgányiu.   That's all right.

(At the end of the day, the students are leaving class:)

Hohksāang

Joigin.   Goodbye.

Sīnsàang

Joigin.   Goodbye.

+ + + + + + + + + + + +

Introduction to Pronunciation:

A. Tones:

You have probably heard that Chinese languages are tone
languages, and know this means that sounds which are the same except
for rise and fall of the voice mean different things. This sometimes leads to confusion and/or merriment when a foreigner gets a
tone wrong in a phrase, and says 'lazy' when he means 'broken,'
'sugar' when he means 'soup,' 'ghost' when he means 'cupboard,'
and so on--and on and on.

In Cantonese there are seven tones, that is seven variations in voice pitch having the power to combine with an otherwise identical syllable to make seven different meanings. This is best illustrated by examples, which your teacher will read to you:

sì	思	think	(High falling tone)
sí	史	history	(High rising tone)
si	試	try	(Mid level tone)
sī	詩	poem	(High level tone)
sìh	時	time	(Low falling tone)
síh	市	a market	(Low rising tone)
sih	事	a matter; business	(Low level tone)

Below is a practice exercise on the seven tones. Close your books and concentrate on listening to the teacher or tape. Repeat loud and clear during the pause after each syllable or group of syllables.

(This practice section on the basic tones was prepared by Prof. James E. Dew.)

1. sì, sì____; sí sí____; si si____; sī sī____; sìh sìh____;
   síh síh____; sih sih____.

2. sì sì sì____; sí sí sí____; si si si sī____; sì sí si sī____;
   sìh síh sih____; sìh síh sih____.

3. sì sí____; sí sì____; sìh síh____; síh sìh____; si sih____;
   sì sih____.

4. sì sìh____; sí síh____; si sih____; sī síh____; sī si sih____;
   sī si sih____.

5. fàn fán fan____; fàn fán fan____; fàn fán fan fān____;
   fàhn fáhn fahn____; fàhn fáhn fahn____.

6. fàn fán____; fàhn fáhn____; fan fān fahn____; fān fan fahn____;
   fàn fàhn____; fán fáhn____; fàn fán fan fān____;
   fàhn fáhn fahn____.

7. bà bá ba____; bà bá ba____; màh máh mah____; màh máh mah____;
   bà bá ba màh máh mah_____.

8. bìn bín bin____; bìn bín bin____; bìn bín bin bīn____;
   mìhn míhn mihn____; mìhn míhn mihn____.

9. bīt bit miht____; bìn bín bin bit bīt____; mìhn míhn mihn
   miht____; bìn bín bin bit bīt____; mìhn míhn mihn miht____.

4

10. sǐ, fàn, bà, bīn____; sí fán bá bǐn____; si, fan, ba, bin____;
    sī, fān, bīn, bīt____; sìh, fàhn, màh, mìhn____; síh fáhn,
    máh, míhn____; sih, fahn, mah, mihn____; sǐ sí si sī,
    sìh síh sih____; bìn bín bin bit bīt, mìhn míhn mihn miht____.

Discussion of Tones:

There are seven tones in Standard Cantonese. Their designations,
together with examples of each tone, are:

1.	high level	sī	詩	fān	分
2.	high falling	sì	思	fàn	婚
3.	high rising	sí	史	fán	粉
4.	mid level	si	試	fan	訓
5.	low falling	sìh	時	fàhn	焚
6.	low rising	síh	市	fáhn	憤
7.	low level	sih	事	fahn	份

You will note that the tones have three contours--level, rising,
and falling.

There are three level tones: high level, mid level, and low
level.

    ex: hl: sī 詩
         ml: si 試
         ll: sih 事

There are two rising tones: high rising and low rising.

    ex: hr: sí 史
         lr: síh 市

There are two falling tones: high falling and low falling.

    ex: hf: sì 思
         lf: sìh 時

Following a chart devised by Y. R. Chao, we graph the tones of
Cantonese on a scale of one to five, thus:

high level	:55	sī	詩
mid level	:33	si	試
low level	:22	sih	事
high rising	:35	sí	史
low rising	:23	síh	市
high falling	:53	sì	思
low falling	:21	sìh	時

5

In present day Standard Cantonese as spoken in Hong Kong the high falling tone seems to be dying out. Many people do not have a high falling tone in their speech, and use high level tone in place of high falling. These people then have just six tones in their speech. In this book we mark seven tones, but your teacher may only have six, and the tapes accompanying the text include the speech of some speakers with only six tones. Copy what you hear. High falling and high level tones are given in the examples below. If you do not hear a difference, your teacher doesn't differentiate.

Ex: high-falling, high-level contrasts:

Ex:	1. sàam	three	三
	sāam	clothing	衫
	2. fàn	divide	分
	fān	minute	分
	3. Hòh Sàang	Mr. Ho	何生
	hohksāang	student	學生
	4. sí	think	思
	sǐ	poetry	詩

Tonal Spelling:

The system of tonal spelling we will use in this book is a modified form of the Huang-Kok Yale romanization. This system divides the tones into two groups, an upper register group and a lower register one. The lower register tones are marked by an <u>h</u> following the vowel of the syllable. This <u>h</u> is silent and simply indicates lower register. The upper register group doesn't have the <u>h</u>:

Ex: Upper register tones:	sí	詩
	sí	思
	sí	史
	si	試
Ex: Lower register:	sìh	時
	sìh	市
	sih	事

The rising, falling, and level contours of the tones are indicated by the presence or absence of diacritics over the vowel

6

of each syllable. The diacritics are: `, ´, ¯, representing
falling, rising, and level respectively.

> Ex: à   falling
>   á   rising
>   ā   level

The absence of a diacritic represents level tone.

> Ex: a

Using three diacritics and the low register symbol h, we spell
the seven tones thus:

ā	high level
a	mid level
ah	low level
à	high falling
àh	low falling
á	high rising
áh	low rising

The low register symbol h follows the vowel of the syllable.
If the syllable ends with a consonant, the h still follows the
vowel, but comes before the final consonant.

> Ex.   sahp   ten
>   sèhng   whole, entire

Traditionally Chinese recite Cantonese tones in upper register-
lower register sequence, in the order falling, rising, level, thus:

sì	思	53
sí	史	35
si	試	33
sìh	時	21
síh	市	23
sih	事	22

This is the way Cantonese themselves recite tones. You will
note that the high level tone is not recited traditionally. There
are historical reasons for this which we won't go into here.

In a few words the consonants m and ng occur as vowels, and
in these cases the diacritics are placed above the n of ng and the
m.

          Ex: m̀h   'not'

              ńgh   'five'

Tones in Sequence:

    <u>Tone Sandhi</u>. Changes in the basic sound of tones when syllables are spoken in sequence is called tone sandhi. The high falling tone in Cantonese undergoes tone sandhi in certain position, as follows:

    1. When high falling tones occur in succession without intervening pause, all but the final one are pronounced as high level.

        Ex: hf + hf becomes hl + hf

燒 豬 1. sìu   jyù ------ sīujyù   燒豬

          roast   pig   roast pork

傷 風 2. sèung   fùng ---- sēung fùng   傷風

          hurt   wind   to catch cold

傷 風添 3. sèung fùng tìm! --sēung fūng tìm! 傷風添

          hurt wind !   caught cold!

    2. When a high falling tone occurs before a high level tone without intervening pause, it is pronounced as high level.

        Ex: hf + hl becomes hl + hl

租 屋 1. jòu   ūk -------jōu ūk   租屋

          rent   house   to rent a house

西 餐 2. sài   chāan --- sāichāan 西餐

          west   meal   western food

    In this book high falling tone has been written high level only when the tone sandhi is within word boundaries. For separate words, the high falling will be marked with its usual diacritic.

        Ex. <u>Separate forms</u>   <u>Combined forms</u>

先 生 sìn   sàang ------- sīnsàang   先生

        first   born   man, teacher, Mr.

張 生 Jèung Sàang ------- Jèung Sàang 張生

        Cheung Mr.   Mr. Cheung

Tones not 'sung.'

    That Cantonese is a tone language does not mean that sentences in it are sung as you would sing a musical phrase. Music has sustained notes and strict rhythmic scheme, the spoken language does not. At first you may feel that Cantonese sounds sing-song,

but practice will bring familiarity and soon it will sound natural
to you.

B. Intonation:

A sentence may be said different ways, to stress different
points in the sentence and also to express what the speaker feels
about what he is saying. To give an English example, the sentence
'So glad you could come,' may be said:

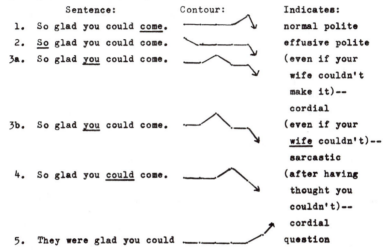

	Sentence:	Contour:	Indicates:
1.	So glad you could <u>come</u>.		normal polite
2.	<u>So</u> glad you could come.		effusive polite
3a.	So glad <u>you</u> could come.		(even if your wife couldn't make it)-- cordial
3b.	So glad <u>you</u> could come.		(even if your <u>wife</u> couldn't)-- sarcastic
4.	So glad you <u>could</u> come.		(after having thought you couldn't)-- cordial
5.	They were glad you could come?		question

The graphs of the sentence contours above represent the rise
and fall of the voice pitch throughout the length of the sentence.
This rise and fall over sentence length we call an "intonation."

You will note that the question sentence (#5) rises in pitch
at the end, and the statement sentences (#1 - 4) all end with falling
pitch, although within their contours rise and fall occurs at
different points. In English sentence-final fall is the norm, and
sentence-final rise expresses doubt.

Intonation also has another job within a sentence--it can
express how the speaker feels about what he is saying. By expressive
rise and fall of his voice, by varying his "tone of voice," the
speaker can indicate that he is angry or happy, doubtful or certain,
being polite or rude, suggesting or demanding.

9

Cantonese sentences too exhibit intonation contours. Sentence-final contours in particular are much more varied in Cantonese than in English, and capable of expressing quite a range of emotional implications.

You may wonder how intonation affects the tone situation in Cantonese, each syllable having as it does its characteristic tone. How the tone contours operate in the framework of sentence contour has been compared to the action of ripples riding on top of waves. Each ripple relates to the one before it and behind it, whether in the trough of the wave or on the crest.

Sentence Stress:

In speaking of sentence stress we mean relative prominence of syllables in a sentence--loud or soft (heavy or light), rapid or slow. Consider the stress pattern of the following English sentences:

      1. I'm John Smith.   (In response to "Which one of you
                                 is John Smith?")

      2. I'm John Smith.   (In response to "I was supposed
                                 to give this letter to Tom
                                 Smith.")

In the sentences above the stressed syllables (those underlined) give prominence to the information requested in the stimulus sentences.

In certain sentences stress differences alone indicate difference in message content. The pair of sentences often quoted in illustration of this is:

      1. Ship sails today.   (The ship will sail today.)
      2. Ship sails today.   (Please ship the sails today.)

Another example, from a headline in a newspaper:

      Boy Scratching Cat Is Caught, Destroyed

How do you stress that one?

Sentence Pause:

Another feature important in establishing natural sentence rhythm is pause--the small silences between groups of syllables. Note the following English sentences:

10

In considering him for the job he took
into account his education, previous
experience, and appraised potential.

There is a pause between "job" and "he" in the sentence above, and
if you read it instead pausing after "took," you find the sentence
doesn't make sense--you have to go back and read it again putting a
pause in the right place.

We will not discuss Cantonese stress and pause features in this
Introduction, other than to say that Cantonese sentences, like
English ones, do exhibit stress and pause phenomena, as well as
intonational ones. What this effectively means for you as a student
is that you must not concentrate solely on learning words as
individual isolated units; but in imitating the teacher's spoken
model, you should be alert to his delivery of phrase-length segments
and whole sentences, and should mimic the stress, pause, and intonation of the phrases you repeat.

C. Consonants and Vowels

We regard the syllable in Cantonese as being composed of an
initial and a final. The initials are consonants. The finals are
vowels, or vowels plus consonants. Tones are also included as part
of the final.

The practices that follow include all the initials and finals
in Cantonese. They were prepared by James E. Dew.

Initials. Repeat after each syllable in the pause provided.
Concentrate on the initial sound of each syllable.

1.	bò	bò	,	pò	pò	,	mò	mò	,	fò	fò
2.	dò	dò	,	tò	tò	,	nò	nò	,	lò	lò
3.	jà	jà	,	chà	chà	,	sà	sà	,	yà	yà
4.	gà	gà	,	kà	kà	,	ngà	ngà	,	hà	hà
5.	gwà	gwà	,	kwà	kwà	,	wà	wà			

Finals. Listen carefully and repeat in the pauses provided.
Concentrate on the finals--the vowels and vowel+consonant combinat-
ions. (Tones are not marked.)

a	e	eu	i	o	u	yu
ga 架	je 借	heu 靴	ji 至	go 個	wu 惡	jyu 註
gaai界 gai計	gei記	geui句		goi 蓋	fui 悔	
gaau敎 gau夠			giu叫	gou告		
gaam監 gam禁			gim劍			
gaan澗 gan艮		deun敦	gin見	gon幹	gun冠	gyun絹
gaang gang更 geng 鏡	geun芫		ging敬	gong鋼	gung供	
gaap甲 gap鴿			gip扱			
baat八 bat筆		cheut出	git結	got割	fut闊	kyut決
baak百 bak北 kek劇	geuk脚		gik	gok覺	guk焗	

The Mechanics of Producing speech sounds:

In speaking we make use of 1) air, 2) the vibration of the vocal chords (i.e. the voice), and 3) the position of the tongue and other members of the mouth to produce speech sounds. The air originates in the lungs and is released through the mouth, the vocal chords vibrate to produce voiced sounds, and the position of the tongue and other members affect the shape of the vocal instrument and thus the sounds it produces.

Consonants:

1) Air:

Air flow, originating in the lungs and released through the mouth, is required for all speech sounds, but different manner of air release produces different sounds. The manner of release is particularly important for consonant sounds. For consonant sounds friction is created at some point in the oral passageway by resistance to the flow of air. The point of resistance to the air flow and the manner of release from this resistance are important contributing factors in how consonants are made. There are several routes through which the air may be released:

A. Nasal release: Air can be released through the nose, producing nasal sounds. Try prolonging the English sounds m and n. mmmmm, nnnnn. While you are prolonging these sounds, hold your nose and you notice you can't say m or n. That's because the air flow is released through the nose in saying m and n.

12

B. **Lateral release**: The air release can be over the surface of the
side of the tongue. Prolong the English sound l. lllll. Then
breathe in and out through your mouth without moving your tongue
from its l position. Can you feel that the air passes laterally
out one or both sides of your mouth? For me, the air release
for l is from both sides. Do you release the air to the right,
or to the left, or from both sides?

C. **Stop and Release, with and without Aspiration**: Another manner
of air release is for the air flow to be blocked at some point
in the mouth and then released, letting the air flow through.
When you make the English sounds p-, t-, k-, you notice that
the air flow is first blocked at different points, and then
released.

The stop releases can be either aspirated or unaspirated.
In reference to language sounds 'aspirated' means released with
a puff of air. Compare the English sounds p-, t-, k-, and
b-, d-, g-. If you put your hand close to your mouth as you
say p-, t-, k-, you will notice that you feel your breath
against your hand. Say b-, d-, g-, and you find you do not
feel your breath against your hand, or at least not as much
so. The p-, t-, k- sounds are aspirated, the b-, d-, g- ones
unaspirated.

Try:

p-	b-
t-	d-
k-	g-

D. **Spirant release**: When air is released through a narrow passage
under pressure, a hissing sound is produced, as in s- sssss,
and h- hhhhh. We refer to this type of air release as spirant
release.

2) **Voicing**:

Voiced and Voiceless Consonants: The vocal chords vibrate to produce some sounds--which we refer to as voiced sounds--and do
not vibrate in the production of other sounds--which are re-
fered to as voiceless. For example, in English the 'z' sound
is a voiced sound and the 's' sound is a voiceless one.

13

Prolong the buzzing sound of 'z'--zzzzz. You can hear the
voicing, and if you put your hand on your throat over the Adam's
apple, you can feel the vibration of the vocal chords. Prolong
the hissing sound of 's'--sssss. Notice that voicing ceases,
the vocal chords do not vibrate. In Cantonese the only consonants that are voiced are the nasals--m, n, and ng.

3) __Position of tongue and other members__: Different position of the
tongue and other members of the mouth forms the third element
in producing speech sounds. Note for example how the difference
in tongue position produces different sounds in the English
words 'tea' and 'key.' For 't,' the tip of tongue touches the
roof of the mouth at the gum ridge behind the upper teeth. Try
it: t-, t-, t-, tea. For 'k,' the back of the tongue touches
the roof of the mouth at the back: k-, k-, k-, key.

We will describe the consonants of Cantonese in terms of
air release, voicing, and position of tongue and other members
of the vocal aparatus. We will concentrate primarily on those
sounds which are problems for Americans.

__Vowels:__

Production of vowels, like production of consonants, is a
matter of air flow, voicing, and positioning.

1. __Air Flow:__

Whereas in making a consonant sound friction is created by
resistance at some point in the passageway to the flow of air,
in making vowels the passageway does not resist the flow of
air, and the sound produced is therefore frictionless. The
presence or absence of friction is a factor distinguishing
consonants and vowels.

2. __Vibrating of vocal chords (Voicing):__

Vowels are voiced sounds. Under certain circumstances,
such as whispering, vowels may be de-voiced, but voicing for
vowels is taken as a given, and when exceptions occur, they
are specifically noted.

A feature of voicing which is potentially significant for
vowels is vowel length. In some languages different vowel

14

length in an otherwise identical syllable can produce different words.

>Example: In German, the following two words differ in
>pronunciation only in the length of their vowels:
>staat [ŝtaˑt]   'state'
>statt [ŝtaˇt]   'place'

3. Positioning:

In positioning for vowel sounds the important contributing factors are how the lips and tongue are placed.

The lips, in making vowel sounds, are described in terms of whether they are rounded or unrounded (spread). For example, in English, the 'i' of 'pit' is a vowel said with lips spread, and the 'u' of 'put' is said with lips rounded. There are vowels which are produced with lips neither markedly rounded or spread, such as 'a' in 'father.' This type is not described in terms of lip position. If a vowel is not described as being rounded or spread, you can assume that the lip position is midway between rounded and spread. We will use the terms 'unrounded' and 'spread' interchangeably.

Tongue position for vowels is described in vertical terms and in horizontal terms. On the vertical we speak of the tongue height of a vowel. For example, take the vowels of 'pit,' 'pet,' and 'pat' in English. You notice that the forward part of the tongue is relatively high towards the roof of the mouth in saying the 'i' of 'pit,' that it drops somewhat to say the 'e' of 'pet,' and drops still lower to say the 'a' of 'pat.' These positions might also be described in terms of how wide the lower jaw opens in making the sounds-- narrow for the 'i,' medium for the 'e,' and wide for the 'a.' However, since description in terms of tongue height has become standard, we will adopt the standard description here, and speak of vowels in terms of high, mid, and low in reference to tongue height. Deviations from these cardinal positions are described in terms of higher-mid, lower-mid, etc.

Horizontally, tongue position is described in terms of front, central, and back. In English the vowels of 'pit,'

'pet,' and 'pat' are all front vowels, with the points of
reference for 'front' being the blade of the tongue and the
dental ridge. 'Pit,' 'pet,' and 'pat' are high front, mid
front, and low front respectively. For the central vowels
the points of reference in the oral passageway are the center
surface of the tongue and the hard palate. In English the
vowels of 'putt' and 'pot' are central vowels. For the back
vowels the points of reference in the passageway are the back
surface of the tongue and the soft palate. In English the
vowels of 'put,' 'pole,' and 'paw' are back vowels. Deviations
are described in terms of being fronted or backed from the
cardinal positions.

Pronunciation Practice:

1. **ch, as in Chàhn**

    ch is an initial consonant in Cantonese. We describe the ch
sound in terms of voicing, air flow, and position of tongue against
the roof of the mouth. Like the American ch sound in "chance," the
Cantonese ch is voiceless. In terms of air air flow the American and
Cantonese ch's are alike--both are stops with aspirated release. The
tongue pressing against the roof of the mouth stops the flow of air
entirely, then lets go and allows the air to flow through again,
accompanied by a puff of air. The tongue position for the American ch
and Cantonese ch differs. For the Cantonese ch sound, the tongue
rests flat against the dental ridge (the ridge just behind the upper
teeth) and the blade part of the tongue, that part just back from the
tip, blocks the air passage at the dental ridge. The blade of the
tongue is pressed flat against the ridge: [ts̹] The American ch the
contact point is the tip of the tongue, not the blade of the tongue;
the tongue is grooved, not flat; and the contact point on the roof
of the mouth is a little farther back on the dental ridge than for
the Cantonese ch sound.

    Compare--Listen and repeat: (Read across)

English:	chance	ch	ch	ch	chance
Cantonese:	Chàhn	ch	ch	ch	Chàhn 陳
	chàn	ch	ch	ch	chàn 親

16

2.　j, as in joigin, jousahn, Jeung, siuje

　　　　J is an initial consonant in Cantonese. We describe the j sound
in terms of voicing, air flow, and position of the tongue against the
roof of the mouth. Unlike the American j sound (in 'joy'), the Cantonese j sound is voiceless. In terms of air flow the American and
Cantonese j's are alike--both are stops with unaspirated release.
The tongue, pressing against the roof of the mouth, stops the flow of
air entirely, then lets go and allows the air to flow through again,
without aspiration (accompanying puff of air). The tongue position
for the Cantonese j is the same as that for the Cantonese ch, different
from that of the American counterpart. For the Cantonese j sound the
blade of the tongue, resting flat against the dental ridge, blocks
the air passage: [tɕ] For the American j the tip of the tongue,
grooved, blocks the air passage at a point a little farther back on
the dental ridge than for the Cantonese j. When air is released, it
flows over a grooved tongue surface for the American sound, a flat
tongue surface for the Cantonese sound.

　　　　　　Compare English and Cantonese similar syllables:
　　　　　　　　Listen and repeat: (Read across)
　　　　　　　　English　　　　　　　　Cantonese
　　　　　　1.　Joe (3 times)　　　jóu (3 times) 早
　　　　　　2.　joy (3 times)　　　joi (3 times) 再
　　　　　　3.　Jess (3 times)　　　jé (3 times) 姐

　　　　The Cantonese j sound is said with lips rounded before rounded
vowels, and spread before unrounded vowels. (Rounded vowels are those
pronounced with the lips rounded, unrounded vowels those that are
not.)

　　　　　　Watch the teacher, listen and repeat: (read across)
　　　　　　Ex:　　　rounded　　　　　unrounded
　　　　　　　　1.　Jóu 早 (3 times)　jé 姐(3 times)
　　　　　　　　2.　joi 再 (3 times)　jé 姐(3 times)

　　　　Some speakers of Standard Cantonese use slightly different tongue
positions for the j sound, depending on whether it comes before a
rounded or unrounded vowel. Other speakers use the tongue position
described for j above throughout. Those that use different positions

before rounded and unrounded vowels use the position described above
before unrounded vowels. Before rounded vowels they retract their
tongue a bit and use the tip of the tongue instead of the part just
behind the tip as contact point for making j. Listen and see if your
teacher's j sounds the same or different before rounded and unrounded
vowels.

Listen: (Watch the teacher:)

rounded	unrounded
jó 左	je 借
joi 再	ja 榨
jóu 早	

What has been said in regard to lip-rounding for the j applies
also to ch sounds in Cantonese, but we will not practice this feature
in relation to ch until it comes up in the Basic Conversations.

3. ng, as in ngóh

ng is a voiced nasal initial consonant in Cantonese. In
position, the back surface of the tongue presses against the roof of
the mouth at the soft palate, in the same position as for the English
word "sing." We refer to this position as velar, making an adjective
of the word velum, the technical term for soft palate. ng is a velar
nasal consonant, which in Cantonese may occupy initial position in
a syllable.

Listen and repeat:

ngóh 我 (6 times)

The only reason this sound may be hard for English speakers is
that we don't have any words beginning with ng in English, though we
have many ending with the same sound.

If you have trouble, try saying "sing on" in English, and then
say the si part of "sing" silently, beginning to voice on the -ng
part:

sing on

(si)ng on

----ng on

Now try initial ng again:

Listen and repeat:

ngóh 我 (5 times)

18

4. o, and in Hòh, ngóh

    o is a final in Cantonese. It is a mid back rounded vowel--[ɔ].
The closest American sound is the vowel sound of general American
"dog," but with more rounding of the lips than in English. In Cantonese a rounded vowel has a rounding effect on a consonant preceding
it in a syllable. Watch your teacher and note that in syllables with
an o vowel, he rounds his lips for the preceding consonant too.

        Listen, watch the teacher, and repeat:
            ngóh 我 (5 times)
            Hòh 何 (5 times)

5. yu, as in deuimhjyuh

    yu is a single vowel spelled with two letters. yu is a high
front rounded vowel--[ü], occuring as a final in Cantonese. There is
no counterpart vowel in American English with a similar sound, but
you can produce the sound by protruding your lips while you sustain
the "ee" [i] sound of the English letter "E." The "long e" [i] sound
in English is a high front unrounded vowel. Rounding the lips produces a high front rounded vowel.

        Listen, watch the teacher, and repeat:
            1. deuimhjyuh jyuh jyuh
            2. jyuh 住 (3 times)
            3. yú 羡 (fish) (3 times)

6. eu

    eu is a single vowel spelled with two letters. eu is a mid front
rounded vowel--[ø], occuring as a final in Cantonese only in a very
few words. There is no counterpart vowel in American English with a
similar sound, but you can produce the sound by protruding your lips
while you sustain the "e" [E] sound of the English word "less." This
"short e" [E] sound in English is a mid front unrounded vowel.
Rounding the lips makes it a rounded vowel. In Cantonese a rounded
vowel has a rounding effect on a consonant preceding it in a syllable.

        Watch your teacher, listen, and repeat:
            lēu   'spit out'
            hēu 靴   'boot'
            dēu   'tiny bit'

19

7. <u>eung</u>, as in Jèung

     <u>eung</u> is a two-part final composed of the mid front rounded vowel <u>eu</u> [ø] plus the velar nasal consonant <u>ng</u>. There is no close English counterpart. As a rounded final, <u>eung</u> has a rounding effect on a consonant preceding it in a syllable.

     Watch the teacher, listen, and repeat:

     Jèung 張 (5 times)

     The <u>eu</u> portion of <u>eung</u> is not nasalized. In English, a vowel before a nasal final is nasalized--that is, part of the air release for the vowel goes through the nose. To illustrate the English situation, hold your nose and say the following English words:

        sue

        soon

        see

        seem

        sit

        sing

     You notice that the vowels of the words with nasal finals (-<u>n</u>, -<u>m</u>, and -<u>ng</u>) are partially blocked when the nose is blocked, thus revealing that for such vowels some of the air is normally released through the nose. The vowels of the words which do not end in a nasal are unaffected by clocking the nasal passage. They are 'open' vowels, not 'nasalized' vowels.

     In Cantonese, a vowel before a nasal final is <u>not</u> nasalized-- All of the air is released through the mouth for the vowel portion. Test whether you can keep the vowel open before nasal final by stopping you nose as you say:

     Jèung   (5 times)

     To practice the open vowel before a nasal final, try saying the following pairs of words in which -<u>eu</u> and -<u>eung</u> are contrasted. To make the -<u>eung</u> sound, pretend through the -<u>eu</u> part that you are going to say -<u>eu</u>, then add the -<u>ng</u> as an after-thought. You will then have an open <u>eu</u> followed by the nasal <u>ng</u> sound.

       -<u>eu</u>   -<u>eung</u>

    1. hēu 靴 boot   hèung 香 fragrant

    2. lēu   to spit out   léuhng 雨 two
    3. geu 鋸 to saw   gèung 羌 ginger
    4. jeuk 著 to wear   Jèung 張 surname Cheung

eui, as in deuiṁhjyuh

    eui is a two-part final composed of the mid front rounded vowel
eu plus the high front rounded vowel **yu** [ü]. (We spell the second
part of this two-part final with **i** instead of **yu**--**eui** instead of **euyu**,
the latter being extremely awkward-looking.) The major force of the
voice falls on the **eu** part, with the **yu** (spelled **i**) part an offglide.

    Listen and repeat:
    1. deuiṁhjyuh 對唔住 (3 times)
    2. deui 對 (3 times)

The tongue position for **eu** before **i** is slightly lower and more
backed than it is for **eu** before **ng**. **eui** = [œü]; **eung** = [ɵŋ].

    Listen and watch for differences in **eu** sound: (Read across)
    1. Jèung 張 Jèung   Jèung   Jèung
    2. deui 對 deui   deui   deui
    3. Jèung 張 deui 對 (4 times)
    4. deui 對 Jèung 張 (4 times)

an, as in Chàhn, jóusàhn, ṁhgányiu

    an is a two-part final composed of the backed mid central vowel
a [ə˒] plus the dental nasal consonant **n**. Tongue height for the
Cantonese **a** [ə˒] is lower than that for American vowel in "cup,"
higher than that for American vowel in "cop," and more backed than
either of the American counterparts. Before the nasal final the
Cantonese vowel is not nasalized, as an American vowel before a
nasal final would be. The Cantonese vowel is shorter and tenser
than the American counterparts.

    Listen, watch the teacher, and repeat:
    1. Chàhn   (4 times)   陳
    2. jóusàhn   (4 times) 早晨
    3. ṁhgányiu (4 times) 唔緊要
Compare English and Cantonese syllables:
Listen and repeat: (Read across)
        English   Cantonese
    1. John   John   Chàhn   Chàhn 陳

21

                    2. sun   sun   san   sàn 中
10. m as in m̀h

        The bilabial nasal consonant m occurs as a vowel, in that the
    consonant m is syllabic in the syllable m̀h.

                    Listen and repeat:
                        1. m̀hhaih   (2 times)
                        2. haih m̀hhaih a?   (2 times)

11. Tone practice with words in Lesson 1:

                    Listen and repeat:
                        1. Jèung, jóu, sing   ; Hòh, Léih, haih   .
                        2. Jèung, jóu, sing   ; Hòh, Léih, haih   .
                        3. Jèung, Jèung   ; Hòh, Hòh   .
                        4. jóu, jóu   ; Léih, Léih   .
                        5. jóu, Léih   ; Léih, jóu   .
                        6. sing, sing   ; haih, haih   .
                        7. sing, haih   ; haih, sing   .
                        8. Jèung, Hòh   ; jóu, Léih   ; sing, haih   .
                        9. Hòh, Jèung   ; Léih, jóu   ; haih, sing   .

                    ——————————————

II. Notes:

A. Culture Notes

    1. Surname and titles.

    a. Titles follow surnames: (Drills 1-6)
        Léih Sàang   'Mr. Lee'
        Léih Táai   'Mrs. Lee'
        Léih Síujé   'Miss Lee'

    b. Sàang/Sīnsàang and Táai/Taaitáai
        Sàang and Sīnsàang, Táai and Taaitáai are alternate forms for
        'Mr.' and 'Mrs.' respectively.
        Léih Sīnsàang   'Mr. Lee'
        Léih Taaitáai   'Mrs. Lee'

            Native speakers differ in respect to their use of Sàang and
        Sīnsàang, and Táai and Taaitáai as titles to surnames. Some say
        that the full forms denote more respect and the short forms are
        used in informal situations only. Others say that as title to

surnames the longer forms are used only in letters and that in speech, Sàang and Táai are used even for subordinates speaking to superiors. Everyone seems to agree that on the telephone both long forms and the short forms are common. In this book we have used the short forms almost exclusively, but you--when you get into a Cantonese speaking situation--keep your ears peeled and imitate what your Cantonese peers are saying. Incidentally, you will notice that what people say and what they say they say do not always coincide exactly. Also, different people may disagree vehemently about what is 'right.' This is confusing to the beginning student. Be advised, however, that the area of dis-agreement is on peripheral matters. If your teachers disagree about two forms, you may safely conclude that both forms are used. taaitáai basically = 'married woman;' sīnsàang = 'man.'

c. Sīnsàang as 'teacher'

Sīnsàang meaning 'teacher' may be used with or without a surname attached. A woman teacher named Wong may be addressed as Sīnsàang or as Wòhng Sīnsàang.

d. Síujé, 'unmarried woman,' used as title

In addressing a woman whose name you do not know, it is appropriate to address her as Síujé, no matter how old she is, and even if you know she is married. In addressing a woman by her maiden name, the appropriate title is Síujé. Ex: Wòhng Síujé. It is the custom for Chinese women to use their maiden names in business life, so it often turns out that someone addressed as Síujé is married.

e. It is inappropriate to refer to oneself by title in a social situation. Avoid saying "Ngóh haih Smith Sàang." Say instead "Ngóh sing Smith." (See Drill 5).

2. sing, V/N to have the surname of; surname

Sing is the surname one is born with. For married women, equivalent to the English née. The English and American custom is for a woman's surname to change at the time of marriage to that of her husband. The Cantonese sing does not change upon marriage. When you ask a woman her surname, ordinarily she gives her maiden name in response. If it is a social gathering, she might add something like "Ngóh sīnsàang sing..., My husband has the surname...."

B. Structure Notes

1. Relationship of Cantonese to other Chinese languages.

Cantonese is traditionally called a dialect of Chinese. The major dialect of Chinese being Mandarin, and other important dialects in addition to Cantonese, are Shanghai, Fukkienese (also called Hokkienese or Amoy), and Hakka. Mandarin is considered the major dialect because it is spoken by the greatest number of people and, more importantly, because it has been prompted as the national standard language by both the Communist Chinese government on Mainland China and the Nationalist Chinese government on Taiwan.

Although historically descended from a single mother tongue, the various Chinese dialects are today different languages. A person who speaks only Cantonese cannot understand a person who speaks only Mandarin, Shanghai, Fukkienese, or Hakka. However, if two speakers of two different Chinese languages can read, they can communicate, since Chinese has a uniform writing system which is not based on sound. (A Western comparison can be made in the number system, in which '2' is intelligible without reference to pronunciation.)

The languages of the Chinese family group are different--and similar--on three levels: vocabulary, grammatical sentence structure, and phonological sound system. The level of greatest similarity is in that of the grammatical sentence structure. Students who have studied another Chinese language will find that in great measure they already 'know' the sentence patterns of Cantonese. In preparing this book we at first planned to make a Cantonese-Mandarin grammatical appendix to list the grammatically different structures, the idea being that they were listable, being so few of them. To draw a parallel we wrote out the Basic Conversations of the first 15 lessons in Mandarin translation and found to our surprise quite a lot more differences than we had expected. The differences, however, were mostly in the nature of 'You could say it that way--that sentence pattern exists in Cantonese--but actually that's not the way we say it, we say it this way.' We therefore didn't make the appendix, but for the benefit of students who have previously studied Mandarin, we have used the Notes section to draw attention to basic grammatical differences where they come up in the text.

On the level of vocabulary there are greater differences than

24

on the level of grammatical structure, but still a great deal of
similarity. A rough check of the first 10 lessons of this book re-
veals that more than 55% of the Cantonese expressions have identical
Mandarin counterparts.

In pronunciation, differences are greater still, but there are
systematic correspondences. For example, ai in Mandarin is oi in
Cantonese. In total, though, the phonological correspondences are
quite complex, as witnessed by a series of articles on the subject
in a Japanese linguistic journal which runs 26 pages long.

2. Sentence Types--full sentences and minor sentences.

  a. Full sentences have two parts--subject and predicate, in that
     order. Examples from the Basic Conversation of Lesson One are:

       1. Ngóh m̀hhaih Léih Táai.   I am not Mrs. Lee.
       2. Ngóh sing Chàhn.   I am surnamed Chan.

     In these sentences Ngóh is the subject and the remainder of
     each sentence is the predicate.

  b. Minor sentences are not in subject-predicate form. Minor
     sentences are common as responses, commands, exclamations.
     In Lesson One there are several minor sentences in the Basic
     Conversation:

       1. Hòh Sàang, jóusàhn.   Good morning, Mr. Ho.
       2. Joigin.   Goodbye.
       3. M̀hgányiu.   That's all right. [literally:
                                   Not important.]

3. Verbs.

     In Cantonese, words which can be preceded by the negative
m̀h are regarded as verbs. There are a few cases in which this rule
doesn't work, but basically, you can test whether a new word you
hear is a verb by asking whether you can say m̀h (new word).
Is ngóh a verb? Ask the teacher whether it's OK to say m̀h ngóh.
Is haih a verb? Ask the teacher whether it's OK to say m̀h haih.

4. Adverbs.

     In Cantonese an adverb is a word or word group which forms
a construction with a verb. In most cases in Cantonese adverbs
precede the verb they belong with. An example from Lesson 1 is
m̀h-, 'not,' which precedes a verb to form the negative.

5. Phrases.

     We give the name 'phrase' to a group of words which has a

specialized meaning as a group. For example, in English, spill +
water = spill the water, and spill + beans = spill the beans.
Spill the water is a simple Verb + Object construction. Spill the
beans may be, but it may also be a phrase whose meaning differs from
the added together meaning of the individual words. This type of
phrase is often called an idiom, or an idiomatic expression. In
this lesson M̀hgányiu, 'It doesn't matter; That's all right; Never
mind,' is such a phrase.

    We also give the name 'phrase' to another kind of construction—
a group of words whose total meaning may be the same as the added
together meaning of the individual words, but which we don't feel
is necessary for you to analyze and learn separately in the first
stage of learning Cantonese. It may even be that the fact that
the construction is grammatically a word group and not a single
word may not be apparent, since the construction may be written
as a single word. Examples are m̀hhóu 'don't' in the Classroom
Phrases of Lesson 1 and sèsíu 'a little' in Lesson 3.

6. Lead Sentences and Follow Sentences.

      a. It's a pretty day today.

      b. How about you?

      c. Where?

a, b and c are all sentences, and all are intelligible, but in b
and c as stated it is not clear what is happening. Without drawing
too rigid lines, we are going to distinguish between lead sentences—
sentences that are intelligible as self-contained units, and follow
sentences, ones which depend upon information supplied by a preceding sentence or the context for full intelligibility.

III. DRILLS

    1. Substitution Drill: Substitute joigin in the position of jóusàhn
       following the pattern of the example sentence.

         Ex: T: Léih Táai, jóusàhn.   T: Good morning, Mrs. Lee.

            S: Léih Táai, joigin.   S: Goodbye, Mrs. Lee.

     1. Chàhn Táai, jóusàhn.   1. Chàhn Táai, joigin.

+ 2. Làuh Sàang, jóusàhn.   2. Làuh Sàang, joigin.
    (Good morning, Mr. Lau.)

+ 3. Jèung Síujé, jóusàhn   3. Jèung Síujé, joigin.
    (Good morning, Miss Cheung.)

+ 4. Máh Sàang, jóusàhn.   4. Máh Sàang, joigin.
    (Good morning, Mr. Ma.)

  5. Léih Táai, jóusàhn.   5. Léih Táai, joigin.

---

2. Substitution Drill: Substitute the cue in the appropriate position
   following the pattern of the example sentence.

    Ex: T: Léih Táai, jóusàhn.   T: Good morning, Mrs. Lee.
       /Chàhn/   /Chan/

      S: Chàhn Táai, jóusàhn.   S: Good morning, Mrs. Chan.

  1. Chàhn Táai, jóusàhn. /Léih/   1. Léih Táai, jóusàhn.

+ 2. Léih Táai, jóusàhn. /Wòhng/   2. Wòhng Táai, jóusàhn.
    (Wong)

  3. Wòhng Táai, jóusàhn. /Hòh/   3. Hòh Táai, jóusàhn.

  4. Hòh Táai, jóusàhn. /Jèung/   4. Jèung Táai, jóusàhn.

  5. Làuh Táai, jóusàhn. /Chàhn/   5. Chàhn Táai, jóusàhn.

---

3. Substitution Drill: Substitute the cue in the appropriate position,
   following the pattern of the example sentence.

    Ex: T: Wòhng Sàang, jóusàhn. T: Good morning, Mr. Wong.
       /Táai/   /Mrs./

      S: Wòhng Táai, jóusàhn.   S: Good morning, Mrs. Wong.

  1. Wòhng Táai, jóusàhn. /Síujé/   1. Wòhng Síujé, jóusàhn.

  2. Wòhng Síujé, jóusàhn. /Làuh/   2. Làuh Síujé, jóusàhn.

  3. Làuh Síujé, jóusàhn. /joigin/   3. Làuh Síujé, joigin.

  4. Làuh Síujé, joigin. /Sàang/   4. Làuh Sàang, joigin.

  5. Làuh Sàang, joigin. /Táai/   5. Làuh Táai, joigin.

---

4. Expansion Drill: Expand the cue sentence as indicated in the
   example.

   Ex: T: Ngóh m̀hhaih Wòhng   T: I'm not Mr. Wong.
          Sàang.

       S: Deuim̀hjyuh, ngóh   S: I beg your pardon, I'm not
          m̀hhaih Wòhng Sàang.   Mr. Wong.

1. Ngóh m̀hhaih Léih Síujé.   1. Deuim̀hjyuh, ngóh m̀hhaih
                                      Léih Síujé.

2. Ngóh m̀hhaih Chàhn Sàang.   2. Deuim̀hjyuh, ngóh m̀hhaih
                                      Chàhn Sàang.

3. Ngóh m̀hhaih Jèung Táai.   3. Deuim̀hjyuh, ngóh m̀hhaih
                                      Jèung Táai.

4. Ngóh m̀hhaih Hòh Sàang.   4. Deuim̀hjyuh, ngóh m̀hhaih Hòh
                                      Sàang.

5. Ngóh m̀hhaih Wòhng Táai.   5. Deuim̀hjyuh, ngóh m̀hhaih
                                      Wòhng Táai.

---

5. Expansion Drill: Expand the cue sentences to conform with the
   pattern of the example.

   Ex: T: Ngóh m̀hhaih Léih   T: I'm not Mrs. Lee. /Cheung/
          Táai. /Jèung/

       S: Ngóh m̀hhaih Léih   S: I'm not Mrs. Lee, my name is
          Táai, ngóh sing   Cheung.
          Jèung.

1. Ngóh m̀hhaih Hòh Táai. /Chàhn/   1. Ngóh m̀hhaih Hòh Táai, ngóh
                                       sing Chàhn.

2. Ngóh m̀hhaih Chàhn Síujé. /Máh/   2. Ngóh m̀hhaih Chàhn Síujé,
                                       ngóh sing Máh.

3. Ngóh m̀hhaih Máh Sàang. /Wòhng/   3. Ngóh m̀hhaih Máh Sàang, ngóh
                                       sing Wòhng.

4. Ngóh m̀hhaih Wòhng Táai. /Jèung/ 4. Ngóh m̀hhaih Wòhng Táai,
                                       ngóh sing Jèung.

5. Ngóh m̀hhaih Léih Táai. /Hòh/   5. Ngóh m̀hhaih Léih Táai, ngóh
                                       sing Hòh.

28

6. Conversation Drill: Carry on the suggested conversation following
   the model of the example.

        Ex: A: Chàhn Sàang, jóusàhn.   A: Good morning Mr. Chan.

            B: Deuimhjyuh, ngóh   B: I beg your pardon, I'm not
               mhhaih Chàhn   Mr. Chan. My name is Cheung.
               Sàang. Ngóh sing
               Jèung.

            A: A, deuimhjyuh,   A: A, excuse me, Mr. Cheung.
               Jèung Sàang.

            B: Mhgányiu.   B: That's OK.

    1. A: Chàhn Síujé........   1. A: Chàhn Síujé, jóusàhn.

       B: ....   B: Deuimhjyuh, ngóh mhhaih
          ....   Chàhn Síujé. Ngóh sing
          ....Wòhng.   Wòhng.

       A: ....   A: A, deuimhjyuh, Wòhng
                                          Síujé.

       B: ....   B: Mhgányiu.

    2. A: Jèung Síujé ....   2. A: Jèung Síujé, jóusàhn.

       B: ....   B: Deuimhjyuh, ngóh mhhaih
          ....   Jèung Síujé. Ngóh sing
          ....Léih.   Léih.

       A: ....   A: A, deuimhjyuh, Léih
                                          Síujé.

       B: ....   B: Mhgányiu.

    3. A: Hòh Sàang ....   3. A: Hòh Sàang, jóusàhn.

       B: ....   B: Deuimhjyuh, ngóh mhhaih
          ....   Hòh Sàang. Ngóh sing
          ....Wòhng.   Wòhng.

       A: ....   A: A, deuimhjyuh, Wòhng
                                          Sàang.

       B: ....   B: Mhgányiu.

    4. A: Jèung Sàang ....   4. A: Jèung Sàang, jóusàhn.

       B: ....   B: Deuimhjyuh, ngóh mhhaih
          ....   Jèung Sàang. Ngóh sing
          ....Léih.   Léih.

       A: ....   A: A, deuimhjyuh, Léih Sàang.

       B: ....   B: Mhgányiu.

    5. A: Chàhn Síujé ....   5. A: Chàhn Síujé, jóusàhn.

       B: ....   B: Deuimhjyuh, ngóh mhhaih
          ....   Chàhn Síujé. Ngóh sing
          ....Làuh.   Làuh.

A: ....   A: A, deuim̀hjyuh, Làuh
                                    Síujé.

B: ....   B: M̀hgányiu.

Vocubulary Checklist for Lesson 1

1. A   ex: Oh
2. Chàhn   sur: Chan
3. deuim̀hjyuh ph: Excuse me; I beg your pardon; I'm sorry.
4. haih   v: is, am, are, were, etc.
5. Hòh   sur: Ho
6. hohksāang   n: student
7. Jèung   sur: Cheung
8. Joigin   Ph: Goodbye
9. Jóusàhn   Ph: Good morning
10. Làuh   sur: Lau
11. Léih   sur: Li
12. Máh   sur: Ma
13. m̀h-   adv: not
14. M̀hgányiu   Ph: That's all right; It doesn't matter; Never mind.
15. ngóh   pro: I, me, my
16. Sàang   t: Mr.
17. sìnsàang   n: man (see notes); teacher
18. Sìnsàang   t: Mr. (see notes)
19. sing   v: have the surname
20. síujé   n: unmarried woman; woman, lady (see notes)
21. Síujé   t: Miss
22. Táai   t: Mrs.
23. taaitáai   n: married woman (see notes)
24. Taaitáai   t: Mrs. (see notes)
25. Wòhng   sur: Wong

CLASSROOM PHRASES

A. Learn to respond to the following classroom instructions:

1. Yìhgā ngóh mahn néih, néih   1. Now I'll ask you, and you answer
   daap ngóh.   me.

2. Yìhgā néihdeih jihgéi mahn,   2. Now you yourselves ask and answer.
   jihgéi daap.

3. Gaijuhk.   3. Continue. (i.e., Do the next
                                       one, Keep going.)

4. Néih jouh __A__, néih jouh   4. You do A, you do B.
   __B__.

B. The following are some comments that the teacher may make on your
   recitations.

5. Ngāam laak. OR Āam laak.   5. That's it. (After student suc-
                                      ceeds in saying something right.)

6. Haih gám laak.   6. That's it. Now you've got it.

7. Haih laak.   7. That's it. Now you've got it.

8. Hóu jéun.   8. Just right. Quite accurate.

9. Góngdāk hóu.   9. Good, spoken well.

10. Góngdāk m̀hhóu.   10. No, that won't do. Not spoken
                                      right.

11. Chàm̀hdō.   11. Approximately. (i.e., Good
                                      enough for now, but not perfect.)

12. Yiu suhk dī.   12. Get it smoother. (When a student's
                                      recitation is halting.)

13. Daaihsēng dī.   13. Louder.

I. BASIC CONVERSATION

A. Buildup:

(At a party in Hong Kong)

sīnsàang	man

<u>Sīnsàang</u>

gwaising	your surname (polite)
a	sentence suffix, to soften abruptness
síujé	woman
Síujé gwaising a?	What is your surname, Miss?

<u>Síujé</u>

Ngóh sing Wòhng.	My name is Wong.

<u>Sīnsàang</u>
(bowing slightly)

Wòhng Síujé.	Miss Wong.

<u>Síujé</u>

nē?	sentence suffix for questions
Sīnsàang nē?	And you? (polite)

<u>Sīnsàang</u>

síusing	my name (polite)
Síusing Làuh.	My name is Lau.

<u>Síujé</u>
(bowing slightly)

Làuh Sàang	Mr. Lau.

<u>Sīnsàang</u>

(Indicating a young lady standing beside Miss Wong)

mātyéh <u>or</u> mēyéh <u>or</u> mīyéh	what?
sing mēyéh a?	have what surname?
pàhngyáuh	friend
néih	your
néih pàhngyáuh	your friend
Néih pàhngyáuh sing mēyéh a?	What is your friend's name?

<u>Síujé</u>

sing Màh	has the name Ma

32

ge	noun-forming boundword. ge suffixed to a Verb Phrase makes it grammatically a Noun Phrase.
sing Máh ge	is a named-Ma one
kéuih	he, she, it
Kéuih sing Máh ge.	Her name is Ma.

Sīnsàang

Gwóngdùng	Kwangtung
yàhn	person
Gwóngdùngyàhn	Cantonese person, a person from Kwangtung province
haih m̀haih a?	is/not-is? a question formula
Kéuih haih m̀haih Gwóngdùngyàhn a?	Is she Cantonese?

Síujé

Seuhnghói	Shanghai
Seuhnghóiyàhn	Shanghai person
M̀haih a. Kéuih haih Seuhnghóiyàhn.	No, she's from Shanghai.

Sīnsàang

gám,...	'Well then, ...', 'Say', ... sentence prefix, resuming the thread of previous discussion.
Gám, néih nē?	And you?

Síujé

dōu	also
dōu haih Seuhnghóiyàhn	also am Shanghai person
Ngóh dōu haih Seuhnghóiyàhn.	I'm also from Shanghai.

B. **Recapitulation:**

(At a party in Hong Kong)

Sīnsàang

Síujé gwaising a?	What is your (sur)name, Miss?

<u>Síujé</u>

Ngóh sing Wòhng.   My name is Wong.

<u>Sīnsàang</u>
(bowing slightly)

Wòhng Síujé.   Miss Wong.

<u>Síujé</u>

Sīnsàang nē?   And you?

<u>Sīnsàang</u>

Síusing Làuh.   My name is Lau.

<u>Síujé</u>
(bowing slightly)

Làuh Sàang.   Mr. Lau.

<u>Sīnsàang</u>

(Indicating a young lady standing beside Miss Wong)

Néih pàhngyáuh sing mēyéh a?   What is your friend's name?

<u>Síujé</u>

Kéuih sing Máh ge.   Her name is Ma.

<u>Sīnsàang</u>

Kéuih haih m̀hhaih Gwóngdùngyàhn   Is she Cantonese?
   a?

<u>Síujé</u>

M̀hhaih a. Kéuih haih Seuhnghóiyàhn.   No, she's from Shanghai.

<u>Sīnsàang</u>

Gám, néih nē?   And you?

<u>Síujé</u>

Ngóh dōu haih Seuhnghóiyàhn.   I'm also from Shanghai.

+ + + + + + + + + + + + +

Problem sounds in Lesson Two: Initials

1. <u>b</u>, <u>d</u>, <u>g</u>, and <u>j</u> (phonetically [p], [t], [k], and [tɕ].

     <u>b</u>, <u>d</u>, <u>g</u>, and <u>j</u> sounds in Cantonese are voiceless, in contrast
to the voiced English sounds spelled with the same letters.
Positioning for Cantonese <u>b</u> and <u>g</u> sounds is the same as for English.
For the <u>d</u> sound the tongue tip is more forward in Cantonese than in
English--against the base of the upper teeth for Cantonese, on the
dental ridge for English. Position for the <u>j</u> sound has been dis-

cussed in Lesson One. The sounds are unaspirated, as are their
English counterparts, but the Cantonese and English sounds contrast
with respect to tenseness--the Cantonese initial consonants being
tense and the English lax in isolated words and in stressed position
in a sentence.

Compare: (left to right, then right to left.)

	English		Cantonese		
b:	bean		bīn go	邊個	who
	beau		bou	布	cloth
	buoy		būi	杯	cup
	bun		bān	賓	guest
	buy		baai	拜	worship
d:	doe		dou	到	arrive
	die		daai	帶	bring
	ding		dīng	丁	surname Ting
	deem		dim	店	shop (Noun)
g:	gay		gei	記	record (Verb)
	gum		gam	噤	so
	guy		gaai	界	border
	guava		Gwóngdùng	廣東	Kwangtung
j:	joy		joi	再	again
	gee		ji	至	until, to
	Jew		jiu	照	reflect
	Joe		jou	灶	stove

2. p, t, k, and ch. As initials, phonetically [p´], [t´], [k´], and
[tɕ´].

    Cantonese p, t, k, and ch sounds are similar to English counter-
part p, t, k, ch sounds in that they are voiceless and aspirated.
Positioning for p and k is the same as for English. For the t
sound the tongue tip is more forward in Cantonese than in English--
against the base of the upper teeth for Cantonese, on the dental
ridge for English. The positioning for ch has been discussed in

Lesson One. The Cantonese consonants are tenser than the American counterparts.

Compare: (left to right, then right to left)

	English		Cantonese		
p:	pingpong		pàhngyáuh	朋友	friend
	pay		pèi	披	to throw over the shoulders
	pie		paai	派	send
	Poe		pou	舖	shop (N)
	putt		pāt	匹	M for horses
t:	tie		tāai	呔	necktie
	team		tìm	添	additional
	top		taap	塔	pagoda
	tong		tong	烫	iron (Verb)
k:	cow		kaau	靠	lean on
	Kay		kei	冀	hope
	cut		kāt	咳	cough
	cup		kāp	級	step (Noun)
ch:	chuck		chāk	測	guess
	chew		chìu	超	exceed
	chow		chau	臭	bad smell
	chip		chip	妾	concubine

3. un, as in Yahtbún, Yahtbúnyàhn

Un is a two-part final composed of the high back rounded vowel u [u] followed by the velar nasal consonant n.

u is a high back rounded vowel, which before n has a slight offglide to high central position: u + n = [u:^{i}n]. The vowel is open, not nasalized, before the nasal final. The Cantonese un is roughly comparable to the oon in general American "boon."

Compare Cantonese and English:
1. bún 本 boon (3 times)
2. boon   bún 本 (3 times)

4. **eui** practice

Listen and repeat--remember to keep the lips rounded throughout, remember that the **-i** of **eui** represents the rounded high front vowel **yu** [ü].

> kéuih   (5 times)   佢
> deuim̀hjyuh   (5 times)   對唔住
> deui   (5 times)   對

5. **iu**

iu is a two-part final composed of the high front unrounded vowel **i** [i] plus the high back rounded vowel **u** [u]. In this sequence the **i** is pronounced as an onglide, with the main force of voicing on the **u** portion of the syllable--[^{i}u].

Listen and repeat:

1. síujé   (3 times)
2. síu   (3 times)

6. **Tone practice**

1. dōu dōu   , sing sing   , haih haih   .
2. dōu sing haih   , haih sing dōu   .
3. dōu sing   , sing haih   , dōu haih   , haih dōu   .
4. dōu dōu   , Jèung Jèung   .
5. Jèung, dōu   , dōu Jèung   .
6. síu síu   , néih néih   .
7. síu néih   , néih síu   .
8. haih yàhn   , yàhn haih   .

II. Notes

A. Culture Notes:

1. A Gwóngdùngyàhn is a person from Kwangtung province. In English such a person is usually referred to as 'Cantonese,' the English name deriving from the city of Canton in Kwangtung province. People from Hong Kong are also included in the term Gwóngdùngyàhn.

2. Polite forms in social conversation:

a) Sīnsàang and síujé are polite formal substitutes for néih-- 'you' as terms of direct address.

    1. Sīnsàang gwaising a?   What is the gentleman's (i.e.,
                                   your) name?

    2. Sìujé gwaising a?   What is the lady's (i.e., your)
                                   name?

   (See Drill _11_)

b) <u>Sìujé</u> is the general polite substitute for <u>néih</u> when addressing
a woman, even if she is a married woman.

    Ex:

      Mr. Lee (to Mrs. Chan):

      Sìujé haih m̀hhaih Gwóng- Is the lady (i.e., Are you)
        dùngyàhn a?   from Kwangtung?

   (See Drill _14_)

c) Surname and title as polite formal substitute for <u>néih</u> as term
of address.

    Ex:

      Mr. Lee (to Miss Chan):

      Chàhn Sìujé haih m̀hhaih Is Miss Chan (i.e., Are you)
        Gwóngdùngyàhn a?   from Kwangtung?

   (See Drill _14_)

d) <u>gwai-</u> and <u>sìu-</u>

    1. <u>gwai-</u> is a polite form meaning "your," referring to the
      person you are talking to.

        Ex: gwaising = your name. The literal meaning of <u>gwai-</u>
            "precious, valuable."

    2. <u>sìu-</u> is a polite form used in referring to oneself when
      talking with another person. It means "my." Ex: sìusing =
      my name. The literal meaning of <u>sìu-</u> is "small."
      (See Drill _11_)

    3. <u>Ngóh sing</u> seems more commonly used than <u>sìusing</u>, but
      <u>gwaising</u> is more common than Néih sing mēyéh a? in social
      conversation. At a doctor's office, or in registering for
      school 'What is your name' would be more apt to be asked
      as '<u>Sing mēyéh</u>?' than as '<u>Gwaising a</u>?'

B. Structure Notes.

    Some people in speaking about Cantonese and other Chinese
languages, say "Cantonese has no grammar." In this they are referring

to the fact that words in Cantonese (and other Chinese languages) do
not undergo the changes of form which English words experience in
relation to tense: see, saw, seen; to number: boy, boys; to case: I,
me, my, mine; to word class: photograph, photographer, photography,
photographic; to subject-verb concord: He sits, They sit.

1. Verb form: Absence of Subject-Verb concord.

There is no subject-verb concord in Cantonese. Whereas
the English verb changes form in concord with the subject--
I am, You are, He is--, the Cantonese verb remains in one
form regardless of the subject.

Ex:

Subject	Verb		
Ngóh	haih	Chàhn Síujé.	I am Miss Chan.
Néih	haih	ngóh pàhngyáuh.	You are my friend.
Kéuih	haih	Gwóngdùngyàhn.	He is Cantonese.
Kéuihdeih	haih	Seuhnghóiyàhn.	They are Shanghai people.

(See Drill   3)

2. Noun form: Absence of Singular/Plural Distinction.

There is no distinction in Chinese nouns between singular
and plural. One form is used for both single and plural
objects, with other parts of the sentence, or sometimes simply
the situational context, giving information regarding number.

Ex: yàhn = person, people

Yìnggwokyàhn = 'Englishman, Englishmen.'

Singular/Plural

(a) Kéuih   haih Yìnggwokyàhn. He is an Englishman.
(b) Kéuihdeih haih Yìnggwokyàhn. They are Englishmen.

(See Drill   3)

3. Pronoun forms.

1. Cantonese has three personal pronouns:

1. ngóh = I, me, my
2. néih = you, your (singular)
3. kéuih = he, she, it, him, her

2. Plurality is marked in personal pronouns by the plural
suffix -deih:

1. ngóh = I
   ngóhdeih = we (both inclusive and exclusive)
2. néih = you (sing.)
   néihdeih = you (plu.)
3. kéuih = he, she, it
   kéuihdeih = they
(See Drill __3__)

4. Modification structures: Noun modification:
   In Cantonese a modifier precedes the noun it modifies:
   Example: <u>Modifier</u> + <u>Noun head</u>

   <u>Ngóh</u>   <u>pàhngyáuh</u> haih Yìnggwokyàhn.

   <u>My</u>   <u>friend</u>   is an Englishman.

   We will refer to this modifier-modified noun structure as a
   Noun Phrase (NP), consisting of modifier and head.
   (See Drills 5a, 12, 13)

5. Sentence suffixes.

   What we call sentence suffixes are also called "final
   particles" and "sentence finals."

   Sentence suffixes are used in conversation, and are a
   means by which the speaker signals the listener what he feels
   about what he's saying--that he is doubtful, definite, sur-
   prised, sympathetic, that he means to be polite, or sar-
   castic.

   Some sentence suffixes have actual content meaning. For
   example, mē, which you will learn in Lesson 3, has interrogative meaning, and suffixed to a statement sentence makes
   it a question. But others operate primarily as described
   above--to add an emotion-carrying coloration to the sentences
   they attach to. As such they have been called also "in-
   tonation-carrying particles," intonation here used in its
   "tone of voice" sense.

   Two sentence suffixes appear in the Basic Conversation
   of this lesson:

   1. Sentence suffix <u>a</u>

       The sentence suffix <u>a</u> has the effect of softening the

sentence to which it is attached, making it less
abrupt than it would otherwise be.

Examples from this lesson:

1. Kéuih haih m̀haih   Is she a Cantonese?
   Gwóngdùngyàhn a?

2. M̀haih a.   No.

In English a courteous tone of voice is perhaps the
best counterpart to the a sentence suffix.

(See Basic Conversation (BC), and Drill 7)

2. Sentence suffix nē

   nē in a follow sentence of structure Noun + nē? is
   an interrogative sentence suffix, meaning 'how
   about...?,' 'And...?' In such a sentence nē is
   interrogative on its own:

   Example:

   Ngóh haih Gwóngdùng-   I am a Cantonese; how
      yàhn; néih nē?   about you?

   Sentence suffix a is not substitutable for nē in
   this type of sentence, a not having an interrogative
   sense of its own.

   (See BC, and Drill 14)

We have used tone marks in writing the sentence suffixes,
but perhaps it would have been better to use other symbols,
maybe arrows pointing up for high, diagonally for rising, to
the right for mid, down for falling. Since some finals can
be said with different pitch contours with the effect of
changing the coloration of what is said but not the content,
they are not truly tonal words. For example, sentence suffix
a, encountered in this lesson, we have described as having
the effect of softening an otherwise rather abrupt sentence.
This final can also be said at high pitch: ā, without changing the sentence-softening aspect, but adding liveliness to
the response.

Ex: A: Néih haih m̀haih   Are you a Cantonese?
       Gwóngdùngyàhn a?

B: M̀hhaih ā. Ngóh haih   No, siree, I'm a Shanghai man.
         Seuhnghóiyàhn.

Beginning students, even advanced students, often have a lot of difficulty with sentence suffixes, because they don't fit into categories which we recognize in English. Partly this is because most of us haven't analyzed the English we use. How would you explain, for example, the English "sentences suffixes" in the following:

1. What do you mean by that, pray?
2. Hand me that pencil, will you?
3. Cut that out, hear?
4. He's not coming, I don't think.

Our advice to students in regard to sentence suffixes is absorb them as you can, don't get bogged down in trying to plumb their "real" meanings--in doing so, you spend more time on them than they warrant.

6. Choice-type Questions.

Questions which in English would be answered by yes or no, are formed in Cantonese by coupling the positive and negative forms of a verb together, and requiring an echo answer of the suitable one. This question form we call the Choice-type Question.

     Example:

     Question: Kéuih haih m̀hhaih   Is he an American?
              Méihgwokyàhn a?   [He is-not is American-
                                         person a?]
     Responses: Haih.   Yes. [Is.]
               M̀hhaih.   No. [Not-is]
     (See BC and Drills 6, 9, 13, 14)

7. Question-word Questions.

Question-word Questions are question sentences using the Cantonese question-word equivalents of what, when, where, why, how, how much, how many, who. mēyéh? 'what?' (variant pronunciations mātyéh? and mīyéh?) is an example of a question-word.

In Cantonese question-word (QW) questions pattern like statement sentences--they have the same word order as statement sentences, with the question-word occupying the same position in the
sentence which the reply word occupies in the statement.

Example: Kéuih sing │mēyéh│ a?   [He is surnamed what?] What
                                     is his name?

         Kéuih sing │Wòhng│.   [He is surnamed Wong.] His
                                     name is Wong.

         (See BC and Drill 12, 13)

8. -ge, noun-forming boundword

     ge attaches to the end of a word or phrase which is not
a noun and makes it into a noun phrase. In such cases it
usually works to translate -ge into English as 'one who' or
'such a one.' When we say ge is a boundword we mean it is
never spoken as a one-word sentence, but always accompanies
some other word.

     Example: 1. Kéuih sing Wòhng ge.   She is one who has the
                                         surname Wong. or
                                         She's a person named
                                         Wong.

         (See BC and Drills 9, 10, 12, 13)

     ga is a fusion of ge + sentence suffix a

     Example: A: Kéuih haih m̀hhaih   Is he named Wong?
                    sing Wòhng ga?

              B: M̀hhaih--kéuih   No, he's not named Wong.
                    m̀hhaih sing Wòhng   His name is Ho.
                    ge. Kéuih sing
                    Hòh.

         (See Drill 9)

9. mātyéh, mēyéh, and mīyéh = variant pronunciations for 'what?'
mātyéh is occasionally used in conversations as an
emphatic form; normally the spoken pronunciation is mēyéh or
mīyéh, some people favoring mēyéh, others mīyéh. We have
written mēyéh uniformly in the text, but on the tapes you
will hear all three forms.

III. DRILLS

1. Transformation Drill: Make negative sentences following the
pattern of the example. Student should point to himself in ngóh
sentences, to another student in kéuih and néih sentences.

Ex: T: Kéuih haih Seuhng-   T: He (or she) is from Shanghai.
        hóiyàhn.   (Shanghai person)

    S: Kéuih m̀haih   S: He (or she) is not from
        Seuhnghóiyàhn.   Shanghai.

1. Kéuih haih Seuhnghóiyàhn   1. Kéuih m̀haih Seuhnghóiyàhn.

+ 2. Kéuihdeih haih Gwóngdùngyàhn.   2. Kéuihdeih m̀haih Gwóngdùng-
     (They are Cantonese.)   yàhn.

+ 3. Ngóh haih Jùnggwokyàhn.   3. Ngóh m̀haih Jùnggwokyàhn.
     (I am a Chinese.)

+ 4. Ngóhdeih haih Jùnggwokyàhn.   4. Ngóhdeih m̀haih Jùnggwokyàhn.
     (We are Chinese.)

+ 5. Néih haih Yìnggwokyàhn.   5. Néih m̀haih Yìnggwokyàhn.
     (You are an Englishman.)

+ 6. Néih haih Méihgwokyàhn.   6. Néih m̀haih Méihgwokyàhn.
     (You are an American)

+ 7. Néihdeih haih Méihgwokyàhn.   7. Néihdeih m̀haih Méihgwok-
     (You (plu.) are Americans.)   yàhn.

+ 8. Ngóh haih Yahtbúnyàhn.   8. Ngóh m̀haih Yahtbúnyàhn.
     (I am a Japanese.)

+ 9. Ngóh haih Tòihsāanyàhn.   9. Ngóh m̀haih Tòihsāanyàhn.
     (I am a Toishan man.)

_____

2. Substitution Drill: Substitute the cue word to make a new sentence, following the pattern of the example.

Ex: T: Kéuihdeih haih   T: They are Cantonese.
        Gwóngdùngyàhn   /Shanghai people/
        /Seuhnghóiyàhn/

S: Kéuihdeih haih   S: They are Shanghai people.
   Seuhnghóiyàhn.

1. Kéuihdeih haih Seuhnghóiyàhn.   1. Kéuihdeih haih Méihgwokyàhn.
   /Méihgwokyàhn/

2. Kéuihdeih haih Méihgwokyàhn.   2. Kéuihdeih haih Yìnggwokyàhn.
   /Yìnggwokyàhn/

3. Kéuihdeih haih Yìnggwokyàhn.   3. Kéuihdeih haih Yahtbúnyàhn.
   /Yahtbúnyàhn/

4. Kéuihdeih haih Yahtbúnyàhn.   4. Kéuihdeih haih Jùnggwokyàhn.
   /Jùnggwokyàhn/

5. Kéuihdeih haih Jùnggwokyàhn.   5. Kéuihdeih haih Gwóngdùng-
   /Gwóngdùngyàhn/   yàhn.

_____

3. Mixed Substitution Drill: Substitute the cue word in the appropriate position, following the pattern of the example.

   Ex: T: Ngóh haih Seuhng-   I am from Shanghai.
          hóiyàhn. /néihdeih/   /you (plu.)/

       S: Néihdeih haih Seuhng-   You (plu.) are from Shanghai.
          hóiyàhn.

       T: Néihdeih haih Seuhng-   You (plu.) are from Shanghai.
          hóiyàhn.   /Chinese/
          /Jùnggwokyàhn/

       S: Néihdeih haih Jùng-   You (plu.) are Chinese.
          gwokyàhn.

1. Kéuih haih Yìnggwokyàhn.   1. Kéuihdeih haih Yìnggwokyàhn.
   /kéuihdeih/

2. Kéuihdeih haih Yìnggwokyàhn. 2. Néihdeih haih Yìnggwokyàhn.
   /néihdeih/

3. Néihdeih haih Yìnggwokyàhn.   3. Néihdeih haih Méihgwokyàhn.
   /Méihgwokyàhn/

4. Néihdeih haih Méihgwokyàhn.   4. Ngóh haih Méihgwokyàhn.
   /ngóh/

5. Ngóh haih hohksàang.   5. Ngóh haih sìnsàang.
   /sìnsàang/

_____

4. Expansion Drill: Expand the cue sentences as indicated in the
   example. Students should gesture to indicate pronouns.

   Ex: T: Kéuih mhhaih Léih   She is not Mrs. Lee.
          Táai.

45

S: Kéuih m̀hhaih Léih   She is not Mrs. Lee, I am.
   Táai, ngóh haih.

1. Kéuih m̀hhaih Jèung Sàang.   1. Kéuih m̀hhaih Jèung Sàang;
                                        ngóh haih.

2. Kéuih m̀hhaih Chàhn Síujé.   2. Kéuih m̀hhaih Chàhn Síujé;
                                        ngóh haih.

3. Kéuih m̀hhaih Hòh Sàang.   3. Kéuih m̀hhaih Hòh Sàang;
                                        ngóh haih.

4. Kéuih m̀hhaih Léih Táai.   4. Kéuih m̀hhaih Léih Táai;
                                        ngóh haih.

5. Kéuih m̀hhaih Chàhn Sàang.   5. Kéuih m̀hhaih Chàhn Sàang;
                                        ngóh haih.

---

5. Transformation Drill: Respond according to the pattern of the
   example. Students gesture pronouns.

        Ex: T: Ngóh haih Méih-   T: I am an American.
               gwokyàhn.

            S: Néih haih m̀hhaih   S: Are you an American?
               Méihgwokyàhn a?

1. Ngóh haih Gwóngdùngyàhn.   1. Néih haih m̀hhaih Gwóng-
                                        dùngyàhn a?

2. Ngóh haih Wòhng Sàang.   2. Néih haih m̀hhaih Wòhng
                                        Sàang a?

3. Kéuih haih Léih Sàang.   3. Kéuih haih m̀hhaih Léih
                                        Sàang a?

4. Ngóh haih Méihgwokyàhn.   4. Néih haih m̀hhaih Méih-
                                        gwokyàhn a?

5. Ngóhdeih haih Yahtbúnyàhn.   5. Néihdeih haih m̀hhaih
                                        Yahtbúnyàhn a?

6. Kéuih haih Jùnggwokyàhn.   6. Kéuih haih m̀hhaih Jùng-
                                        gwokyàhn a?

    a. Do the above sentences as an expansion drill, expanding
       with pàhngyáuh thus:

       T: Ngóh haih Gwóngdùngyàhn.

       S: Ngóh pàhngyáuh haih Gwóngdùngyàhn.

---

6. Response Drill: Respond according to the pattern of the example.

Ex: T: Jèung Síujé haih   T: Is Miss Cheung an American?
       m̀hhaih Méihgwokyàhn   /English-person/
       a? /Yìnggwokyàhn/

    S: M̀hhaih. Kéuih haih S: No, she's English.
       Yìnggwokyàhn.

1. Néih haih m̀hhaih Yìnggwokyàhn   1. M̀hhaih. Ngóh haih Méih-
   a? /Méihgwokyàhn/   gwokyàhn.

2. Néih haih m̀hhaih Seuhng-   2. M̀hhaih. Ngóh haih Gwóng-
   hóiyàhn a? /Gwóngdùngyàhn/   dùngyàhn.

3. Jèung Sàang haih m̀hhaih   3. M̀hhaih. Kéuih haih Seuhng-
   Gwóngdùngyàhn a?   hóiyàhn.
   /Seuhnghóiyàhn/

4. Máh Táai haih m̀hhaih Yìng-   4. M̀hhaih. Kéuih haih Méihgwokyàhn a? /Méihgwokyàhn/   gwokyàhn.

5. Kéuih haih m̀hhaih Seuhng-   5. M̀hhaih. Kéuih haih Tòih-
   hóiyàhn a? /Tòihsāanyàhn/   sāanyàhn.

---

7. Conversation Exercise: Carry on the suggested Conversations
   following the pattern of the example.

Ex: A: Néih haih m̀hhaih   A: Are you Miss Cheung?
       Jèung Síujé a?

    B: M̀hhaih. Ngóh sing   B: No, my name is Chan.
       Chàhn.

1. A: .... Chàhn Sàang a?   1. A: Néih haih m̀hhaih Chàhn
                                         Sàang a?
   B: .... Hòh.   B: M̀hhaih a. Ngóh sing Hòh.

2. A: .... Léih Síujé a?   2. A: Néih haih m̀hhaih Léih
                                         Síujé a?
   B: .... Jèung.   B: M̀hhaih a. Ngóh sing
                                         Jèung.

3. A: .... Chàhn Táai a?   3. A: Néih haih m̀hhaih Chàhn
                                         Táai a?
   B: .... Hòh.   B: M̀hhaih a. Ngóh sing Hòh.

4. A: .... Léih Sàang a?   4. A: Néih haih m̀hhaih Léih
                                         Sàang a?
   B: .... Jèung.   B: M̀hhaih a. Ngóh sing
                                         Jèung.

5. A: .... Hòh Síujé a?   5. A: Néih haih m̀hhaih Hòh
                                         Síujé a?

47

B: .... Chàhn.   B: M̀hhaih a. Ngóh sing Chàhn.

7a. Continue, with student A using a name at random and
student B using his own name in response.

---

8. Response Drill: Respond according to the pattern of the example:

Ex: T: Kéuih sing Wòhng.   T: Her name is Wong. /Cheung/
          /Jèung/

    S: Kéuih m̀hhaih sing   S: Her name is not Wong, it's
          Wòhng, sing Jèung.   Cheung.

1. Kéuih sing Jèung. /Hòh/   1. Kéuih m̀hhaih sing Jèung,
                                         sing Hòh.

2. Kéuih sing Hòh. /Chàhn/   2. Kéuih m̀hhaih sing Hòh, sing
                                         Chàhn.

3. Kéuih sing Chàhn. /Léih/   3. Kéuih m̀hhaih sing Chàhn,
                                         sing Léih.

4. Kéuih sing Léih. /Làuh/   4. Kéuih m̀hhaih sing Léih, sing
                                         Làuh.

5. Kéuih sing Máh. /Wòhng/   5. Kéuih m̀hhaih sing Máh, sing
                                         Wòhng.

---

9. Response Drill

Ex: T: Kéuih haih m̀hhaih sing   Is her name Chan? /Ho/
 +   Chàhn <u>ga</u>? /Hòh/

    S: M̀hhaih. Kéuih sing Hòh   No, her name is Ho.
          ge.

1. Kéuih haih m̀hhaih sing Léih   1. M̀hhaih. Kéuih sing Chàhn ge.
      ga? /Chàhn/

2. Kéuih haih m̀hhaih sing Máh   2. M̀hhaih. Kéuih sing Hòh ge.
      ga? /Hòh/

3. Kéuih haih m̀hhaih sing Jèung   3. M̀hhaih. Kéuih sing Léih ge.
      ga? /Léih/

4. Kéuih haih m̀hhaih sing Chàhn   4. M̀hhaih. Kéuih sing Máh ge.
      ga? /Máh/

5. Kéuih haih m̀hhaih sing Hòh   5. M̀hhaih. Kéuih sing Jèung ge.
      ga? /Jèung/

Comment:

a. Sentence suffix <u>ga</u> is a fusion of <u>ge</u> + <u>a</u> = <u>ga</u>.

48

b. In the choice-type question form, <u>sing</u> is preceded by
haih m̀hhaih to make the question.

---

10. Expansion Drill:

Ex: T: Néihdeih haih Méihgwokyàhn.
/ngóhdeih/

      You are Americans. /we/

S: Néihdeih haih Méih-
gwokyàhn; ngóhdeih
dōu haih Méihgwok-
yàhn.

      You are Americans; we are also
Americans.

1. Kéuihdeih haih Yìnggwokyàhn.
/ngóhdeih/

    1. Kéuihdeih haih Yìnggwokyàhn;
ngóhdeih dōu haih Yìng-
gwokyàhn.

2. Ngóhdeih haih Seuhnghóiyàhn.
/kéuihdeih/

    2. Ngóhdeih haih Seuhnghóiyàhn;
kéuihdeih dōu haih Seuhnghóiyàhn.

3. Wòhng Táai haih ngóh pàhngyáuh. /kéuih/

    3. Wòhng Táai haih ngóh pàhng-
yáuh; kéuih dōu haih ngóh
pàhngyáuh.

4. Kéuihdeih haih Gwóngdùngyàhn.
/néihdeih/

    4. Kéuihdeih haih Gwóngdùngyàhn;
néihdeih dōu haih Gwóng-
dùngyàhn.

5. Ngóhdeih haih sing Chàhn ge.
/kéuihdeih/

    5. Ngóhdeih haih sing Chàhn ge;
kéuihdeih dōu haih sing
Chàhn ge.

---

11. Conversation Exercise

Example:

1. A: Síujé gwaising a?

    (To a woman) What is your name?

   B: Síusing Hòh.

    My name is Ho.

   A: Hòh Síujé.

    Miss Ho.

2. A: Sīnsàang gwaising a?

    (To a man) What is your name?

   B: Síusing Làuh.

    My name is Lau.

   A: Làuh Sàang.

    Mr. Lau.

1. A: Sīnsàang ....?

    1. A: Sīnsàang gwaising a?

   B: ....Léih.

      B: Síusing Léih.

   A: ....

      A: Léih Sàang.

49

2. A: Sīnsàang ....?
   B: ....Chàhn.
   A: ....

2. A: Sīnsàang gwaising a?
   B: Sìusing Chàhn.
   A: Chàhn Sàang.

3. A: Sīnsàang ....?
   B: ....Jèung.
   A: ....

3. A: Sīnsàang gwaising a?
   B: Sìusing Jèung.
   A: Jèung Sàang.

4. A: Sìujé ....?
   B: ....Wòhng.
   A: ....

4. A: Sìujé gwaising a?
   B: Sìusing Wòhng.
   A: Wòhng Sìujé.

5. A: Sìujé ....?
   B: ....Hòh.
   A: ....

5. A: Sìujé gwaising a?
   B: Sìusing Hòh.
   A: Hòh Sìujé.

---

12. Conversation Drill

Ex: A: Néih pàhngyáuh sing mēyéh a?

What is your friend's name?

B: Kéuih sing Wòhng ge.

His name is Wong.

1. A: ....?

   B: ......Hòh........

1. A: Néih pàhngyáuh sing mēyéh a?

   B: Kéuih sing Hòh ge.

2. A: ....?

   B: ......Làuh.......

2. A: Néih pàhngyáuh sing mēyéh a?

   B: Kéuih sing Làuh ge.

3. A: ....?

   B: ......Wòhng......

3. A: Néih pàhngyáuh sing mēyéh a?

   B: Kéuih sing Wòhng ge.

4. A: ....?

   B: ......Jèung......

4. A: Néih pàhngyáuh sing mēyéh a?

   B: Kéuih sing Jèung ge.

5. A: ....?

   B: ......Léih.......

5. A: Néih pàhngyáuh sing mēyéh a?

   B: Kéuih sing Léih ge.

50

13. Conversation Drill

  Ex: A: Néih pàhngyáuh sing A: What is your friend's name?
     mēyéh a?

    B: Kéuih sing Wòhng ge. B: His name is Wong.

    A: Kéuih haih m̀hhaih A: Is he a Cantonese?
     Gwóngdùngyàhn a?

    B: M̀hhaih. Kéuih haih B: No, he's a Japanese.
     Yahtbúnyàhn.

1. A: ....?   1. A: Néih pàhngyáuh sing
                 mēyéh a?

 B: ....Hòh.   B: Kéuih sing Hòh ge.

 A: ....Yìnggwokyàhn a?   A: Kéuih haih m̀hhaih
                 Yìnggwokyàhn a?

 B: ......Méihgwokyàhn.   B: M̀hhaih. Kéuih haih
                 Méihgwokyàhn.

2. A: ....?   2. A: Néih pàhngyáuh sing
                 mēyéh a?

 B: ....Léih.   B: Kéuih sing Léih ge.

 A: ...Seuhnghóiyàhn a?   A: Kéuih haih m̀hhaih
                 Seuhnghóiyàhn a?

 B: ......Tòihsāanyàhn.   B: M̀hhaih. Kéuih haih
                 Tòihsāanyàhn.

3. A: ....?   3. A: Néih pàhngyáuh sing
                 mēyéh a?

 B: ....Chàhn.   B: Kéuih sing Chàhn ge.

 A: ....Méihgwokyàhn a?   A: Kéuih haih m̀hhaih Méih-
                 gwokyàhn a?

 B: ......Yìnggwokyàhn.   B: M̀hhaih. Kéuih haih
                 Yìnggwokyàhn.

4. A: ....?   4. A: Néih pàhngyáuh sing
                 mēyéh a?

 B: ....Máh.   B: Kéuih sing Máh ge.

 A: ...Gwóngdùngyàhn a?   A: Kéuih haih m̀hhaih Gwóng-
                 dùngyàhn a?

 B: .....Seuhnghóiyàhn.   B: M̀hhaih. Kéuih haih
                 Seuhnghóiyàhn.

5. A: ....?   5. A: Néih pàhngyáuh sing
                 mēyéh a?

 B: ....Wòhng.   B: Kéuih sing Wòhng ge.

A: .....Yahtbúnyàhn a?

A: Kéuih haih m̀hhaih Yahtbúnyàhn a?

B: ......Jùnggwokyàhn.

B: M̀hhaih. Kéuih haih Jùnggwokyàhn.

6. A: ....?

6. A: Néih pàhngyáuh sing
mēyéh a?

B: ....Jèung.

B: Kéuih sing Jèung ge.

A: ...Seuhnghóiyàhn a?

A: Kéuih haih m̀hhaih Seuhnghóiyàhn a?

B: ....Yahtbúnyàhn.

B: M̀hhaih. Kéuih haih Yahtbúnyàhn.

---

14. Conversation Drill: Carry on the suggested conversations following
the pattern of the example.

Ex: A: Sīnsàang haih m̀hhaih
Méihgwokyàhn a?

Is the gentleman (i.e. Are you)
an American?

B: M̀hhaih--ngóh haih
Yìnggwokyàhn.
Síujé nē?

No, I'm an Englishman. And
the lady (i.e. you)?

A: Ngóh haih Gwóngdùng-
yàhn.

I am a Cantonese.

1. A: (Woman): Sīnsàang .....
....Gwóngdùngyàhn.

A: Sīnsàang haih m̀hhaih
Gwóngdùngyàhn a?

B: (Man) : ....Seuhnghóiyàhn.

B: M̀hhaih. Ngóh haih Seuhnghóiyàhn. Síujé nē?

A: (Woman): .....Yahtbúnyàhn.

A: Ngóh haih Yahtbúnyàhn.

2. A: (Man) : Síujé ....
......Yahtbúnyàhn...

A: Síujé haih m̀hhaih Yahtbúnyàhn a?

B: (Woman): ....Jùnggwokyàhn...

B: M̀hhaih. Ngóh haih Jùng-
gwoyàhn. Sīnsàang nē?

A: (Man) : .....Méihgwokyàhn..

A: Ngóh haih Méihgwokyàhn.

3. A: (Man) : Sīnsàang ....
......Yìnggwokyàhn

A: Sīnsàang haih m̀hhaih
Yìnggwokyàhn a?

B: (Man) : .....Méihgwokyàhn.

B: M̀hhaih. Ngóh haih Méihgwokyàhn. Sīnsàang nē?

A: (Man) : .....Gwóngdùngyàhn.

A: Ngóh haih Gwóngdùngyàhn.

4. A: (Woman): Máh Sīnsàang ....
.....Yahtbúnyàhn.

A: Máh Sīnsàang haih m̀hhaih
Yahtbúnyàhn a?

B: (Man)   : ..... Jùnggwokyàhn.   B: Mhhaih. Ngóh haih Jùng-
           ....Chàhn Síujé...?   gwokyàhn. Chàhn Síujé
                                        nè?

A: (Woman): .....Yìnggwokyàhn.   A: Ngóh haih Yìnggwokyàhn.

   a. Continue, students using their own situation to carry
      on the suggested conversations.

V. CONVERSATIONS FOR LISTENING

    The text of these conversations is written out in Appendix 1.

    Listen to the tape with your book closed, checking the text
afterward, if necessary.

. SAY IT IN CANTONESE:

    In this section you get directed practice in using some of the
Cantonese you have learned, using the English sentences to prompt
you. This is not to be thought of as a translation exercise--the
English is just to get you going. Try to put the ideas into Cantonese,
saying it the way the Cantonese would. Often there will be quite a
few ways to say the same thing.

A. Ask the person sitting next   And he answers:
    to you:

   1. What is your name?   1. My name is _____.

   2. Are you an Englishman?   2. No, I'm an American.

   3. Is your friend also an   3. Yes, he is.
      American?

   4. Is Miss Ho from Shanghai?   4. No, she's from Toishan.

   5. Is Mr. Lau a Toishan man?   5. Yes, he is.

   6. What is your friend's name?   6. His name is Lee.

   7. Are you Mr(s). Wong?   7. I'm not Mr(s). Wong, my name
                                is _____.

   8. Are you a student?   8. No, I'm not a student, I'm a
                                teacher.

B. At a party:

1. Mr. Wong asks Mr. Ho his name.
2. Mr. Ho replies that his name is Ho, and asks Mr. Wong his name.
3. Mr. Wong gives his name, and asks Mr. Ho if he is a Kwangtung man.
4. Mr. Ho answers that he is. He asks Mr. Ho if he also is from Kwangtung.
5. Mr. Wong says no, that he is a Shanghai man.

C. A and B, two new students, wait for the teacher to come to class:

1. A asks B what his name is. (students use actual names)
2. B replies and inquires A's name.
3. A gives his name, and asks B if he is Japanese.
4. B replies, and asks A if he is an Englishman.
5. A replies, and asks B what C's name is.
6. B replies, adding that C is Chinese.

Vocabulary Checklist for Lesson 2

1. a	ss:	sen. suf., to soften abruptness	
2. dōu	Adv:	also	
3. ga	ss:	sen. suf., fusion of ge + a = ga	
4. Gám	sp:	'Well then, ...' 'Say,...' sen. prefix resuming the thread of previous discussion	
5. -ge	bf:	noun-forming boundword; -ge added to a Verb Phrase makes it a Noun Phrase	
6. gwaising?	Ph:	what is (your) surname? [polite]	
7. Gwóngdùng	pw:	Kwangtung, a province in SE China	
8. Gwóngdùngyàhn [go]	n:	Cantonese person, person from Kwangtung Province	
9. Jùnggwokyàhn	n:	Chinese person	
10. kéuih	Pro:	he, him, his	
11. kéuihdeih	Pro:	they, them, their	
12. mātyéh?	QW:	what?	

13. Měihgwokyàhn	n:	American
14. mēyéh?	QW:	what?
15. mīyéh?	QW:	what?
16. nē	ss:	sen. suf. for questions
17. néih	Pro:	you, your
18. néihdeih	Pro:	you, your (plu.)
19. ngóhdeih	Pro:	we, our, us
20. pàhngyáuh [gò]	n:	friend
21. Seuhnghói	pw:	Shanghai
22. Seuhnghóiyàhn	n:	person from Shanghai
23. Sīnsàang	n:	"Sir," term of direct address
24. sīnsàang	n:	man
25. síujé	n:	'Miss,' Madame, term of direct address
26. síusing	Ph:	my surname is (polite)
27. Tòihsāan	pw:	Toishan, a county in southern Kwangtung about 100 miles west of Hong Kong.
28. Tòihsāanyàhn	n:	person from Toishan
29. yàhn	n:	person
30. Yahtbúnyàhn	n:	Japanese person
31. Yīnggwokyàhn	n:	Englishman, person from England

CLASSROOM PHRASES

Learn to respond to the following classroom instructions. First look at the English equivalents as the teacher reads the Cantonese instructions. Then close your books and listen to the teacher and watch his gestures to help you understand. Check your book if you have difficulty. The teacher will say each sentence several times to help you become familiar with the instructions. Your goal is to be able to respond to the Cantonese without doing mental translations into English. Knowing the scope of what to expect will make the details stand out clearly.

1. Ngóh jídou bĭngo, bĭngo jauh góng.

1. I'll point to someone, and that person should speak.

2. Yìhgā ngóh duhk, néihdeih sĭn tèng.

2. Now I'll read aloud and you (plu.) first listen.

3. Yìhgā néihdeih m̀hhóu tái syù, gànjyuh ngóh duhk.

3. Now don't look at your books, and recite after me.

4. Yìhgā néihdeih gànjyuh laihgeui gám jouh.

4. Do (the problems) according to the pattern set in the example sentence.

5. Yìhgā ngóhdeih tái daih yāt go lihnjaahp.

5. Now we'll look at the first exercise.

6. Yìhgā ngóhdeih tái daih yāt geui.

6. Now we'll look at the first sentence.

7. Yáuh móuh mahntàih?

7. Are there any questions? OR Do you have any questions?

Responses:

Yáuh.

Have. (i.e., Yes, I have a question)

Móuh.

Don't have. (i.e., No, I don't have any questions.)

8. Nihng táu.

8. Shake the head.

9. Ngahp táu.

9. Nod the head.

56

I. BASIC CONVERSATION

A. <u>Buildup</u>:

           (Three colleagues, returning from lunch, are waiting
           for the elevator in their office building. Next to
           them two other businessmen are engaged in conversations)

Wòhng Síujé

wá	language
mēyéh wá a?	what language?
góng	speak
góng mēyéh wá a?	speak what language?
Kéuihdeih góng mēyéh wá a?	What language are they speaking?
jí <u>or</u> jídou	know
jí m̀hjí a?	know/not know?
Néih jí m̀hjí kéuihdeih góng mēyéh wá a?	Do you know what language they are speaking?
Gwokyúh	Mandarin
góng Gwokyúh	speak Mandarin
Haih m̀hhaih góng Gwokyúh a?	Are they speaking Mandarin?

Chàhn Sàang

M̀hhaih.	(They) are not.
Seuhnghóiwá	Shanghai dialect
Kéuihdeih góng Seuhnghóiwá.	They're speaking the Shanghai dialect.

Jèung Síujé

sīk	know (how)
sīk góng Seuhnghóiwá	know how to speak Shanghai dialect, be able to speak Shanghai dialect.
mē?	sentence suf., indicating surprised question
Néih sīk góng Seuhnghóiwá mē?	You can speak Shanghai dialect?!

Chàhn Sàang

sèsíu	a little, somewhat

57

jē   sentence suf., indicating
                                      'merely', 'only', 'that's
                                      all'

Sīk sèsíu jē.   I know a little, that's all.

Wòhng Síujé

tùhng   and
Seuhnghóiwá tùhng Gwokyúh   Shanghai dialect and
                                      Mandarin

dōu   both
kéuih dōu sīk góng   he speaks both
Seuhnghóiwá tùhng Gwokyúh   he speaks both Shanghai
  kéuih dōu sīk góng   dialect and Mandarin.
ga   sen. suf. for matter of
                                      fact assertion.

Seuhnghóiwá tùhng Gwokyúh kéuih   He speaks both Shanghai dialect
  dōu sīk góng ga.   and Mandarin.

Jèung Síujé

Yìngmán or Yìngmàhn   English language
Gám, néih sīk m̀hsīk Yìngmán a?   Well, do you know English?

Chàhn Sàang

sīk góng sèsíu   can speak a little
sé   write
m̀hsīk sé   can't write
daahnhaih   but
daahnhaih m̀hsīk sé   but can't write
Sīk góng sèsíu, daahnhaih m̀hsīk   I can speak a little, but I
sé.   can't write.

Jèung Síujé

hohk   study, learn
séung   wish to, want to, would
                                      like to

séung hohk   would like to learn
séung hohk Yìngmán   would like to learn English
dī   a little, some
séung hohk dī Yìngmán   would like to learn a
                                      little English

Ngóh séung hohk dī Yìngmán--   I'd like to learn a little
                                  English--

  dím a?   how?
  dím góng a?   how (do you) say?
  Yìngmán, dím góng a?   how is it said in English?
  yāt yih sàam sei ńgh   one two three four five
Yāt yih sàam sei ńgh, Yìngmán   How do you say 'one two three
  dím góng a?   four five' in English?

<u>Chàhn Sàang</u>

One two three four five.   One two three four five.

<u>Jèung Síujé</u>

  chìngchó   clear
  m̀hchìngchó   not clear
Ngóh tèng m̀hchìngchó.   I didn't hear clearly.
  yāt chi   one time, once
  góng yāt chi   say (it) one time
  joi   again
  joi góng yāt chi   say (it) once again
  m̀hgòi néih   Would you please ...
M̀hgòi néih joi góng yāt chi.   Would you please say it once
                                  again?

B. <u>Recapitulation</u>:

<u>Wòhng Síujé</u>:

Néih jì m̀hjì kéuihdeih góng mēyéh   What language are they speaking?
  wá a? Haih m̀hhaih góng Gwokyúh a? Are they speaking Mandarin?

<u>Chàhn Sàang</u>:

M̀hhaih. Kéuihdeih góng Seuhnghói- (They) are not. They're
  wá.   speaking the Shanghai
                                   dialect.

<u>Jèung Síujé</u>:

Néih sīk góng Seuhnghóiwá mē?   You can speak the Shanghai
                                   dialect?

<u>Chàhn Sàang</u>:

Sīk sèsíu jē.   I know a little, that's all.

Wòhng Síujé:

Seuhnghóiwá tùhng Gwokyúh kéuih dōu sīk góng ga.	He speaks both Shanghai dialect and Mandarin.

Jèung Síujé:

Gám, néih sīk m̀hsīk Yìngmán a?	Well, do you know English?

Chàhn Sàang:

Sīk góng sèsíu, daahnhaih m̀hsīk sé.	I can speak a little, but I can't write.

Jèung Síujé:

Ngóh séung hohk dī Yìngmán-- Yāt yih sàam sei ńgh, Yìngmán dím góng a?	I'd like to learn a little English--How do you say 'one two three four five' in English?

Chàhn Sàang:

One two three four five.	One two three four five.

Jèung Síujé:

Ngóh tèng m̀hchìngchó. M̀hgòi néih joi góng yāt chi.	I didn't hear clearly. Would you please say it once again.

+ + + + + + + + + + + +

Pronunciation

1. Open vowels before nasal consonants:

Practice the open vowel before a nasal final in the syllables of that structure you have had thus far in the text. Hold your nose, listen, and repeat:

-m: gám 敢 gám   , sàam 衫 sàam   .

-n: Yahtbún 日本 Yahtbún   ,
   Chàhn 陳 Chàhn   , jóusàhn 早晨 jóusàhn   .

-ng: séung 想 séung   , Jèung 張 Jèung   ,
   góng 講 góng   , sīnsàang 先生 sīnsàang   ,
   sing 姓 sing   , gwaising 貴姓 gwaising   .

2. Nasalized vowel following nasal consonant:

Vowels following nasal consonants in the same syllable are nasalized in Cantonese, whereas in English a vowel following a nasal consonant in the same syllable is open.

Listen to your teacher as he holds his nose and says:

ngóh 我

60

néih 你

nē 呢

Máh 馬

Yìngmán 英文

You notice that the vowels are partially blocked when the nose is blocked, revealing that some air is normally released through the nose. Repeat the above words after your teacher, holding your nose to test if you are nasalizing the vowel.

If you can't quite say these right your pronunciation will sound foreign accented, but it won't make any significant different because what you say won't have some other meaning, as it might if you got the tone wrong.

3. eung practice:

    1. séung   séung   séung

    2. Jèung   Jèung   Jèung

4. eui practice: (Remember that the -i here represents the lip-rounded yu sound.)

    1. kéuih   kéuih   kéuih

    2. deuimhjyuh   deui   deui

5. eui/oi contrast practice:

    1. deui   deui   deui

    2. joi   joi   joi

    3. deui   joi   , deui   joi   , deui   joi   .

    4. joi   deui   , joi   deui   , joi   deui   .

6. ok, as in hohk, Jùnggwok

-k: k in final position is produced by the back of the tongue pressing against the roof of the mouth, stopping the air flow at the junction of the hard and soft palates. In final position k is un-released--[k˺].

o: o before k has the same value as o elsewhere--mid back rounded vowel: [ɔ].

Listen and repeat:

    1. hohk 學 (5 times)

    2. Jùnggwok 中國 (5 times)

    3. ngóh hohk 我學 , ngóh hohk   , ngóh hohk   .

    4. joi hohk 再學, joi hohk   , joi hohk   .

5. hohk 學 góng 講 , hohk   góng   , hohk   góng   .

7. **ng as in ńgh**

The velar nasal consonant **ng** occurs as a vowel, in that the consonant **ng** is syllabic in the syllable **ńgh**. (There are also two surnames using the syllable **ng**.)

Listen and repeat:

想   五   1. séung séung   , ńgh ńgh   .

我   五   2. ngóh ngóh   , ńgh ńgh   ,

一二三四五 3. yāt yih sàam sei ńgh   .

II. NOTES

A. Culture Notes:

1. Chinese languages

Gwóngdùngwá: The language spoken in the area roughly coinciding
with Kwangtung Province in SE China is called <u>Gwóng-
dùngwá</u> 'Kwangtung - speech.' In English it is referred
to as 'Cantonese,' named after the major city in
which it was spoken when Westerners arrived in China
and began to learn it.

There are many dialects of <u>Gwóngdùngwá</u>, of which
the recognized standard is the language of Canton and
Hong Kong. This book will not concern itself with the
many dialects, but will concentrate solely on Standard Cantonese. (The dialect of Cantonese spoken by
most American Chinese is <u>Tòihsāanwá</u>, spoken in
Toishan county in Southern Kwangtung, from whence
most American Chinese emigrated.)

Gwokyúh: [national-language] called in English 'Mandarin,' is
the native language of the greater part of north and
northwest China. Mandarin has been promoted as the
national language by both the Communist Chinese and
the Nationalists and is the language of instruction
in the school systems of both China and Taiwan.

Seuhnghóiwá: 'Shanghai dialect' spoken in the area around Shanghai
on the East Coast of China.

2. Dialect differences in Standard Cantonese: initial <u>n</u> <u>l</u>

In Standard Cantonese as spoken in Hong Kong there exist
variations in pronunciation which cannot be called substandard,
since they are used by educated persons. One such variation
is to substitute an <u>l</u> sound for an <u>n</u> sound in words and syllables
which begin with <u>n</u>. Some educated speakers do not have initial
<u>n</u> in their speech, and substitute <u>l</u> wherever <u>n</u> occurs. This is
quite common in Hong Kong.

> Ex: néih ──→ léih   'you (sing.)'
> néihdeih ──→ léihdeih   'you (plu.)'

B. Structure Notes:

1. <u>Uninflected verb forms in Cantonese:</u>

Verbs in English have compulsory differences in form (inflec-
tions) to represent action in progress (is eating), intended
action (going to eat), past action (ate), general statement (eats),
and others.

Broadly speaking, Cantonese verbs do not have the same compulsory differences in form. One form may cover action in progress,
intended action, past action, general statement. For example:
<u>Kéuih gaau Gwóngdùngwá</u> can mean: He is teaching Cantonese, He
taught Cantonese, He teaches Cantonese.

> (See Drill <u>1, 6</u>)

Additional clements <u>may</u> be used by the speaker to particularize
action in progress, repeated action, accomplished action, etc.,
but their use is not the compulsory feature of the language that
it is in English.

2. <u>Verbs in series</u>: affirmative, negative, and question forms.

1. When two verbs occur together in series, it is the first verb
   which forms a set with the negative and the choice-type
   question.

> Example: Kéuih <u>sīk góng</u> Gwokyúh.   He can speak Mandarin.
> Kéuih <u>m̀hsīk góng</u> Gwokyúh. He can't speak Mandarin.
> Kéuih <u>sīk m̀hsīk góng</u>   Can he speak Mandarin?
> Gwokyúh a?

63

2. haih is frequently used in series with action verbs in the
   negative and in choice questions, but not normally in the
   affirmative or in question-word questions.

   (QWQ): Kéuihdeih góng mēyéh   What language are they
          wá a?   speaking?

   (CHQ): Haih m̀haih góng   Are they speaking Mandarin?
          Gwokyúh a?

   (Neg): M̀haih góng Gwokyúh--   (They're) not speaking
                                          Mandarin--

   (Aff): Kéuihdeih góng Seuhng-   They're speaking Shanghai
          hóiwá.   dialect.
                    (See BC)

3. Sentence suffix mē

      mē is an interrogative sentence suffix indicating surprised
   question. mē makes a question sentence of the statement sentence
   it attaches to, with the force of "What?! I can hardly believe
   it!"

      Ex: Néih sīk góng Seuhnghóiwá mē?!   What?! You can speak Shang-
                                           hai dialect?!

                    (See BC and Drill 2)

4. Sentence suffix jē.

      jē has the force of "merely," "only," "that's all." Alternate
   pronunciations are ja, or je.

      Ex: Sīk góng sèsíu jē.   I can speak just a bit,
                                        that's all.

5. Sentence suffix ga

   1. Sentence suffix ga (usually pronounced [kə], similar to the gu
      sound in the English word "Gus") attaches to a sentence,
      giving a matter-of-fact connotation to the sentiment expressed.

         Ex. (from Basic Conversation):

            Seuhnghóiwá tùhng Gwokyúh   Shanghai dialect and Manda-
              Kéuih dōu sīk góng ga.   rin, he can speak both,
                                         that's a fact.
      The implication is that there's nothing extraordinary about
      it, that's simply the way it is.

64

2. Matter-of-fact __ga__ and NP forming __ge__.

These two are sometimes difficult to differentiate. A test
is that a NP __ge__ sentence either uses the verb __haih__ or can be
expanded with __haih__, but a matter-of-fact __ga__ sentence can't
always be expanded with __haih__.

Ex: 1. Kéuih haih gaau Yìng-   He is someone who teaches
       mán ge.   English.
            (See Drill 18)

2. Kéuih (haih) sing   He is someone named Wong.
   Wòhng ge.

3. Seuhnghóiwá tùhng   Shanghai dialect and Manda-
   Gwokyúh kéuih dōu sīk   rin, he can speak both,
   góng ga.   that's a fact.

6. __Loose relationship of Subject-Predicate in Cantonese__: Subject +
   Predicate as Topic + Comment.

We described full sentences above in Lesson One as being
composed of Subject and Predicate, in that order.

Below are examples of Subject-Predicate sentences:

Subject	Predicate
1. Ngóh	sing Chàhn.
2. Kéuih	sīk góng Seuhnghóiwá mē?!
3. Néih pàhngyáuh	góng mēyéh wá a?
4. Síujé	gwaising a?
5. Yìngmán	dím góng?
6. Yāt yih sàam	Yìngmán dím góng a?
7. Seuhnghóiwá	
tùhng Gwokyúh	kéuih dōu sīk góng ga.
8. Néih jî mhjî	kéuihdeih góng mēyéh wá a?

You will note from the sentences above that Subject in
Cantonese does not cover the same territory that Subject in English
does. For example, Sentence No. 7 above might be rendered in
English: "Shanghai dialect and Mandarin--he can speak both."
The subject of that sentence is "he." If you were to say "Shanghai
dialect and Mandarin are both spoken by him," the subject would
be "Shanghai dialect and Mandarin." In English the subject of

65

the sentence is that which governs the verb. But in Cantonese the
subject doesn't govern the verb--there is no subject-verb concord
(He speaks, They speak, It is spoken), and the ground rules are
different. In Cantonese the subject comes first in a sentence,
and is what is being talked about; the predicate follows, and is
what is said about the subject. The subject is thus the topic
of the sentence, and the predicate is the comment. In Seuhnghóiwá
tùhng Gwokyúh kéuih dōu sīk góng ga, the subject, or topic,--
what is being talked about--is Seuhnghóiwá tùhng Gwókyúh "Shanghai
dialect and Mandarin," the predicate or comment,--what is said
about the topic--is "kéuih dōu sīk góng ga," "he knows how to
speak both."

In Sentence No. 5 above, Yìngmán dím góng a? the topic is
Yìngmán, "English," and the comment dím góng a? "how say?" Ex-
tended, in Sentence No. 6, to "Yāt yih sàam Yìngmán dím góng a?"
the subject, or topic, is Yāt yih sàam, the predicate, or comment,
is Yìngmán dím góng a?

The relationship of Subject and Predicate in Cantonese is
looser than that of Subject and Predicate in English. In English
Subject and Predicate are tied together by the verb of the predicate being governed by the status of the Subject. In Cantonese
Subject and Predicate are bound together by simple juxtaposition.

7. Types of Predicates

   a. Verbal Predicate. The most common predicate is the verbal
   predicate, consisting of a verb phrase (VP). A Verb Phrase
   consists of a verb alone, a verb and preceding modifier(s), or
   a verb and its following object(s), or a combination of these.

   Ex: Subject   Predicate
                 (modifier) Verb (Object)

Ngóh		jìdou.	I know.
Ngóh	m̀h	jì.	I don't know.
Kéuih		góng Gwokyúh.	He's speaking Mandarin.

   b. Nominal Predicate. Another type of predicate is the nominal
   predicate, consisting of a nominal expression. Examples are:

Subject	Predicate	
	Nominal Expression	
Síusing	Hòh.	My name (is) Ho.
Síujé	gwaising a?	Miss your name?

c. Sentence Predicate. The predicate can be in itself a full
Subject-Predicate sentence.

Ex: Subject   Predicate

Ngóh m̀hjì   kéuihdeih góng   I don't know what
             meyéh wá?   language they are
                                speaking.

Yāt yih sàam Yìngmán dím góng a? How do you say, one
                                   two three in
                                   English?

Yāt yih sàam kéuih dōu m̀hsīk   He can't even say one
              góng.   two three.

8. **Subject-Verb-Object (SVO) Sentence.**

A Subject-Predicate sentence in which the predicate contains
a verb and its object is a very frequent sentence type in Cantonese.
We take Subject-Verb-Object (SVO) as the base form of the Cantonese
sentence.

Ex: Subject: Predicate:
    subject   verb   object
    Kéuihdeih góng Seuhnghóiwá.

9. **Absence of pronoun object.**

Compare Cantonese and English:

1A. Néih sīk m̀hsīk Yìngmán a?   1A. Do you know English?

B. Ngóh sīk góng, m̀hsīk sé.   B. I can speak (it), can't
                                    write (it).

2. M̀hgòi néih joi góng yāt chi. 2. Please say (it) once again.

Note that English requires a pronoun object, and Cantonese
does not.

10. **Subjectless sentence.** The predicate sentence with no subject is
a very common sentence type in Chinese.

Ex: Sīk sèsíu jē. = (I) know just a little.

Note that the counterpart English sentence requires stated
subject. (We are referring here to statement sentences ('I study'),
not to imperative sentences ('study!'), which we will take up in
Lesson 5.)

11. tùhng and yauh

   1. tùhng, 'and,' links nominal expressions.

          Seuhnghóiwá tùhng Gwokyúh kéuih dōu sīk góng ga.

              He knows how to speak both Shanghai dialect and Mandarin.

              (See Drills 10, 11)

   2. yauh, 'and,' links verbal expressions. It is classed as an
      adverb because it is always linked to a verb, preceding it.

          Kéuih sīk góng yauh sīk sé.

              He can speak and write.

                  (See Drill 9)

   3. yauh can be in a set with a second yauh, with the force of
      'both... and ...'

          Kéuih yauh sīk góng yauh sīk sé.

              He can both speak and write.

                  (See Drill 9)

12. dōu 'also,' 'both,' 'all'; 'even'

          dōu is classed as an adverb, because it appears always linked
          to a verb, preceding it.

              Ex: 1. Ngóh dōu haih Seuhng-   I am also a Shanghai
                     hóiyàhn.   person.

                  2. Kéuih dōu sīk góng   He also can speak
                     Gwokyúh.   Mandarin.

                  3. Seuhnghóiwá tùhng   He can speak both Shanghai
                     Gwokyúh kéuih   dialect and Mandarin.
                     dōu sīk góng ga.

13. dōu, 'even'

          In the Subject-Predicate pattern X dōu negative Verb, dōu
          translates into English as 'even'.

              Ex: Yāt yih sàam (kéuih)   (He) can't even say 'one
                  dōu mhsīk góng.   two three.'

                  (See Drill 14)

14. Auxiliary verbs.

          Auxiliary verbs take other verbs as their objects. Two
      auxiliary verbs appear in Lesson Three: sīk, 'know (how),' and
      séung 'want to, plan to, be considering, have (it) in mind to ...'

          Ex: 1. Néih sīk góng Seuhnghóiwá mē?!

                 You know how to speak Shanghai dialect?!

2. Ngóh séung hohk dî Yìngmán.

   I want to learn a little English.

   (See BC and Drill 2, 3, 4, 7)

15. sīk 'know (how),' 'be acquainted with'; 'know (someone)'

    sīk operates both as an auxiliary verb and as a main verb.

    1. As an auxiliary verb:

       Ex: Kéuih sīk góng Gwokyúh.   He can speak Mandarin.

                    (See Drill _2_)

    2. As a main verb:

       Ex: 1. Kéuih m̀hsīk Seuhnghóiwá. He is unacquainted with

                                          Shanghai dialect.

                    (See Drill _2a_)

           2. Ngóh m̀hsīk kéuih.   I don't know him.

                    (See Drill _13_)

II. DRILLS

1. Transformation Drill: Transform the sentences from question to
   statement, following the pattern of the example.

         Ex: T: Kéuih góng mēyéh   T: What language is he speaking?
       +   wá a? /Gwóngdùngwá/   /Cantonese/
                (Cantonese)

           S: Kéuih góng Gwóng-   S: He's speaking Cantonese.
              dùngwá.

   1. Kéuih góng mēyéh wá a?   1. Kéuih góng Seuhnghóiwá.
      /Seuhnghóiwá/

   2. Kéuih góng mēyéh wá a?   2. Kéuih góng Gwokyúh.

   3. Kéuih góng mēyéh wá a?   3. Kéuih góng Yìngmàhn.
      Yìngmàhn/

 + 4. Kéuih góng mēyéh wá a?   4. Kéuih góng Yahtbúnwá.
      /Yahtbúnwá/   He's speaking Japanese.
      (Japanese spoken language)

   5. Kéuih góng mēyéh wá a?   5. Kéuih góng Gwóngdùngwá.
      /Gwóngdùngwá/

   Comment: The examples in this drill could also serve as
            general statements:

            T: What language(s) does he speak?

            S: He speaks Cantonese.

2. Substitution Drill

Ex: T: Kéuihdeih sīk góng   T: They can speak Cantonese.
       Gwóngdùngwá.   /Shanghai dialect/
       /Seuhnghóiwá/

    S: Kéuihdeih sīk góng   S: They can speak Shanghai
       Seuhnghóiwá.   dialect.

1. Kéuih sīk góng Yìngmàhn.   1. Kéuih sīk góng Gwóngdùngwá.
   /Gwóngdùngwa/

2. Wòhng Sàang sīk góng   2. Wòhng Sàang sīk góng
   Gwóngdùngwá.   Gwokyúh.

3. Hòh Táai sīk góng Gwokyúh   3. Hòh Táai sīk góng Seuhng-
   /Seuhnghóiwá/   hóiwá.

4. Hòh Sīnsàang sīk góng   4. Hòh Sīnsàang sīk góng
   Seuhnghóiwá. /Yìngmán/   Yìngmán.

5. Chàhn Síujé sīk góng Yìngmán. 5. Chàhn Síujé sīk góng
   /Yahtbúnwá/   Yahtbúnwá.

    a. Repeat, omitting góng:

       T: Kéuihdeih sīk Gwóng-   They know Cantonese.
          dùngwá. /Seuhng-   /Shanghai dialect/
          hóiwá/

       S: Kéuihdeih sīk   They know Shanghai dialect.
          Seuhnghóiwá.

    b. Repeat, adding mē:

       T: Kéuihdeih sīk góng   They know Cantonese.
          Gwóngdùngwá.

       S: Kéuihdeih sīk góng   They know Cantonese?!?
          Gwóngdùngwá mē!?

---

3. Transformation Drill

Ex: T: Méihgwokyàhn m̀hsīk   Americans can't speak Cantonese.
       góng Gwóngdùngwá.

    S: Méihgwokyàhn sīk   Can Americans speak Cantonese?
       m̀hsīk góng Gwóng-
       dùngwá a?

1. Kéuih m̀hsīk góng Yìngmán.   1. Kéuih sīk m̀hsīk góng Yìng-
                                    mán a?

2. Hòh Síujé sīk góng Seuhng-   2. Hòh Síujé sīk m̀hsīk góng
   hóiwá.   Seuhnghóiwá a?

70

3. Kéuihdeih sīk góng Gwokyúh.

+ 4. Méihgwokyàhn m̀hsīk sé
   <u>Jùngmàhn</u>.
   Americans can't write
   <u>Chinese</u>.

+ 5. Kéuih sīk <u>gaau</u> Yahtbúnwá.
   He knows how to <u>teach</u>
   spoken Japanese.

3. Kéuihdeih sīk m̀hsīk góng
   Gwokyúh a?

4. Méihgwokyàhn sīk m̀hsīk sé
   Jùngmàhn a?
   Do Americans know how to
   write Chinese.

5. Kéuih sīk m̀hsīk gaau Yahtbúnwá a?

---

4. Response Drill

   Ex: T: Kéuih hohk Gwóng-   T: He studies Cantonese.
        dùngwá.   /Shanghai dialect/
        /Seuhnghóiwá/

       S: Gám, kéuih hohk   S: Well, then, does he study
        m̀hhohk Seuhnghóiwá   Shanghai dialect?
        a?

   1. Kéuih sīk Yīngmán. /Jùngmàhn/   1. Gám, kéuih sīk m̀hsīk Jùngmán
                                            a?

   2. Kéuih gaau Gwóngdùngwá.   2. Gám, kéuih gaau m̀hgaau Gwok-
      /Gwokyúh/   yúh a?

   3. Kéuih sīk góng Gwokyúh.   3. Gám, kéuih sīk m̀hsīk góng
      /Seuhnghóiwá/   Seuhnghóiwá a?

   4. Kéuih sīk sé Jùngmàhn.   4. Gám, kéuih sīk m̀hsīk sé
      /Yīngmán/   Yīngmàhn a?

   5. Kéuih sīk gaau Yīngmán.   5. Gám, kéuih sīk m̀hsīk gaau
      /Gwóngdùngwá/   Gwóngdùngwá a?

   Comment: <u>gám</u> is a sentence prefix with the connotation of
            continuing from before, resuming the thread of pre-
            vious discourse. The closet English approximations
            would be 'In that case,...', 'Then,...', 'Well,
            then,...' but these don't always fit. <u>Gám</u> is very
            frequent in Cantonese, but if translated in counter-
            part English sentences is not usually idiomatic. We
            will usually not translate <u>gám</u> in the English
            sentences. In the above examples <u>gám</u> is translated
            as 'Well, then,' suggesting continuation from the
            previous statement.

---

5. Transformation Drill

   Ex: T: Wòhng Sàang hohk   T: Mr. Wong is studying Cantonese.
        Gwóngdùngwá.
                          71

S: Wòhng Sàang haih
  m̀hhaih hohk
  Gwóngdùngwá a?

S: Is Mr. Wong studying Cantonese?

1. Léih Táai gaau Gwokyúh.

 1. Léih Táai haih m̀hhaih gaau
  Gwokyúh a?

2. Hòh Sàang góng Yìngmán.

 2. Hòh Sàang haih m̀hhaih góng
  Yìngmán a?

3. Chàhn Síujé sé Jùngmàhn.

 3. Chàhn Síujé haih m̀hhaih sé
  Jùngmàhn a?

4. Jèung Sàang sīk góng
  Yahtbúnwá.

 4. Jèung Sàang haih m̀hhaih sīk
  góng Yahtbúnwá a?

5. Làuh Táai sīk gaau Gwóngdùngwá.

 5. Làuh Táai haih m̀hhaih sīk
  gaau Gwóngdùngwá a?

---

6. Question and Answer Drill

  Ex: T: Wòhng Sàang sé
    Yìngmàhn.
  + /Yahtmàhn/(or)
    Yahtmán/

Mr. Wong is writing English
(right now). /Japanese/

  S$_1$: Wòhng Sàang haih
    m̀hhaih sé Yahtmán a?

Is Mr. Wong writing Japanese?

  S$_2$: M̀hhaih. Kéuih m̀hhaih
    sé Yahtmán; kéuih
    sé Yìngmàhn.

No, he's not writing Japanese,
he's writing English.

1. Jèung Táai góng Gwokyúh.
 /Seuhnghóiwá/

 1. S$_1$: Jèung Táai haih m̀hhaih
    góng Seuhnghóiwá a?

  S$_2$: M̀hhaih. Kéuih m̀hhaih
    góng Seuhnghóiwá,
    kéuih góng Gwokyúh.

2. Wòhng Táai gaau Gwóngdùngwá.
 /Yìngmàhn/

 2. S$_1$: Wòhng Táai haih m̀hhaih
    gaau Yìngmàhn a?

  S$_2$: M̀hhaih. Kéuih m̀hhaih
    gaau Yìngmàhn; kéuih
    gaau Gwóngdùngwá.

3. Léih Sàang hohk Yìngmàhn.
 /Yahtbúnwá/

 3. S$_1$: Léih Sàang haih m̀hhaih
    hohk Yahtbúnwá a?

  S$_2$: M̀hhaih. Kéuih m̀hhaih
    hohk Yahtbúnwá; kéuih
    hohk Yìngmàhn.

 Comment: The above sentence may also be translated 'He writes'
    instead of 'He is writing,' etc. For example:
    sé Yìngmàhn, 'writes English'--not knows how to,

but does it as a habit, custom or general rule. For
instance, He writes English at the office. Likewise
for sentences with main verb <u>hohk</u>, <u>gaau</u>, and <u>góng</u>.
The situational context, not the structural form
of the Cantonese verb, makes the meaning clear.

7. Expansion Drill

    Ex: T: Ngóh sīk góng Gwokyúh.   I can speak Mandarin.
        /Seuhnghóiwá/   /Shanghai dialect/

       S: Ngóh sīk góng Gwokyúh, I can speak Mandarin, but not
          daahnhaih m̀hsīk góng   the Shanghai dialect.
          Seuhnghóiwá.

1. Ngóh sīk góng Gwóngdùngwá.   1. Ngóh sīk góng Gwóngdùngwá,
   /Seuhnghóiwá/   daahnhaih m̀hsīk góng
                          Seuhnghóiwá.

2. Kéuih sīk góng Yìngmán.   2. Kéuih sīk góng Yìngmán,
   /Gwokyúh/   daahnhaih m̀hsīk góng
                          Gwokyúh.

+ 3. Kéuihdeih sīk góng <u>Tòihsāanwá.</u> 3. Kéuihdeih sīk góng Tòihsāan-
   They can speak <u>Toishan</u>   wá, daahnhaih m̀hsīk góng
   dialect. /Yìngmán/   Yìngmán.

4. Hòh Táai sīk góng Gwokyúh.   4. Hòh Táai sīk góng Gwokyúh,
   /Gwóngdùngwá/   daahnhaih m̀hsīk góng
                          Gwóngdùngwá.

5. Chàhn Táai sīk góng Yìngmán. 5. Chàhn Táai sīk góng Yìng-
   /Yahtbúnwá/   mán, daahnhaih m̀hsīk góng
                          Yahtbúnwá.

8. Expansion Drill

    Ex: T: Ngóh sīk góng Yìng-   I can speak English. /Cantonese/
        màhn. /Gwóngdùngwá/

       S: Ngóh sīk góng Yìngmàhn; I can speak English; (and I)
          dōu sīk góng Gwóng-   can also speak Cantonese.
          dùngwá.

1. Ngóh sīk góng Gwóngdùngwá.   1. Ngóh sīk góng Gwóngdùngwá´
   /Seuhnghóiwá/   dōu sīk góng Seuhnghóiwá.

2. Kéuih sīk Gwokyúh. /Yìngmán/ 2. Kéuih sīk góng Gwokyúh;
                          dōu sīk góng Yìngmán.

3. Léih Sàang sīk góng Seuhng- 3. Léih Sàang sīk góng Seuhnghóiwá. /Gwokyúh/   hóiwá;dōu sīk góng Gwokyúh.

4. Chàhn Táai sīk góng Yìngmán.
   /Gwóngdùngwá/

5. Hòh Síujé sīk góng Seuhnghóiwá.
   /Gwóngdùngwá/

4. Chàhn Táai sīk góng Yìngmán; dōu sīk góng Gwóngdùngwá.

5. Hòh Síujé sīk góng Seuhnghóiwá; dōu sīk góng Gwóngdùngwá.

---

9. Expansion Drill

Ex: T: Kéuih sīk góng Gwóng-   He can speak Cantonese.
       dùngwá. /Gwokyúh/   /Mandarin/

  + S: Kéuih (yauh) sīk góng   He can speak Cantonese and
       Gwóngdùngwá, yauh   Mandarin. or
       sīk góng Gwokyúh.   He can speak both Cantonese
       [(both) ... and ...]   and Mandarin.

1. Kéuih hohk Yahtmàhn./Yìngmán/   1. Kéuih yauh hohk Yahtmán,
                                      yauh hohk Yìngmán.
                                      He's studying written
                                      Japanese and English.

2. Ngóh gaau Jùngmàhn. /Yìngmán/   2. Ngóh yauh gaau Jùngmán,
                                      yauh gaau Yìngmán.

3. Kéuih sīk sé Yìngmàhn.   3. Kéuih yauh sīk sé Yìngmàhn,
   /Yahtmàhn/   yauh sīk sé Yahtmàhn.

4. Kéuih m̀hhaih Méihgwokyàhn.   4. Kéuih yauh m̀hhaih Méihgwok-
   /Yìnggwokyàhn/   yàhn, yauh m̀hhaih Yìng-
                                      gwokyàhn.

5. Ngóh m̀hhohk góng Gwokyúh.   5. Ngóh yauh m̀hhohk góng Gwok-
   /Seuhnghóiwá/   yúh, yauh m̀hhohk góng
                                      Seuhnghóiwá.

---

10. Expansion Drill

Ex: T: Léih Sàang haih Seuhng- Mr. Lee is from Shanghai
       hóiyàhn. /Léih Táai/   /Mrs. Lee/

    S: Léih Sàang tùhng Léih   Mr. [Lee] and Mrs. Lee are
       Táai dōu haih Seuhng-   both from Shanghai.
       hóiyàhn.

1. Wòhng Táai sīk góng Gwokyúh.   1. Wòhng Táai tùhng Chàhn Síujé
   /Chàhn Síujé/   dōu sīk góng Gwokyúh.

2. Kéuih sīk Wòhng Sàang. /ngóh/ 2. Kéuih tùhng ngóh dōu sīk
                                      Wòhng Sàang.

74

3. Jèung Síujé hohk Gwóngdùngwá.
   /kéuih pàhngyáuh/

3. Jèung Síujé tùhng kéuih
   pàhngyáuh dōu hohk Gwóngdùngwá.

4. Ngóh haih sing Jèung ge.
   /kéuih/

4. Ngóh tùhng kéuih dōu haih
   sing Jèung ge.

5. Hòh Táai sīk sé Yahtmàhn.
   /Chàhn Síujé/

5. Hòh Táai tùhng Chàhn Síujé
   dōu sīk sé Yahtmàhn.

---

11. Expansion Drill

Ex: T: Kéuih sīk góng Gwokyúh.   He can speak Mandarin. /Canton-
    /Gwóngdùngwá/   ese/

    S: Kéuih sīk góng Gwokyúh   He can speak Mandarin and
       tùhng Gwóngdùngwá.   Cantonese.

1. Kéuih hohk Yìngmán. /Yahtmán/   1. Kéuih hohk Yìngmán tùhng
                                      Yahtmán.

2. Kéuihdeih gaau Jùngmàhn.   2. Kéuihdeih gaau Jùngmàhn
   /Yìngmán/   tùhng Yìngmán.

3. Léih Táai sīk sé Yahtmàhn.
   /Jùngmán/   3. Léih Táai sīk sé Yahtmán
                                      tùhng Jùngmàhn.

+ 4. Ngóh sīk Léih Sàang. /Léih   4. Ngóh sīk Léih Sàang tùhng
     Táai/ (know (someone))   Léih Táai.
                                      I know Mr. and Mrs Lee.

---

12. Substitution Drill

+ Ex: T: Bīngo gaau Gwóng-   Who teaches Cantonese?
        dùngwá a?
        /Léih Sàang/

      S: Léih Sàang gaau Gwóng-   Mr. Lee teaches Cantonese.
         dùngwá.

1. Bīngo góng Seuhnghóiwá a?   1. Hòh Táai góng Seuhnghóiwá.
   /Hòh Táai/

2. Bīngo hohk Gwokyúh a?   2. Wòhng Sàang hohk Gwokyúh.
   /Wòhng Sàang/

3. Bīngo gaau Yìngmàhn a?   3. Chàhn Síujé gaau Yìngmàhn.
   /Chàhn Síujé/

4. Bīngo sīk góng Yahtbúnwá a?   4. Jèung Sàang sīk góng Yaht-
   /Jèung Sàang/   búnwá.

75

5. Bīngo sīk gaau Gwóngdùngwá   5. Léih Táai sīk gaau Gwóng-
   a? /Léih Táai/   dùngwá.

---

13. Response & Expansion Drill

    Ex: 1.T: Néih sīk mhsīk   T: Do you know Mr. Wong?
           Wòhng Sàang a?
           /nod/

        S. Ngóh sīk kéuih.   S: Yes, he is a friend of mine.
           Kéuih haih ngóh
           pàhngyáuh.

        2.T: Néih sīk mhsīk   T: Do you know Mr. Wong?
           Wòhng Sàang a?
           /shake/

        S: Ngóh mhsīk kéuih.   S: No, who is he?
           Kéuih haih bīngo
           a?

    1. Néih sīk mhsīk Hòh Táai a?   1. Ngóh sīk kéuih. Kéuih haih
       /nod/   ngóh pàhngyáuh.

    2. Néih sīk mhsīk Chàhn Sàang a?   2. Ngóh mhsīk kéuih. Kéuih haih
       /shake/   bīngo a?

    3. Néih sīk mhsīk Jèung Síujé a?   3. Ngóh sīk kéuih. Kéuih haih
       /nod/   ngóh pàhngyáuh.

    4. Néih sīk mhsīk Léih Sàang a?   4. Ngóh mhsīk kéuih. Kéuih haih
       /shake/   bīngo a?

---

14. Response Drill

    Ex: T: Néih sīk mhsīk góng   T: Do you know how to speak
          Yahtbúnwá a?   Japanese? /shake/
          /shake/

        S: Mhsīk. Yahtbúnwá   S: No. I don't even know one
     +   ngóh yāt geui dōu   sentence in Japanese.
          mhsīk góng.

        T: /nod/

        S: Sīk sèsíu jē.   S: (I) know just a little.

    1. Néih sīk mhsīk góng Gwóng-   1. Mhsīk. Gwóngdùngwá ngóh
       dùngwá a? /shake/   yāt geui dōu mhsīk góng.

    2. Néih sīk mhsīk góng Gwokyúh a? 2. Mhsīk. Gwokyúh ngóh yāt geui
       /shake/   dōu mhsīk góng.

3. Néih sīk m̀hsīk góng Seuhng-   3. Sīk sèsíu jē.
   hóiwá a? /nod/

4. Néih sīk m̀hsīk góng Yìngmàhn a? 4. Sīk sèsíu jē.
   /nod/

5. Néih sīk m̀hsīk góng Yahtbúnwá   5. M̀hsīk. Yahtbúnwá ngóh yāt
   a? /shake/   geui dōu m̀hsīk góng.

---

15. Expansion Drill

        Ex: T: Kéuihdeih góng   T: What language are they s aking?
               mēyéh wá a?

            S: Néih jī m̀hjī kéuih- S: Do you know what language
               deih góng mēyéh   they're speaking?
               wá a?

    1. Kéuih sing mēyéh a?   1. Néih jī m̀hjī kéuih sing
       What is his name?   mēyéh a?
                                      Do you know what his name
                                      is?

    2. Kéuih gaau mēyéh wá a?   2. Néih jī m̀hjī kéuih gaau
       What language does he teach?   mēyéh wá a?

    3. Kéuih sé mēyéh a?   3. Néih jī m̀hjī kéuih sé mēyéh
       What is he writing?   a?

    4. Kéuih haih bīngo a?   4. Néih jī m̀hjī kéuih haih
       Who is he?   bīngo a?

    5. Kéuih haihm̀hhaih sing Hòh   5. Néih jī m̀hjī kéuih haih
       ga?   m̀hhaih sing Hòh ga?
       Is her name Ho?   Do you know if her name
                                      is Ho?

---

16. Translation Drill

        Ex: T: "Pàhngyáuh" Yìngmán T: How do you say "friend" in
               dím góng a?   English

            S: Friend   S: Friend.

    1. "Hohk," Yìngmán dím góng a? 1. "Learn".

    2. "Gaau," Yìngmán dím góng a? 2. "Teach!"

    3. "Daahnhaih," Yìngmán dím góng 3. "But."
       a?

    4. "Sèsíu," Yìngmán dím góng a? 4. "A little!"

    5. "Gwokyúh," Yìngmán dím góng a? 5. "Mandarin!"

6. "Jídou", Yìngmán dím góng a?

7. "Sīk", Yìngmán dím góng a?

8. "Sé", Yìngmán dím góng a?

9. "Hohksāang, "Yìngmán dím góng a?

6. "Know" (something)."

7. "Know how to or know (a person)."

8. "Write."

9. "Student."

---

17. Translation Drill

Ex: T: "Two" Gwóngdùngwá dím góng a?

T: How do you say "two" in Cantonese?

S: "Yih".

S: "Yih".

1. "Three" Gwóngdùngwá dím góng a?

1. "Sàam."

2. "Teach" Gwóngdùngwá dím góng a?

2. "Gaau."

3. "They" Gwóngdùngwá dím góng a?

3. "Kéuihdeih."

4. "Who" Gwóngdùngwá dím góng a?

4. "Bīngo."

5. "Know how" Gwóngdùngwá dím góng a?

5. "Sīk."

6. "But" Gwóngdùngwá dím góng a?

6. "Daahnhaih."

7. "Please say it again" Gwóng-dùngwá dím góng a?

7. "Mhgòi néih joi góng yāt chi."

8. "I don't know" Gwóngdùngwá dím góng a?

8. "Ngóh mhjì."

9. "Teacher" Gwóngdùngwá dím góng a?

9. "Sīnsàang."

10. "Four" Gwóngdùngwá dím góng a?

10. "Sei."

11. "Five" Gwóngdùngwá dím góng a?

11. "Ńgh."

---

18. Response Drill:

Ex: T: Kéuih haih bīngo a? /gaau Yìngmán/

T: Who is he? /teach English/

S: Kéuih haih gaau Yìngmán ge.

S: He's someone who teaches English.

1. Kéuih haih bīngo a?
   /sing Wòhng/
2. Kéuih haih bīngo a?
   /gaau Gwóngdùngwá/
3. Kéuih haih bīngo a?
   /gaau Yìngmán/
4. Kéuih haih bīngo a?
   /hohk Gwokyúh/

1. Kéuih haih sing Wòhng ge.
2. Kéuih haih gaau Gwóngdùngwá ge.
3. Kéuih haih gaau Yìngmán ge.
4. Kéuih haih hohk Gwokyúh ge.

a. Repeat, teacher cueing with right hand column, students
   responding with correspond haih m̀hhaih question sentence,
   thus:

   T: Kéuih gaau ngóh Yìngmán ge.

   S: Kéuih haih m̀hhaih gaau néih Yìngmán ga?

. CONVERSATIONS FOR LISTENING

   (On tape. Listen to tape with book closed.)

SAY IT IN CANTONESE:

A. Ask your neighbor:

1. if he can speak the
   Shanghai dialect.
2. who teaches him to speak
   Cantonese.
3. if Mrs. Wong teaches
   Cantonese.
4. if his friend can speak
   Cantonese.
5. how to say 'Good morning'
   in Cantonese.
6. if he can write Chinese.
7. if Mr. Chan can speak the
   Taishan dialect.
8. if Mr. Cheung can speak
   Japanese and English.

B. And he answers:

1. that he can't, but that he can
   speak Mandarin.
2. that Mr. Cheung does.
3. that she doesn't; she teaches
   English.
4. that he can't say even one
   sentence.
5. that he didn't hear you (hear
   clearly)--would you repeat.
6. that he can't write it, but
   can speak a little.
7. that he can speak Taishan
   dialect and also can speak
   Shanghai dialect.
8. Yes, he can speak both Japanese
   and English.

9. if he knows what language   9. they're speaking English.
   they are speaking.

10. whether his student is   10. No, he's not an American, he's
    American.   an Englishman.

Vocabulary Checklist for Lesson 3

1.	bīngo?	QW:	who?
2.	chi	m:	time, occasion
3.	chīngchó	adj:	clear
4.	daahnhaih	cj:	but
5.	dī	m:	a little, some
6.	dím?	QW:	how?
7.	dōu	adv:	both
8.	gaau	v:	teach
9.	ga/ge/g	ss:	sen. suf. for matter of fact assertion
10.	geui	m:	sentence
11.	góng	v:	speak
12.	Gwokyúh	n:	Mandarin spoken language
13.	Gwóngdùngwá	n:	Cantonese spoken language
14.	hohk	v:	study, learn
15.	jē	ss:	sen. suf. only, merely; that's all
16.	jī(dou)	v:	know (something)
17.	joi	adv:	again
18.	Joi góng yātchi	Ph:	Say it again.
19.	Jùngmàhn	n:	Chinese (written) language
20.	mē	ss:	sen. suf. for question indicating surprise
21.	Mhgòi néih...	Ph:	Please..., Would you please....
			sen. pre. preceding a request
22.	ńgh	nu:	five
23.	sàam	nu:	three
24.	sé	v:	write
25.	sèsíu	Ph:	a little
26.	sei	nu:	four
27.	Seuhnghóiwá	n:	Shanghai dialect (spoken language)

28. séung	aux v:	wish to, want to, would like to, am considering, be of a mind to
29. sĭk	v:	to know someone
30. sĭk	aux v/v:	know how (to do something)
31. tèng	v:	hear, listen
32. Tòihsāanwá	n:	Toishan dialect
33. tùhng	cj:	and (connects nouns)
34. wá	n:	spoken language, dialect
35. Yahtbúnwá	n:	Japanese (spoken) language
36. Yahtmán	n:	Japanese (written) language
37. Yahtmàhn	n:	Japanese (written) language
38. yāt	nu:	one
39. yāt chi	Ph:	once [one-time]
40. yauh	adv:	also (connects Verb Phrases)
41. yauh V̲, yauh V̲.	PAdv:	both..., and ....
42. yih	nu:	two
43. Yìngmàhn	n:	English language
44. Yìngmán	n:	English language

CLASSROOM PHRASES

Learn to respond to the following classroom instructions. First look at the English equivalents as the teacher reads the Cantonese instructions. Then close your books and listen to the teacher and watch his gestures to help you understand. Check your book if you have difficulty. The teacher will say the sentences several times to help you become familiar with them. Your goal is to be able to respond to the Cantonese without needing to do mental translations into English.

1. Yìhgā néihdeih tái daih __1__ yihp.

1. Now look at page __1__.

2. Dáhòi néih bún syù, daih __1__ yihp.

2. Open your book to page ____.

3. Yìhgā ngóhdeih duhk daih __4__ fo gèibún wuihwá.

3. Now we'll read aloud Lesson __4__, Basic Conversation.

4. Yìhgā ngóhdeih wānjaahp daih __3__ fo.

4. Now we'll review Lesson __3__.

5. Kàhmyaht gaaudou bīndouh a?

5. Where did we get to [lit. teach to] yesterday?

6. Seuhng chi gaaudou bīndouh a?

6. Where did we get to last time?

7. Kàhmyaht gaaudou daih __2__ yihp, daih __2__ fo, daih __2__ go, lihnjaahp, daih __2__ geui.

7. Yesterday we got to page __2__, Lesson __2__, Drill __2__, Sentence __2__.

8. Dāk meih?
   Responses:
      Dāk laak.
      Meih dāk a. or Meih dāk.

8. Are you ready yet?
      Ready.
      Not ready yet.

I. BASIC CONVERSATION

A. Buildup:

Léih Baak-chiu appears at the door of Làuh Gwok-jūng's office. The two had planned to have lunch together, and Mr. Léih has come to get Mr. Làuh.

Léih:

dāk meih?	ready?
Baak-chiu, dāk meih?	Baak-chiu, are you ready?

Làuh:

meih	not yet
Meih a.	Not yet.
dímjūng <u>or</u> dím	hour, o'clock
géidím <u>or</u> géidímjūng?	what time?
Géidím a?	What time is it?

Léih:

yihgā	now
daahp yāt	five after the hour
yāt dím daahp yāt	five after one
Yihgā ... (he looks at his watch)	It's ...five after one.
yāt dím daahp yāt.	

Làuh:

wá?	sentence suffix 'what did you say?'
Géidím wá?	What time did you say?

Léih:

yāt go jih	five minutes
Yāt dím yāt go jih.	It's one oh five.

Làuh:

jéun	accurate
jéun mhjéun a?	accurate/not accurate
bīu	wristwatch, watch
go bīu	a watch
néih go bīu	your watch
Néih go bīu jéun mhjéun ga?	Your watch accurate one? (i.e. Is your watch accurate?)

<u>Léih</u>

Chàhmdō--   Approximately--
    faai   fast
    la   sentence suffix indicating
                                            change from previous
                                            condition: 'has become'.
    faai sèsíu la   gotten a bit fast
    lā = la + raised sentence   raised final intonation =
        final intonation   a sentence suffix indi-
                                                cating casualness.
    waahkjé   maybe, or
Waahkjé faai sèsíu lā.   Maybe it's a little fast. <u>or</u>
                                        Or a little fast.

<u>Làuh</u>

    fānjūng   minute(s)
    géi   several
    géi fānjūng   several minutes
    dáng   wait
    dáng géi fānjūng   wait a few minutes
    dáng ngóh géi fānjūng   wait for me a few minutes
    joi dáng ngóh géi fānjūng   again wait for me a few
                                            minutes
    tìm   in addition, also, more
    lā   sentence suffix for
                                            suggestion--polite
                                            imperative.
Gám, joi dáng ngóh géi fānjūng   Well, wait for me a few minutes
    tìm lā.   more, please.

<u>Léih</u>
    hóu   OK, all right, fine
Hóu, ngóh dáng néih lā.   OK, I'll wait for you.

<u>Làuh</u>
    mhhóu yisi   I'm sorry. <u>or</u> It's
                                            embarrassing. (used in
                                            apologizing for social
                                            gaffe.)

84

bo	sentence suffix, expressing certainty.
Ṁhhóu yisi bo.	I'm sorry.

Léih

Ṁhgányiu.	It's all right.

B. Recapitulation:

Léih

Baak-chíu, dāk meih?	Baak-chíu, are you ready?

Làuh

Meih a. Géidím a?	Not yet. What time is it?

Léih

Yihgā ... (he looks at his watch) ... yāt dím daahp yāt.	It's ... five after one.

Làuh

Géidím wá?	What time did you say?

Léih

Yāt dím yāt go jih.	It's one oh five.

Làuh

Néih go bíu jéun ṁhjéun ga?	Is your watch accurate? [Your watch accurate one?]

Léih

Chàṁhdō--waahkjé faai sèsíu lā.	Approximately--or a little fast.

Làuh

Gám, joi dáng ngóh géi fānjūng tìm lā.	Well, wait for me a few minutes more, please.

Léih

Hóu, ngóh dáng néih lā.	OK, I'll wait for you.

Làuh

Ṁhhóu yisi bo.	I'm sorry.

Léih

Ṁhgányiu.	That's all right.

+ + + + + + + + + + + + +

85

PRONUNCIATION PRACTICE

1. **aa**, (written in our text as **a** when it is in syllable-final position)
   as in **yìhgā**, **Máh**, **wá**

   aa as syllable final is a low back vowel [ɑ]. It is similar to the
   vowel in the American word "Pa," though the American vowel is less
   backed than the Cantonese one. (American [a]; Cantonese [ɑ].
   Some Americans have the backed vowel in their pronunciation of the
   English word "balm." [bɑm] Since the backed mid-central vowel in
   Cantonese [ə·] which we write with the letter **a** does not occur as a
   syllable final but only as the first part of a two-part final, we
   use a single **a** to write the lowback vowel **aa** [ɑ] when it is final
   in its syllable.

   Listen and repeat:
   1. Máh   , Máh   , Máh   . 馬
   2. wá   , wá   , wá   . 話
   3. yìhgā , yìhgā , yìhgā . 而家

2. **aap**, as in **daahp**

   aap is a two-part final composed of the low back vowel **aa** [ɑ]
   plus the bilabial stop consonant **p** [p]. As a final **p** is unreleased:
   [p˺]. **aa** before **p** is produced the same way as **aa** finally, as a low
   back vowel, relatively long in an isolated syllable [ɑ·p˺]. The
   nearest American counterpart is the **op** in the American word "pop,"
   but the vowel portion is more backed than the American vowel.
   (American [a], Cantonese [ɑ]).

   Listen and repeat:
   daahp   , daahp   , daahp   . 踏

3. **ap**, as in **sahp**, '10'

   ap is a two-part final composed of the backed mid-central vowel
   a [ə·] plus the bilabial stop consonant **p** [p]. As a final **p** is
   unreleased: [p˺]. The **a** is relatively short in an isolated syllable: [ə·p˺], but it can be attenuated in sentence context under
   certain conditions. The nearest American counterpart to **ap** is the
   mid-central vowel [ə] in the **up** of general American "cup," [kəp],
   but the Cantonese vowel is more backed than the American one
   (Cantonese [ə·], American [ə]).

Listen and repeat:

sahp , sahp , sahp , sahp . 拾

4. **ap/aap** contrasts

Listen and repeat:

1. sahp , sahp , sahp . 拾
2. daahp , daahp , daahp . 踏
3. sahp daahp , sahp daahp , sahp daahp 拾踏 .
4. daahp sahp , daahp sahp , daahp sahp 踏拾 .

5. **eung** practice

1. léuhng (5 times) 兩
2. séung (5 times) 想
3. Jèung (5 times) 張

6. **eun**, as in **jéun**

eun is a two-part final composed of the lower mid-central rounded vowel **eu** [œ] plus the dental nasal **n**. **eu** before **n** is lower and more backed than the same vowel before **ng**. **eun** = [œ n]; eung = [∅ ŋ] The vowel **eu** before **n** is relatively long: [œ :n]. The vowel is an open vowel before the nasal final. The rounded **eu** has a rounding effect on a consonant preceding and following it. There is no close counterpart in English.

Listen and repeat: (Watch the teacher, copy his lip position)

準準準 1. jéun, jéun, jéun ; jéun, jéun, jéun .
準 唔準呀? 2. jéun mhjéun a? , jéun mhjéun a? ,
jéun mhjéun a? .

7. **eun/eung** contrast

1. jéun (3 times) , séung (3 times) .
2. jéun (3 times) , Jèung (3 times) .
3. jéun (3 times) , léuhng (3 times)
4. séung, Jèung, léuhng , jéun jéun jéun ;
5. jéun, jéun, jéun , séung, Jèung, léuhng .

8. **eun/eui** contrast

1. jéun jéun deui deui
2. jéun deui , deui jéun , jéun deui ,
deui jéun .

87

9. uk, as in luhk, 'six'

     uk is a two-part final composed of the high back rounded
vowel u plus the velar stop consonant k. k as a final is unreleased: [kᵀ] Before k, the tongue position for u is considerably
lowered in regard to tongue height from cardinal high position to
upper-mid position: [o]. The vowel is relatively short before k:
[o k]. The closest American counterpart is the ook of "look," but
the Cantonese vowel is lower than the American one. (Cantonese
[oˇk], American [Uk].)

                    Listen and repeat:
                         1. luhk luhk luhk
                         2. luhk   , luhk   , luhk   . 六

10. ung, as in tùhng

     ung is a two-part final composed of the high back rounded vowel
u plus the velar nasal consonant ng: [ŋ]. The tongue position
for u before ng is the same as that of u before k--lowered from
cardinal high back position to upper mid position: [oŋ]. The
vowel is an open vowel before the nasal final. Lips are rounded.

                    Listen and repeat:
                         1. tùhng tùhng tùhng
                         2. tùhng   , tùhng   , tùhng   . 同

11. ung/uk contrast

                         1. luhk tùhng   , luhk tùhng   , luhk tùhng   .
                         2. tùhng luhk   , tùhng luhk   , tùhng luhk   .
                         3. luhk tùhng   , tùhng luhk   ,
                              tùhng luhk   , luhk tùhng   .

12. un/ung contrast [uᵗn]/[o ŋ]

                    Compare: Listen and repeat:
                         1. tùhng tùhng 同 , bun bun 半 .
                         2. bun tùhng   , tùhng bun   .
                         3. tùhng bun tùhng
                         4. bun tùhng bun

                                 88

I. NOTES

A. Culture Notes:

Greetings. When two Americans meet for the first time during the
day they use some sort of greeting before ordinary talk begins. Hi,
hello, good morning, good afternoon, whatever seems appropriate to
the situation. In English it is a bit rude not to offer a greeting
before getting down to the business at hand. But Cantonese doesn't
have one to one correspondences with American greetings and uses
greeting forms more sparingly than English does. A good all-purpose
greeting is just to greet the addressee by name.

        Ex: Mr. Chan (to Mr. Lee): Léih Sàang.
            Mr. Lee: A, Chàhn Sàang.

In this connection notice the first lines of dialogue in the opening
conversation.

        Ex: When A comes to B's office to get him for lunch:
            A: Bāk-chìu dāk meih?   Bāk-chìu, are you ready?
            B: Meih a.   Not yet.

In an equivalent English situation, A would be likely to say "Hi" or
some such greeting before saying "Ready yet?"

B. Structure Notes:

1. 'Dāk meih?'

Dāk means 'OK, all right' and meih, 'not yet,' Together they
form a positive-negative question--'OK?, or not yet?,' i.e.,
"Ready yet?"

Responses to Dāk meih? are:
        Dāk la. = Ready.
        Meih dāk.= Not ready yet.

2. Time Expressions

1. The following time expressions are used in telling time in
Cantonese:

        dīm or dīmjūng = hour, o'clock
        fānjūng   = minute (not used as much in Cantonese as
                         in English)
        gwāt   = quarter-hour sections of the hour (trans-
                         literation of English "quarter")
        jih   = five-minute sections of the hour (jih

89

literally means "figure," here the 12
numbers on the clock dial.)

2. The above time-words combine as follows:

   1. yāt dím (jūng) = one o'clock

   2. yāt dím yāt fānjūng = one minute after one o'clock

   3. yāt dím yāt go jih = five minutes after one

              (See Drill _7_)

   4. yāt dím yāt go gwāt = a quarter after one

              (See Drill _6_)

   5. yāt dím bun = half past one

              (See Drill _3_)

3. **daahp** in time expressions

    daahp, literally "tread on" is used in reference to the
number on the clock face to which the minute hand points to
tell time:

       Ex: yāt dím daahp yāt = five minutes after one

          yāt dím daahp yih = ten minutes after one

           (See BC and Drills 4, 7)

4. **géi?** 'which number?' in time expressions

                  in time expressions operates as an
interrogative number, and occupies the position in the sentence
which the reply number occupies.

       Ex: 1. géi dím a? = what time is it? [What number o'clock?]

            Ńgh dím. = It's five o'clock.

         2. Yìhgā daahp géi a? = What time is it? [Now treads

                          on what number?]

         Yìhgā daahp sei. = It's 20 after. [Now treads 4.]

         (See BC and Drills 1, 3, 4)

5. **Positioning of time expressions in relation to main verbs:**

   1. **A time expression which precedes the verb** in the sentence
      indicates the time that the action represented by the verb
      took/takes/will take place. We refer to the pre-verb time
      expression as a 'time when' expression.

       Ex: Kéuih sahp dímjùng gaau   He teaches Cantonese **at**
          Gwóngdùngwá.   **10 o'clock.**

          (See Drill _10_)

2. A time expression which follows the verb indicates the
length of time the action represented by the verb took/
takes/will take **place**. We refer to the post-verb time
expression as a "time spent" expression.

 Ex: M̀hgòi néih joi dáng   Would you mind waiting for
   ngóh géi fānjūng tìm   me a few more minutes.
   lā.

    (See Drill _12_)

3. Sentence suffix wá?

 wá is an interrogative sentence suffix attaching to
question-word questions, asking for a repeat of the preceding sentence.
It has the force of "_???_ did you (or he, etc.) say?"

 Ex: 1. Géidím wá?   What time did you say it was?
   2. Bīngo gaau néih wá?   Who did you say taught you?
   3. Kéuih sing mēyéh wá?   What did you say his name
              was?

    (See Drill _11_)

4. Measures:

 A Measure is a word in Cantonese which comes between a
number (or a limited set of other entities) and a noun.

 Ex: go   = representative of a class of words
        called Measures.

  Ngóh go bīu= my [Measure] watch = my watch

  yāt go jih = one [Measure] figure = one figure, i.e.,
         (in relation to time on the clock dial)
         five minutes past the hour

 Inasmuch as ordinary English nouns do not have a category of word standing between number (and certain other
modifiers) and noun, Measures are usually not translatable
in English equivalent sentences.

  sàam go gwāt = 3 [M] quarters = three quarters

 In follow sentences the Measure substitutes for the
noun.

 Ex: Kéuih go bīu jéun m̀hjéun   His [M] watch--is it
   ga?   accurate?

Kéuih <u>go</u> m̀hjéun.   His one isn't accurate.
            (See Drill <u>8</u>)

    We defer fuller treatment of Measures to Lessons 6 and 7.

5. <u>Adjectives</u>:

    Adjectives in Cantonese are descriptive words. Examples
in this lesson are <u>jéun</u>, 'accurate,' <u>faai</u>, 'fast,' <u>maahn</u>,
'slow.'

    Adjectives are classed with Verbs, since they can be
preceded by the negative <u>m̀h</u>.

    Ex: Néih go bīu jéun m̀h-
            jéun ga?   Is your watch accurate?
        Ngóh go bīu m̀hjéun.   My watch isn't accurate.
                (See BC)

    Note that whereas in English an appropriate form of the
verb "be" is needed when an adjective is used in the predicate, in Cantonese adjectives are used in the predicate
without any other verb.

        Compare:

Subject	Predicate
My watch	is not accurate.
Ngóh go bīu	m̀hjéun.

    This class of words which we call "adjectives," some
other writers refer to as "stative verbs.'

    Adjectives will be treated more fully in Lesson 8.

6. <u>Numbers</u>:

    1. Simple numerals

        a. From 1 to 10:

            1. yāt   6. luhk
            2. yih   7. chāt
            3. sàam   8. baat
            4. sei   9. gáu
            5. ńgh   10. sahp

        b. From 11 to 19 Cantonese numbers use an adding formula:
           ten-one, ten-two, etc:

            11. sahpyāt   13. sahpsàam
            12. sahpyih   14. sahpsei

92

15. sahpńgh   18. sahpbaat
16. sahpluhk   19. sahpgáu
17. sahpchāt

2. yih and léuhng = "2"

yih and léuhng both represent "2."

yih is used in counting off: yāt, yih, sàam, 'one, two, three,' and in compound numbers: sahpyih, '12,' yihsahp, '20,' yihsahpyih, '22,' etc.

léuhng represents "2" usually, but not in every case, before Measures.

Ex: léung dím   = 2:00
    léuhng dím yāt go jih   = 2:05
    léuhng dím léuhng go jih = 2:10

(See Drills 1, 2, 5, 7)

We recommend that students not try to generalize at first about when to use léuhng and when to use yih, but simply learn them as vocabulary in the places where they occur.

7. Sentence suffix la

la is a sentence suffix indicating that the condition described in the sentence to which it is attached is changed from the way it used to be.

Ex: Ngóh go bīu faai   My watch has gotten a little
    sèsíu la.   fast.

More on sentence suffix la in Lesson 5.

8. Raised final intonation.'

In the Basic Conversation of this lesson, raised final intonation transforms sentence suffix la into lā in the following:

Waahkjé faai sèsíu lā.   Maybe (it's) a little fast.

Raised final intonation here indicates uncertainty, doubt.

9. Sentence suffix lā

lā attaches to imperative sentences, with the effect of making the imperative a gentle one, definitely a suggestion politely intended rather than a command. (By imperative we

93

mean 'inciting to action,' including everything from per-
emptory commands to polite requests and also self-imperatives,
such as the equivalent of 'I'll do such and such.') Perhaps
the closest English equivalent for lā is a polite tone of
voice. The connotation is 'please,' 'Would you mind...' and
for the self-imperative, 'I'll...'

<blockquote>
Ex: 1. M̀hgòi néih dáng ngóh   Would you please wait for
       géi fānjūng tìm lā.   me a few minutes more.

    2. Hóu, ngóh dáng néih   OK, I'll wait for you.
       lā.
</blockquote>

(See BC)

10. Dialect variations: <u>(ng)āam(ng)āam</u> and others

Words in Cantonese which begin with <u>aa</u>, <u>o</u>, and <u>u</u> have a
variant pronunciation in Standard Cantonese in which the
initial vowel is preceded by <u>ng</u>.

<blockquote>
Examples: āamāam, ngāamngāam   'exactly; just'

          oi, ngoi   'want'

          ūk, ngūk   'house'
</blockquote>

(See Drill <u>5</u>)

III. DRILLS

Preliminary Number Drill: 6-10

1. Students listen.
+   Teacher counts off from one to   Yāt yih sàam sei ńgh (1 time)
    five, then from six to ten,   <u>luhk chāt baat gáu sahp</u>
    gesturing with fingers.   (six seven eight nine ten)
                          (do 10 times)

2. Students in chorus count simul-
    taneously with teacher.
    Teacher counts from 6 to 10,   luhk chāt baat gáu sahp
    using hand signals.   (10 times)

3. Teacher silent, signals to an   luhk chāt baat gáu sahp
    individual student to recite
    by himself.

4. Random order count: Teacher   sahp, luhk, gáu. etc.
    indicates one finger at a time   (approximately 30 numbers)
    in random order, signalling
    students either individually
    or in chorus to call out
    appropriate number.

94

1. Listen and repeat: number drill: clock hours. Teacher uses pointer
   and blackboard clock. The students repeat after the teacher in
   the pauses provided.

   1. yāt (pause)   yāt dím. (pause)   yāt dímjūng. (pause)   1,   1:00.
   + 2. yih (pause)   léuhng dím   léuhng dímjūng. (pause) 2,   2:00.
                      (pause)
   3. sàam (pause)   sàam dím. (pause)   sàam dímjūng. (pause)   3,   3:00.
   4. sei (pause)   sei dím. (pause)   sei dímjūng. (pause)   4,   4:00.
   5. ńgh (pause)   ńgh dím. (pause)   ńgh dímjūng. (pause)   5,   5:00.
   6. luhk (pause)   luhk dím. (pause)   luhk dímjūng. (pause)   6,   6:00.
   7. chāt (pause)   chāt dím. (pause)   chāt dímjūng. (pause)   7,   7:00.
   8. baat (pause)   baat dím. (pause)   baat dímjūng. (pause)   8,   8:00.
   9. gáu (pause)   gáu dím. (pause)   gáu dímjūng. (pause)   9,   9:00.
   10. sahp (pause) sahp dím. (pause)   sahp dímjūng. (pause)   10, 10:00.
   + 11. sahpyāt   sahpyāt dím.   sahpyāt dímjūng.   11, 11:00.
        (pause)   (pause)   (pause)
   + 12. sahpyih   sahpyih dím.   sahpyih dímjūng.   12, 12:00.
        (pause)   (pause)   (pause)
   13. géi (pause)   géidím? (pause)   géidímjūng? (pause)
       Which   What o'clock?   What o'clock?
       number?

       a. Random order. Teacher silent, points to different numbers
          on clock dial in random order, students call out time.
          Individual or group response, or both.

       Comment: géi? 'which?' is an interrogative pronoun of number.

       _____

2. Expansion Drill: Props: A big clock drawn on blackboard. Teacher
   silent, gives visual cues by pointing to numbers on clock.

       Ex: T: (points to 7 on the clock dial)
           S: Yìhgā chāt dím.   It's seven o'clock. [Now
                                       seven o'clock.]

       1. (3)   1. Yìhgā sàam dím.
       2. (6)   2. Yìhgā luhk dím.
       3. (9)   3. Yìhgā gáu dím.
       4. (8)   4. Yìhgā baat dím.
       5. (2)   5. Yìhgā léuhng dím.

       a. Continue, teacher pointing to numbers on clock to cue
          students. Teacher signals for choral or individual response.

3. Expansion Drill: Props: A big clock drawn on blackboard. Teacher points to number and says cue word.

Ex: T: /yāt/   T: /one/

    S: Yihgā daahp yat.   S: It's five after.

1. /sàam/   1. Yìhgā daahp sàam.
2. /baat/   2. Yìhgā daahp baat.
3. /gáu/   3. Yìhgā daahp gáu.
4. /sei/   4. Yìhgā daahp sei.
5. /chāt/   5. Yìhgā daahp chāt.
6. /yih/   6. Yìhgā daahp yih.
7. /sahpyat/   7. Yìhgā daahp sahpyāt.
+ 8. /<u>bun</u>/   8. Yìhgā daahp bun.
      <u>half</u>   It's half past.
9. /ńgh/   9. Yìhgā daahp ńgh.

---

4. Conversation Drill: Props: A big clock drawn on blackboard. Teacher provides visual cues only, by pointing to number on clock.

Ex: T: 1

    S_1: Yìhgā daahp géi a?   T: What time is it?

    S_2: Yìhgā daahp yāt.   S: It's five after.

1.   5   1. A. Yìhgā daahp géi a?
                                   B. Yìhgā daahp ńgh.
2.   7   2. A. Yìhgā daahp géi a?
                                   B. Yìhgā daahp chāt.
3.   11   3. A. Yìhgā daahp géi a?
                                   B. Yìhgā daahp sahpyāt.
4.   8   4. A. Yìhgā daahp géi a?
                                   B. Yìhgā daahp baat.
5.   6   5. A. Yìhgā daahp géi a?
+   B. Yìhgā <u>daahp bun</u>.
                                      (<u>daahp bun = half past</u>)
6.   2   6. A. Yìhgā daahp géi a?
                                   B. Yìhgā daahp yih.

96

5. Expansion Drill: Props: Blackboard clock. Teacher points first
   to hour number then to the half-hour number, as he voices the
   cue sentence.

     Ex: T: Yìhgā sàam dím bun.   T: It's half past three.
                                  [Now three o'clock half.]

    + S: Yìhgā ngāamngāam   S: It's exactly half past three.
          sàam dím bun.
          (ng)āam(ng)āam =
          exactly, just.

1. Yìhgā léuhng dím bun.   1. Yìhgā ngāamngāam léuhng dím
                              bun.

2. Yìhgā ńgh dím bun.   2. Yìhgā ngāamngāam ńgh dím bun.

3. Yìhgā luhk dím bun.   3. Yìhgā ngāamngāam luhk dím
                              bun.

4. Yìhgā baat dím bun.   4. Yìhgā ngāamngāam baat dím
                              bun.

5. Yìhgā sahp dím bun.   5. Yìhgā ngāamngāam sahp dím
                              bun.

---

6. Expansion Drill: Props: Blackboard clock. Teacher says cue then
   points to the quarter hour on the clock to signal students'
   response.

     Ex: T: Sahp dím.   T: Ten o'clock

       S: Yìhgā sahp dím   S: It's a quarter after ten.
       +   yāt go gwāt.   [Now ten o'clock one quarter.]

1. yāt dím   1. Yìhgā yāt dím yāt go gwāt.

2. sei dím   2. Yìhgā sei dím yāt go gwāt.

3. chāt dím   3. Yìhgā chāt dím yāt go gwāt.

4. ńgh dím   4. Yìhgā ńgh dím yāt go gwāt.

5. sàam dím   5. Yìhgā sàam dím yāt go gwāt.

6. léuhng dím   6. Yìhgā léuhng dím yāt go gwāt.

   Comment: gwāt 'quarter', a transliteration from English.
            Grammatically gwāt is a Noun, having the Measure go.
            It occurs in combination with numbers 1 and 3 to
            form time phrases marking the 2 quarter-hours:

           sàam dím yāt go gwāt - Three o'clock one quarter
                                      = 3:15

           sàam dím sàam go gwāt - Three o'clock three quart-
                                      ers = 3:45

7. Alteration Drill:

   Ex: T: Yìhgā sàam dím   It's five after three.
         daahp yāt.   or It's three-oh-five.
                                [three touch one]

       S: Yìhgā sàam dím   It's five after three.
         yāt go jih.   or It's three-oh-five.
                                [Now three o'clock one figure.]

       (TO STUDENT: Take out paper & pencil and write a column
                    of numbers from 1 to 7. As you respond orally,
                    write down the times on paper (e.g. 3:05.)
                    After the exercise, the teacher will give
                    responses in English, and you correct your
                    paper.)

   1. Yìhgā sàam dím daahp yih.   1. Yìhgā sàam dím léuhng go jih.
   2. Yìhgā sàam dím daahp séi.   2. Yìhga sàam dím séi go jih.
   3. Yìhgā sàam dím daahp chāt.   3. Yìhga sàam dím chāt go jih.
   4. Yìhgā sàam dim daahp sàam.   4. Yìhgā sàam dím sàam go jih.
   5. Yìhgā sàam dim daahp sahp.   5. Yìhgā sàam dím sahp go jih.

   Comment: a. jih, 'figure'. Grammatically jih is a Noun, having
              the Meaaure go. It occurs in combination with the
              numbers 1 through 11 to form a series of time
              phrases marking the five-minutes subdivisions of the
              hour.

              yāt go jih = 5 after

              léuhng go jih = 10 after, etc.

           b. The go jih part of the above phrases may be omitted,
              with the meaning unchanged:

              sàam dím sàam go jih - sàam dím sàam = 3:15

8. Expansion Drill:

   Ex: T: Léih Táai go bíu   Mrs. Lee's watch is a little
         faai sèsiu.   fast. /slow a little/
         /maahn sèsiu/

       B: Léih Táai go bíu faai   Mrs. Lee's watch is a little
         sèsiu; ngóh go   fast, mine's a little slow.
         maahn sèsiu.

   1. Léih Táai go bíu maahn sèsiu.   1. Léih Táai go bíu maahn
      /faai sesiu/   sèsiu, ngóh go faai sèsiu.

   2. Léih Táai go bíu faai yātgo-   2. Léih Táai go bíu faai yātgo-
      jih. /maahn yātgojih/   jih, ngóh go maahn yātgo-
                                           jih.

3. Léih Táai go bíu maahn
   yāt fānjūng /faai yāt fān-
   jūng/
   Mrs. Lee's watch is one
   minute slow.

3. Léih Táai go bíu maahn yāt
   fānjūng, ngóh go faai yāt
   fānjūng.

4. Chàhn Táai go bíu faai sèsíu.
   /maahn sèsíu/

4. Chàhn Táai go bíu faai sèsíu,
   ngóh go maahn sèsíu.

5. Chàhn Táai go bíu maahn léuhng-
   gojih./faai yāt go gwāt/

5. Chàhn Táai go bíu maahn
   léuhng_go jih,_ngóh go
   faai yāt go gwāt.

---

9. Response Drill:

    Ex: T: Kéuihdeih haih m̀hhaih   Are they English?
           Yìnggwokyàhn a?   /Americans/
           /Méihgwokyàhn/

       S: Ngóh m̀hjí. Waahkjé   I don't know - They may be
          haih Yìnggwokyàhn,   English, may be Americans.
          waahkjé haih
          Méihgwokyàhn.

1. Kéuih haih m̀hhaih Gwóng-   1. Ngóh m̀hjí, waahkjé haih
   dùngyàhn a? /Seuhnghóiyàhn/   Gwóngdùngyàhn, waahkjé
                                        haih Seuhnghóiyàhn.

2. Kéuih haih m̀hhaih Méihgwok-   2. Ngóh m̀hjí, waahkjé haih
   yàhn a? /Yìnggwokyàhn/   Méihgwokyàhn, waahkjé
                                        haih Yìnggwokyàhn.

3. Kéuih haih m̀hhaih Seuhnghói-   3. Ngóh m̀hjí, waahkjé haih
   yàhn a? /Gwóngdùngyàhn/   Seuhnghóiyàhn; waahkjé
                                        haih Gwóngdùngyàhn.

4. Kéuih haih m̀hhaih Jùnggwok-   4. Ngóh m̀hjí, waahkjé haih
   yàhn a? /Yahtbúnyàhn/   Jùnggwokyàhn; waahkjé
                                        haih Yahtbúnyàhn.

   a. Repeat, Teacher giving the two fillers only, students
      taking both parts of conversation, thus:

        T: /Yìnggwokyàhn/ Méihgwokyàhn/

        S1: Kéuih haih m̀hhaih Yìnggwokyàhn a?

        S2: Waahkjé haih Yìnggwokyàhn, waahkjé haih Méihgwokyàhn.

---

10. Combining Drill:

    Ex: T: Yìhgā sahp dím bun.   T: It's ten thirty.
        Kéuihdeih hohk   They study Cantonese.
        Gwóngdùngwá.

S: Kéuihdeih sahp dím   S: They study Cantonese at 10:30.
bun hohk Gwóngdùng-
wá.

1. Yìhgā gáu dímjūng.   1. Kéuih gáu dímjūng gaau
   Kéuih gaau bīngo a?   bīngo a?

2. Yìhgā léuhng dím yātgogwāt. 2. Bīngo léuhng dím yātgogwāt
   Bīngo hohk Yìngmàhn a?   hohk Yìngmàhn a?

3. Yìhgā sàam dím sàamgogwāt.   3. Léih Sàang sàam dím sàamgo-
   Léih Sàang hohk mēyéh a?   gwāt hohk mēyéh a?

4. Yìhgā sahpyāt dím bun.   4. Ngóhdeih sahpyāt dím bun
   Ngóhdeih hohk sé Jùngmàhn.   hohk sé Jùngmàhn.

5. Yìhgā sei dím bun.   5. Hòh Síujé sei dím bun gaau
   Hòh Síujé gaau Méihgwokyàhn   Méihgwokyàhn Gwokyúh.
   Gwokyúh.

6. Yìhgā baat dím sàamgogwāt.   6. Jèung Táai baat dím sàamgo-
   Jèung Táai gaau néih góng   gwāt gaau néih góng
   Gwóngdùngwá.   Gwóngdùngwá.

Comment: A time phrase which indicates the time that the
action represented by the verb takes place, precedes
the verb in the sentence.

----

11. Response Drill: Make a wá? question out of each statement, sub-
    stituting the appropriate question word for the expression
    underlined in the cue sentence.

        Ex: T: Yìhgā sahpdím bun.   T: It is now 10:30.

            S: Yìhgā géidím wá?   S: What time did you say it was
                                        now?

1. Kéuih sing Làuh.   1. Kéuih sing mēyéh wá?

2. Kéuih haih ngóh hohksàang.   2. Bīngo haih néih hohksàang
                                   wá?

3. Hòh Síujé gaau ngóh Seuhng- 3. Bīngo gaau néih Seuhnghói-
   hóiwá.   wá wá?

4. Chàhn Táai haih kéuih sìnsàang. 4. Bīngo haih kéuih sìnsàang
   Mrs. Chan is her teacher.   wá?

5. Léih Sàang haih Méihgwokyàhn. 5. Bīngo haih Méihgwokyàhn wá?

----

12. Substitution Drill: Repeat the first sentence, then substitute
    as directed.

1. Ńhgòi néih dáng ngóh géi   1. Ńhgòi néih dáng ngóh géi
   fānjūng.   fānjūng.

2. /géi go jih/   2. Ñhgòi néih dáng ngóh géi
                                      go jih.

3. /yāt go jih/   3. Ñhgòi néih dáng ngóh yāt
                                      go jih.

4. /léuhng fānjūng/   4. Ñhgòi néih dáng ngóh léuhng
                                      fānjūng.

5. /léuhng go jih/   5. Ñhgòi néih dáng ngóh léuhng
                                      go jih.

V. CONVERSATIONS FOR LISTENING

    (On tape. Listen to tape with book closed.)

. SAY IT IN CANTONESE.

A. Ask your neighbor: B. And he replies:

   1. if his watch is accurate.   1. that it is a little slow.

   2. what time Mr. Chan teaches   2. that he is sorry but he doesn't
      English.   know.

   3. if Mr. Wong teaches English   3. no, he teaches English at
      at 2:15.   2:45.

   4. how to say 'five after   4. telling you two ways to say
      three' in Cantonese.   it.

   5. to wait for you 10 more   5. OK, he'll wait.
      minutes.

   6. if he's ready.   6. that he is.

   7. if he's ready.   7. that he's not--and asks you
                                          to wait a few minutes.

   8. what time he said it was.   8. 10:30.

   9. if Mr. and Mrs. Chan are   9. that Mr. Chan is from Shanghai
      from Shanghai.   but Mrs. Chan is from
                                          Taishan.

  10. what time his watch has,   10. that it's exactly 11:02.
      adding that your own
      might not be accurate.

101

Vocabulary Checklist for Lesson 4

1.	āamāam	adv:	exactly
2.	baat	nu:	eight
3.	bīu	n:	watch
4.	bo	ss:	sen. suf. for certainty
5.	bun	nu:	half
6.	chàmhdō	Ph:	approximately
7.	chāt	nu:	seven
8.	daahp	v:	tread on
9.	daahp bun	TW:	half past
10.	daahp géi?	TW:	how many five minutes past the hour?
11.	Dāk meih?	Ph:	Ready?
12.	dáng	v:	wait (for)
13.	dím(jūng)	m:	o'clock
14.	faai	adj:	fast
15.	fānjūng	m:	minute(s)
16.	gáu	nu:	nine
17.	géi	nu:	several
18.	géi?	QW:	which number?
19.	géidím(jūng)?	Ph:	What o'clock? What time?
20.	go	m:	M. for nouns
21.	gwāt	(bf)n:	quarter (hour)
22.	Hóu	adj:	OK. All right. (response used in agreeing with someone.)
23.	jéun	adj:	accurate, right
24.	jih	n:	written figure; word
25.	lā	ss:	sen. suf. la for change + raised intonation for doubt.
26.	lā	ss:	sen. suf. for polite suggestion
27.	la	ss:	sen. suf. indicating change from previous condition.
28.	léuhng	nu:	two
29.	luhk	nu:	six
30.	maahn	adj:	slow
31.	Meih	adv:	Not yet.

32. Ṁhhóu yisi	Ph:	I'm sorry; It's embarassing.
33. ngāamngāam	adv:	exactly (see āamāam)
34. sàam go gwāt	Ph:	three quarters after the hour
35. sahp	nu:	ten
36. sahpyāt	nu:	eleven
37. sahpyih	nu:	twelve
38. tìm	ss:	in addition, also, more
39. wá	ss:	interrogative sen. suf. calling for repeat of preceding sentence. i.e., ____ did you say?'
40. waahkjé	cj:	maybe; or
41. yāt go gwāt	Ph:	a quarter after the hour
42. yāt go jih	Ph:	five minutes
43. yìhgā	TW:	now

I. BASIC CONVERSATION

A. Buildup:

Mrs. Wòhng stops in to see her friend Mrs. Jèung at home.

jyúyàhn   host, hostess

Jyúyàhn

chóh   sit

chèuihbín   As you wish, at your
                                            convenience

Chèuihbín chóh là.   Sit anywhere you like.

yàhnhaak   guest

Yàhnhaak

mhgòi   thank you

Hóu, mhgòi.   All right, thank you.

(The hostess extends a pack of cigarettes)

Jyúyàhn

yīn   tobacco

sihk   eat

sihk yīn   smoke tobacco, smoke

Sihk yīn là.   Have a cigarette.

Yàhnhaak

haakhei   polite

mhsái   unnecessary, no need to

Mhsái haakhei.   You don't need to be polite.
                                            (i.e., no thanks)

Jyúyàhn

mhhóu   don't ... (as a command)
                                            [not good to ...]

Mhhóu haakhei a.   Don't be polite. (i.e., Do
                                            have one)

Yàhnhaak

Hóu, mhgòi.   All right, thanks.

Jyúyàhn

Mhsái mhgòi.   No need to thank. (i.e.,
                                            You're welcome.)

(A servant brings in tea and cakes.)

Jyúhàhn

chàh	tea
yám	drink
Yám chàh lā.	Have some tea.

Yàhnhaak

Ṁhgòi.	Thank you.

Jyúyàhn

béng	cake(s), cookie(s)
Sihk béng lā.	Have some cookies.

Yàhnhaak

laak	sentence suffix la indicating change or potential change + k = lively. la + k = laak.
Ṁhsái laak; ṁhgòi.	No thanks.

Jyúyàhn

si	try
Siháh lā.	Try a little.

Yàhnhaak

jànhaih	really
léh	sentence suffix for definiteness.
Jànhaih ṁhsái haakhei léh.	No thanks--really.

(They talk awhile, then the guest prepares to leave.)

Yàhnhaak

aiya!	exclamation of consternation
Aiya! Ngh dím la.	Oh--oh. It's five o'clock.
jáu	leave
yiu jáu	must go
Ngóh yiu jáu laak.	I must be going.

Jyúyàhn

faai	fast
gam	so
gam faai	so fast, so soon
gam faai jáu	go so soon

Ṁhhóu gam faai jáu lā.	Don't go so soon!

Yàhnhaak

Ṁhhaih a--	No--
Jànhaih yiu jáu laak.	I really must go.

B. Recapitulation:

Mrs. Wòhng stops in to see her friend Mrs. Jèung at home.

Jyúyàhn

Chèuihbín chóh lā.	Sit anywhere you like.

Yàhnhaak

Hóu, ṁhgòi.	All right; thanks.

(The hostess extends a pack of cigarettes.)

Jyúyàhn

Sihk yīn lā.	Have a cigarette.

Yàhnhaak

Ṁhsái haakhei.	You don't have to be polite. (i.e., No thanks.)

Jyúyàhn

Ṁhhóu haakhei a.	Don't be polite. (i.e., Do have one.)

Yàhnhaak

Hóu, ṁhgòi.	All right, thanks.

Jyúyàhn

Ṁhsái ṁhgòi.	No need to thank. (i.e., you're welcome.)

(A servant brings in tea and cakes.)

Jyúyàhn

Yám chàh lā.	Have some tea.

Yàhnhaak

Ṁhgòi.	Thank you.

Jyúyàhn

Sihk béng lā.	Have some cookies.

Yàhnhaak

Ṁhsái laak; ṁhgòi.	No thanks.

106

Jyúyàhn

Siháh lā.   Try a little.

Yàhnhaak

Jànhaih m̀hsái haakhei léh.   No thanks--really.

   (They talk awhile, then the guest prepares to leave.)

Yàhnhaak

Aiya! Ǹgh dím laak. Ngóh yiu   Oh--oh. It's five o'clock. I
  jáu laak.   must be going.

Jyúyàhn

M̀hhóu gam faai jáu lā.   Don't go so soon!

Yàhnhaak

M̀hhaih a--   No--
  Jànhaih yiu jáu laak.   I really must go.

+ + + + + + + + + + + + + +

Pronunciation:

. ai

   ai is a two-part final composed of the backed mid central vowel
a [ə˞] plus high front unrounded offglide i [ə˞ⁱ]. The a portion is
quite short in an isolated syllable--[ə˞ⁱ]. The syllable may be
lengthened when it occurs in stress position in a sentence, in which
case it is the i part that lengthens, not the a part.

      m̀hsái   (5 times) 唔使

. aai

   aai is a two-part final composed of the low back vowel aa [ɑ]
plus high front unrounded offglide i, which following aa is somewhat
lower than it is following a, [ɑᴵ]. The aa portion is relatively
long in an isolated syllable--[ɑːᴵ]. The aai syllable may be
lengthened when it occurs in stress position in a sentence, in which
case it is the aa part that lengthens, not the i part. The Cantonese
aai is similar to the ie of the American words 'fie,' 'die,' 'tie.'

      Listen and repeat:

        1. faai   (five times) 快
        2. táai   (five times) 太

. ai/aai contrasts

      Listen and repeat:

        1. m̀hsái, faai   . (5 times)

        2. faai, m̀hsái   . (5 times)

4. <u>ang</u> in <u>dáng</u> (Lesson 4)

      <u>ang</u> is a two-part final composed of the backed mid central vowel
<u>a</u> [ə˥] plus the velar nasal consonant <u>ng</u>. The closest American
counterpart to the Cantonese vowel is the mid central vowel in the
English "dung." The Cantonese vowel is shorter than the American one,
more backed, and not nasalized before the nasal final.

          Compare English and Cantonese--Listen:

            dung dáng (5 times) 凍 等

          Listen and repeat:

            dáng (5 times) 等

5. <u>aang</u> in <u>cháang</u>

      <u>aang</u> is a two-part final composed of the low back vowel <u>aa</u> [a]
plus the velar nasal consonant <u>ng</u>. The <u>aa</u> before <u>ng</u> is pronounced
the same way as <u>aa</u> before <u>p</u> and before <u>i</u>. The closest American
counterpart is the low central vowel of "dong" [a] in "ding dong,"
but the Cantonese <u>aa</u> [ɑ] is more backed and not nasalized before the
final nasal consonant.

          Compare English and Cantonese--Listen:

            dong cháang (5 times)   橙

          Listen and repeat:

            cháang (5 times) 橙

            sīnsàang (5 times) 先生

6. <u>ang</u>/<u>aang</u> contrasts

          Listen and repeat:

            1. dáng (3 times)

            2. cháang (3 times)

            3. dáng cháang (3 times)

            4. cháang dáng (3 times)

7. <u>ak</u> in <u>dāk</u> (Lesson 4)

     <u>ak</u> is a two-part final composed of the backed mid central vowel
<u>a</u> [ə˥] plus velar stop consonant <u>k</u>. As a final <u>k</u> is unreleased--[k˺],
<u>a</u> is as elsewhere--short in an isolated unstressed syllable, more
backed than its closest American counterpart, which is the [ə] of
"duck." It is also tenser than the American counterpart.

Compare English and Cantonese:

duck dāk   (5 times)

Listen and repeat:

dāk   (5 times)

Compare the a before k with the a elsewhere:--

Listen and repeat:

1. dāk   (3 times)
2. chāt   (3 times)
3. sahp   (3 times)
4. dāk chāt sahp   (3 times)
5. gám   (3 times)
6. Chàhn   (3 times)
7. dáng   (3 times)
8. gám, Chàhn, dáng
9. m̀hsái

• **aak in yàhnhaak, haakhei**

aak is a two-part final composed of the low back vowel aa [ɑ] plus the velar stop k. As a final k is unreleased [k˥], aa is produced the same way as before -ng, -p and elsewhere. It is somewhat more backed than the vowel of "hock," the closest general American counter-part.

Listen and repeat:

1. yàhnhaak   (3 times)   人客
2. haakhei   (3 times)   客氣

• **ak/aak contrasts**

Listen and repeat:

1. meih dāk   (3 times)   未得
2. yàhnhaak   (3 times)   人客
3. meih dāk, yàhnhaak   (3 times)
4. yàhnhaak, meih dāk   (3 times)

• **Fast speech forms.**

Listen to fast speech pronunciation:

1. haakhei   客氣
2. M̀hsái haakhei   唔使客氣
3. M̀hhóu haakhei   唔好客氣

Comments: 1. You notice that there is a tendency for
the friction of the <u>h</u> consonant to dis-
appear in fast speech. This is particularly true in such ritual courtesy forms
as the above. We similarly abbreviate
courtesy forms in English without perhaps
noticing it. Ex: 'anksalot' = Thanks a
lot.

2. The <u>k</u> in syllable final but not word
final position has a tendency in fast
speech to be pronounced as a glottal
stop rather than as a velar stop. Listen:

     1. waahkjé   (3 times)
     2. Jùnggwokyàhn   (3 times)
     3. haakhei   (3 times)
     4. hohksāang   (3 times)

We are not going to give much specific
attention to fast speech forms in this
text. It is probably just as well for
you not to try to produce them, because
chances are you would notice some and not
others.

11. The <u>-k</u> final of sentence suffix <u>laak</u>.

     We have used <u>k</u> to represent the final sound in the sentence
suffix <u>laak</u>. This sound is a glottal stop, rather than the velar stop
which is the sound <u>k</u> normally represents. Linguistically this is a
messy way to handle this situation, but in practice, restricted as
it is to sentence suffix position, it has not given previous students
difficulty.

     The <u>laak</u> spelling derives thus:

        <u>la</u> is initial <u>l</u> plus the low back <u>aa</u> vowel [a], which we
spell <u>a</u> when it is final in a syllable. (The mid central <u>a</u>
vowel [$ə$] never occurs in syllable final position.)
Adding <u>k</u> as final makes the <u>aa</u> not final in its syllable,
so its spelling is represented as <u>aa</u>: <u>la</u> + <u>-k</u> = <u>laak</u>

            Ex: Ngóh haih yàhnhaak.   I am a guest.

                Ngóh yiu jáu laak.   I must go now.

. au as in jáu, gáu

     au is a two-part final composed of the backed mid central vowel
a [ə⁾] and the high back rounded vowel u [u]. The a before u has
a tongue position slightly lower than in other positions (before
-i, -p, -k, etc.). The nearest American counterpart is general
American ow in "cow."

          Listen and repeat:

             1. jáu   (3 times) 酒

             2. bējáu (3 times) 啤酒

             3. gáu   (3 times) 九

             4. jáu jái ("son")酒仔, jáu jái   , jáu jái   .

. aau in gaau

     aau is a two-part final composed of the low back vowel aa
and the high back rounded vowel u [u]. In this position the aa
is more fronted [aᶜ] than in other positions. The nearest American
counterpart is in the relatively fronted vowel of the Southern
Pronunciation of "cow," the vowel of which begins with the low front
a [æ] of "cat."

          Listen and repeat:

            gaau   (5 times)

. au/aau

          Listen and repeat, comparing au and aau:

             1. jáu gaau   (3 times) 酒 教

             2. gaau jáu   (3 times) 教 酒

             3. gáu gaau   (3 times) 九 教

             4. gau ('enough') gaau   (3 times) 夠 教

             5. gaau gau   (3 times) 教 夠

II. NOTES

A. <u>Culture Notes</u>

1. <u>Customs of polite behavior for host and guest.</u>

In a host-guest situation in Cantonese, it is standard courtesy for the host to offer some refreshment, for the guest to politely decline, and for the host to urge the guest again to have some, at which point the guest politely accepts or declines as he wishes.

Since it is customary to decline offered refreshments, in offering them it is best to avoid phrasing your offer in a choice-type question, because your Cantonese friends will feel it pushy to answer yes when asked this way. If the food is already at hand it is better to use the polite suggestion form: <u>Sihk béng lā</u>. 'Have some cookies.' If the refreshments are not right at hand, use the question-word question: <u>Yám dī mēyéh a</u>? [Drink a little what?] 'What would you like to drink?

2. <u>sihk faahn</u> [eat rice] means 'to have a meal,' 'to eat.' It may also mean to eat Chinese food, in contrast to eating Western food.

3. <u>yám chàh</u>, 'drink tea.'

<u>yám chàh</u> also has a wider meaning, reflecting a distinctively Cantonese custom. This is the custom of going to the teahouse in the morning to drink tea and eat hot snacks, generally steamed shrimp dumplings [hā gāau] and steamed dumplings of minced pork and mushrooms [sīu màai]. This is called 'going out to <u>yám chàh</u>!' It is on the whole a morning custom, though in Hong Kong, perhaps influenced by the British custom of afternoon tea, some teahouse also serve tea and snacks in the afternoon. <u>yám chàh</u> doesn't correspond to the coffee break; instead it substitutes for a regular meal, either breakfast or lunch. At a 'regular' meal you have rice, but when you go to a teahouse to <u>yám chàh</u>, by tradition you don't get rice. Now that custom too is breaking down, and you may, though the chances are against it, get rice with a <u>yám chàh</u> meal.

4. **Aiya!** is an exclamation of consternation. English equivalents are very much dependent on the speaker, ranging from "Oh, my!" to "Good Lord!" to "Oh my god!" etc.

    Aiya! is said to be used more by women than by men. Men use **Wah!** more often instead.

5. **mhgòi,** 'thank you' is appropriate for thanking someone for a service. When someone gives you some information or does you a favor, you thank them with **mhgòi.** There is another word, **dòjeh,** 'thank you,' which is appropriate for thanking someone for a gift. (We encounter this word is the text of Lesson 14.)

    In the Conversation which opens this lesson, the guest accepted a cigarette with **mhgòi**--viewing this as more of a courtesy than a gift.

(See BC and Drills 7, 8, 9)

B. Structure Notes

1. Sentence suffix **laak.**

    laak is a fusion of sentence suffix **la** indicating change-- (that change has occurred, or is about to occur, or may occur)-- plus **k**, which is suffixed to a few sentence suffixes, giving the sentence a lively air.

    Whether **la** or **laak** is used depends partly on the speaker-- some speakers habitually tend to use **laak** more than **la**--, partly on whether the conversation is spirited or matter-of-fact, **laak** tending to be used more in spirited than in matter-of-fact discourses.

    Because **la/laak** has to do with change, it works pretty well to translate it in English as "now," keeping in mind that it contrasts the present situation to some previous or future one.

    Examples from the Basic Conversation:

1. Mhsái laak, mhgòi.   (In response to being offered some cookies:) Not [necessary] now, thanks. (It's not that I don't want your cookies, I might change and have some later, but not just now, thanks.)

2. Aiya! Ńgh dìm laak!   Wow! It's five o'clock already (I didn't realize it had gotten so late.)

113

3. Ngóh yiu jáu laak.   I must be going now.

    (See BC and Drills 7, 8, 9)

2. -k for lively speech.

    -k is a glottal stop ending to certain sentence suffixes--
for example, la and a which adds liveliness.

    (See BC, Drills 7, 8, 9, and Structure Notes 1, 3)

3. Sentence suffix aak.

    aak is a fusion of sentence suffix a (which softens abrupt-
ness) and the final -k, giving a lively air.

    a + k = aak (cf: la + -k = laak)

        Example:

        Host: Sihk yīn lā.   Have a cigarette.

        Guest: Hóu aak, m̀hgòi. OK, thanks.

           (See Drills 7, 8, 9)

4. Sentence suffix léh.

    léh is an emphatic sentence suffix, adding the connotation
that you are quite definite about what you say. (léh is probably
derived from sentence suffix la.) The tone of voice is polite.

    Example from the Basic Conversation:

      Jànhaih m̀hsái haakhei   (Declining cookies which the
        léh.   host has urged you twice to
                          take) No thanks, really.

        (See BC and Drill 11)

5. Sentence suffix lā for polite suggestion.

    This lesson has many examples of sentence suffix lā, first
encountered in Lesson 4.

    lā is suffixed to command sentences, softening the command to
a polite suggestion.

        Ex: Sihk yīn lā.   Have a cigarette. (polite tone
                                of voice.)

    (See BC and Drills 1, 2, 4, 5, 7, 8, 9)

6. Imperative sentences without sentence suffix.

    Without a softening sentence suffix an imperative sentence
has the force of a command rather than a suggestion.

        Example:

        M̀hhóu sihk béng.   Don't eat those cookies.

        (See Drill 5)

The above sentence might be one said by a father or mother to a child.

7. **-háh,** Verb suffix for casualness.

    -hah is a verb suffix which gives a somewhat casual air to the verb it attaches to. In this lesson -háh attaches to the verb si, 'try.' Siháh has the force of 'give it a try,'--a bit more casual than 'thr it.'

(See BC)

8. **yiu,** 'must,' and **mhsái,** 'mustn't;' 'needn't'

    yiu used as an auxiliary verb preceding another verb can have the meaning 'must _V_,' ' have to _V_,' 'need to _V_.' The basic meaning of yiu is 'require,' and it can be used as a full verb, though in this lesson it is introduced only in its auxiliary verb use.

      Ex: yiu jáu   =   must leave, have to be going
          Ngóh yiu jáu laak.   I must be going.

    To express that you needn't do something, or to ask if something is necessary, Cantonese doesn't use the negative and question forms of yiu, but uses the negative and question forms of the verb sái, 'need,' 'have to.'

    Ex: Ngóh yìhgā | yiu   hohk | Yìngmàhn.   I have to study English right now.

         Ngóh yìhgā | mhsái hohk | Yìngmàhn.   I don't have to study English right now.

         Néih yìhgā | sái mhsái hohk | Yìngmàhn a?   Do you have to study English right now?

(See BC)

115

III. DRILLS

    1. Substitution Drill

            Ex: T: Sihk béng lā.   T: Have a cookie [polite].
                    /yĭn/   /tobacco/

                                             or
                                             Have some cookies [polite].

                S: Sihk yĭn lā.   S: Have a cigarette [polite].

    + 1. Sihk yĭn lā. /faahn/   1. Sihk faahn lā.
                     (rice)   Dinner is ready; come eat.
    + 2. Sihk faahn lā. /pìhnggwó/   2. Sihk pìhnggwó lā.
                      (apple)   Have an apple.
    + 3. /cháang/   3. Sihk cháang lā.
              (orange)   Have an orange.
      4. /béng/   4. Sihk béng lā.
      5. /yĭn/   5. Sihk yĭn lā.
    + 6. /jĭu/   6. Sihk jĭu lā.
              (banana)

    _____

    2. Substitution Drill

    +   Ex: T: Yám chàh lā! /gafē/   T: Have some tea! [polite] /coffee/
                S: Yám gafē lā!   S: Have some coffee!

      1. Yám chàh lā. /gafē/   1. Yám gafē lā.
    + 2. Yám gafē lā. /heiséui/   2. Yám heiséui lā.
                     (soft drink)   Have a soft drink.
    + 3. Yám heiséui lā. /bējáu/   3. Yám bējáu lā.
                        (beer)   Have a beer.
    + 4. Yám bējáu lā. /séui/   4. Yám séui lā.
                      (water)   Have some water.
      5. Yám séui lā. /chàh/   5. Yám chàh lā.
    + 6. /ngàuhnáaih/   6. Yám ngàuhnáaih lā.
              (milk)
    + 7. /jáu/   7. Yám jáu lā.
              (alcoholic beverage)

    _____

116

3. Substitution Drill

    Ex: T: Yám m̀hyám heiséui a?   T: Would you like a soft drink?
         /bējáu/   /beer/
      S: Yám m̀hyám bējáu a?   S: Would you like a beer?

1. /gafē/   1. Yám m̀hyám gafē a?
2. /heiséui/   2. Yám m̀hyám heiséui a?
3. /séui/   3. Yám m̀hyám séui a?
4. /bējáu/   4. Yám m̀hyám bējáu a?
5. /ngàuhnáaih/   5. Yám m̀hyám ngàuhnáaih a?

Comment: The above sentences could also mean 'Do you drink?'
        (as a custom, as opposed to an intention)

Social comment: Chinese custom makes one feel awkward to an-
        swer choice type question affirmatively.
        It is better to ask 'Yám dī mēyéh a?' 'You'll
        drink a little what?', i.e. "What'll you
        have to drink?"

---

4. Expansion Drill

    Ex: 1. T: chàh   T: tea
          S: Yám chàh lā!   S: Have some tea.
       2. T: béng   T: cookies
          S: Sihk béng lā!   S: Have a cookie.
                       or
                     Have some cookies.

1. gafē   1. Yám gafē lā!
2. heiséui   2. Yám heiséui lā!
3. faahn   3. Sihk faahn lā!
4. bējáu   4. Yám bējáu lā!
5. yīn   5. Sihk yīn lā!
6. pìhnggwó   6. Sihk pìhnggwó lā!
7. séui   7. Yám séui lā!
8. cháang   8. Sihk cháang lā!
9. béng   9. Sihk béng lā!
10. chàh   10. Yám chàh lā!
11. jáu   11. Yám jáu lā!
12. jīu   12. Sihk jīu lā!

5. Transformation Drill

> Ex: T: Sihk yīn lā!   T: Have a cigarette. (polite
>   invitation)
>
>   S: Ṁhhóu sihk yīn!   S: Don't smoke! (abrupt; note
>   absence of lā)

1. Yám bējáu lā.   1. Ṁhhóu yám bējáu!
2. Sihk yīn lā.   2. Ṁhhóu sihk yīn!
3. Yám gafē lā.   3. Ṁhhóu yám gafē!
4. Sihk béng lā.   4. Ṁhhóu sihk béng!
5. Yám heiséui lā.   5. Ṁhhóu yám heiséui!

   a. Repeat. as **polite** negative request, thus:

>   T: Sihk yīn lā!   T: Have a cigarette.
>   S: Ṁhhóu sihk yīn lā.   S: Please don't smoke.

---

6. Expansion Drill

> Ex: T: Kéuih yám chàh.   T: He drinks tea. /coffee/
>   /gafē/
>
>   S: Kéuih yám cháh,   S: He drinks tea, but he doesn't
>   daahnhaih ṁhyám   drink coffee.
>   gafē.
>   **or**
>
>   He drinks tea, but not coffee.

1. Kéuih yám heiséui. /bējáu/   1. Kéuih yám heiséui,
                                      daahnhaih ṁhyám bējáu.

2. Kéuih yám gafē. /chàh/   2. Kéuih yám gafē, daahnhaih
                                      ṁhyám chàh.

3. Kéuih sihk pìhnggwó. /cháang/   3. Kéuih sihk pìhnggwó, daahn-
                                      haih ṁhsihk cháang.

4. Kéuih sihk béng. /yám chàh/   4. Kéuih sihk béng, daahnhaih
                                      ṁhyám chàh.

5. Kéuih sīk sé Jùngmàhn. /Yìng-   5. Kéuih sé Jùngmán, daahnhaih
   mán/   ṁhsīk sé Yìngmàhn.

118

7. Response Drill

	Ex: 1.	T: Yám gafē lā? /nod/	T: Would you like some coffee? /nod/
+		S: Hóu aak. M̀hgòi.	S: Yes; thanks.
	2.	T: Yám gafē lā? /shake/	T: Would you like some coffee? /shake/
		S: M̀hyám laak, m̀hgòi.	S: No thanks, not right now.

1. Yám chàh lā? /nod/	1. Hóu aak. M̀hgòi.
2. Yám bējáu lā? /nod/	2. Hóu aak. M̀hgòi.
3. Yám heiséui lā? /shake/	3. M̀hyám laak, m̀hgòi.
4. Yám gafē lā? /shake/	4. M̀hyám laak, m̀hgòi.
5. Yám séui lā? /nod/	5. Hóu aak. M̀hgòi.

Comment: aak occurs in a set with hóu as a fixed phrase,
followed by pause: Hóu aak. 'Agreed.', 'OK.' But
hóu, when it introduces a comment, is not followed
by aak. Compare the pausing of:

Hóu, m̀hgòi.   OK, thanks.

Hóu aak. M̀hgòi.   OK. Thanks.

---

8. Response Drill

	Ex: 1.	T: Sihk béng lā! /nod/	T: Have a cookie. /nod/
		S: Hóu aak. M̀hgòi.	S: All right. Thanks you.
	2.	T: Sihk béng lā! /shake/	T: Have a cookie. /shake/
		S: M̀hsihk laak; m̀hgòi.	S: Not just now, thanks.

1. Sihk pìhnggwó lā! /nod/	1. Hóu aak. M̀hgòi.
2. Sihk yīn lā! /nod/	2. Hóu aak. M̀hgòi.
3. Sihk faahn lā! /shake/	3. M̀hsihk laak; m̀hgòi.
4. Sihk cháang lā! /shake/	4. M̀hsihk laak; m̀hgòi.
5. Sihk béng lā! /nod/	5. Hóu aak. M̀hgòi.
6. Sihk jīu lā! /nod/	6. Hóu aak. M̀hgòi.

Comment: If you don't smoke, the way to say so colloquially,
when you are invited to have a cigarette, is:
"Síu sihk", 'smoke very little', 'seldom smoke',
i.e. "I don't smoke."

9. Response Drill: Respond appropriately, following patterns established in Drills 7 and 8. (For the negative use m̀hsihk and
   m̀hyám, although m̀hsái is equally appropriate.)

   1. Yám chàh lā? /nod/   1. Hóu aak. M̀hgòi.
   2. Yám bējáu lā? /shake/   2. M̀hyám laak. M̀hgòi.
   3. Sihk yīn lā! /nod/   3. Hóu aak. M̀hgòi.
   4. Sihk béng lā! /shake/   4. M̀hsihk laak. M̀hgòi.
   5. Yám gafē lā? /nod/   5. Hóu aak. M̀hgòi.
   6. Sihk pìhnggwó lā! /nod/   6. Hóu aak. M̀hgòi.
   7. Yám heiséui lā? /shake/   7. M̀hyám laak. M̀hgòi.
   8. Sihk cháang lā? /shake/   8. M̀hsihk laak. M̀hgòi.

   a. Repeat, teacher cueing nouns only, students doing Q&A,
      answering M̀hsái laak, m̀hgòi. 'No, thanks.'

---

10. Substitution Drill: Substitute in Subject or Object position as
    appropriate.

    Ex: 1. T: Néih yám mēyéh   T: What would you like to drink?
              a? /néih   /your friend/
              pàhngyáuh/

          S: Néih pàhngyáuh   S: What would your friend like
             yám mēyéh a?   to drink?

          T: Néih pàhngyáuh   T: What would your friend like
             yám mēyéh a?   to drink? /soft drink/
             /heiséui/

          S: Néih pàhngyáuh   S: Your friend would like a soft
             yám heiséui.   drink.

    1. Kéuih yám mēyéh a? /kéuih   1. Kéuih pàhngyáuh yám mēyéh
       pàhngyáuh/   a?
    2. /séui/   2. Kéuih pàhngyáuh yám séui.
    3. /jáu/   3. Kéuih pàhngyáuh yám jáu.
    4. /ngóhdeih pàhngyáuh/   4. Ngóhdeih pàhngyáuh yám jáu.
    5. /néih pàhngyáuh/   5. Néih pàhngyáuh yám jáu.
    6. /bīngo/   6. Bīngo yám jáu a?
    7. /kéuih/   7. Kéuih yám jáu.
    8. /mēyéh/   8. Kéuih yám mēyéh a?

    Comment: Yám Object can mean (1) 'intend to yám object' and
              it can mean (2) in process of yám-ing object or
              could mean (3) 'customarily yám object'. The
              situation governs which interpretation is appropriate.
              This follows for all the sentences in this drill.

11. Conversation Drill

Ex: Host: Sihk béng lā?   Host: Won't you have some cookies?
    Guest: M̀hsái haakhei.   Guest: Ah, no, thank you.
    Host: M̀hhóu haakhei a.   Host: Oh, do have some.
    Guest: (shake) Ngóh   Guest: No thanks, really not.
        jànhaih m̀hsihk
        léh.

    or   or
    Guest: (nod) Hóu aak.   Guest: Well, all right, thanks.
        m̀hgòi.
    Host: M̀hsái m̀hgòi.   Host: You're welcome. or
                                           Not at all.

1. A. Sihk pìhnggwó lā?   1. A. Sihk pìhnggwó lā?
   B. ....   B. M̀hsái haakhei.
   A. ....   A. M̀hhóu haakhei a.
   B. (shake)   B. Ngóh jànhaih m̀hsihk léh.

2. A. Yám gafē lā?   2. A. Yám gafē lā?
   B. ....   B. M̀hsái haakhei.
   A. ....   A. M̀hhóu haakhei a.
   B. (nod)   B. Hóu aak, m̀hgòi.
   A. ....   A. M̀hsái m̀hgòi.

3. A. Sihk cháang lā?   3. A. Sihk cháang lā?
   B. ....   B. M̀hsái haakhei.
   A. ....   A. M̀hhóu haakhei a.
   B. (shake)   B. Ngóh jànhaih m̀hsihk léh.

4. A. Sihk yīn lā?   4. A. Sihk yīn lā?
   B. ....   B. M̀hsái haakhei.
   A. ....   A. M̀hhóu haakhei a.
   B. (shake)   B. Ngóh jànhaih m̀hsihk léh.

5. A. Yám bējáu lā?   5. A. Yám bējáu lā?
   B. ....   B. M̀hsái haakhei.
   A. ....   A. M̀hhóu haakhei a.
   B. (shake)   B. Ngóh jànhaih m̀hyám léh.

12. Conversion Drill

Ex: Waiter: Yám mēyéh a?   A: What'll you have to drink?

Customer: Ngóh yám chàh.   B: I'll have tea.

Waiter: Síujé haih   A: Will the young lady have tea
        mhhaih dōu   too?
        yám chàh a?

Customer: Mhhaih. Kéuih   B: No, she'll have coffee.
          yám gafē.

1. W. ....?   1. W. Yám mēyéh a?

   C. ...... bējáu.   C. Ngóh yám bējáu.

   W. Néih pàhngyáuh ......?   W. Néih pàhngyáuh haih
                                      mhhaih dōu yám bējáu a?

   C. ......gafē.   C. Mhhaih. Kéuih yám gafē.

2. W. ....?   2. W. Yám mēyéh a?

   C. ......heiséui.   C. Ngóh yám heiséui.

   W. Kéuih ......?   W. Kéuih haih mhhaih dōu
                                      yám heiséui a?

   C. ...... bējáu.   C. Mhhaih. Kéuih yám bējáu.

3. W. SĪnsàang ......?   3. W. SĪnsàang yám mēyéh a?
                                      What will you have to
                                      drink, sir?

   C. ...... chàh.   C. Ngóh yám chàh.

   W. Síujé ......?   W. Síujé haih mhhaih dōu
                                      yám chàh a?
                                      Will the young lady
                                      have tea too?

   C. ......heiséui.   C. Mhhaih.Kéuih yám heiséui.

4. W. Hòh Sàang ......?   4. W. Hòh Sàang yám mēyéh a?
                                      What'll you have to
                                      drink, Mr. Ho?

   C. ...... bējáu.   C. Ngóh yám bējáu.

   W. Hòh Táai ......?   W. Hòh Táai haih mhhaih dōu
                                      yám bējáu a?
                                      Will Mrs. Ho have beer
                                      too?

   C. ......heiséui.   C. Mhhaih.Kéuih yám heiséui.

Comment: In a different situation the Example conversation
         (and likewise those below) could also be appro-
         priately interpreted as:

         A. What's that you're drinking?

B: I'm drinking tea.

A: Is he drinking tea too?

A: No, he's drinking coffee.

---

13. Conversation Drill

Ex: Guest: Aiya! Yìhgā
          sahp dím daahp
          chāt. Ngóh yiu
          jáu laak.

    Guest: Oh-oh! It's 10:35.
           I must be going.

    Host: Mhhóu gam faai
         jáu lā!

    Host: Oh don't go so soon!

    Guest: Mhhaih a. Jàn-
         haih yiu jáu
         laak.

    Guest: No. Really, I must go.

1.

1. A. Aiya! Yìhgā yāt dím daahp
      chāt. Ngóh yiu jáu laak.

  B. Mhhóu gam faai jáu lā!

  A. Mhhaih a. Jànhaih yiu
     jáu laak.

2.

2. A. Aiya! Yìhgā sàam dím
      sàamgogwāt. Ngóh yiu
      jáu laak.

  B. Mhhóu gam faai jáu lā!

  A. Mhhaih a. Jànhaih yiu
     jáu laak.

3.

3. A. Aiya! Yìhgā luhk dím
      daahp sahp. Ngóh yiu
      jáu laak.

  B. Mhhóu gam faai jáu lā!

  A. Mhhaih a. Jànhaih yiu
     jáu laak.

4.

4. A. Aiya! Yìhgā sahpyih dím
      daahp sei. Ngóh yiu
      jáu laak.

  B. Mhhóu gam faai jáu lā!

  A. Mhhaih a. Jànhaih yiu
     jáu laak.

123

5.

5. A. Aiya! Yìhgā baat dìm yāt-
      gogwāt. Ngóh yiu jáu
      laak.

   B. Mhhóu gam faai jáu lā!

   A. Mhhaih a. Jànhaih yiu
      jáu laak.

IV. CONVERSATIONS FOR LISTENING

    (On tape. Listen to tape with book closed.)

V. SAY IT IN CANTONESE

    A. Student A to Student B: B. Student B replies:

       1. offers him tea.   1. Thank you.

       2. Have some cookies.   2. No thanks.

       3. It's 6:30--I have to go.   3. Don't go so soon!

       4. Sit anywhere you like.   4. Thanks.

       5. (acting the part of a   5. I'll have beer.
          waiter:) What'll you have
          to drink?

       6. Don't go so soon!   6. No, I really have to go.

       7. (offering cookies to a guest   7. I really don't care for
          who has politely declined   any, thanks. [really not
          them already:)   eat]
          Do try some!

Vocabulary Checklist for Lesson 5

1. aak	ss:	sen. suf. a to soften abruptness + -k for liveliness
2. Aiya!	ex:	exclamation of consternation
3. bējáu	m:	beer
4. béng	n:	cake
5. cháang	n:	orange
6. chàh	n:	tea
7. chèuihbín	adv:	As you wish, At your convenience
8. chèuihbín chóh lā.	Ph:	'Sit anywhere you like.'
9. chóh	v:	sit
10. faahn	n:	rice (cooked)
11. gafē	n:	coffee
12. gam	adv:	so, such
13. haakhei	adj:	polite
14. -háh	Vsuf:	Verb suffix for casual effect
15. heiséui	n:	soft drink
16. Hóu aak	Ph:	OK. Agreed. Response indicating agreement.
17. jànhaih	adv:	really, indeed
18. jáu	n:	alcoholic beverage
19. jáu	v:	leave, depart
20. jīu	n:	banana
21. jyúyàhn	n:	host, hostess
22. -k	ss:	a glottal stop ending to certain sentence suffixes, giving sentence a lively air.
23. la	ss:	sen. suf. indicating potential change
24. laak	ss:	sen. suf. la (change) + sen. suf. -k (liveliness)
25. léh	ss:	sen. suf. for definiteness
26. M̀hgòi	Ph:	Thank you (for service)
27. m̀hhóu	Ph:	don't (as a command)
28. M̀hhóu haakhei	Ph:	'Don't be polite.'
29. M̀hsái	Ph:	no need to, not necessary
30. M̀hsái la(ak)	Ph:	No thanks (when offered something) [not necessary now]

125

31. m̀hsái m̀hgòi.	Ph:	You're welcome. [not necessary] Polite response when someone thanks you for doing him a service
32. m̀hsái haakhei	Ph:	[don't need to be polite.] "No thanks." (to an offer) "You're welcome." (when someone thanks you.)
33. ngàuhnáaih	n:	milk
34. pìhnggwó	n:	apple
35. séui	n:	water
36. si	v:	try
37. siháh	Vsuf:	give it a try
38. sihk	v:	eat
39. sihk yīn	vo:	to smoke
40. Síu sihk	Ph:	'I don't smoke.' non-smoker's response in refusing a cigarette. [seldom-smoke]
41. yàhnhaak	n:	guest
42. yám	v:	drink
43. yīn	(bw)n:	tobacco; smoke
44. yiu	auxV:	must, need, have to

126

I. BASIC CONVERSATION

  A. Buildup:

          (Clerk and Customer in a department store)
          sauhfoyùhn   sales clerk
                         Sauhfoyùhn

          máaih   buy
          Máaih mēyéh a?   Buy what? (i.e., May I help
                                              you?)

          guhaak   customer
                         Guhaak

          sēutsāam   shirt
          gihn   measure for clothing
          séung máaih   wish to buy, want to buy
          Ngóh séung máaih gihn sēutsāam.   I want to buy a shirt.
          chín   money
          géidō?   how much?
          géidō chín a?   how much money?
          nī   this
          nī gihn   this one (this 'measure')
          NĪ gihn géidō chín a?   How much is this one?

                         Sauhfoyùhn

          mān   dollar
          yahsei   twenty-four
          yahsei mān $24
          NĪ gihn yahsei mān.   This one is $24.

                         Guhaak

          gó   that
          gó gihn   that one (that 'measure')
          gó léuhng gihn   those two
          dōu haih yahsei mān   is also $24, are also $24.
          haih m̀haih dōu haih   are (they) also $24? or
             yahsei mān a?   is (it) also $24?
          Gó léuhng gihn haih m̀haih   Those two, are they also $24
             dōu haih yahsei mān gihn a?   each?

                              127

Sauhfoyùhn

| Ṁhhaih; yihsahp māan jē. | No; twenty dollars only |
| Ṁhhaih--yihsahp māan gihn jē. | No--Only $20 each. |

Guhaak

béi	give
béi ngóh	give me
béi nī gihn ngóh	give this one (to) me
Hóu, béi nī gihn ngóh lā.	OK, give me this one.

Sauhfoyùhn

| géidō gihn | how many ones |
| Yiu géidō gihn a? | How many do you want? |

Guhaak

| gau | enough |
| Yāt gihn gau laak. | One is enough. |

Sauhfoyùhn

| Gám, néih máaih ṁhmáaih gó léuhng gihn a? | Are you going to buy those two? |

Guhaak

| Ṁhmáaih laak. | Not buy. |

B. Recapitulation:

Sauhfoyùhn

| Máaih mēyéh a? | What would you like to buy? |

Guhaak

| Ngóh séung máaih gihn sēutsāam. NĪ gihn géidō chín a? | I'm looking for a shirt. How much is this one? |

Sauhfoyùhn

| NĪ gihn yahsei māan. | This one is $24. |

Guhaak

| Gó léuhng gihn haih ṁhhaih dōu haih yahsei māan gihn a? | Are those two also $24 each? |

Sauhfoyùhn

| Ṁhhaih; yihsahp māan gihn jē. | No; only $20 each. |

Guhaak

| Hóu, béi nī gihn ngóh lā. | OK, give me this one. |

Sauhfoyùhn

Yiu géidö gihn a?   How many do you want?

Guhaak

Yāt gihn gau laak.   One is enough.

Sauhfoyùhn

Gám, néih máaih ṁhmáaih gó   Are you going to buy those two?
léuhng gihn a?

Guhaak

Ṁhmáaih laak.   Not now, thanks.

+ + + + + + + + + + + + +

Pronunciation:

1. at in chāt, bāt, maht

      at is a two-part final composed of the mid central vowel a [ə˘],
plus the consonant stop t. To produce t the tongue tip stops the flow
of air at the dental ridge, close to the base of the lower teeth.
In final position the t is unreleased:--[t˺]. The closest American
counterpart to the Cantonese at is the ut of general American "but,"
but the Cantonese syllable is shorter in an isolated syllable, more
backed, and tenser.

                Listen and repeat:
                    chāt   (3 times) 七
                    bāt   (3 times) 筆
                    maht   (3 times) 勿

2. aat in baat

      aat is two-part final composed of the low back unrounded vowel
aa [ɑ], plus the consonant stop t. t is produced as described above,
with the tongue tip stopping the air flow at the dental ridge at the
base of the upper teeth, with the air unreleased. aa before t is
produced the same way as before the other final stops (-k and -p).
The nearest American counterpart to aat is the ot sound in general
American "hot," [ɑ], but the Cantonese syllable is more backed, and
somewhat longer in the isolated syllable.

3. <u>at/aat</u> contrasts

      Listen and repeat:

          1. bāt baat   (3 times)

          2. baat bāt   (3 times)

          3. baat baat bāt bāt   (3 times)

          4. bāt bāt baat baat   (3 times)

          5. chāt baat baat chāt   (3 times)

          6. maht baat   (3 times)

          7. baat maht   (3 times)

          8. baat maht maht baat   (3 times)

          9. chāt baat maht   (3 times)

          10. maht baat chāt   (3 times)

4. <u>eui</u>

      Listen and repeat–(Remember that the <u>eui</u> final is rounded
      throughout, that the <u>i</u> part here represents that rounded <u>yu</u> [ü]
      sound, and that a rounded **vowel** has a rounding effect on a
      consonant preceding it in a syllable):

          1. chèuihbín   (3 times)   隨便

          2. chèuih   (3 times)   隨

          3. séui   (3 times)   水

          4. deuimhjyuh   (3 times)   對唔住

          5. deui   (3 times)   對

5. <u>au/aau</u> practice

      Listen and repeat: (Watch the teacher)

          1. gau , gau , gau .   夠

          2. gaau , gaau , gaau .   教

          3. gau gaau , gau gaau , gau gaau .

          4. gaau gau , gaau gau , gaau gau .

          5. gau gaau gaau gau

          6. gaau gau gau gaau

          7. mhgau 唔夠, mhgaau 唔教.

          8. gau mhgau a? , gaau mhgaau a? .

          9. Jáu gau mhgau a? 酒夠唔夠呀?

          10. Mhgau jáu.

6. <u>eut</u>, as in <u>sēutsāam</u>

   <u>eut</u> is a two-part final composed of the single vowel <u>eu</u> and the
consonant stop <u>t</u>. <u>eu</u> before <u>t</u> is a lowered mid front rounded vowel
[œ] produced the same way as before <u>n</u> and <u>i</u>. The <u>t</u> as final is
produced as elsewhere as final, with the tongue tip stopping the flow
of air at the dental ridge, near the base of the upper teeth, un-
released--[t˥]. There is no close comparison in American English to
the <u>eut</u> sound, though the "sēut" of "sēutsāam" is a transliteration
into Cantonese of the English word "shirt."

   Listen and repeat: (Remember that the rounded vowel has a rounding
      effect on the consonant preceding it in a syllable)
      1. sēutsāam   (3 times) 恤衫
      2. sēut sēut sēut   , sēut sēut sēut   . 恤 恤 恤
      3. sēut séui   (3 times) 恤 水
      4. séui sēut   (3 times) 水 恤
      5. sēut jéun   (3 times) 恤 準
      6. jéun sēut   (3 times) 準 恤

7. <u>eu</u> before dentals in contrast to <u>eu</u> before velars: Notice the difference in tongue height of <u>eu</u> before the dentals <u>t</u>, <u>n</u>, and <u>yu</u>
   (spelled <u>i</u> following <u>eu</u>); and <u>eu</u> before the velar nasal <u>ng</u>. The <u>eu</u>
   is relatively lowered before the dentals, raised before the velar.
      1. sēut sēun séung séung
      2. sēut sēut léuhng léuhng
      3. séui séui séung séung
      4. deui deui Jèung Jèung
      5. jéun jéun Jèung Jèung
      6. jéun jéun séung séung

II. NOTES

1. Numbers 20 - 99

a. 20 through 90. For the even 10's the Cantonese use a multiplying
formula: two-ten's, three-ten's, etc.

20.	yihsahp	60.	luhksahp
30.	sàamsahp	70.	chātsahp
40.	seisahp	80.	baatsahp
50.	ńghsahp	90.	gáusahp

b. 21 through 99. For these numbers which are not the even 10's, a
combination of the multiplying and adding formula is used: two-
ten's-one, two-ten's-two, etc.

21. yihsahpyāt

22. yihsahpyih

23. yihsahpsàam etc., to

99. gáusahpgáu

c. Full forms and abbreviated forms:

There is a full form and an abbreviated form for the numbers
from twenty to ninety-nine. Both forms are used in everyday
speech. The contracted form shortens the sahp element to -ah-.

Ex:		Full form	Abbreviated form
	20	yihsahp	yah
	21	yihsahpyāt	yahyāt
	22	yihsahpyih	yahyih
	30	sàamsahp	sà'ah
	31	sàamsahpyāt	sà'ahyāt
	40	seisahp	sei'ah
	50	ńghsahp	ńgh'ah
	60	luhksahp	luhk'ah
	70	chātsahp	chāt'ah
	80	baatsahp	baat'ah
	90	gáusahp	gáu'ah
	99	gáusahpgáu	gáu'ahgáu

(See Drill 6)

132

2. Measures

In Lesson 4 we touched briefly on Measures, saying they were
a class of word in Cantonese which comes between a number (or a
limited set of other entities) and a noun.

Ex:	M	N	
ngóh	go	bīu	my watch
sàam	go	gwāt	three-quarters

In English some nouns are counted in terms of a measure of their
volume or size or shape. For example, we do not ordinarily say
'a water,' but rather 'a glass of water,' 'a gallon of water,'
'a tub of water,' etc. In English 'glass, gallon, tub' type words are
measures used in counting nouns perceived as a mass--(sand, bread,
milk, tobacco, etc.) but not ordinarily in counting nouns perceived
as individual units--(pencil, man, shirt, etc.)

In Chinese, however, a measure word precedes every noun when
it is counted. For a mass-type noun the measure is variable--one
cup, bowl, pound, etc. of rice, for example--but every individual-
type noun has its own invariable measure which is by nature a pronoun
standing in apposition to the noun.

a. Individual Measures

In Lesson Six you will encounter several new individual
measures.

Ex:		M	Noun	
1.	yāt	tìuh	tāai	one [M] tie = one tie
2.	ngóh	bá	jē	my umbrella = my umbrella
3.	kéuih	gihn	sēutsāam	his [M] shirt = his shirt

The individual measures are in apposition to the noun that
follows. Some individual measures have a degree of independent
meaning apart from their structural function. For example, bá
means 'handle,' and is a measure for objects having handles,
tìuh means 'strip' and is a measure for objects which are long and
narrow in shape. However, go, statistically the most frequent
measure, has no independent meaning of its own.

What we have called individual measures some writers have
called classifiers, indicating that nouns are classified according

133

to shape. We use the wider term 'measure' to cover individual
measures and other types of measure as well.

(See Drills 1, 2, 3, 4)

b. Group Measures

In addition to individual measures, there are other types of
measures. One type is the group measure. An example is deui, 'pair.'
Structurally group measures do not differ from individual measures--
they fill the same position in a sentence that individual measures
do, and combine with the same kinds of words. Semantically, of
course, a group measure differs from an individual measure.

Ex:	Measure	+ Noun	
yāt	deui	hàaih	one pair shoes = one pair of shoes
yāt	jek	hàaih	one [M] shoe = one shoe

What we call group measures some writers have called
'collective' measures.

c. Standard Measures

Another type of measure is the standard measure. In English
we talk of 'standard weights and measures'--pounds, inches, gal-
lons, etc. This is the type involved in the Cantonese category
of standard measure. The standard measure is of itself a meaning-
ful unit. Some examples which you have encountered so far are:

Number	+ Standard Measure	
yāt	mān	one dollar
yāt	dím	one o'clock (hour)
yāt	fānjūng	one minute

Standard measures, like all measures, may follow a number
directly. They differ from individual and group measures in that
they are not in apposition to a following noun, and do not depend
on a following noun to give them meaning. Thus they are measures
only in the grammatical sense; they behave like measures in that
they follow numerals directly. Semantically they are like nouns.

134

3. Nouns

A word which requires a measure between a number and itself is classed as a noun in Cantonese.

Ex: Number + Measure + Noun

léuhng	gihn	sēutsāam	two shirts
sàam	go	bīu	three watches
sei	go	jih	4 figures (in reference to time, 4 numbers on the clock dial, i.e. 20 minutes)

4. Measure as substitute for noun.

In a follow sentence a measure substitutes for the noun it represents. In this way a measure operates like a pronoun.

Ex: A. Ngóh máaih léuhng   I'm buying two [M] ties.
          tiuh tāai.

       B. Bīn léuhng tiuh a?   Which two [ones]?

       C. Nī léuhng tiuh.   These two [ones].

          (See BC and Drills 3,4)

5. Measure without preceding number.

We noted in Lesson 2 that nouns do not indicate singular and plural in Cantonese. (sēutsāam = shirt, shirts) The use of a measure without a number preceding it indicates singular number.

Ex: 1. Kéuih séung máaih   1. He wants to buy some
       sēutsāam.   shirts. or
                                      He wants to buy a
                                      shirt.

    2. Kéuih séung máaih gihn   2. He wants to buy a
       sēutsāam.   shirt.

          (See BC)

6. m̀hsái not used in affirmative.

The verb sái 'need,' 'have to,' is used in the negative and in choice-type question, but not in the affirmative.

Ex: Q: Sái m̀hsái máaih luhk   Do you need to buy 6--
       gihn gàm dò a?   so many? (doubtful
                                      that it is necessary)

    A: M̀hsái máaih luhk gihn--   I don't need 6--3 are
       sàam gihn gau laak.   enough.

          (See Drills 1, 3, 12)

To answer a sái m̀hsái? question affirmatively you use yiu
'require,' 'need,' 'have to.'

> Ex: Q: Sái m̀hsái máaih luhk   Do you need to buy so
>   gihn gàm dò a?   many as six?
>
>   A: Yiu máaih luhk gihn--   I need to buy six--
>   sàam gihn m̀hgau.   three aren't enough.
>
>   (See Drill 12)

7. Free words and boundwords

Words in Cantonese which can be spoken as one word sentences
are free words, and ones which are never spoken as a one-word
sentence, but always with some other word accompanying, are boundwords.
Words which are always bound to an element which follows them we call
right-bound (b-), and ones which are always bound to an element which
precedes them we call left-bound (-b). Some boundwords can be bound
in either direction.

8. nī, 'this,' and gó, 'that' classed as specifiers.

nī, 'this,' and gó, 'that,' are boundwords functioning as
modifier in a Noun Phrase (NP). They are right bound, bound to a
following element or elements, commonly a measure, or a number +
measure:

> Ex: nī/gó   nu.   M
>
> nī   gihn   = this one [this M]
>
> gó   léuhng   go   = those two [that-two-M]
>
>   (See BC and Drills 2, 3, 11)

Note the word order of nī/gó constructions:

	N/Pro.	nī/gó	Nu.	M	N	
1.		nī	léuhng	gihn	sēutsāam	these two shirts
2.		gó	sei	bá	jē	those 4 umbrellas
3.	ngóh	nī	léuhng	tìuh	tāai	these two ties of mine

>   (See Drills 1, 11)

nī and gó fill a position in a sentence that can be occupied
by only a few words. bīn? 'which?' fills this same position. We use
the class name Specifier to refer to this small group.

We call nī and gó 'this' and 'that' to give you memory-aid
definitions. More specifically, nī refers to what is relatively
near, and gó to what is relatively distant.

9. __Relative word order of direct and indirect object.__

Some verbs, such as __béi__, 'give,' take two objects: a direct
object (thing), and indirect object (usually a person). In Cantonese
the word order is Verb + Direct object + Indirect object.

>   Verb + Direct obj + Indirect obj
>   Béi   nī gihn   ngóh   lā. Give this one (to) me.
>   Béi   sàam màn   kéuih   lā. Give $3 (to) him.
>   (See BC and Drills 11, 12, 15)

10. __géi(dō)?__, 'how many, how much?' as an interrogative number.

__géidō?__ and
occupying the position in a question-word sentence that a number
occupies in the response sentence. In this frame __géi(dō)__ is classed
as an interrogative number. As a number it precedes a measure.

Ex:	Number	Measure	
Kéuih máaih	géi(dō)	gihn	a? How many is he going to buy?
Kéuih máaih	sàam	gihn.	He's going to buy three.

>   (See BC and Drill _9_)

You will remember that __géi__ has another meaning which you encountered in Lesson Four. __géi__, 'several' is an approximate number
and is distinguished from __géi?__, 'how many?' in a sentence by the presence of the sentence suffix __a__ in the question sentence but not in
the statement sentence.

>   Ex: 1. Kéuih séung máaih géi   He's thinking of buying
>   gihn.   several.
>
>   2. Kéuih séung máaih géi   How many is he thinking of
>   gihn a?   buying?

11. __géidō?__, 'how many?' and __géi-?__, 'how many?' differentiated.

The difference between __géi-?__ and __géidō?__ is that __géi-?__ is a boundword
bound to a following Measure, and __géidō?__ is a free word which can be
bound to a following measure as modifier (in which case it is interchangeable with __géi-?__), but may also be head in a nominal construction, which
__gei-?__ cannot.

>   Ex: 1. Kéuih séung máaih ⎰géi ⎱gihn a?   1. How many [Ms] does he
>   ⎱géidō⎰   want?
>
>   2. Kéuih séung máaih géidō   a?   2. How many does he want?

137

12. <u>Ṁhjì</u>...$\begin{Bmatrix} n\bar{e}? \\ a? \end{Bmatrix}$, as polite question form: 'I wonder...?,' i.e., 'I wonder (if you could tell me)...?

    By extension <u>ṁhjì</u>, 'don't know,' may be taken to mean something like 'I wonder...?' 'Could you tell me...?' a polite way of making a question without being abrupt. By adding the sentence suffix <u>a</u> or <u>nē</u> to the end of the negative sentence, the negative is transformed to the polite 'I wonder...?' question.

Ex: Ṁhjì yiu géidō chin.	(I) don't know how much it costs.
Ṁhjì yiu géidō chin $\begin{Bmatrix} n\bar{e} \\ a \end{Bmatrix}$?	(I) wonder how much it costs? (You assume that the person you're talking to <u>does</u> know and in this indirect way prompt him to tell you.)

II. DRILLS

   1. Expansion Drill: (Students repeat sentence after the teacher.

  + 1. a. Máaih <u>yúhlāu</u>.   1. a. Buy a <u>raincoat/raincoats</u>.

      b. Máaih gihn yúhlāu.   b. Buy a raincoat.

      c. Máaih ńgh gihn yúhlāu.   c. Buy 5 raincoats.

      d. Máaih nī ńgh gihn yúhlāu.   d. Buy these 5 raincoats.

      e. Ngóh máaih nī ńgh gihn yúhlāu. e. I'll take these 5 rain-
                                  coats.

  + 2. a. Máaih <u>fu</u>.   2. a. Buy slacks.
        (<u>slacks</u>, <u>trousers</u>, <u>long-</u>
        <u>pants</u>)

    + b. Máaih <u>tìuh</u> fu.   b. Buy a pair of slacks.
        (<u>M. for trousers</u>)

      c. Máaih léuhng tìuh fu.   c. Buy two pairs of slacks.

      d. Máaih nī léuhng tìuh fu.   d. Buy these two pairs of
                                  slacks.

      e. Máaih nī léuhng tìuh fu lā! e. Buy these two pairs of
                                  slacks!

  + 3. a. Máaih <u>maht</u>.   3. a. Buy <u>socks</u>.

    + b. Máaih <u>deui</u> maht.   b. Buy a <u>pair</u> of socks.

      c. Máaih sàam deui maht.   c. Buy three pairs of socks.

      d. Ṁhsái máaih sàam deui maht. d. You don't need to buy
                                  three pairs of socks.

      e. Ṁhsái máaih sàam deui maht   e. You don't need to buy 3
        laak.   pairs of socks just
                                  now.

  + 4. a. Máaih <u>bāt</u>.   4. a. Buy pens (<u>or</u> pencils)
        (<u>writing implements</u>)

    + b. Máaih <u>jì</u> bāt.   b. Buy a pen (<u>or</u> pencil)
        (<u>M. for bāt</u>)

    + c. Máaih jì <u>yùhnbāt</u>.   c. Buy a <u>pencil</u>.

      d. Séung máaih jì yùhnbāt.   d. Want to buy a pencil

      e. Ṁhséung máaih jì yùhnbāt.   e. Don't want to buy a
                                  pencil.

      f. Séung ṁhséung máaih jì   f. Do (you) want to buy a
        yùhnbāt a?   pencil?

                                  <u>or</u>

                                Are you planning to buy
                                a pencil?

<table>
<tr><td></td><td>or</td></tr>
</table>

or

Would you like to buy a pencil?

+ 5. a. <u>Jūng</u>.　　　　　　　　　5. a. Clock

   b. Máaih jūng.　　　　　　　　b. Buy clock(s)

   c. Máaih go jūng.　　　　　　　c. Buy a clock.

   d. Séung máaih go jūng.　　　　d. Plan to buy a clock.

   e. Séung máaih léuhng go jūng.　e. Plan to buy two clocks.

   f. Ngóh séung máaih léuhng go jūng.　f. I plan to buy two clocks.

+ 6. a. <u>Kwàhn</u>.　　　　　　　　6. a. Skirt

   b. Máaih kwàhn.　　　　　　　b. Buy skirt(s).

   c. Máaih tìuh kwàhn.　　　　　c. Buy a skirt.

+   d. Máaih tìuh <u>dáikwàhn</u> (<u>slip</u>, <u>petticoat</u>)　d. Buy a slip.

   e. Máaih léuhng tìuh dáikwàhn.　e. Buy two slips.

   f. Séung máaih léuhng tìuh dáikwàhn.　f. Wish to buy two slips.

   g. Ngóh séung máaih léuhng tìuh dáikwàhn.　g. I wish to buy two slips.

 7. a. Síujé　　　　　　　　　7. a. Lady

+   b. Go <u>wái</u> síujé　　　　　　b. That lady (<u>wái</u> = polite <u>M for person</u>)

   c. Sīk go wái síujé.　　　　　c. Know that lady

   d. Mhsīk go wái síujé.　　　　d. Not know that lady.

   e. Ngóh mhsīk go wái síujé.　e. I don't know that lady.

+ 8. a. <u>Jē</u>　　　　　　　　　　8. a. Umbrella

+   b. <u>Bá</u> jē (<u>M. for umbrella</u>)　b. An umbrella

   c. Máaih nī bá jē.　　　　　　c. Buy this umbrella.

   d. Máaih nī bá jē, géidō chín a?　d. How much does this raincoat cost?

+   e. Máaih nī bá jē <u>yiu</u> géidō chín a? (yiu + money expression = want X amount, costs X amount, i.e., the asking price)　e. How much (do you) want for this raincoat?

140

f. Ngóh m̀hjì máaih nī bá jē yiu géidō chín.	f. I don't know how much this umbrella is.
+ g. <u>Ngóh m̀hjì</u> máaih nī bá jē yiu géidō chín a? [(Ngóh) m̀hjì...a? = I wonder...? i.e. polite question introduction]	g. I wonder how much this raincoat is?

2. Transformation Drill: Transform the sentences from affirmative to choice type question.

Ex: T: Nī gihn sēutsāam sahpsàam mān.

T: This shirt is thirteen dollars.

S: Nī gihn sēutsāam haih m̀hhaih sahpsàam mān a?

S: Is this shirt thirteen dollars?

1. Nī gihn sēutsāam sahpyāt mān.

1. Nī gihn sēutsāam haih m̀hhaih sahpyāt mān a?

+ 2. Gó tiuh <u>tāai</u> sei mān. That <u>tie</u> is four dollars.

2. Gó tiuh tāai haih m̀hhaih sei mān a?

3. Nī tiuh fu sahpsàam mān.

3. Nī tiuh fu haih m̀hhaih sahpsàam mān a?

+ 4. Gó deui <u>hàaih</u> yahńgh mān. That pair of <u>shoes</u> is twenty-five dollars.

4. Gó deui hàaih haih m̀hhaih yahńgh mān a?

5. Nī deui maht sàam mān.

5. Nī deui maht haih m̀hhaih sàam mān a?

6. Gó bá jē sahpyāt mān.

6. Gó bá jē haih m̀hhaih sahpyāt mān a?

7. Nī gihn yúhlāu sahpgáu mān.

7. Nī gihn yúhlāu haih m̀hhaih sahpgáu mān a?

8. Nī go bīu ńgh'ahgáu mān.

8. Nī go bīu haih m̀hhaih ńgh'ahgáu mān a?

+ 9. Gó jī <u>yùhnjíbāt</u> yāt mān. That <u>ball point pen</u> is one dollar.

9. Gó jī yùhnjíbāt haih m̀hhaih yāt mān a?

3. Response Drill: Teacher should point to a spot near himself for <u>nī</u>-, students should point away for <u>gó</u>-, to link the words with the situation.

Ex: T: Nī gihn sahpyāt mān.

T: This one is eleven dollars.

S: Gó gihn dōu yiu sahpyāt mān.

S: That one is eleven dollars.

141

1. Nī tiuh sahpsei mān.
2. Nī deui luhk mān.
3. Nī gihn sahpbaat mān.
4. Nī jí yāt mān.
5. Nī go yahgáu mān.
+ 6. Nī tiuh <u>dáifu</u> ńgh mān.
    (underpants, undershorts)

1. Gó tiuh dōu yiu sahpsei mān.
2. Gó deui dōu yiu luhk mān.
3. Gó gihn dōu yiu sahpbaat mān.
4. Gó jí dōu yiu yāt mān.
5. Gó go dōu yiu yahgáu mān.
6. Gó tiuh dáifu dōu yiu ńgh mān.

Comment: Note that in the sentences above, numbered money
expressions stand as predicate without the inclusion
of a verb. The inclusion of <u>haih</u> is, however, also
permitted: <u>Nī gihn haih sahpyāt mān</u>. 'This one is
$11'.

---

4. Expansion Drill

    Ex: T: Nī gihn yúhlāu sahp
        mān.

      S: Nī gihn yúhlāu sahp
        mān, gó gihn dōu
        haih sahp mān.

    T: This raincoat is $10.

    S: This raincoat is $10.
       That one is also $10.

1. Nī gihn sēutsāam sahpńgh mān.

2. Nī deui hàaih yahluhk mān.

3. Nī bá jē sahpchāt mān.

4. Nī tiuh fu yahyih mān.

5. Nī tiuh tāai baat mān.

1. Nī gihn sēutsāam sahpńgh mān,
gó gihn dōu haih sahp-
ńgh mān.

2. Nī deui hàaih yahluhk mān,
gó deui dōu haih yahluhk
mān.

3. Nī bá jē sahpchāt mān,
gó bá dōu haih sahpchāt
mān.

4. Nī tiuh fu yahyih mān, gó
tiuh dōu haih yahyih mān.

5. Nī tiuh tāai baat mān,
gó tiuh dōu haih baat mān.

---

5. Substitution Drill: Repeat the first sentence after the teacher,
then substitute the cues as appropriate to make new sentences.

1. Ngóh séung máaih gihn yúhlāu.
   I want to buy a raincoat.
2. /gó go yàhn/

1. Ngóh séung máaih gihn
yúhlāu.
2. Gó go yàhn séung máaih gihn
yúhlāu.

That man wants to buy this
raincoat.

3. Gó go Yǐnggwokyàhn.

3. Gó go Yǐnggwokyàhn séung
   máaih gihn yùhlāu.

4. deui maht

4. Gó go Yǐnggwokyàhn séung
   máaih deui maht.

+ 5. Gó go síujé
     (woman)

5. Gó go síujé séung máaih deui
   maht.
   That lady wants to buy a
   pair of socks.

+ 6. Gó wái sǐnsàang
     (man)

6. Gó wái sǐnsàang séung máaih
   deui maht.

7. tiuh fu

7. Gó wái sǐnsàang séung máaih
   tiuh fu.

---

6. Transformation Drill: Transform the numbers from full form to
   abbreviated form.

   Ex: T: Nǐ tiuh sàamsahp màn.   T: This one is thirty dollars.
       S: Nǐ tiuh sà'ah màn.   S: This one is thirty dollars.

1. Nǐ tiuh yihsahpsei màn.
   [24]

1. Nǐ tiuh yahsei màn.

2. Nǐ tiuh yihsahpchāt màn.
   [27]

2. Nǐ tiuh yahchāt màn.

3. Nǐ tiuh sàamsahpńgh màn.
   [35]

3. Nǐ tiuh sà'ahńgh màn.

4. Nǐ tiuh sàamsahpyih màn.
   [32]

4. Nǐ tiuh sà'ahyih màn.

5. Nǐ tiuh seisahpbaat màn.
   [48]

5. Nǐ tiuh sei'ahbaat màn.

6. Nǐ tiuh seisahpluhk màn.
   [46]

6. Nǐ tiuh sei'ahluhk màn.

7. Nǐ tiuh ńghsahpsei màn.
   [54]

7. Nǐ tiuh ńgh'ahsei màn.

8. Nǐ tiuh ńghsahpyih màn.
   [51]

8. Nǐ tiuh ńgh'ahyih màn.

9. Nǐ tiuh luhksahpńgh màn.
   [65]

9. Nǐ tiuh luhk'ahńgh màn.

10. Nǐ tiuh luhksahpgáu màn.
    [69]

10. Nǐ tiuh luhk'ahgáu màn.

---

7. **Response Drill:** Teacher points away for gó-, students near for nī-.

Ex: T: Gó tìuh fu sahp   T: That pair of trousers is ten
       màn. /baat màn/   dollars.

     S: Nī tìuh baat màn jē.   S: This pair is only eight dollars.

1. Gó deui haaih yahsàam màn.   1. Nī deui yahyāt màn jē.
   /yahyāt màn/

2. Gó deui maht luhk màn. /sei màn/   2. Nī deui sei màn jē.

3. Gó tìuh fu sahpyìh màn.   3. Nī tìuh sahp màn jē.
   /sahp màn/

4. Gó go bīu sà'ahngh màn.   4. Nī go yahchāt màn jē.
   /yahchāt màn/

5. Gó gihn yúhlāu yihsahp màn.   5. Nī gihn sahpgáu màn jē.
   /sahpgáu màn/

------

8. **Response Drill**

Ex: T: Nī gihn sahpluhk   T: This one is sixteen dollars.
       màn.

     S: Gám, gó gihn haih   S: Well, is that one sixteen
       mhhaih dōu haih   dollars too?
       sahpluhk màn a?

1. Nī bá sahpbaat màn.   1. Gám, gó bá haih mhhaih dōu
                    haih sahpbaat màn a?

2. Nī tìuh ńgh màn.   2. Gám, gó tìuh haih mhhaih
                 dōu haih ńgh màn a?

3. Nī gihn sahpsei màn.   3. Gám, gó gihn haih mhhaih
                 dōu haih sahpsei màn a?

4. Nī deui yahsàam màn.   4. Gám, gó deui haih mhhaih
                 dōu haih yahsàam màn a?

5. Kéuih haih Gwòngdùngyàhn.   5. Gám, kéuih pàhngyáuh haih
   /kéuih pàhngyáuh/   mhhaih dōu haih Gwóng-
                 dùngyàhn a?

------

9. **Response Drill**

Ex: T: Néih máaih géidō   T: How many do you want to buy?
       gihn a? /ńgh/   are you going to get?
                        /5/

     S: Ngóh máaih ńgh gihn.   S: I want five.

144

1. Néih máaih géidō bá a? /léuhng/	1. Ngóh máaih léuhng bá.
2. Néih máaih géidō tiuh a? /sàam/	2. Ngóh máaih sàam tiuh.
3. Néih máaih géidō deui a? /luhk/	3. Ngóh máaih luhk deui.
4. Néih máaih géidō gihn a? /sei/	4. Ngóh máaih sei gihn.
5. Néih máaih géidō jí a? /sei/	5. Ngóh máaih sei jí.
6. Néih máaih géidō go a? / /sahpyih/	6. Ngóh máaih sahpyih go.

a. Repeat, teacher cuing with Measure and number only, students giving question and answer, thus:

T: /gihn/ńgh/	T: /M:/5/
Sl: Néih máaih géidō gihn a?	Sl: How many are you going to buy?
S2: Ngóh máaih ńgh gihn.	S2: I'm going to buy 5.

---

10. Expansion Drill

Ex: T: Máaih sēutsāam.	T: Buy shirts.
S: Kéuih máaih gihn sēutsāam.	S: She's buying a shirt.

Note that the measure is not cued, that student must supply it.

1. Máaih fu.	1. Kéuih máaih tiuh fu.
2. Máaih tāai.	2. Kéuih máaih tiuh tāai.
3. Máaih maht.	3. Kéuih máaih deui maht.
4. Máaih jē.	4. Kéuih máaih bá jē.
5. Máaih hàaih.	5. Kéuih máaih deui hàaih.
6. Máaih yúhlāu.	6. Kéuih máaih gihn yúhlāu.
7. Máaih sēutsāam.	7. Kéuih máaih gihn sēutsāam.
8. Máaih bīu.	8. Kéuih máaih go bīu.
9. Máaih cháang.	9. Kéuih máaih go cháang.
10. Máaih kwàhn.	10. Kéuih máaih tiuh kwàhn.
11. Máaih dáikwàhn.	11. Kéuih máaih tiuh dáikwàhn.
12. Máaih pìhnggwó.	12. Kéuih máaih go pìhnggwó.
13. Máaih bāt.	13. Kéuih máaih jí bāt.
14. Máaih yùhnbāt.	14. Kéuih máaih jí yùhnbāt.
15. Máaih yùhnjíbāt.	15. Kéuih máaih jí yùhnjíbāt.

16. Máaih bējáu.   16. Kéuih máaih jï bējáu.

17. Máaih jūng.   17. Kéuih máaih go jūng.

---

11. Expansion Drill: Expand the given sentence by adding the cue word
    in the appropriate place.

    Ex: T: Béi léuhng tìuh   T: Give me two ties. /this/
         tāai ngóh lā. /nǐ/

       S: Béi nǐ léuhng tìuh   S: Give me these two ties.
         tāai ngóh lā.

1. Béi bá ngóh lā. /nǐ/   1. Béi nǐ bá ngóh lā.

2. Béi tìuh fu ngóh lā. /gó/   2. Béi gó tìuh fu ngóh lā.

3. Béi deui maht ngóh lā. /luhk/   3. Béi luhk deui maht ngóh lā.

4. Béi sàam gihn ngóh lā. /gó/   4. Béi gó sàam gihn ngóh lā.

5. Béi sàam tìuh ngóh lā. /nǐ/   5. Béi nǐ sàam tìuh ngóh lā.

6. Béi léuhng tìuh ngóh lā. /tāai/   6. Béi léuhng tìuh tāai ngóh
                                        lā.

7. Béi gó deui hàaih ngóh lā.   7. Béi gó léuhng deui hàaih
   /léuhng/   ngóh lā.

8. Béi léuhng gihn sēutsāam ngóh   8. Béi gó léuhng gihn sēutsāam
   lā. /gó/   ngóh lā.

9. Béi tìuh kwàhn ngóh lā. /gó/   9. Béi gó tìuh kwàhn ngóh lā.

---

12. Response Drill

    Ex: 1. T: Néih máaih m̀h-   T: Are you going to get this pair
          máaih nǐ deui   of shoes? Do you want this
          hàaih a? /nod/   pair of shoes?

         S: Hóu, béi nǐ deui   S: OK, give me that pair.
          ngóh lā.

       2. T: Néih máaih m̀h-   T: Do you want this pair of
          máaih nǐ deui   shoes?
          hàaih a? /shake/

         S: M̀hmáaih laak.   S: Not today, thanks. [not buy
                          now.]

1. Néih máaih m̀hmáaih nǐ gihn   1. Hóu, béi nǐ gihn ngóh lā.
   sēutsāam a? /nod/

2. Néih máaih m̀hmáaih nǐ gihn   2. Hóu, béi nǐ gihn ngóh lā.
   yùhlāu a? /nod/

3. Néih máaih m̀hmáaih nī bá jē
   a? /shake/

3. M̀hmáaih laak.

4. Néih máaih m̀hmáaih nī tiuh
   fu a? /shake/

4. M̀hmáaih laak.

5. Néih máaih m̀hmáaih nī deui maht
   a? /nod/

5. Hóu, béi nī deui ngóh lā.

6. Néih máaih m̀hmáaih nī tiuh
   tāai a? /shake/

6. M̀hmáaih laak.

7. Néih máaih m̀hmáaih nī deui
   hàaih a? /nod/

7. Hóu, béi nī deui ngóh lā.

8. Néih máaih m̀hmáaih nī jì
   yùhnbāt a? /shake/

8. M̀hmáaih laak.

9. Néih máaih m̀hmáaih nī go bīu
   a? /nod/

9. Hóu, béi nī go ngóh lā.

Comment: In these sentences idiomatic English counterparts for
máaih might be 'take,' 'get,' 'want,' as well as
'buy.'

---

13. Expansion/Substitution Drill: Expand or substitute as appropriate
with the cue provided.

Ex: T: Máaih nī gihn.
      /ngóh/

T: Buy this one. /I/

S: Ngóh máaih nī gihn.

S: I'll take this one.
    (said to clerk in store)

T: /gó gihn/

T: That one.

S: Ngóh máaih gó gihn.

S: I'll take that one.
    (said to clerk)

1. Gó go yàhn máaih sēutsāam.
   /séung/
   That man is buying shirts.

1. Gó go yàhn séung máaih
   sēutsāam.
   That man wants to buy
   shirts.

2. /gihn/

2. Gó go yàhn séung máaih gihn
   sēutsāam.

3. /léuhng/

3. Gó go yàhn séung máaih
   léuhng gihn sēutsāam.

4. /géidō/

4. Gó go yàhn séung máaih
   géidō gihn sēutsāam a?

5. /sei/

5. Gó go yàhn séung máaih sei
   gihn sēutsāam.

6. /m̀hséung/

6. Gó go yàhn m̀hséung máaih
   sei gihn sēutsāam.

7. /séung mhséung a?/

7. Gó gó yàhn séung mhséung
   máaih sei gihn seutsāam a?

8. /léuhng tiuh tāai/

8. Gó go yàhn séung mhséung
   máaih léuhng tiuh tāai a?

---

14. Conversation Exercise:

Ex: A: Mhsái máaih luhk
gihn seutsāam,
sàam gihn gau laak.

A: You needn't buy 6 shirts;
3 is enough.

B: Mhhaih. Sàam gihn
mhgau; yiu máaih
luhk gihn.

B: No, 3 isn't enough; I need to
get 6.

1. A. ...sàam deui maht;
Yāt deui ......

B. ....

1. A. Mhsái máaih sàam deui
maht; yāt deui gau laak.

B. Mhhaih. Yāt deui mhgau;
yiu máaih sàam deui.

2. A. ...léuhng bá jē;
Yāt bá......

B. ....

2. A. Mhsái máaih léuhng bá jē;
yāt bá gau laak.

B. Mhhaih. Yāt bá mhgau;
yiu máaih léuhng bá.

3. A. ...sahp go cháang;
Gáu go......

B. ....

3. A. Mhsái máaih sahp go
cháang; gáu go gau laak.

B. Mhhaih. Gáu go mhgau;
yiu máaih sahp go.

4. A. ...chāt jì bējáu;
luhk jì......

B. ....

4. A. Mhsái máaih chāt jì bējáu;
luhk jì gau laak.

B. Mhhaih. Luhk jì mhgau;
yiu máaih chāt jì.

5. A. ...sei go béng;
Léuhng go......

B. ....

5. A. Mhsái máaih sei go béng;
léuhng go gau laak.

B. Mhhaih. Léuhng go mhgau;
yiu máaih sei go.

---

15. Response Drill: Respond affirmatively or negatively as directed, following the pattern of the example.

Ex: 1. T: Yāt bá jē gau
m̀hgau a? /nod/

T: Is one umbrella enough?

   S: Gau laak. Yāt bá
gau laak.

S: Yes, one is enough.

2. T: Yāt bá jē gau
m̀hgau a? /shake/

T: Is one umbrella enough?

   S: Yāt bá m̀hgau.
m̀hgòi néih béi
léuhng bá ngóh
lā.

S: One is not enough. Please give
me two.

1. Léuhng jì yùhnjíbāt gau
m̀hgau a? /nod/

1. Gau laak. Léuhng jì gau laak.

2. Yāt gihn yúhlāu gau m̀hgau a?
/shake/

2. Yāt gihn m̀hgau. M̀hgòi néih
béi léuhng gihn ngóh lā.

3. Luhk jì heiséui gau m̀hgau a?
/nod/

3. Gau laak. Luhk jì gau laak.

4. Yāt deui hàaih gau m̀hgau a?
/shake/

4. Yāt deui m̀hgau. M̀hgòi néih
béi léuhng deui ngóh lā.

5. Sàam go pìhnggwó gau m̀hgau a?
/shake/

5. Sàam go m̀hgau. M̀hgòi néih
béi sei go ngóh lā.

6. Léuhng go bīu gau m̀hgau a?
/nod/

6. Gau laak. Léuhng go gau
laak.

7. Sahp go béng gau m̀hgau a?
/shake/

7. Sahp go m̀hgau. M̀hgòi néih
béi sahpyāt go ngóh lā.

V. CONVERSATIONS FOR LISTENING

   (On tape. Listen to tape with book closed.)

. SAY IT IN CANTONESE

A. You ask your neighbor:

   1. What he wants to buy.

   2. How many (ties) he wants.

   3. How much these shoes cost.

   4. Whether those (shoes) are
also $60.00 a pair.

B. And he replies:

   1. That he wants to buy a tie.

   2. He wants to buy two.

   3. They are $60 a pair.

   4. No, they are $65.

5. Whether three pairs of socks are enough.

5. That he doesn't need three pairs--two pairs are enough.

6. How much that ballpoint pen is.

6. That it is $1--two sell for $1.90.

7. Whether 5 pencils are enough.

7. That five aren't enough--he wants ten.

8. How much that petticoat costs.

8. That it sells for $12.50.

9. Who that gentleman is.

9. That he doesn't know.

10. Who that lady is.

10. That her name is Chan--she teaches Cantonese.

Vocabulary Checklist for Lesson 6

1. bá	m:	M. for things with handles, such as umbrellas
2. bāt	n:	writing implement; pen or pencil
3. béi	v:	give
4. chín	n/m:	money
5. dáifu	n:	underpants, undershorts
6. dáikwàhn	n:	slip, petticoat
7. deui	m:	pair; group measure for shoes, socks, chopsticks
8. fu	n:	trousers
9. gau	adj:	enough
10. géi(dō)	QW/nu:	how much? how many?
11. gihn	m:	M. for clothes
12. gó	sp:	that
13. go	m:	general M. for nouns
14. guhaak	n:	customer (restricted use)
15. hàaih	n:	shoes
16. jē	n:	umbrella
17. jī	m:	M. for pen, pencil, bottles
18. jūng	n:	clock
19. kwàhn	n:	skirt
20. máaih	v:	buy
21. maht	n:	socks

150

22. mān   m: dollar
23. Mhjí(dou)...a?   Ph: I wonder...?
24. nī   sp: this
25. sauhfoyùhn   n: Salesclerk [sell-goods-personnel]
26. sēutsāam   n: shirt
27. sīnsàang   n: man
28. síujé   n: lady, woman
29. tāai   n: tie
30. tìuh   m: M. for trousers, ties, roads
31. wái   m: polite M. for persons
32. yàhn   n: person
33. yiu + money expression   v: wants X amount, costs X amount, (i.e.,
                                      the asking price is X amount.)
34. yúhlāu   n: raincoat
35. yùhnbāt   n: pencil
36. yùhnjíbāt   n: ball point pen

CLASSROOM PHRASES

Below are some sentences for students to say to the teacher. Don't try to memorize them all at once, but learn them as you find them useful.

1. Ngóh m̀hjī ____ dím gáai.
   I don't know what ____ means.
   [lit. I don't know how ____ is explained.]

2. M̀hgòi néih gáaisīkháh.
   Please explain.

3. M̀hgòi néih géui go laih làih táiháh.
   Please give an example to demonstrate.

4. M̀hgòi néih yuhng ____ jouh yāt geui béi ngóh tèngháh.
   Please use ____ to make a sentence for me to hear.

5. Hái mēyéh sìhhauh sìnji góng?
   When do you say that? (i.e., in what kind of situation?)

6. Hái mēyéh chìhngyìhng sìnji góng?
   In what circumstances is that said?

7. A____ tùhng B____ yáuh móuh fànbiht?
   Is there any difference between A____ and B____?

8. A____ tùhng B____ yáuh mēyéh fànbiht?
   What is the difference between A____ and B____?

9. Ngóh nī geui yáuh dī mahntàih.
   I have a question about this sentence.

10. Ngóh nī go jih yáuh dī mahntàih.
    I have a question about this word.

11. Gám góng dāk m̀hdāk a?
    Is it OK to say it this/that way?

12. ____ hóu m̀hhóu tèng?
    Does ____ sound right?

13. ____ duhk mēyéh sīng a?
    What tone is ____?

. BASIC CONVERSATION

A. **Buildup**:

(Customer and clerk in a grocery store:)

Fógei

fógei	clerk
Máaih mēyéh a?	What will you have?

Guhaak

haih ... làih ge	is...(grammatical structure emphasizing enclosed noun.)
haih mēyéh làih ga?	is what?
dī	mass measure; plural measure
nī dī	this (mass); these (units)
Nī dī haih mēyéh làih ga?	What's **this**?

Fógei

ngàuhyuhk	beef
Nī dīhaih ngàuhyuhk.	This is beef.
oi, or ngoi	want, want to possess, want to have
oi àhoi, or ngoi àhngoi	want/not want?
Néih oi àhoi nē?	Do you want some?

Guhaak

jyùyuhk	pork
dī jyùyuhk	some pork
Àhoi, ngóh séung oi dī jyùyuhk.	No, I don't; I want to get some pork.
gàn	catty (unit of measure = 600 gms. ca. 1 1/3 pounds)
Géidō chín gàn a?	How much is it per catty?

Fógei

sei go luhk	$4.60 [4 measure 6 (dimes)]
ngàhnchín	money [silver-money]
sei go luhk ngàhnchín	$4.60 [4 dollars 6 (dimes)]
sei go luhk ngàhnchín gàn	$4.60 per catty
Nī dī sei go luhk ngàhnchín gàn.	This is $4.60 per catty.

Guhaak

béi ngóh lā	give (it to) me please
léuhng gàn	two catties
Béi léuhng gàn ngóh lā.	Please give me two catties.

(They go over to the fruit section.)

Guhaak

maaih	sell
dím maaih nē?	how sell?
cháang dím maaih nē?	oranges--how sell?
Dī cháang dím maaih nē?	What do the oranges sell for?

Fógei

hòuh(jí)	dime
Ńgh hòuhjí go.	50¢ [5 dimes] each.

Guhaak

Dī pìhnggwó nē?	And the apples?

Fógei

yātyeuhng	same
Yātyeuhng--ńgh hòuhji go.	The same--50¢ each.

Guhaak

tòhng	sugar
bohng tòhng	a pound of sugar
léuhng bohng tòhng	two pounds of sugar
A! Ngóh dōu séung máaih léuhng bohng tòhng.	Oh! I also want to buy two pounds of sugar.
géi chín a?	how much money?
Géidō chín bohng a?	How much is it per pound?

Fógei

luhk hòuh bun	65¢ [6 dimes + half]
luhk hòuh bun jí	65¢ [6 dimes half dime]
Luhk hòuh bun jí bohng.	65¢ per pound.

B. **Recapitulation**:

Fógei

Máaih mēyéh a?	What will you have?

Guhaak

Nī dī haih mēyéh làih ga?   What's _this_?

Fógei

Nī dī haih ngàuhyuhk. Néih oi   This is beef. Do you want
àhoi nē?   some?

Guhaak

Ãhoi, ngóh séung oi dī jyùyuhk.   No, I don't; I want to get
Géidō chín gàn a?   some pork. How much is it
                                             per catty?

Fógei

Nī dī sei go luhk ngàhnchín   This is $4.60 per catty.
gàn.

Guhaak

Béi léuhng gàn ngóh lā.   Please give me two catties.

(They go over to the fruit counter.)

Guhaak

Dī cháang dím maaih nē?   What do the oranges sell for?

Fógei

Ñgh hòuhjí go.   50¢ [5 dimes] each.

Guhaak

Dī pìhnggwó nē?   And the apples?

Fógei

Yātyeuhng--ñgh hòuhjí go.   The same--50¢ each.

Guhaak

A! Ngóh dōu séung máaih léuhng   Oh! I also want to buy two
bohng tòhng. Géidō chín   pounds of sugar. How much
bohng a?   is it per pound?

Fógei

Luhk hòuh bun jí bohng.   65¢ per pound.

Note to teacher: In drill #2 of this lesson there are some
                          visual props needed which you may want to
                          assemble early.

+ + + + + + + + + + + + +

155

Pronunciation

1. Tone practice:

A. Tone practice with Measures: Repeat during the pauses provided:
   1. máh (= yard (in length) (3 times)
   2. yāt jí   , yāt bá   , yāt go   ; yāt tìuh   , yāt máh   ,
       yāt gihn   .
   3. yāt jí, yāt bá, yāt go   ; yāt tìuh, yāt máh, yāt gihn
   4. yāt jí, yāt tìuh   , (3 times)
   5. yāt go, yāt gihn   (3 times); yāt gihn, yāt go   . (3 times)
   6. yāt bá, yāt máh   (3 times); yāt máh, yāt bá   . (3 times)
   7. yāt gihn, yāt tìuh   (3 times)
   8. chēut (= M. for movie)   . (3 times)
   9. yāt chēut, yāt go, yāt gihn   ; yāt gihn, yāt go, yāt chēut
   10. jí bá go chēut   , tìuh máh gihn   .
   11. jí bá go chēut tìuh máh gihn   .

B. Tone practice with Numbers:
   1. lìhng (= 'zero')   . (3 times)
   2. sàam, gáu sei   ; lìhng, ńgh, yih   .
   3. sàam, gáu, sei, lìhng, ńgh, yih   .
   4. sàam, gáu, sei, chāt   ; lìhng, ńgh, yih   .
   5. sàam, gáu, sei, chāt, lìhng, ńgh, yih   .
   6. chāt sei   , sei chāt   ; yih sei   , sei yih   .
   7. gáu ńgh   , ńgh gáu   .
   8. lìhng yih   , yih lìhng   .
   9. chāt go, baat go, sahp go   , sahp go, baat go, chāt go   .
   10. sahp go, baat go; baat go, sahp go   .
   11. chāt go, baat go   , baat go, chāt go   .
   12. gáu go, léuhng go   , léuhng go, gáu go   .

2. <u>ai/aai</u> contrasts

                Listen and repeat: (Notice that <u>ai</u> is shorter and
                tenser in an isolated syllable than is <u>aai</u>; that the
                <u>a</u> of <u>ai</u> is a mid central vowel, whereas the <u>aa</u> of
                <u>aai</u> is a low back vowel; that <u>i</u> after <u>a</u> is high
                front unrounded, after <u>aa</u> is somewhat lower (<u>i</u> after
                <u>a</u> is more like the <u>ee</u> sound of English "see," after

156

aa it is more like the i sound of English "is.")

1. gāi gāi gāi 雞 , tāai tāai tāai 太 .
2. gāi tāai   , tāai gāi   .
3. haih haih haih   , maaih maaih maaih   .
4. haih m̀hhaih a?   , maaih m̀hmaaih a?   .
5. haih m̀hhaih a?   , máaih m̀hmáaih a?   .
6. Gó wái taaitáai haih m̀hhaih máaih hàaih a?
7. Jànhaih m̀hsái máaih hàaih.

3. maaih and máaih

    Listen and repeat:

    1. maaih, maaih   , máaih, máaih   .
    2. máaih, máaih   , maaih, maaih   .
    3. máaih m̀hmáaih a?   , maaih m̀hmáaih a?   .
    4. maaih m̀hmáaih a?   , máaih m̀hmáaih a?   .
    5. m̀hséung maaih   , m̀hséung máaih   .
    6. máaih léuhng go, máaih léuhng go   ,
       maaih léuhng go   , maaih léuhng go   .

4. yuk = y + uk

    yuk is a syllable composed of y as initial and uk as a two-part
final, composed of the high back rounded vowel u plus the velar
consonant stop k. The high front rounded yu [ü] plus velar stop
consonant k doesn't occur as a two-part final in Cantonese. Therefore the spelling yuk, which on paper could be ambiguously inter-
preted as either yu + k or y + uk, can only be y + uk.

    Listen and repeat:

    1. jyùyuhk jyùyuhk   豬肉
    2. yuhk yuhk   肉肉
    3. luhk luhk   六肉
    4. yuhk luhk   (2 times)肉六

A. NOTES

1. **dī** 'some,' as general plural measure for individual nouns

    a. Plurality unspecified in number is expressed by the plural measure
        dī, 'some.'

            1.   go pìhnggwó = the apple, an apple
                dī pìhnggwó = the apples, some apples
            2. nī go pìhnggwó = this apple
                nī dī pìhnggwó = these apples

    b. Individual nouns have different individual measures, but **dī** serves
        as plural measure for all individual nouns.

            Ex: 1. bá jē   = the umbrella, an umbrella
                  dī jē   = the umbrellas, some umbrellas
               2. tìuh tāai = the tie, a tie
                  dī tāai = the ties, some ties
               3. go cháang = the orange, an orange
                  dī cháang = the oranges, some oranges
               (See BC and Drill _4_)

    c. In a follow sentence **dī** substitutes for the noun it represents,
        serving in such position as an impersonal pronoun.

        Béi gó dī cháang ngóh lā. = Give me those [M] oranges.
        Béi gó dī   ngóh lā. = Give me those. [distant ones]

    d. **dī** is not used as Measure following a number. When number is
        specified, the individual measure follows the number.

            Ex: <u>sp+nu +m +n</u>
                nī   dī jē   = these umbrellas
                   sàam bá jē   = three umbrellas
                nī sàam bá jē   = these three umbrellas
            (-)   sàam dī jē -- doesn't occur
           (-)nī sàam dī jē -- doesn't occur
              (See BC and Drills **1.5, 1.6**)

2. Mass Nouns
   a. Mass nouns designate substances which are perceived in the mass
      rather than as discrete units. For example:

      tòhng   - 'sugar'
      séui   - 'water'
      jyùyuhk - 'pork'

   b. When counted, mass nouns do not use individual measures. Instead
      they are counted in terms of their length, weight, or some
      other standard; or in terms of a container of their volume; or
      in terms of a segment of their whole.

      Ex: <u>Nu</u>. + <u>M</u> + <u>N</u>
          sàam   bohng   tòhng   = three pounds of sugar
          sàam   máh   bou   = three yards of cloth
          sàam   bùi   chàh   = three cups of tea
          sàam   faai   pāi   = three pieces of pie

      Certain individual nouns may also be counted in terms of weight
      or other standard; but they are not limited to being counted
      this way:

      Ex: sàam   bohng   cháang   = three pounds of oranges
          sàam   go   cháang   = three oranges

   c. Similarities and differences between individual and mass measures.
          The standard/container/segment measures used in counting
      mass nouns occupy the same position in the sentence that indivi-
      dual measures occupy. The measures for mass nouns, however, differ
      from individual measures in not being in apposition with the
      following noun. They also differ in having independent meaning.

3. dī, general measure for mass nouns.
          When mass nouns are particularized but not counted by number,
      the plural measure dī serves as general mass measure for all mass
      nouns. It is translated in English as 'the' in subject position,
      'some,' 'a little,' in object position. Incorporated into a nī or gó
      compound, it translates as 'this' or 'that' in both subject and
      object positions.

Ex: 1. Nǐdī ngàuhyuhk yiu luhk   1. This beef costs $6.00
       màn gàn.   a catty.

    2. Dǐ faahn dungjó.   2. The rice has totten cold.

    3. Ngǒh séung máaih dī   3. I'd like to buy some beef.
       ngàuhyuhk.

    4. Néih séung yám dī mēyéh   4. You'd like to drink a little
       a?   what? (i.e. What would
                                         you like to drink?)

        (See BC and Drills 6, 7, 10, 11, 12 for
        subject position examples: See BC and Drills
        1, 2, 3 for object position examples.)

4. haih .. X .. làih ga?
                   ge.

    haih .. X .. làih ga? (& ge) is a phrase frame which has the effect
of emphasizing the noun it envelopes.

        Ex: Nǐ dī haih mēyéh a?   What's this?

            Nǐ dī haih mēyéh làih   What in the world is this?
            ga?

            Gó go haih bīngo làih   Who in the world is that?
            ga?

                (See BC and Drill 14)

    Note that the question: Nǐ dī haih mēyéh làih ga? permits the
mass/plural dī regardless of whether the object referred to is unit
or mass, or whether, if unit, is singular or plural. If the item is
singular, using the singular pronoun is also permitted.

        Ex: Q: Nǐ jī haih mēyéh   What's this?
               làih ga?

            A: Nǐ jī haih yùhnbāt   It's a pencil.
               làih ge.

        or Q: Nǐ dī haih mēyéh   What's this?
               làih ga?

            A: Nǐ dī haih yùhnbāt   It's a pencil.
               làih ge.

5. Money Measures.

    The unit of currency in Hong Kong is the Hong Kong dollar.
HK$1.00 = US$0.16 2/3; US$1.00 = approximately HK$6.00 in 1970.

a. The money measures used in counting money are the following:

    1. màn = measure for 'dollar,' used when the figure is a
        round number. The word is derived from the first syllable
        of the English word 'money.'

160

2. **go ngàhnchìn** = measure + noun. The compound of the two is used to represent 'dollar' when the figure is a round number. This form less common than the **mān** form for round number dollar figures. The basic meaning of ngàhnchìn is 'money,' [literally 'silver-money']

    Ex: sàam gò ngàhnchìn = three dollars

3. **go** = measure for 'dollar' when the figure is not a round number.

    Ex: $3.10 = sàam go yāt = three dollars one (dime)
            = $3.10

4. **hòuh(jì)** = measure for 'dime,' used when the amount is less than one dollar.

    Ex: sàam hòuh(jì) = three dimes, i.e. thirty cents

    Note (in #3 above) that when dimes are part of a money expression which is larger than a dollar the dime measure is not stated. That a number following the dollar measure would indicate the dime number is predictable on the basis of the decimal system used in counting money.

5. The penny measure is not used in Hong Kong, except perhaps in banking. 5¢ is expressed, however, thus:

    sei hòuh bun = 4 dimes (and) half = 45¢

    In fact **bun** following any measure is left-bound to that measure, and means 'plus half that measure.'

    Ex: sàam go bun = three dollars and a half

b. '$1.00 apiece,' '$1.00 a pound' type phrases.

In 'one dollar apiece' expressions in Cantonese the order of parts is irreversible with the money part coming first. (In English the order is often reversible: '5 cents for two/two for 5 cents.'

In the Cantonese phrase, the last number of the money measure must not directly precede the noun measure.

    Ex: (read across)

	Nu	M	Nu	M		Nu	M	
1.	sei	go	sei	ngàhnchín			bá	} 4 dollars 4 dimes
2.	sei	go	sei		yāt		bá	} for one [M] =
3.	sei	go	sei	ngàhnchín	yāt		bá	} $4.40 each.
(-) 4.	sei	go	sei				bá	(not said this way)
5.	sei	go	sei	ngàhnchín	léuhng	bá:		4 dollars 4 dimes for two [M] = 2 for $4.40

(See BC and Drills 1, 6, 16.1)

c. Omission of <u>yāt</u> in certain 'one dollar' phrases.

　　　When the dollar amount is one dollar and a fraction, the numeral <u>yāt</u> preceding the dollar measure <u>go</u> is ordinarily omitted in the spoken language.

> Ex: <u>go yāt</u> = a dollar ten cents ($1.10)
>
> <u>go yāt ngàhnchín bohng</u> = a dollar ten cents a pound
> <u>or go yāt yāt bohng</u>　　($1.10 per pound)
>
> (See Drill 1.3)

　　　<u>Yāt</u> is required, however, if the expression reaches a three-figure number.

> Ex: yāt go baat <u>hòuh</u> bun jí bohng = $1.85 per pound
> yāt go baat hòuh bun　　　= $1.85

6. Words belonging to more than one grammatical category.

> Ex: ngàhnchín = noun and measure: 'money' [silver-money]

<u>nu</u> + m + nu + m　　　(+ n)　　+ nu　+ m.

1.	sei go sàam ngàhnchín		léuhng bohng	= $4.30 for 2 pounds
2.		sàam go	ngàhnchín léuhng bohng	= $3.00 for 2 pounds
3.		sàam māan	léuhng bohng	= $3.00 for 2 pounds

　　　In Sentence #1 above, <u>ngàhnchín</u> is a measure, in #2 a noun. In comparison with English, there are relatively few words in Cantonese which belong to more than one grammatical category.

162

II. DRILLS

1. Expansion Drill: Repeat after the teacher:

    1. a. Gàn.
       b. Géidō chín gàn a?
       c. Ngàuhyuhk géidō chín gàn a?

       d. Dī ngàuhyuhk géidō chín gàn a?

       e. Dī ngàuhyuhk maaih géidō chín gàn a?
       f. Gó dī ngàuhyuhk maaih géidō chín gàn a?
       g. Gó dī ngàuhyuhk maaih ńgh màn gàn.

    + 2. a. Yú
         b. Dī yú.

         c. Nī dī yú.

         d. Nī dī yú géidō chín gàn a?

         e. Nī dī yú sàam go sei ngàhnchín gàn.

    3. a. Go yih.
         (go + number, in a money phrase = one dollar and X number dimes)
         b. Go yih ngàhnchín.
    +   c. Go yih ngàhnchín bàau.
    +   d. Yīnjái go yih ngàhnchín bàau.

         e. Dī yīnjái go yih ngàhnchín bàau.

         f. Nī dī yīnjái go yih ngàhnchín bàau.

         g. Kéuih wah nī dī yīnjái go yih ngàhnchín bàau.

    + 4. a. máh
         b. Géidō chín máh a?
    +   c. Dī bou géidō chín máh a?
            [cloth, fabric, material]

---

    1. a. Catty (1-1/3 pounds)
       b. How much per catty?
       c. How much is beef per catty.

       d. How much is the beef per catty?

       e. How much does the beef sell for per catty?
       f. How much does that beef sell for per catty?
       g. That beef sells for five dollars per catty.

    2. a. Fish
         b. The fish (in the mass) or These fish.

         c. This fish (in the mass) or These fish.

         d. How much is this fish per catty? or ...are these fish.

         e. This fish is $3.40 per catty. or These are ...

    3. a. $1.20

         b. $1.20
         c. $1.20 per pack(age)
         d. Cigarettes are $1.20 per pack.

         e. The cigarettes are $1.20 per pack.

         f. These cigarettes are $1.20 per pack.

         g. He says these cigarettes are $1.20 per pack.

    4. a. yard (in length)
         b. How much per yard?
         c. How much is the cloth per yard?

163

d. Nī dī bou géidō chín máh a?

d. How much is this cloth per yard?

e. Nī dī bou géidō chín léuhng máh a?

e. How much is this cloth for 2 yards? How much is 2 yards of this cloth?

f. Nī dī bou yahgáu mān léuhng máh.

f. This cloth is $29 for 2 yards.

+ 5. a. <u>syù</u>

5. a. <u>book</u>

+ b. <u>bún</u> syù (<u>M. for book</u>)

b. a/the book

c. Nī bún syù

c. this book

d. Nī bún syù dím maaih a?

d. How much is this book? <u>or</u> How much does this book sell for?

e. Nī léuhng bún syù dím maaih a?

e. How much do these 2 books sell for?

f. Nī léuhng bún syù maaih yah mān.

f. These two books are $20.00.

g. Nī léuhng bún syù maaih yihsahp mān bún.

g. These two books are $20.00 each.

+ 6. a. <u>Gāi</u>.

6. a. <u>Chicken</u>.

+ b. <u>Jek gāi</u>. (<u>M. for chicken</u>)

b. A/the chicken.

c. Léuhng jek gāi.

c. 2 chickens

d. Nī léuhng jek gāi.

d. These 2 chickens.

e. Nī léuhng jek gāi sei mān gàn.

e. These 2 chickens are $4 a catty.

f. Nī léuhng jek gāi maaih sei mān gàn.

f. These 2 chickens sell for $4 per catty.

g. Nī léuhng jek gāi maaih sei go bun ngàhnchín gàn.

g. These 2 chickens sell for $4.50 per catty.

h. Kéuih wah nī léuhng jek gāi maaih sei go bun ngàhnchín gàn.

h. He says these 2 chickens sell for $4.50 per catty.

+ 7. a. <u>Hàaih</u>.

7. a. <u>Shoe</u>

b. Jek hàaih.

b. the/a shoe

c. Béi jek hàaih ngóh.

c. Give me the shoe.

d. Ṁhgói néih béi jek hàaih ngóh.

d. Please give me the shoe.

Comment: <u>jek</u> is also the M. for <u>maht</u>, 'socks,' 'stockings.'

2. Response Drill

    Ex: T: Ngóh séung máaih   T: I want to buy some beef.
           dī ngàuhyuhk.

        S: Kéuih dōu séung   S: He also wants to buy some beef.
           máaih dī ngàuhyuhk.

1. Ngóh séung máaih bá jē.   1. Kéuih dōu séung máaih bá jē.

2. Ngóh séung máaih dī jyùyuhk.   2. Kéuih dōu séung máaih dī jyùyuhk.

3. Ngóh séung máaih bāau yīnjái.   3. Kéuih dōu séung máaih bāau yīnjái.

4. Ngóh séung máaih dī tòhng.   4. Kéuih dōu séung máaih dī tòhng.

5. Ngóh séung máaih tiuh yú.   5. Kéuih dōu séung máaih tiuh yú.

6. Ngóh séung máaih jī bējáu.   6. Kéuih dōu séung máaih jī bējáu.

7. Ngóh séung máaih gihn sēutsāam.   7. Kéuih dōu séung máaih gihn sēutsāam.

---

3. Conversation Drill

    Ex: T: /dī jyùyuhk/   T: /some pork/
        S1: Máaih mēyéh a?   S1: May I help you?
        S2: Ngóh séung máaih dī S2: I'd like to buy some pork.
           jyùyuhk.

1. /dī ngàuhyuhk/   1. A. Máaih mēyéh a?
                     B. Ngóh séung máaih dī ngàuhyuhk.

2. /bāau yīnjái/   2. A. Máaih mēyéh a?
                     B. Ngóh séung máaih bāau yīnjái.

3. /jek gāi/   3. A. Máaih mēyéh a?
                     B. Ngóh séung máaih jek gāi.

4. /bohng tòhng/   4. A. Máaih mēyéh a?
                     B. Ngóh séung máaih bohng tòhng.

5. /dī jyùyuhk/   5. A. Máaih mēyéh a?
                     B. Ngóh séung máaih dī jyùyuhk.

6. /tìuh yú/

    6. A. Máaih mēyéh a?

       B. Ngóh séung máaih tìuh yú.

7. /deui hàaih/

    7. A. Máaih mēyéh a?

       B. Ngóh séung máaih deui hàaih.

---

4. **Transformation Drill**

    Ex: T: Nī gihn sēutsāam géidō chín a?

        How much is this shirt?

       S: Nī dī sēutsāam géidō chín gihn a?

        How much are these shirts apiece?

1. Nī bāau yīnjái géidō chín a?

   1. Nī dī yīnjái géidō chín bāau a?

2. Nī bá jē géidō chín a?

   2. Nī dī jē géidō chín bá a?

3. Nī deui hàaih géidō chín a?

   3. Nī dī hàaih géidō chín deui a?

4. Nī gihn yúhlāu géidō chín a?

   4. Nī dī yúhlāu géidō chín gihn a?

5. Nī tìuh fu géidō chín a?

   5. Nī dī fu géidō chín tìuh a?

6. Nī gihn sāam géidō chín a?

   6. Nī dī sāam géidō chín gihn a?

    Comment: The individual Measures mean 'apiece,' 'each,' following a money phrase: Standard Measures mean 'per M.'

        Ex: Nī dī gāi sei màn gàn.

          These chickens are $4.00 per catty.

        Nī dī yùhnbāt sàam hòuhjí jí.

          These pencils are 30¢ each.

        Nī dī yùhnbāt luhk hòuhjí léuhng jí.

          These pencils are 60¢ for two.

---

5. **Substitution Drill**

    Ex: T: jyùyuhk /gàn/

        T: pork /catty/

       S: Nī dī jyùyuhk géidō chín gàn a?

        S: How much is this pork per catty?

1. /ngàuhyuhk /gàn/

   1. Nī dī ngàuhyuhk géidō chín gàn a?

166

2. /sēutsāam/gihn/

3. /gāi/jek/

4. /bējáu/jì/

5. /yīnjái/bāau/

6. /tòhng/bohng/

7. /cháang/go/

8. /pìhnggwó/go/

9. /jíu/gàn/

10. /dáifu/tìuh/

2. Nǐ dǐ sēutsāam géidō chín gihn a?

3. Nǐ dǐ gāi géidō chín jek a?

4. Nǐ dǐ bējáu géidō chín jì a?

5. Nǐ dǐ yīnjái géidō chín bāau a?

6. Nǐ dǐ tòhng géidō chín bohng a?

7. Nǐ dǐ cháang géidō chín go a?

8. Nǐ dǐ pìhnggwó géidō chín go a?

9. Nǐ dǐ jíu géidō chín gàn a?

10. Nǐ dǐ dáifu géidō chín tìuh a?

---

6. Transformation Drill

Ex: T: Nǐ dǐ ngàuhyuhk sāam go luhk ngàhnchín gàn.

T: This beef is $3.60 per catty.

S1: Nǐ dǐ ngàuyuhk géidō chín gàn a?

S1: How much is this beef per catty?

S2: Sāam go luhk ngàhnchín gàn.

$3.60 per catty.

1. Nǐ dǐ jyùyuhk sei man gàn.

1. A. Nǐ dǐ jyùyuhk géidō chín gàn a?

B. Sei māan gàn.

2. Nǐ dǐ ngàuhyuhk ńgh māan bohng.

2. A. Nǐ dǐ ngàuhyuhk géidō chín bohng a?

B. Ńgh māan bohng.

3. Nǐ dǐ yīnjái go yih ngàhnchín bāau.

3. A. Nǐ dǐ yīnjái géidō chín bāau a?

B. Go yih ngàhnchín bāau.

4. Nǐ dǐ dáikwàhn léuhng māan tìuh.

4. A. Nǐ dǐ dáikwàhn géidō chín tìuh a?

B. Léuhng māan tìuh.

5. Nǐ dǐ dáikwàhn go yih ngàhnchín gihn.

5. A. Nǐ dǐ dáikwàhn géidō chín gihn a?

B. Go yih ngàhnchín gihn.

---

7. Alteration Drill

Ex: T: Nī dī ngàuhyuhk   T: How do you sell this beef? or
       dīm maaih a?   What does this beef sell for?

    S: Nī dī ngàuhyuhk géi-   S: How much is this beef per
       dō chìn gàn a?   catty?

1. Nī dī jyùyuhk dīm maaih a?   1. Nī dī jyùyuhk géidō chìn
   /gàn/   gàn a?

2. Nī dī gāi dīm maaih a? /gàn/ 2. Nī dī gāi géidō chìn gàn a?

3. Nī dī yú dīm maaih a? /gàn/   3. Nī dī yú géidō chìn gàn a?

4. Nī dī bējáu dīm maaih a? /jì/ 4. Nī dī bējáu géidō chìn jì a?

5. Nī dī tòhng dīm maaih a?   5. Nī dī tòhng géidō chìn
   /bohng/   bohng a?

6. Nī dī yīnjái dīm maaih a?   6. Nī dī yīnjái géidō chìn
   /bāau/   bāau a?

---

8. Response Drill: Answer with '2' each time.

Ex: T: Néih oi m̀hoi yīnjái   T: Do you want cigarettes?
       a?

    S: Oi - Béi léuhng   S: Yes - Give me two packs
       baau ngóh lā.   please.

1. Néih oi m̀hoi bējáu a?   1. Oi - Béi léuhng jì ngóh lā.

2. Néih oi m̀hoi yīnjái a?   2. Oi - Béi léuhng bāau ngóh
                                    lā.

3. Néih oi m̀hoi ngàuhyuhk a?   3. Oi - Béi léuhng gàn ngóh lā.

4. Néih oi m̀hoi tòhng a?   4. Oi - Béi léuhng bohng ngóh
                                    lā.

5. Néih oi m̀hoi heiséui a?   5. Oi - Béi léuhng jì ngóh lā.

6. Néih oi m̀hoi yīnjái a? /jì/ 6. Oi - Béi léuhng jì ngóh lā.

       (M for one cigarette)

---

9. Response Drill

Ex: 1. T: Ǹgh bohng gau   T: Is five pounds enough?
          m̀gau a? /nod/

       S: Gau laak.   S: That's enough.

168

2. T: Ńgh bohng gau   T: Is five pounds enough?
      mhgau a? /shake/

   S: Mhgau. Ngóh oi luhk S: No, I want to get six pounds.
      bohng.

   Note: Answer with one more than the given number in
         response to the negative cue.

1. Sei bohng gau mhgau a? /nod/   1. Gau laak.
2. Léuhng bāau gau mhgau a? /shake/   2. Mhgau. Ngóh oi sàam bāau.
3. Luhk gàn gau mhgau a? /shake/   3. Mhgau. Ngóh oi chāt gàn.
4. Sàam jì gau mhgau a? /nod/   4. Gau laak.
5. Yāt jek gau mhgau a? /shake/   5. Mhgau. Ngóh oi léuhng jek.
6. Chāt gihn gau mhgau a? /nod/   6. Gau laak.
7. Ńgh tìuh gau mhgau a? /nod/   7. Gau laak.
8. Baat deui gau mhgau a? /shake/   8. Mhgau. Ngóh oi gáu deui.
9. Gáu go gau mhgau a? /shake/   9. Mhgau. Ngóh oi sahp go.

———————

10. Conversation Drill

    Ex: A: Nī dī yīnjái dím   A. What do these cigarettes sell
           maaih a?   for?

        B: Go yih ngàhnchín   B. $1.20 per pack. How many packs
           bāau. Néih máaih   do you want?
           géidō bāau a?

        A: Yāt bāau gau laak.   A. One pack is enough.

1. A. Nī dī jyùyuhk ......?   1. A. Nī dī jyùhyuhk dím
                                        maaih a?

   B. Ńgh go sei ngàhnchín gàn.   B. Ńgh go sei ngàhnchín gàn.
                                        Néih máaih géidō gàn
                                        a?

   A. Yāt ....   A. Yāt gàn gau laak.
2. A. Nī dī bējáu ......?   2. A. Nī dī bējáu dím maaih a?

   B. Go baat ngàhnchín jì.   B. Go baat ngàhnchín jì.
                                        Néih máaih géidō jì a?

   A. Luhk ......   A. Luhk jì gau laak.
3. A. Nī dī fu ....?   3. A. Nī dī fu dím maaih a?

   B. Yahluhk go baat ngàhnchín   B. Yahluhk go baat ngàhnchín
      tìuh.   tìuh. Néih máaih géidō
                                        tìuh a?

   A. Yāt ....   A. Yāt tìuh gau laak.

169

4. A. Nī dī bou ....
   B. Sahpchāt mān máh ......

   A. Sàam ....
5. A. Nī dī tòhng ....?
   B. Luhk hòuhjí bohng....

   A. Yāt ....
6. A. Nī dī maht ....
   B. Léuhng go bun ngàhnchín
      deui ....

   A. Léuhng ....

4. A. Nī dī bou dím maaih a?
   B. Sahpchāt mān máh.
      Néih máaih géidō máh a?
   A. Sàam máh gau laak.
5. A. Nī dī tòhng dím maaih a?
   B. Luhk hòuhjí bohng.
      Néih máaih géidō bohng
      a?
   A. Yāt bohng gau laak.
6. A. Nī dī maht dím maaih a?
   B. Léuhng go bun ngàhnchín
      deui. Néih máaih géidō
      deui a?
   A. Léuhng deui gau laak.

---

11. Combining Drill

Ex: T: Nī dī haih tòhng.
       Béi sàam bohng
       ngóh lā.

     S: Béi sàam bohng nī
       dī ngóh lā.

T: This is sugar.
    Give me three pounds.

S: Give me three pounds of this.

1. Nī dī haih pìhnggwó.
   Béi luhk go pìhnggwó ngóh lā.
2. Nī dī haih bou.
   Béi léuhng máh bou ngóh lā.
3. Nī dī haih yùhnbāt.
   Béi sei jì yùhnbāt ngóh lā.
4. Nī dī haih syù.
   Béi bún syù ngóh lā.
5. Nī dī haih heiséui.
   Béi sàam jì heiséui ngóh lā.
6. Nī dī haih yú.
   Béi tìuh yú ngóh lā.

1. Béi luhk go nī dī ngóh lā.
   Give me six of these.
2. Béi léuhng máh nī dī ngóh
   lā.
3. Béi sei jì nī dī ngóh lā.

4. Béi bún nī dī ngóh lā.

5. Béi sàam jì nī dī ngóh lā.

6. Béi tìuh nī dī ngóh lā.

---

12. Response Drill

    Ex: T: Nī dī haih jē.   T: These are umbrellas.

        S: Mhgòi néih béi bá   S: Please give me one.
           ngóh lā!

1. Nī dī haih bāt.   1. Mhgòi néih béi jī ngóh lā!
2. Nī dī haih syù.   2. Mhgòi néih béi bún ngóh lā!
3. Nī dī haih yùhnbāt.   3. Mhgòi néih béi jī ngóh lā!
4. Nī dī haih pìhnggwó.   4. Mhgòi néih béi go ngóh lā!
5. Nī dī haih béng.   5. Mhgòi néih béi go ngóh lā!

---

13. Conversation Drill:

    Ex: T: géi jek jīu   a few bananas

      S1: Mhgòi béi géi jek   Please give me a few bananas.
         jīu ngóh lā.

      S2: Béi géi jek mēyéh wá? Give a few whats, did you say?

      S1: Géi jek jīu.   A few bananas.

1. géi go pìhnggwó   1. S1: Mhgòi béi géi go pìhng-
                           gwó ngóh lā.

                       S2: Béi géi go mēyéh wá?

                       S1: Géi go pìhnggwó.

2. géi tìuh tāai   2. S1: Mhgòi béi géi tìuh tāai
                           ngóh lā.

                       S2: Béi géi tìuh mēyéh wá?

                       S1: Géi tìuh tāai.

3. géi go cháang   3. S1: Mhgòi béi géi go cháang
                           ngóh lā.

                       S2: Béi géi go mēyéh wá?

                       S1: Géi go cháang.

4. géi jī yùhnjíbāt   4. S1: Mhgòi béi géi jī yùhn-
                           jíbāt ngóh lā.

                       S2: Béi géi jī mēyéh wá?

                       S1: Géi jī yùhnjíbāt.

5. géi bāau yīn   5. S1: Mhgòi béi géi bāau yīn
                           ngóh lā.

                       S2: Béi géi bāau mēyéh wá?

                       S1: Géi bāau yīn.

14. Question & Answer Drill: Teacher gives cue by pointing to objects,
or pictures of them. Props required: apple, orange, ball point pen,
etc.

    Ex: T: (pencil)

        S1: NĪ dĪ haih mēyéh   S1: What's this?
            làih ga?

        S2: Yùhnbāt. Gó dĪ   S2: A pencil. ᵀhat's a pencil. <u>or</u>
            haih yùhnbāt.   Pencils. Those are pencils.

        S1: Géidō jí nē? /4/   S1: How many? /unit/
            (holds up fingers)

        S2: Sei jí.   S2: 4.

1. (apple)   1. A. Nĭ dĭ haih mēyéh làih ga?

                    B. Pìhnggwó. Gó dĭ haih
                       pìhnggwó.

                    A. Géidō go nē? /3/

                    B. Sàam go.

2. (orange)   2. A. Nĭ dĭ haih mēyéh làih ga?

                    B. Cháang. Gó dĭ haih cháang.

                    A. Géidō go nē? /1/

                    B. Yāt go.

3. (ball point pen)   3. A. Nĭ dĭ haih mēyéh làih ga?

                    B. Yùhnjíbāt. Gó dĭ haih
                       yùhnjíbāt.

                    A. Géidō jí nē? /6/

                    B. Luhk jí.

4. (pack of cigarettes)   4. A. Nĭ dĭ haih mēyéh làih ga?

                    B. Yīnjái. Gó dĭ haih yīnjái.

                    A. Géidō bāau nē? /2/

                    B. Léuhng bāau.

5. (book)   5. A. Gó dĭ haih mēyéh làih ga?

                    B. Syù. Gó dĭ haih syù.

                    A. Géidō bún nē? /1/

                    B. Yāt bún.

---

15. Substitution Drill: Teacher writes numbers on the blackboard to
cue the students.

    Ex: T: $12.40   T: $12.40

15. Substitution Drill: Teacher writes numbers on the blackboard to cue the students.

      Ex: T: $12.40   T: $12.40

          S: Nī gihn sēutsāam   S: This shirt sells for $12.40.
             maaih sahpyih go
             sei.

1. $12.20   1. Nī gihn sēutsāam maaih
                         sahpyih go yih.

2. $13.60   2. Nī gihn sēutsāam maaih
                         sahpsàam go luhk.

3. $13.20   3. Nī gihn sēutsāam maaih
                         sahpsàam go yih.

4. $13.50   4. Nī gihn sēutsāam maaih
                         sahpsàam go bun.

5. $15.90   5. Nī gihn sēutsāam maaih
                         sahpńgh go gáu.

      a. Continue, with other numbers.

---

16. Expansion Drill

    1. a. ngàuhnáaih.   a. milk

       b. Dī ngàuhnáaih.   b. the milk, or some milk

       c. Dī ngàuhnáaih go baat   c. The milk is $1.80 a bottle.
          ngàhnchín jì.

       d. Dī ngàuhnáaih yiu go baat d. The milk costs $1.80 a
          ngàhnchín jì.   bottle.

    2. a. jīu   a. bananas

       b. dī jīu.   b. the bananas <u>or</u> some bananas

       c. dī jīu ńgh hòuhjí gàn.   c. the bananas are 50¢ a catty.

       d. Dī jīu maaih ńgh hòuhjí   d. The bananas sell for 50¢ a
          gàn.   catty.

       e. Dī jīu haih mhhaih maaih e. Do the bananas sell for
          ńgh hòuhjí gàn a?   50¢ a catty?

IV. CONVERSATIONS FOR LISTENING

      (On tape. Listen to tape with book closed.)

V. SAY IT IN CANTONESE

A. In a grocery store, the clerk asks:

   1. What do you want to buy?

   2. Is 5 pounds of sugar enough?

   3. Whether you'd like to buy some fish.

   4. How many packs (of cigarettes) do you want?

B. And the customer answers:

   1. I want some beef, and also some pork and milk.

   2. 5 pounds is not enough-- give me 10 pounds.

   3. Yes, I'd like to buy one fish.

   4. Two packs are enough.

C. In a grocery store, the customer asks:

   1. How much does the beef sell for?

   2. How much are these cigarettes?

   3. Is this fish $3.00 a catty?

   4. What is this?

   5. These bananas are 80¢ a catty, aren't they?

   6. These apples are 30¢ each, aren't they?

   7. How much is the sugar per pound?

D: And the clerk answers:

   1. It's $5.80 a catty.

   2. They're $1.20 a pack.

   3. No, this is $2.80 a catty-- those (pointing) are $3.00 a catty.

   4. That's pork--would you like some?

   5. Yes, 80¢ a catty.--how many catties would you like?

   6. No, the apples are 50¢ each-- the oranges are 30¢ each.

   7. It's 75¢ a pound.

---

ocabulary Checklist for Lesson 7

1.	bàau	m:	package, M. for cigarette pack
2.	bohng	m:	pound
3.	bou	n:	cloth
4.	bún	m:	M. for book
5.	-bun	nu:	half
6.	dī	m:	some, the
7.	gāi	n:	chicken
8.	gàn	m:	catty, unit of weight ca 1 1/3 lb
9.	gó dī	sp+m:	those (in reference to unit nouns); that (in reference to mass nouns)
10.	haih...làih ge	Ph:	is..(grammatical structure giving emphasis to enclosed noun)
11.	hòuh(jí)	m:	dime
12.	jek	m:	M. for chicken, shoe, sock, ship.
13.	jì	m:	M. for cigarette
14.	jyùyuhk	n:	pork
15.	...làih ge		see: haih...làih ge
16.	maaih	v:	sell
17.	máh	m:	yard (in length)
18.	ngàhnchín	n/m:	money [silver-money]
19.	ngàuhyuhk	n:	beef
20.	nī dī	sp+m:	these (in reference to unit nouns) this (in reference to mass nouns)
21.	ngoi	v:	var. of oi, want, want to have, want to possess
22.	oi	v:	want, want to have, want to possess
23.	syù	n:	book
24.	tòhng	n:	sugar
25.	yātyeuhng	nuM/adj:	same
26.	yīnjái	n:	cigarette
27.	yú	n:	fish

I. BASIC CONVERSATION

A. Buildup:

(Buying socks at a department store:)

Guhaak

dyún	short
dyún maht	socks
baahk-	white
baahk dyún maht	white socks
yáuh	have; there is/are
móuh	not have; there is/are not
yáuh móuh?	have/not have? do you have? is there? are there?
yáuh móuh maht?	do (you) have socks?
yáuh móuh baahk dyún maht	do you have white socks? or are there any white socks?

Yáuh móuh baahk dyún maht   Do you have white socks for
  maaih a?   sale?

Sauhfoyùhn

Yáuh.   Yes. [Have]

  jeuk   wear (clothes)

Haih m̀haih néih jeuk ga?   Are they for you? [ones for
                                                        you to wear?]

Guhaak

Haih.   That's right.

Sauhfoyùhn

  houh   number; size
  géi houh?   what size?
Jeuk géi houh a?   What size do you wear?

Guhaak

Gáu houh.   Number nine.

Sauhfoyùhn

  pèhng   cheap
  leng   pretty
  yauh   also

176

yauh pèhng yauh leng

Nī dī yauh pèhng yauh leng.

jùngyi

jùng m̀hjùngyi a?

Néih jùng m̀hjùngyi a?

Guhaak

hóu

géi hóu

daaih

m̀hgau daaih

Géi hóu, daahnhaih m̀hgau daaih.

-dī

daaihdī

daaihdī ge

Yáuhmóuh daaihdī ge nē?

Sauhfoyùhn

-saai

maaihsaai laak.

Deuim̀hjyuh--daaihdī ge dōu

maaihsaai laak.

hāak-

hāaksīk

hóu m̀hhóu?

Hāaksīk, hóu m̀hhóu a?

Hāaksīk dōu hóu leng ga.

Guhaak

Hóu aak.

Sauhfoyùhn

Nī dī sàam mān, nīdī sàam go

bun.

bīn-?

júng

both cheap and pretty

These are both cheap and
pretty.

like; like to

do you like (it/them)?

Do you like them?

good, nice

quite nice, pretty nice

big

not big enough

They're quite nice, but they're
not big enough.

somewhat--, a little bit--

a little larger

larger one (or ones)

Do you have any little bit
larger ones?

completely

all sold out

I'm sorry, the larger ones are
all sold out.

black

black color

is (that) all right?

Would black be all right?

The black are also very pretty.

All right.

These are three dollars, and
these are three and a half.

which?

kind, type

177

Néih ngoi bĪn júng a?   Which ones do you want?

<u>Guhaak</u>

    sàam go bun ge   the three-fifty ones (or
                                                    one)

Oi sàam go bun ge lā.   I'd like the $3.50 ones.

<u>Sauhfoyùhn</u>

    dā   dozen
    máaih bun dā   buy half a dozen
    àh   sentence suffix adding force
                                                    of 'I suppose' to sentence
                                                    it attaches to.

Máaih bun dā àh.   You'll take a half a dozen, I
                                                    suppose.

<u>Guhaak</u>

    dò   much, many
Ḿhsái gam dò.   (I) don't need that many.
Sàam deui gau laak.   Three pairs are enough.

B. Recapitulation:

<u>Guhaak</u>

Yáuh móuh baahk dyún maht   Do you have white socks for
   maaih a?   sale?

<u>Sauhfoyùhn</u>

Yáuh. Haih ṁhhaih néih jeuk ga?   Yes. Are they for you?

<u>Guhaak</u>

Haih.   That's right.

<u>Sauhfoyùhn</u>

Jeuk géi houh a?   What size do you wear?

<u>Guhaak</u>

Gáu houh.   Number nine.

<u>Sauhfoyùhn</u>

NĪ dĪ yauh pèhng yauh leng.   These are both cheap and
   Néih jùng ṁhjùngyi a?   pretty. Do you like them?

<u>Guhaak</u>

Géi hóu, daahṁhaih ṁhgau   They're quite nice, but they're

178

daaih.	not big enough.
Yáuh móuh daaihdī ge nē?	Do you have any larger ones?

Sauhfoyùhn

Deuimhjyuh--daaihdī ge	I'm sorry, the larger ones are
dōu maaihsaai laak.	all sold out.
Hāaksīk, hóu mhhóu a?	Would black be all right?
Hāaksīk dōu hóu leng ga.	The black are also very pretty.

Guhaak

Hóu aak.	All right.

Sauhfoyùhn

Nī dī sàam mān, nī dī sàam	These are three dollars, these
go bun.	are $3.50.
Néih ngoi bīa júng nē?	Which ones do you want?

Guhaak

Oi sàam go bun ge lā.	I'd like the three-fifty ones,
	please.

Sauhfoyùhn

Máaih bun dā àh.	Half a dozen, I suppose.

Guhaak

Mhsái gam dò. Sàam deui gau	I don't need so many. Three
laak.	pairs are enough.

+ + + + + + + + + + + + +

Pronunciation Practice:

1. **yun** as in **dyún**

   yun is a two-part final composed of the high front rounded vowel
   yu [ü], plus the dental nasal consonant **n**. The **yu** is an open vowel
   before the nasal final, and being a rounded vowel, has a rounding
   effect on a consonant preceding it in the same syllable, as well as
   the consonant following it.

   Listen and repeat:

   短　　1. dyún , dyún , dyún .
   鉛筆　2. yùhnbāt (5 times separately)
   短鉛　3. dyún yùhn , yùhn dyún . 鉛短
   鉛短　4. yùhn dyún , dyún yùhn . 短鉛

179

2. **yu/yun** contrasts

>   Listen and repeat: (Watch the teacher)
>   1. yú yú 魚 , dyún dyún 短 .
>   2. dyún dyún   , yú yú   .
>   3. dyún yú   , yú dyún   .

3. **euk** in **jeuk, (ng)āamjeuk**

>   **euk** is a two-part final composed of the rounded mid front vowel
> **eu** plus the velar stop consonant **k**. In final position in a syllable,
> **k** is unreleased--[kˀ]. Before **k**, the positioning for **eu** is the same
> as that for **eu** before **ng**--raised mid front rounded--[ø]. Lips are
> rounded for the vowel and also for consonants preceding and following
> it in a syllable.

>   Listen and repeat: (Watch the teacher)
> 著   1. jeuk jeuk jeuk   ; jeuk   , jeuk   ,
>   jeuk .
> 唔著 2. āamjeuk āamjeuk   .
>   3. ngāamjeuk ngāamjeuk   .

4. **euk/eung** contrasts

>   Listen and repeat: (Note that tongue and lip position
>   is the same for **eu** before **k** as it is for **eu** before
>   **ng**.)
>   1. jeuk, jeuk   , Jèung, Jèung   .
>   2. jeuk Jèung   , Jèung jeuk   .
>   3. jeuk séung   , jeuk léuhng   ,
>   4. jeuk chèuhng   , jeuk yātyèuhng   .

5. **euk/eut** contrasts

>   Listen and repeat: (Note that the tongue position for
>   **eu** before the dental **t** is somewhat lower than its
>   position before the velar **k**.)
>   1. jeuk jeuk   , sēut sēut   .
>   2. jeuk sāam   , sēutsāam   .
>   3. sēutsāam   , jeuk sāam   .

6. **ek** as in **jek**

>   **ek** is a two-part final composed of the mid front unrounded vowel
> **e** [E] plus the velar stop consonant **k**. In final position in a
> syllable, **k** is unreleased--[kˀ]. The American counterpart of the

Cantonese ek is the eck in 'peck,' although in final position the
American k is not necessarily unreleased--it may or may not be, with
no significant difference.

Listen and repeat:

jek   (5 times) 隻

. eng as in leng, pèhng, béng, tèng

    eng is a two-part final composed of the mid front unrounded vowel
e [E] plus the velar nasal consonant ng. The e is like the e in the
American 'bet.' It is an open vowel before the nasal final.

Listen and repeat, comparing English and Cantonese:

(Read across)

	English	Cantonese	
1.	bet	béng	餅
2.	pet	pèhng	平
3.	let	leng	靚
4.	Tet	tèng	聽

. ut as in fut, 'wide' (See Drill _3_)

    ut is a two-part final composed of the high back rounded vowel u
plus the dental stop consonant t. The tongue position for t is like
that for English words ending with t--the tip of the tongue stops the
flow of air at the dental ridge behind the upper teeth. In final
position the Cantonese t is unreleased--[t⁷]. u before t is produced
the same as was u finally and u before n--as a high back rounded vowel
[u] with tongue position somewhat higher than for u before k and ng.
Before t the u is relatively long and has a slight offglide to high
central position--[u·ᵘ] [u·ᵘt].

Listen and repeat:

濶   fut   , fut   , fut   , fut   , fut   .

. u/ut contrasts

    u before t is similar to u as a one-part final; both are **high**
back rounded vowels, but u before t has a slight offglide to high
central position [uᵘt].

Listen and repeat:

褲   1. fu fu fu   , fu fu fu   .
濶   2. fut fut fut   , fut fut fut   .

181

3. fu fut   , fu fut   , fu fut   ,
fut fu   , fut fu   , fut fu   .

10. <u>ut</u>/<u>un</u> contrasts

<u>u</u> before <u>t</u> is pronounced the same as <u>u</u> before <u>n</u>, rather long, and with a slight forward offglide before the final consonant--[u·ᵘt̚], [u:ᵘn].

Listen and repeat:

1. fut fut   , bun bun   .
2. fut bun   , bun fut   .
3. bun bun   , fut fut   .

11. <u>ut</u>/<u>uk</u> contrasts

Tongue position for <u>u</u> before <u>k</u> is slightly lower than that for <u>u</u> before <u>t</u>, and the vowel is relatively short before <u>k</u> and long before <u>t</u>--[Uˇk̚], [u:ᵘt̚].

Listen and repeat:

1. fut fut   , luhk luhk   .
2. ngàuhyuhk yuhk, yuhk   , fut fut   .
3. fut yuhk   , fut luhk   , luhk yuhk fut
fut   .

12. <u>ak</u>/<u>aak</u> contrasts

Listen and repeat:

1. dāk dāk 得 , hāak hāak 黑 .
2. dāk hāak   , hāak dāk   .
3. jaak jaak ('narrow') 窄 , jaak dāk   .
4. hāak dāk   , jaak dāk   , baahk dāk   .
5. hāak hāak   , jaak jaak   , baahk baahk   ,
dāk dāk   .

I. NOTES

1. The verb yáuh, 'have,' 'there is/are'

   a. yáuh is irregular in that its negative is not 'm̀hyáuh' but móuh.
      It patterns like other verbs in the affirmative, negative
      and choice questions:

      Ex: aff: yáuh   = have; there is
          neg: móuh   = don't have; there isn't
          q: yáuh móuh ...? = do (you) have?; is there?
          (See BC and Drills 1.1, 1.3, 8)

2. Adjectives

   a. Adjectives are descriptive words. Words like daaih, 'big,' and
      dyún, 'short,' are adjectives.

   b. From the grammatical point of view an adjective is a word that
      fits into certain positions in a sentence. A word which may
      be preceded by the following words and word groups is classed
      as an adjective in Cantonese:

      hóu   very
      géi   quite
      m̀hhaih géi   not very
      m̀hhaih hóu   not exceptionally
              (See BC and Drills 4, 5)

   c. A word which is an adjective in Cantonese may translate into
      another part of speech in English. For example, ngāamjeuk
      'fits, fits well' is an adjective in Cantonese, because it
      patterns like an adjective, whereas the English equivalent
      expression 'fit' is a verb:

      Nī gihn sēutsāam = This shirt fits well.
        hóu ngāamjeuk.   [This shirt is very well-fitting.]

      hóusihk 'good to eat,' 'tasty,' and hóuyám 'good to
      drink,' 'tasty,' are also adjectives, since they pattern like
      adjectives. They can be modified with the set of words, 'géi,'
      'hóu,' etc. that modify adjectives.

          1. Nī go pìhnggwó hóu   This apple is very tasty.
             hóusihk.   (i.e., tastes good.)
          2. Dī bējáu hóu hóuyám.   The beer is very tasty.
                                     (i.e., tastes good.)
                  (See Drill 2)
                       183

d. Adjectives in Cantonese, unlike English, do not require the
   equivalent of the verb 'is' to serve as the predicate.
      Compare:

Cantonese:		English:	
Subject	Predicate	Subject	Predicate
	Adj.		Verb + Adj.
Nī gihn	daaih.	This one	is big.
Nī dī	hóu leng.	Those	are very pretty.

Since adjectives share this characteristic of verbs, and
share also the characteristic of being able to be preceded
directly by m̄h, 'not,' we consider adjectives in Cantonese to be
a sub-category of verbs. Some writers call this category of word
'stative verb' rather than adjective.

e. Adjectives modified and unmodified.

1. An adjective modified by géi 'quite' or hóu 'very' carries
   the force which an unmodified adjective does in English:
      Ex: Nī gihn géi leng.

                            This one is pretty.
      Nī gihn hóu leng.

2. An unmodified adjective indicates an implied comparison in
   a Cantonese sentence with a single adjective as predicate.
      Ex: A: Néih wah bīn gihn   Which one do you think is
             leng a?   pretty?
          B: Nī gihn leng.   This one is pretty. (i.e.
                                      prettier than the other)

3. With two adjectives in the predicate, a yauh...yauh...
   construction is required, and in such a case, the unmodified
   adjective is the norm.
      Ex: Nī go pìhnggwó yauh   This apple is both cheap
             pèhng yauh leng.   and good.
          (See BC and Drill 10)

4. The choice-type question follows the verbal pattern of V m̄hV,
   yielding Adj m̄hAdj.
      Ex: Nī gihn gwai m̄hgwai a? Is this one expensive?
          (See Drills 3, 11)

To say 'Is this one very expensive?' requires a <u>haih</u>
<u>m̀hhaih</u> question:

Ex: Nī gihn haih m̀hhaih   Is this one very expensive?
      hóu gwai a?

f. Adj + <u>ge</u> combination = noun phrase (NP).

An adjective is frequently used to form a noun phrase by
adding the noun-forming suffix <u>ge</u>.

Ex: 1. M̀hhaih daaih ge, haih   1. It's not the big one, it's
        sai ge.   the small one. <u>or</u>
                                         They aren't the big ones,
                                         they are the small ones.

      2. yiu daaihdī ge.   2. Want a large one (<u>or</u> ones).
        (See Drill _13_)

Note that when an adjective combines with <u>ge</u> to form a noun
construction, it is necessary to add <u>haih</u> or another verb to form
a sentence.

3. <u>dī</u> as adj. suffix, 'a little,' '<u>Adj-er</u>.'

In Cantonese <u>Adj-dī</u> has a comparative sense, but the English
equivalents are translated variously, depending on context as:
'somewhat,' 'a little;' and also the comparative '-er.'

Ex: Ngóh go bīu faaidī.   [My watch is a bit faster (than
                                  the right time).]
                                  My watch is a little fast.

NI gihn láangsāam   [This sweater is a little
    daaihdī.   larger (than the size I
                                  need).]
                                  This sweater is a little too
                                  large.

Yáuh móuh saidī ge nē?   Do you have a smaller one?
                                  (<u>or</u> smaller ones)

        (See BC and Drills 13, 15)

4. Two syllable verbs and adjectives form the choice-type questions by
    using only the first syllable before the m̀h, and the whole word
    after:

    <u>V/Adj.</u>   <u>Choice question</u>
    jùngyi   like   jùng m̀hjùngyi a?   (do you) like (it)?
    ngāamjeuk well-fitting   ngāam m̀hngāamjeuk a? (Does it) fit?

        (See BC)

185

5. ặh sentence suffix, adding force of 'I suppose' to sentence it
   attaches to. It makes the sentence a rhetorical question. The
   speaker indicates with the ặh final that he knows the response
   to his sentence will be in agreement with what he says. The
   intonation has the sentence-final fall characteristic of statement
   sentences.

   Ex: Máaih bún dā ặh.   (You'll) buy a half dozen,
                                 I suppose.
                (See BC and Drill _9_)

   Compare the two following English sentences, of which the
   second has a connotation similar to the Cantonese ặh sentences:

          1. He's drinking tea, isn't he? (you're not sure)
          2. He's drinking tea, isn't he. (you're sure he is)

6. Further use of sentence suffix nē?

   A question sentence which continues a topic already being
   discussed often uses the sentence suffix nē?, with force of:
   '...then?;' '...And...?'

   Ex: Yáuh móuh daaihdī   Do you have any larger ones,
       ge nē?   then? (Having been shown
                                  smaller ones)
                (See BC and Drill _16_)

   This nē? is the same final you encountered in Lesson 2 in the
   sentence composed of Noun + nē:

       Sīnsàang nē?   'And you, Sir?'

   The use of nē in this lesson is new in that it is here a
   final in a sentence which is itself a question. This use of nē
   is apparently used more frequently by women than by men, and its
   frequent use by men is said to give an effiminate cast to their
   speech. Sentence suffix a can be substituted for nē in all cases
   in which nē is a sentence suffix to a sentence which is itself
   a question.

186

7. Noun modification structures.

    a. Noun as modifier to a following noun head:

        1. Nouns as modifiers directly precede the noun they modify:

Ex:	Yìnggwok hàaih	English shoes
	Yahtbún bējáu	Japanese beer
	bou hàaih	cloth shoes
	pìhnggwó pāi	apple pie

        2. When the noun head is already established, ge may substitute for the noun head in a follow sentence, keeping modification structures intact:

Ex:	a. Ngóh yiu máaih jì Yahtbún bējáu. Yáuh móuh a?	I want to buy a bottle of Japanese beer [Japan beer]. Do you have any?
	b. Móuh a. Máaih jì Méihgwok ge, hóu m̀hhóu a?	No, we don't. How about getting an American one? [America-one]

        (See Drill _8_)

    b. Adjectives as modifiers to a following noun head:

        1. A one syllable adjective as modifier directly preceeds the noun it modifies:

Ex:	1. Néih gihn sàn sēutsāam hóu leng.	Your new shirt is pretty.
	2. Ngóh m̀hjùngyi jeuk dyún fu.	I don't like to wear shorts. [short trousers]

        2. Adjectives that are pre-modified add ge when modifying a following noun:

1. chèuhng yùhnbāt	long pencil
2. hóu_chèuhng ge yùhn-bāt	very long pencil
3. hóu gwai ge chèuhng yùhnbāt	very expensive long pencil

        (See Drill 1.3)

8. dò 'many'

    1. dò, 'many,' patterns like an adjective in taking the adjective
       modifiers hóu, géi, etc. and the adjective suffix dī, but
       within the larger framework of the sentence it patterns
       differently from adjectives. dò is a boundword, bound either
       to a preceding adverb or a following measure; adjectives are
       free words. Adjectives when pre-modified add ge when modifying
       a following noun, but dò does not:

           Ex: hóu pèhng ge syù   very cheap books
              hóu dò syù   very many books

      A dò phrase patterns like a noun in that it can be the object
       of a verb without adding ge; but adjectives add ge when
       nominalized.

           Ex: Kéuih yáuh hóu dò.   He has many.
              Kéuih yáuh hóu   He has a big one (or ones.)
              daaih ge.

      dò also shares some characteristics with numbers and can be
       viewed as an indefinite number. It is, in fact, a case unto
       itself, and you will learn its various faces bit by bit.

9. bīn- _M_ ? = 'which _M_ ?'

      bīn-? is an interrogative boundword, bound to a following measure.
It occupies the same position in a sentence as nī-, 'this' and gó-, 'that'
and is classed with them as a specifier.

        Ex: A: Néih séung máaih bīn gihn a? Which one are you going to
                                      buy?
         B: Ngóh   máaih nī gihn laak. I'll buy this one.

             (See BC and Drill _14_)

III. DRILLS

1. Expansion Drill: Students repeat after the teacher.

+ 1. a. chèuhng.
     b. chèuhng fu.

     c. yáuh tìuh chèuhng fu.
     d. Yáuh tìuh hāak chèuhng fu.

     e. Yáuh tìuh hāak sīk ge
        chèuhng fu.

1. a. long.
   b. slacks, trousers.
      [long trousers]

   c. Have a pair of slacks.
   d. Have a pair of black
      slacks.

   e. Have a pair of black
      coloured slacks.

+ 2. a. gwai
+   b. géi gwai

+   c. m̀hhaih géi gwai

     d. Dī bou m̀hhaih géi gwai.

     e. Dī Yahtbún bou m̀hhaih
        géi gwai.

2. a. expensive.
   b. rather expensive,
      quite expensive

   c. not very expensive, not
      expensive

   d. The cloth is not too
      expensive.

   e. The Japanese cloth is not
      expensive.

  3. a. Jì yùhnbāt.
     b. Yáuh jì yùhnbāt.
     c. Ngóh yáuh jì yùhnbāt.
     d. Ngóh yáuh jì chèuhng yùhnbāt.
     e. Ngóh yáuh jì hóu gwai ge
        chèuhng yùhnbāt.

3. a. A (or The) pencil.
   b. Have a pencil.
   c. I have a pencil.
   d. I have a long pencil.
   e. I have a very expensive
      long pencil.

+ 4. a. Gihn lāangsāam.
+   b. Gihn sàn lāangsāam.
     c. Ngóh gihn sàn lāangsāam.
     d. Ngóh gihn sàn lāangsāam
        hóu gwai.
     e. Kéuih m̀hjìdou ngóh gihn sàn
        lāangsāam hóu gwai.

4. a. The (or a) sweater.
   b. The new sweater.
   c. My new sweater.
   d. My new sweater is very
      expensive.
   e. He does not know (that)
      my new sweater is very
      expensive.

+ 5. a. gauh
     b. gauh bāt
     c. Jì gauh bāt.
     d. Jì gauh yùhnjíbāt.

5. a. old
   b. old pen.
   c. The old pen (or pencil).
   d. The old ball-point pen.

2. Substitution Drill: Adjectives

Ex: T: Nī dī géi daaih. /leng/	T: These are (or this (mass) is) quite big. /pretty/
S: Nī dī géi leng.	S: These are very pretty. <u>or</u> This (mass) is very pretty.

1. Nī dī géi gwai. /pèhng/   1. Nī dī géi pèhng.

+ 2. /sai/
  (small)

3. /daaih/

+ 4. /hóuyám/
  (tasty, good to drink.)

+ 5. /hóusihk/
  (tasty, good to eat.)

+ 6. /ngāamjeuk (or āamjeuk)
  (well fitting, fits properly)

2. Nī dī géi sai.
  These are (or This (mass)
  is) quite small.

3. Nī dī géi daaih.

4. Nī dī géi hóuyám.
  These are (or This is)
  very tasty. - very good to
  drink.

5. Nī dī géi hóusihk
  These are (or This is)
  very tasty. - very good
  to eat.

6. Nī dī géi ngāamjeuk.
  These fit well.

---

3. Expansion Drill: Fluency practice.

Ex: 1. T: Leng m̀hleng a?	Is it pretty?
+ S: Néih <u>wah</u> leng m̀hleng a? (<u>say, think</u>)	Do you think it's pretty?
2. T: Hóu m̀hhóusihk a?	Is it tasty?
S: Néih wah hóu m̀hhóusihk a?	Do you think it's tasty?

1. Ngāam m̀hngāamjeuk a?	1. Néih wah ngāam m̀hngāam jeuk a?
2. Gwai m̀hgwai a?	2. Néih wah gwai m̀hgwai a?
3. Pèhng m̀hpèhng a?	3. Néih wah pèhng m̀hpèhng a?
4. Sai m̀hsai a?	4. Néih wah sai m̀hsai a?
5. Daaih m̀hdaaih a?	5. Néih wah daaih m̀hdaaih a?
6. Hóu m̀hhóuyám a?	6. Néih wah hóu m̀hhóuyám a?
7. Hóu m̀hhóusihk a?	7. Néih wah hóu m̀hhóusihk a?
8. Leng m̀hleng a?	8. Néih wah leng m̀hleng a?

9. Gauh m̀hgauh a?   9. Néih wah gauh m̀hgauh a?
+ 10. <u>Fut</u> m̀hfut a? (<u>wide</u>)   10. Néih wah fut m̀hfut a?
+ 11. <u>Jaak</u> m̀hjaak a? (<u>narrow</u>) 11. Néih wah jaak m̀hjaak a?

---

4. Substitution Drill: Pre-modifiers of Adjectives

      Ex: T: Gó tìuh fu géi   Those slacks are quite cheap.
            pèhng. /hóu/   /very/

          S: Gó tìuh fu hóu pèhng. Those slacks are very cheap.

   1. Gó tìuh fu géi pèhng. /hóu/   1. Gó tìuh fu hóu pèhng.

   2. Gó tìuh fu hóu gwai.   2. Gó tìuh fu m̀hhaih géi gwai.
      /m̀hhaih géi/   Those slacks aren't very
                                        expensive.

   3. Gó tìuh fu m̀hhaih géi gwai.   3. Gó tìuh fu géi gwai.
      /géi/

   4. Gó tìuh fu géi pèhng. /m̀h/   4. Gó tìuh fu m̀h pèhng.

 + 5. Gó tìuh fu m̀h pèhng.   5. Gó tìuh fu m̀hhaih hóu pèhng.
      /m̀hhaih hóu/ (<u>not very</u>)

---

5. Substitution Drill: Mixed: Nouns and Adjectives

      Ex: 1. T: Gó tìuh yú géi   That fish is pretty cheap.
               pèhng. /hóu/   /very/

             S: Gó tìuh yú hóu   That fish is very cheap.
                pèhng.

          2. T: Gó tìuh yú hóu   That fish is very cheap.
                pèhng. /go bìu/   /watch/

             S: Gó go bìu hóu   That watch is very cheap.
                pèhng.

   1. Kéuih deui maht hóu leng.   1. Kéuih deui maht m̀hhaih géi
      /m̀hhaih géi/   leng.

   2. /tìuh dyún fu/   2. Kéuih tìuh dyún fu m̀hhaih
                                        géi leng.

   3. /hóu gwai/   3. Kéuih tìuh dyún fu hóu gwai.

   4. /nī dī yīnjái/   4. Nī dī yīnjái hóu gwai.

   5. /hóu hóusihk/   5. Nī dī yīnjái hóu hóusihk.

191

6. Substitution Drill: Adjectives as predicates

      Ex: T: Nī gihn lāangsāam   T: This sweater is pretty.
            hóu leng. /hóu
            jaak/

         S: Nī gihn lāangsāam   S: This sweater is narrow.
            hóu jaak.

1. Nī gihn lāangsāam hóu jaak.   1. Nī gihn lāangsāam hóu
   hóu ngāamjeuk.   ngāamjeuk.

2. Hóu gwai.   2. Nī gihn lāangsāam hóu gwai.

3. Gwaidī.   3. Nī gihn lāangsāam gwaidī.

4. Sai sèsíu.   4. Nī gihn lāangsāam sai sèsíu.

5. Daaihdī.   5. Nī gihn lāangsāam daaihdī.

6. Hóu pèhng.   6. Nī gihn lāangsāam hóu pèhng.

7. Mhhaih géi gwai.   7. Nī gihn lāangsāam mhhaih
                         géi gwai.

8. Mhhaih hóu leng.   8. Nī gihn lāangsāam mhhaih
   Not very pretty.   hóu leng.

9. Hóu jaak.   9. Nī gihn lāangsāam hóu jaak.

---

7. Substitution Drill: Repeat the first sentence, then substitute
   as directed.

1. Kéuih mhjùngyi jeuk dyún fu.   1. Kéuih mhjùngyi jeuk dyún fu.
   She doesn't like to wear
   shorts.

+ 2. /chèuhngsāam/(cheongsaam)   2. Kéuih mhjùngyi jeuk chèuhng-
                               sāam.
                               She doesn't like to wear
                               cheongsaams.

3. /dyún maht/(socks)   3. Kéuih mhjùngyi jeuk dyún
                               maht.

4. /chèuhng maht/(stockings)   4. Kéuih mhjùngyi jeuk chèuhng
                                 maht.

5. /lāangsāam/   5. Kéuih mhjùngyi jeuk lāang-
                               sāam.

6. /chèuhng fu/(long pants)   6. Kéuih mhjùngyi jeuk chèuhng
                                 fu.

    Comment: A cheongsaam is the style of dress worn by Chinese
        women, with a high collar and the skirt slit at
        the sides.

---

8. Response Drill

Ex: T: Yáuh móuh cháang
    maaih a?
    /pìhnggwó/

T: Are there oranges for sale
   [to sell] (here)? or
   (Do you) have oranges for
   sale? /apples?

S: Deuim̀hjyuh, maaih-
   saai laak. Pìhng-
   gwó hóu m̀hhóu a?

S: Sorry, they're all sold out.
   Would apples be OK?

1. Yáuh móuh Yìnggwok hàaih maaih
  + a? /Méihgwok ge/
   Do you have English shoes
   for sale? /American ones/
   (ge as noun substitute)

1. Deuim̀hjyuh, maaihsaai laak.
   Méihgwok ge hóu m̀hhóu a?
   I'm sorry, they're all
   sold out. Would American
   ones be all right?

2. Yáuh móuh Méihgwok yìnjái
   maaih a? /Yìnggwok ge/

2. Deuim̀hjyuh, maaihsaai laak.
   Yìnggwok ge hóu m̀hhóu a?

3. Yáuh móuh jyùyuhk maaih a?
   /ngàuhyuhk/

3. Deuim̀hjyuh, maaihsaai laak.
   Ngàuhyuhk hóu m̀hhóu a?

Comment: ge can substitute for a noun in a follow sentence.
       The structure modifier + ge substitutes for
       modifier + Noun. See #1 and #2 above.

---

9. Response Drill

Ex: 1. T: Néih yáuh móuh
      sahp mān a?
      /nod/

1. T: Do you have ten dollars?

    S: Yáuh. Néih yiu
      àh!

S: Yes I do. You want it, huh.

  2. T: Néih yáuh móuh
      sahp mān a?
      /shake/

2. T: Do you have $10?

    S: Móuh a. Deui-
      m̀hjyuh laak.

S: No I don't, I'm sorry.

1. Néih yáuh móuh tòhng a?
   /shake/

1. Móuh a. Deuim̀hjyuh laak.

2. Néih yáuh móuh yìnjái a?
   /shake/

2. Móuh a. Deuim̀hjyuh laak.

3. Néih yáuh móuh jē a? /shake/

3. Móuh a. Deuim̀hjyuh laak.

4. Néih yáuh móuh go bun ngàhnchín a? /nod/

4. Yáuh. Néih yiu àh.

5. Néih yáuh móuh yih sahp mān
   a? /shake/

5. Móuh a. Deuim̀hjyuh laak.

6. Néih yáuh móuh léuhng go bun   6. Yáuh. Néih yiu àh!
   ngàhnchín a? /nod/

7. Néih yáuh móuh yāt dā bējáu   7. Yáuh. Néih yiu àh!
   a? /nod/

Comment: Móuh a. and Móuh laak. compared as follow sentences to
         a yáuh móuh? question:

         Móuh a. indicates simple negative 'Don't have any.'

         Móuh laak. indicates that you used to have some, but
         you don't have any any more.

---

10. Expansion Drill

    Ex: T: Nī go pìhnggwó hóu   T: This apple is cheap. /delicious/
           pèhng. /housihk/

        S: Nī go pìhnggwó yauh   S: This apple is both cheap and
           pèhng yauh hóusihk.   delicious.

    1. Nī go cháang hóu gwai.   1. Nī go cháang yauh gwai yauh
       /m̀hhóusihk/   m̀hhóusihk.

    2. Nī go bīu hóu pèhng. /jéun/ 2. Nī dī bīu yauh pèhng yáuh
                                      jéun.

    3. Gó dī béng hóu sai. /gwai/ 3. Gó dī béng yauh sai yauh
                                      gwai.

    4. Kéuih gihn sēutsāam hóu   4. Kéuih gihn sēutsāam yauh
       chèuhng. /daaih/   chèuhng yauh daaih.

    5. Nī tiuh kwàhn hóu fut.   5. Nī tiuh kwàhn yauh fut yauh
       /daaih/   daaih.

    6. Nī júng bāt hóu pèhng. /leng/ 6. Nī júng bāt yauh pèhng yauh
                                       leng.

---

11. Transformation Drill

    Ex: T: Kéuih gihn yúhlāu   T: Her raincoat is pretty.
           hóu leng.

        S: Kéuih gihn yúhlāu   S: Is her raincoat pretty?
           leng m̀hleng a?

    1. Kéuih gó tiuh fu hóu ngāam- 1. Kéuih gó tiuh fu ngāam
       jeuk.   m̀hngāamjeuk a?
       Those trousers of his fit
       very well.

194

2. Sahp mān m̀hgwai.   2. Sahp mān gwai m̀hgwai a?

3. Nī dī maht hóu pèhng.   3. Nī dī maht pèhng m̀hpèhng a?

4. Hāak sīk ge m̀hhaih géi leng.   4. Hāak sīk ge leng m̀hleng a?

5. Gó dī jyùyuhk gei hóusihk.   5. Gó dī jyùyuhk hóu m̀hhóu
                                           sihk a?

6. Gó tiuh saidī.   6. Gó tiuh sai m̀hsai a?

7. Nī gihn baahk sēutsāam daaihdī.   7. Nī gihn baahk sēutsāam daaih
                                           m̀hdaaih a?

8. Kéuih gihn sāam hóu leng.   8. Kéuih gihn sāam leng m̀hleng
                                           a?

9. Kéuih gó deui hàaih hóu jaak.   9. Kéuih gó deui hàaih jaak
                                           m̀hjaak a?

---

12. **Transformation Drill:** Transform the cue sentence into a **wá?** question
sentence, following the pattern of the example.

    Ex: T: Kéuih sing Wòhng.   His name is Wong.

        S: Kéuih sing mēyéh wá?   You said his name was what?

1. Wòhng Sàang séung máaih   1. Wòhng Sàang séung máaih
   tiuh fu.   mēyéh wá?

2. Léih Síujé jùngyi ngóh.   2. Léih Síujé jùngyi bīngo wá?

3. Kéuih máaih nī gihn.   3. Kéuih máaih bīn gihn wá?
   She wants this one.   which one does she want?

4. Kéuih séung oi gó tiuh.   4. Kéuih séung oi bīn tiuh wá?
   He wants to have that one.   Which one does he want?

5. Kéuih sihk béng.   5. Kéuih sihk mēyéh wá?

6. Kéuih jeuk gáu houh.   6. Kéuih jeuk géidō houh wá?

7. Yìhgā daahp yāt.   7. Yìhgā daahp géi wá?

8. Yìhgā sāam dím bun.   8. Yìhgā géidímjùng wá?

9. Kéuih máaih sei deui.   9. Kéuih máaih géidō deui wá?

10. Kéuih yáuh sahp mān.   10. Kéuih yáuh géidō chín wá?

---

13. Expansion Drill

Ex: T: Nī gihn yúhlāu   This raincoat is a bit small.
        saidī.

    S: Nī gihn yúhlāu saidī,   This raincoat is a bit small;
       yauh móuh daaihdī   do you have any larger ones?
       ge nē?

1. Nī dī yú gwaidī.   1. Nī dī yú gwaidī, yáuh móuh
                                pèhngdī ge nē?

2. Nī tìuh fu daaihdī.   2. Nī tìuh fu daaihdī, yáuh
                                móuh saidī ge nē?

3. Nī gihn lāangsāam chèuhngdī. 3. Nī gihn lāangsāam chèuhngdī,
                                yáuh móuh dyúndī ge nē?

+ 4. Nī gihn dáisāam saidī.   4. Nī gihn dáisāam saidī, yáuh
     (underwear)   móuh daaihdī ge nē?

5. Nī tìuh fu jaak dī.   5. Nī tìuh fu jaak dī, yáuh
                                móuh fut dī ge nē?

---

14. Response Drill

Ex: T: Néih oi bīn gihn   Which shirt do you want?
        sēutsāam nē?   /white color/
        /baahk sīk/

    S: Ngóh oi baahk sīk   I want that (or the) white one.
       gó gihn.

1. Néih oi bīn deui maht nē? 1. Ngóh oi hāak sīk gó deui.
   /hāak sīk/

2. Néih oi bīn bá jē nē? /daaih- 2. Ngóh oi daaihdī gó bá.
   dī/

3. Néih oi bīn tìuh fu nē?   3. Ngóh oi chèuhngdī gó tìuh.
   /chèuhngdī/

4. Néih oi bīn bāau yīnjái nē? 4. Ngóh oi saidī gó bāau.
   /saidī/

5. Néih oi bīn jek gāi nē?   5. Ngóh oi gwaidī gó jek.
   /gwaidī/

196

15. Alteration Drill

      Ex: T: Ngóh ngoi gihn   I want a larger one.
           daaihdĭ ge.

         S: Béi gihn daaihdĭ   Give me a larger one.
           ge ngóh lā!

1. Ngóh ngoi tĭuh futdĭ ge.   1. Béi tĭuh futdĭ ge ngóh lā!

2. Ngóh ngoi deui jaakdĭ ge.   2. Béi deui jaakdĭ ge ngóh lā!

3. Ngóh ngoi bá lengdĭ ge.   3. Béi bá lengdĭ ge ngóh lā!

4. Ngóh ngoi jĭ saidĭ ge.   4. Béi jĭ saidĭ ge ngóh lā!

5. Ngóh ngoi go pèhngdĭ ge.   5. Béi go pèhngdĭ ge ngóh lā!

6. Ngóh ngoi géi gihn saidĭ ge. 6. Béi géi gihn saidĭ ge ngóh
                                   lā!

7. Ngóh ngoi géi tĭuh chèuhngdĭ 7. Béi géi tĭuh chèuhngdĭ ge
    ge.   ngóh lā!

---

16. Response Drill

      Ex: T: Ngóh séung máaih   T: I want to buy two ties.
           léuhng tĭuh tāai.

         S: Máaih bĭn léuhng   S: Which two do you want?
           tĭuh nē?

1. Ngóh séung máaih tĭuh tāai.   1. Máaih bĭn tĭuh nē?

2. Ngóh séung máaih dĭ yùhnbāt. 2. Máaih bĭn dĭ nē?

3. Ngóh séung máaih dĭ bou.   3. Máaih bĭn dĭ nē?

4. Ngóh séung oi sàam deui   4. Oi bĭn sàam deui nē?
    dyún maht.
    I want to get three pairs
    of socks.

IV. CONVERSATIONS FOR LISTENING

    (On tape. Listen to tape with book closed.)

V. SAY IT IN CANTONESE

A. In a store, the customer says:

1. These shoes are pretty--
   do you have (are there?)
   size eight for sale?

2. I don't like the black ones--
   are there white ones
   (do you have white ones)?

3. This sweater is a little
   too wide--I want a smaller
   one.

4. I'll take a dozen of these
   socks.

5. This sweater is pretty, but
   it doesn't fit--do you
   have larger one?

6. These shoes are a bit expensive, do you have any
   cheaper ones?

7. How much do these shorts
   cost?

8. This one (sweater) is pretty
   and fits well, but it's a
   bit expensive--$30, OK?

B. And the clerk responds:

1. I'm sorry, size eight is
   all sold out.

2. Yes, what size do you want?

3. This one is narrower--try
   it.

4. Fine, what size do you wear?

5. Yes.

6. Yes, those are cheaper--do
   you like them?

7. This one is $15.00 and that
   one is $15.50--which one
   do you want?

8. OK.

Vocabulary Checklist for Lesson 8

1. āamjeuk	adj:	fits well, well-fitting
2. àh	ss:	sen. suf. with force of 'I suppose'
3. baahk	adj:	white
4. bīn?	QW:	which?
5. chèuhng	adj:	long (in length)
6. chèuhngsāam	n:	cheongsaam
7. dā	m:	dozen
8. daaih	adj:	large
9. daaihdī	Ph:	a little larger
10. dáisāam	n:	underwear
11. -dī	adj.s:	attaches to adjectives to mean 'a little Adj; somewhat adj; Adj--er.

12. dò	bf:	much, many
13. dyún	adj:	short
14. fut	adj:	wide
15. gauh	adj:	old (not new)
16. -ge	bf:	one(s) = (noun substitute)
17. géi	adv:	rather, quite
18. gwai	adj:	expensive
19. hāak	adj:	black
20. hóu	adv:	very
21. hóu	adj:	good
22. Hóu m̀hhóu a?	Ph:	OK? Is (that) all right?
23. houh	m:	number
24. hóusihk	adj:	good to eat; tasty
25. hóuyám	adj:	good to drink; tasty
26. jaak	adj:	narrow
27. jeuk	v:	wear; put on (clothes)
28. júng	m:	type
29. jùngyi	auxV/v:	like, prefer; like to
30. lāangsāam	n:	sweater
31. leng	adj:	pretty; good-looking; good, nice (for foods)
32. Máaihsaai laak	Ph:	All sold out.
33. m̀hhaih géi	adv:	not very..., not....
34. m̀hhaih hóu	adv:	not very
35. móuh	v:	not have, there isn't (aren't)
36. ngāamjeuk	adj:	well fitting (for clothes), fits well (var. of āamjeuk)
37. pèhng	adj:	cheap
38. -saai	Vsuf:	completely
39. sai	adj:	small
40. sàn	adj:	new
41. sīk	(bf)n:	color
42. wah	v:	say, opine
43. yáuh	v:	have, there is (are)

I. **BASIC CONVERSATION**

A. **Buildup:**

gùngyàhn	servant

Gùngyàhn

Wéi.	Hello.
wán	look for, search
Wán bīnwái a?	Who are you calling?

Jèung Sàang

dihnwá	telephone
tèng	listen, hear
tèng dihnwá	talk [listen] on the telephone
giu	instruct, order, tell
giu kéuih tèng dihnwá	ask her to come to the phone
Ñhgòi néih giu Léih Táai tèng dihnwá.	Please ask Mrs. Lee to come to the phone.

Gùngyàhn

Wán bīnwái wá? Ngóh tèng àhchìngchó.	Who did you say you were looking for? I didn't hear.
daaihsēngdī	louder voice
Ñhgòi daaihsēngdī lā.	Please speak louder.

Jèung Sàang

Léih Taaitáai.	Mrs. Lee.

Gùngyàhn

heui gāai	go out [go street]
jó	Verb suffix, indicating fulfillment of an expectation.
heuijó gāai	has gone out, went out
Kéuih heuijó gāai bo.	She's gone out.
Gwaising wán kéuih a?	Who is calling please?

Jèung Sàang

Sing Jèung ge.	My name is Cheung.
fàanlàih	come back, return

géisìh (géisí)   when?
Kéuih géisìh fàanlaih a?   When will she be back?

Gùngyàhn

sahpyih dím   12 o'clock
-lèhng-   -and some odd. Added to a
                                   number phrase.

Waahkjé sahpyih dím lèhng lā.   Probably a little after 12.
sihk aan or sihk ngaan   eat the midday meal
yiu   going to, intend to
Kéuih yiu fàanlàih sihk ngaan   She's going to come home for
gé.   lunch.
sih   business, affair, matter
yáuh sih   have something to attend
                                   to; have errand, business
Yáuh mēyéh sih a?   What is it you want? (i.e.,
                                   What matter are you calling
                                   about?)

Jèung Sàang

dá dihnwá   make a phone call, to
                                  telephone.

dá dihnwá béi ngóh   telephone me
giu kéuih dá dihnwá béi   tell her to phone me
ngóh
ṁhgòi néih giu kéuih dá   please ask her to phone
dihnwá béi Jèung Sàang lā.   Mr. Cheung.
Gám, kéuih fàanlàih, ṁhgòi   Well, when she comes home,
néih giu kéuih dá dihnwá   please ask her to call Mr.
béi Jèung Sàang lā.   Cheung.

Gùngyàhn

néih ge dihnwá   your telephone
géidō houh?   what number?
néih ge dihnwá géidō houh a?   what is your telephone
                                   number?

Kéuih jí ṁhjí néih ge dihnwá   Does she know your telephone
géidō houh a?   number?

201

Jèung Sàang

Kéuih m̀hjî ga.	She doesn't know.
Ngóh ge dihnwá haih chāt baat ...	My telephone number is 7 8 ...

Gùngyàhn

ló	fetch, go get
dáng ngóh	let me; wait while I ...
dáng ngóh ló jî bāt sîn	let me get a pen first.
Dáng ngóh ló jî bāt sîn lā.	Let me get a pen first ...

(She returns with a pen:)

Gùngyàhn

Wéi, géidō houh wá?	Hello, what number did you say?

Jèung Sàang

lìhng	zero
Chāt baat luhk lìhng ńgh gáu.	786059

Gùngyàhn

Chāt baat luhk lìhng ńgh gáu.	786059
wah kéuih jî	tell her
ngóh wah kéuih jî	I'll tell her
Hóu, kéuih fàanlàih, ngóh wah kéuih jî lā.	All right--when she comes back, I'll tell her.

Jèung Sàang

Hóu, m̀hgòi.	Fine; thanks.

B. **Recapitulation:**

Gùngyàhn

Wéi. Wán bīnwái a?	Hello. Who are you calling?

Jèung Sàang

M̀hgòi néih giu Leih Táai tèng dihnwá.	Please ask Mrs. Lee to come to the phone.

Gùngyàhn

Wán bīnwái wá? Ngóh tèng m̀hchìngchó. M̀hgòi daaihsēng-dī lā.	Who did you say you wanted? I couldn't hear. Please speak louder.

Jèung Sàang

Lèih Taaitáai.

Mrs. Lee.

Gùngyàhn

Kéuih heuijó gāai bo.
Gwaising wán kéuih a?

She's gone out. Who is calling
please?

Jèung Sàang

Sing Jèung ge. Kéuih géisìh
fàanlàih a?

My name is Cheung. When will
she be back?

Gùngyàhn

Waahkjé sahpyih dím lèhng lā.
Kéuih yiu fàanlàih sihk aan
gé. Yáuh mēyéh sih a?

Probably a little after 12.
She's going to come home for
lunch. What is it you want?

Jèung Sàang

Gám, kéuih fàanlàih, mhgòi
néih giu kéuih dá dihnwá
béi Jèung Sàang lā.

Well, (when) she comes home,
please ask her to call Mr.
Cheung.

Gùngyàhn

Kéuih jí mhjí néih ge dihnwá
géidō houh a?

Does she know your telephone
number?

Jèung Sàang

Kéuih mhji ga. Ngóh ge dihnwá
haih chāt baat ...

She doesn't know. My telephone number is 7 8 ...

Gùngyàhn

Dáng ngóh ló jí bāt sìn lā.

Let me get a pen first.

(She returns with a pen:)

Gùngyàhn

Wéi, géidō houh wá?

Hello, what number did you
say?

Jèung Sàang

Chāt baat luhk lìhng ńgh gáu.

786059

Gùngyàhn

Chāt baat luhk lìhng ńgh gáu.
Hóu, kéuih fàanlàih, ngóh
wah kéuih jí lā.

786059
All right--when she comes back,
I'll tell her.

Jēung Sàang

Hóu, m̀hgòi.   Fine; thanks.

+ + + + + + + + + + + + +

Pronunciation Practice:

1. i as in si, chi, jì, dì, nì, sìh, sih, hòuhjì

    i as syllable final is a high front unrounded vowel--[i].

              Listen and repeat:

              1. nì nì   .

              2. si si   .

              3. sih sih   .

              4. sìh sìh   .

              5. jì jì   .

2. ik as in sìk, sihk

    ik is a two-part final composed of the high front unrounded vowel
    i plus the velar stop consonant k. Before k the tongue position for
    i approaches higher-mid front unrounded [e], tenser and lower than
    the American i in "sick,"--[I], closer to the French é in été,
    'summer.' The tongue position of k following the front vowel is more
    forward than that of k following the back vowels u, o, and a --
    [Ik⌐].

              Listen and repeat:

              1. sìk sìk sìk   . 識
              2. sihk sihk sihk . 食

3. i/ik contrasts

    Note that in addition to the difference in tongue position for i
    as a final and before k as described, there is also a length differ-
    ence. i before k is shorter than i as final--[I˅k] or [e ˅k], and
    [i:].

              Listen and repeat:

              1. sih sih   , sihk sihk   .
              2. sih sihk   , sihk sih   .

4. ing as in lìhng, sing, pìhnggwó, chìngchó

    ing is a two-part final composed of the high front unrounded
    vowel i and the velar nasal ng. The tongue position for i before ng
    is similar to that of i before k--lowered from high front position.
    The vowel is open before the nasal final.

Listen and repeat:

1. sing sing 姓 , lìhng lìhng 零 , chìng chìng 清 .
2. chìng sing lìhng   .清 姓 零
3. lìhng lìhng 零 , pìhng pìhng 蘋 .

. ing/eng contrasts

Listen and repeat:

1. lìhng lìhng 零 , pèhng pèhng 平 .
2. pìhng pìhng pìhnggwó   .蘋蘋蘋果
3. pìhng pèhng 蘋平, pìhng pèhng   .
4. leng sing 靚姓, sing leng 姓靚.

. ing/ik contrasts

Listen and repeat:

1. sīk sīk 識 , sing sing 姓 .
2. sihk sihk 食 , sing sing   .

. eu finals

A. eut, eun, and eui

Listen and repeat:

1. chēut, sēut 出 恤
2. deui, heui 對 去
3. jéun, jéun 準 準

B. eung and euk

Listen and repeat:

1. Jèung chèuhng 張 長
2. séung, léuhng 想 雨
3. jeuk, jeuk 著 著

. s as in sing, sihk, si, sé, sei, séung, sàang, sahp, séui.

s is an initial consonant in Cantonese. Like the American s (as
in 'see'), the Cantonese s is voiceless. In terms of air flow the
American and Cantonese s sounds are the same--both are spirants, that
is to say, the air is forced through a narrow passage under friction,
producing a hissing sound. The tongue position for the Cantonese s
differs from that of the American s. The friction points for the
Cantonese sound are the blade of the tongue (that part just back from
the tip) and the dental ridge. The flat surface of the blade of the
tongue comes close to the dental ridge (the tip of the tongue is at

rest, approximately near the base of the upper teeth) and air is forced
through the passage thus provided. For the American s, the friction
points are the tip of the tongue, not the blade, and the dental ridge.
For the American s the grooved tip of the tongue approaches the dental
ridge and air is forced through this passageway. For the Cantonese
sound the lips are rounded before a rounded vowel and spread before
an unrounded one.

    1. Compare American and Cantonese s sounds:

American	Cantonese
1. see see see	si si si
2. sing sing sing	sing sing sing
3. set set set	sé sé sé
4. say say say	sei sei sei
5. son son son	sàn sàn sàn
6. soot soot soot	sēut sēut sēut

    2. Listen and repeat:

        1. si   , si   , si   .
        2. sih   , sih   , sih   .
        3. sé   , sé   , sé   .
        4. sing   , sing   , sing   .
        5. sēut , sēut , sēut .

9. s/j/ch compared.

    There are some similarities of tongue positioning among these
sounds. To make s the blade of the tongue approaches close to the
dental ridge at the point where the tongue touches the ridge to make
the j and ch sounds. The flat surface of the blade is the friction
point for all three sounds.

    Listen and repeat:

        1. ji 至 , chi 次 , si 識 .
        2. jing 正 , chìng 清 , sing 姓 .
        3. jē 姐 , chē 車 , sé 寫 .
        4. jái 仔 , chàih 齊 , sai 細 .

I. NOTES

1. bo = sentence suffix expressing definiteness, conviction.

    Ex: Kéuih chēutjó gāai laak.   She's gone out. (change from
                                         former condition)

        Kéuih chēutjó gāai bo.   She's gone out, that s
                                       definite.

                   (See BC)

2. -jó verb suffix indicating accomplishment of intended action.

    This will be treated in detail in later lessons. At present
learn it in the set phrases you will be apt to need to say and comprehend over the telephone:

    Ex: Kéuih fàanjó gùng.   He's gone to work.
                                    [return-jó work]

        Kéuih heuijó gāai.   She's gone out (from her own
                                    house). [go-jó street]

        Kéuih fàanjó ngūkkéi.   He's gone home.
                                    [return-jó home]

         (See BC and Drills 1.3, 4, 5, 6, 7)

3. ge translated as possessive.

    ge is suffixed to personal nouns and pronouns to show ownership,
'belonging to,' referred to in grammatical terms as the possessive.
ge operates as possessive in noun phrases both in head and modifier
structures:

   a. In head structures:

        ge combines with a preceding personal noun (or pronoun)
        to form the head of a noun phrase.

        Ex: 1. Gó dī / Gó bún syù haih Léih   **Those** / **That** book(s) is/are
                 Siujé ge.   Miss Lee's.

           2. Nī dī / Nī bún haih ngóh ge.   These are / This one is mine.

           3. Léih Siujé ge haih   Miss Lee's is a new one.
              san ge.   are   ones.

           4. Ngóh ge haih gauh ge.   Mine are   old ones.
                                           is an   one.

    In a head structure ge cannot be omitted from the N-ge combination.

        (See Drills 10, 11)

207

b. In modification structures:

ge combines with personal nouns (and pronouns) to form a
possessive modifier to a following noun head.

Ex: 1. Ngóh ge dihnwá haih   My telephone number is....
       ...houh.

    2. Kéuihdeih ge néuih-   Their girlfriends have gone
       pàhngyáuh fàanjó   home.
       ngūkkéi laak.

    3. Ngóh m̀hjùngyi Léih   I don't like Miss Lee's new
       Síujé ge sàn   sweater.
       lāangsāam.

              (See BC)

4. ge/Measure overlap.

    ge may replace the measure in a modification structure.

    Ex: 1. Ngón go néui m̀hhái   My daughter is not here.
           douh.

        2. Ngóh dī néui m̀hhái   My daughters are not here.
           douh.

        3. Ngóh ge néui m̀hhái   My daughter(s) is (are) not
           douh.   here.

5. Possessive modification without ge or Measure.

    A few nouns accept modification by personal nouns and pronouns
directly. Pàhngyáuh, (ng)ūkkéi, and gùngyàhn are the only nouns
of this type we have studied so far.

       Ex: Ngóh pàhngyáuh   My friend/friends

           Léih Síujé (ng)ūkkéi   Miss Lee's home

    But even for these nouns, ge must be used with bīngo ge, whose?
to differentiate from bīn go, which (M)?

       Ex: Bīn go pàhngyáuh?   Which friend?

           Bīngo ge pàhngyáuh?   Whose friend?

       Compare:

           bīngo ge pàhngyáuh?   whose friend?

           bīn go pàhngyáuh?   which friend?

           Léih Táai gaau bīngo   Whose friend does Mrs. Lee
           ge pàhngyáuh?   teach?

           Léih Táai gaau bīn go   Which friend does Mrs. Lee
           pàhngyáuh?   teach?

    The nouns that accept direct modification by personal noun/

                     208

pronoun will be treated as exceptions and noted as such. As a rule
of thumb, such nouns must be of more than one syllable.

6. yiu..V..;séung..V.. differentiated.

   yiu..V.. = definitely intend to ..V..

   séung..V.. = plan to ..V.. (but maybe it won't happen)

   In English yiu can be translated as 'going to' if the sentence
is one of future reference. Yiu contrasts with séung in such sentences in that with séung the implication is that it's iffy whether
or not the action expressed by the following verb will actually
take place, but with yiu the person has definitely made up his mind
to do the action.

   Ex: 1. Kéuih wah ngóh jī   She told me she was planning
          kéuih séung fàan-   to come home for lunch.
          làih sihk aan.

       2. Kéuih wah ngóh jī   She told me she was coming
          kéuih yiu fàanlàih   home for lunch.
          sihk aan.

7. séung..V.. and jùngyi..V..differentiated.

   séung = would like to ..V..; think I'll ..V..

   jùngyi = like (as a general statement)

       Ex: Ngóh séung yám dī chàh.   I'd like some tea.

           Ngóh séung sihk go   I'd like an apple.
           pìhnggwó.

           Ngóh hóu jùngyi yám chàh.   I like to drink tea.
                                       I like tea.

   The differentiation of meaning between jùngyi and séung breaks
down with a mēyéh question, where the jùngyi pattern is used as a
polite way to ask what the addressee wishes. (The jùngyi mēyéh?
question may also mean: What do you like?)

           Ex: Néih séung yám dī   What would you like to drink?
               mēyéh a?

               Néih jùngyi yám dī   What would you like to drink?
               mēyéh a?

                   (See Drill 12)

8. Omission of <u>yāt</u> in certain 'one o'clock' phrases.

  The numeral <u>yāt</u> is ordinarily omitted in the spoken language before the time measure <u>dím</u>, 'o'clock,' when <u>dím</u> is followed by <u>géi</u>, <u>lèhng</u> or <u>bun</u>.

    Ex: 1. dím géi jūng = sometime after one o'clock
       2. dím lèhng (jūng) = a little after one o'clock
       3. dím bun = half past one
         (See Drill <u>7</u>)

In all other phrases concerning one o'clock, <u>yāt</u> cannot be omitted.

9. Omission of <u>go jih</u> in a time phrase.

  <u>go jih</u> is frequently omitted in the spoken language as the final element in a time phrase.

    Ex: sàam dím yāt = 3:05
       sàam dím sàam = 3:15
       sàam dím sei = 3:20

  Note in these abbreviated forms that the numeral following <u>dím</u> is in construction with an unspoken <u>go jih</u>, not with <u>go gwāt</u>. Thus <u>sàam dím sàam</u> is 3:15, not 3:45. X:30 is never stated as <u>X dím luhk</u>, but as <u>X dím bún</u>.

       (See Drill <u>7</u>)

  Although infrequent, <u>X dím yih</u> rather than (-) <u>X dím léuhng</u> is the abbreviated form for <u>X dím léuhng go jih</u>.

II. DRILLS

    1. Substitution Drill: Repeat the first sentence, then substitute as
       directed.

        1. Mhgòi néih giu Léih Táai   1. Mhgòi néih giu Léih Tāai
            tèng dihnwá lā.   tèng dihnwá lā.
            Please call Mrs. Lee to the
            telephone.

        2. Hòh Táai   2. Mhgòi néih giu Hòh Táai
                                        tèng dihnwá lā.

        3. Hòh Síujé   3. Mhgòi néih giu Hòh Síujé
                                          tèng dihnwá lā.

        4. Jèung Sàang   4. Mhgòi néih giu Jèung Sàang
                                          tèng dihnwá lā.

        5. Chàhn Táai   5. Mhgòi néih giu Chàhn Táai
                                          tèng dihnwá lā.

---

    2. Expansion Drill

        Ex: T: Jèung Sàang,   T: Mr. Cheung, telephone!
                tèng dihnwá.

           S: Mhgòi néih giu   S: Please ask Mr. Cheung to come
                Jèung Sàang   to the phone.
                tèng dihnwá.

        1. Chàhn Sàang, tèng dihnwá.   1. Mhgòi néih giu Chàhn Sàang
                                          tèng dihnwá.

        2. Léih Táai, tèng dihnwá.   2. Mhgòi néih giu Léih Táai
                                          tèng dihnwá.

        3. Hòh Síujé, tèng dihnwá.   3. Mhgòi néih giu Hòh Síujé
                                          tèng dihnwá.

        4. Wòhng Sáang, tèng dihnwá.   4. Mhgòi néih giu Wòhng Sáang
                                          tèng dihnwá.

        5. Làuh Táai, tèng dihnwá.   5. Mhgòi néih giu Làuh Táai
                                          tèng dihnwá.

---

    3. Expansion Drill: telephone talk; listen and repeat:

    + 1. <u>cho</u>   <u>mistake, make a mistake</u>

    +   cho <u>sin</u> (<u>line, thread</u>)   wrong line

    +   <u>Daap cho sin</u>   Wrong number! [connected the
                                                wrong line]

2. dáng   wait

+   dáng (yāt)jahn (var: (yāt)ján)   wait awhile

    Mhgòi néih dáng yātjahn.   Just a moment, please.
                                            [Please wait awhile]

    Mhgòi néih dáng yātjahn lā.   Just a moment, please!

+ 3. fàan   go [return] to place you
                                            habitually go to.

+   fàan gùng   go [return] to work

    fàanjó gùng   has gone [or went] to work

    Kéuih fàanjó gùng.   (S)He's gone to work.

    Kéuih fàanjó gùng bo.   I am sorry, but he's gone to
                                            work.

+ 4. chēut gāai   go out [out (to) street]

    chēutjó gāai   has gone [or went] out

    Kéuih chēutjó gāai.   (S)He's gone out.

    Kéuih chēutjó gāai bo.   I'm sorry, but she's gone out.

+ 5. fàan (ng)ūkkéi   go [return] home

    fàanjó (ng)ūkkéi   has gone [or went] home

    Kéuih fàanjó (ng)ūkkéi   (S)He's gone home.

    Kéuih fàanjó (ng)ūkkéi bo.   I'm sorry, but he's gone home.

+ 6. fàan hohk   go [return] to school

    fàanjó hohk   gone to school, left for school

    Kéuih fàanjó hohk la.   He's gone to school.

+ 7. heui gāai   go out [go (to) street]

    heuijó gāai   has gone (or went) out

    Kéuih heuijó gāai.   (S)He's gone out.

    Kéuih heuijó gāai bo.   I'm sorry, but he's gone out.

+ 8. joi dálàih   call back (on the phone)

    dángjahn joi dálàih   call back later

    Dángjahn joi dálàih lā.   Call back later.

    a. Repeat the final sentence of each of the above problem
       sentences as a Listen and Repeat drill, students repeating
       after the teacher.

    b. Repeat, teacher giving the English of the final sentences,
       students called on individually to give Cantonese equiva-
       lents.

4. Conversation Drill: Carry on the suggested conversations following
   the pattern of the example.

Ex: 1. T: Néih wán mēyéh   T: What are you looking for?
         a? /jì yùhn-   /a pencil/
         bāt/

      S: Ngóh wán jì yùhn-   S: I'm looking for a pencil.
         bāt.

    2. T: Néih wán bīngo a?   T: Who are you looking for?
         /Chàhn Sàang/   /Mr. Chan/

      S: Ngóh wán Chàhn   S: I'm looking for Mr. Chan.
         Sàang.

1. Néih wán mēyéh a? /bàau   1. Ngóh wán bàau yīnjái.
   yīnjái/

2. Néih wán mēyéh a? /bá jē/   2. Ngóh wán bá jē.

3. Néih wán bīngo a? /Wòhng Táai/ 3. Ngóh wán Wòhng Táai.

4. Néih wán bīngo a? /Làuh Síujé/ 4. Ngóh wán Làuh Síujé.

5. Néih wán mēyéh a? /jì yùhnjí-   5. Ngóh wán jì yùhnjíbāt.
   bāt/

6. Néih wán bīngo a? /Jèung   6. Ngóh wán Jèung Sàang.
   Sàang/

a. Repeat as Conversation Drill, thus:

   1. T: /yùhnbāt/

     S1: Néih wán mēyéh a?

     S2: Ngóh wán jì yùhnbāt.

   2. T: /Chàhn Sàang/

     S1: Néih wán bīngo a?

     S2: Ngóh wán Chàhn Sàang.

_____

5. Conversation Drill

Ex: A: Ṁhgòi néih giu   A: Please ask Mr. Wong to come
       Wòhng Sàang tèng   to the phone.
       dihnwá lā.

    B: Kéuih chēutjó gāai   B: I'm sorry but he's gone out.
       bo. Gwaising wán   Who is calling please?
       kéuih a?

    A: Sing Jèung ge.   A: My name is Cheung.

1. A. ......Hòh Táai ......   1. A. Ṁhgòi néih giu Hòh Táai
                                    tèng dihnwá lā.

B. ....   B. Kéuih chēutjó gāai bo.
                               Gwaising wán kéuih a?

A. ...... Léih ......   A. Sing Léih ge.

2. A. ...... Jèung Sàang ......   2. A. Mhgòi néih giu Jèung
                                         Sàang tèng dihnwá lā.

B. ....   B. Kéuih chēutjó gāai bo.
                               Gwaising wán kéuih a?

A. ...... Máh ......   A. Sing Máh ge.

3. A. ...... Chàhn Síujé ......   3. A. Mhgòi néih giu Chàhn
                                         Síujé tèng dihnwá lā.

B. ....   B. Kéuih chēutjó gāai bo.
                               Gwaising wán kéuih a?

A. ...... Wòhng ......   A. Sing Wòhng ge.

   a. Continue, using actual names of students.

   Comment: Bīnwái?, who? (polite) may be substituted for
            Gwaising thus:

            Gwaising wán kéuih a?
            Bīnwái wán kéuih a?   Who is calling her?

---

6. Translation & Conversation Drill

   Ex: S1: Mhgòi néih giu   S1: Please ask Mr. Lee to come to
           Léih Sàang tèng   the phone.
           dihnwá lā.

       S2: Kéuih heuijó gāai   S2: I'm sorry, but he's gone out.
           bo.

1. A. ....   1. A. Mhgòi néih giu Léih
                                         Sàang tèng dihnwá lā.

   T. Wrong number!

   B. ....   B. Daap cho sin.

2. A. ....   2. A. Mhgòi néih giu Léih
                                         Sàang tèng dihnwá lā.

   T. Just a moment, please.

   B. ....   B. Mhgòi néih dáng yātján
                                         lā.

3. A. ....   3. A. Mhgòi néih giu Léih
                                         Sàang tèng dihnwá lā.

T. He's gone to work.

B. ....   B. Kéuih fàanjó gùng bo.

4. A. ....   4. A. Mhgòi néih giu Léih
                                   Sàang tèng dihnwá lā.

T. He's gone out.

B. ....   B. Kéuih chēutjó gāai bo.

                               or

                               Kéuih heuijó gāai bo.

5. A. ....   5. A. Mhgòi néih giu Léih
                                   Sàang tèng dihnwá lā.

T. He's gone home.

B. ....   B. Kéuih fàanjó ngūkkéi bo.

6. A. ....   6. A. Mhgòi néih giu Léih
                                   Sàang tèng dihnwá lā.

T. He's gone to school.

B. ....   B. Kéuih fàanjó hohk bo.

---

7. Expansion Drill:

Ex: T: chāt dím   T: 7 o'clock.

    S: Yìhgā chāt dím   S: It's about 7 o'clock.
+   gamseuhnghá lā.
       (approximately)

    T: Nī tìuh dyúnfu sahp   T: These shorts are $10.
       mān.

    S: Nī tìuh dyúnfu sahp   S: These shorts are about $10.
       mān gamseuhnghá lā.

+ 1. dím bun.   1. Yìhga dím bun gamseuhnghá lā.
     1:30 (time expression)   It's about 1:30.

  2. luhk dím sàam   2. Yìhga luhk dím sàam
     six-fifteen   gamseuhnghá lā.
     (short for luhk dim
     sàamgojih)

  3. Nī gihn chèuhngsāam   3. Nī gihn chèuhng sàam yahńgh
     yahńgh mān.   mān gamseuhnghá lā.

  4. Nī tìuh chèuhngfu sahpluhk 4. Nī tìuh chèuhngfu sahpluhk
     mān.   mān gamseuhnghá lā.

  5. Nī gihn lāangsāam sà'ahsei man. 5. Nī gihn lāangsāam sà'ahsei
                                     mān gamseuhnghá lā.

215

Comments: a. <u>gamseuhnghá</u> attaches to the end of a number expression, to make it an approximate number.

---

8. Expansion Drill

Ex: T: Léih Táai wah nī
gihn sahp mān.

T: Mrs. Lee says this one is ten
dollars.

S: Léih Táai wah ngóh
jī nī gihn sahp mān

S: Mrs. Lee told me this one is
ten dollars.

1. Léih Sàang wah kéuih sahp
dím fàanlàih.

1. Léih Sàang wah ngóh jī
kéuih sahp dím fàan-
làih.

2. Kéuih wah gó go yàhn haih
sing Wòhng ge.

2. Kéuih wah ngóh jī gó go
yàhn haih sing Wòhng ge.

3. Chàhn Táai wah kéuih hohk
Gwóngdùngwá.

3. Chàhn Táai wah ngóh jī
kéuih hohk Gwóngdùngwá.

4. Hòh Síujé wah kéuih go bíu
hóu pèhng.

4. Hòh Síujé wah ngóh jī kéuih
go bíu hóu pèhng.

5. Kéuih wah kéuih sahpyih dím
yiu jáu laak.

5. Kéuih wah ngóh jī kéuih
sahpyih dím yiu jáu laak.

Comment: <u>wah (Person jī)</u>,'tell someone', is interchangeable with
<u>góng (Person) tèng</u>, <u>góng (Person) jī</u>, and <u>wah (Person)</u>
<u>tèng</u>.

Learn to recognize the alternate ways when you hear
them.

---

9. Expansion Drill

Ex: T: Kéuih sihk faahn.

T: He is eating dinner.

S: Giu kéuih sihk faahn
lā!

S: Tell him to come to dinner!
(i.e. Dinner is on the
table-come eat.)

1. Léih Táai, tèng dihnwá.
Telephone for you, Mrs. Lee.

1. Giu Léih Táai tèng dihnwá lā!
Tell Mrs. Lee to come to
the phone.

2. Kéuih yìhgā fàanlàih.
He's coming back now.

2. Giu kéuih yìhgā fàanlàih lā!
Tell him to come back
right now.

3. Kéuih dáng jahn joi dá làih.

3. Giu kéuih dáng jahn joi
dá làih lā!

He'll call back in a little while.	Tell him to call back in a little while.
4. Kéuih léuhng dím làih ngóh.	4. Giu kéuih léuhng dím làih wán ngóh lā!
She's coming to see me [lit: look for me] at two o'clock.	Tell her to come see me at 2 o'clock.

+   (heui wán yàhn = go see someone)

5. Kéuih gaau ngóh góng Gwóngdùngwá.	5. Giu kéuih gaau ngóh góng Gwóngdùngwá lā!

---

10. Response Drill

Ex: T: Nī bún syù haih bīngo ga? /ngóh/	T: Whose book is this? /I/
+ S: Haih ngóh ge.	S: It's mine.
(ge = possessive marker)	
1. Gó bá jē haih bīngo ga? /ngóh gùngyàhn/	1. Haih ngóh gùngyàhn ge.
2. Nī dī bāt haih bīngo ga? /Léih Síujé/	2. Haih Léih Síujé ge.
3. Gó dī maht haih bīngo ga? /Wòhng Sàang/	3. Haih Wòhng Sàang ge.
4. Nī léuhng jī bējáu haih bīngo ga? /ngóh pàhngyáuh/	4. Haih ngóh pàhngyáuh ge.
5. Gó sàam go pìhnggwó haih bīngo ga? /gó go Yìnggwokyàhn/	5. Haih gó go Yìnggwokyàhn ge.

---

11. Response Drill

Ex: T: Bīn jī yùhnjíbāt haih néih ga? /hāak sīk/	T: Which ball point pen is yours?
S: Hāaksīk gó jī.	S: That (or the) black one.
1. Bīn gihn sēutsāam haih néih pàhngyáuh ga? /chèuhngdī/	1. Chèuhngdī gó gihn.
2. Bīn bá jē haih néih ga? /daaihdī/	2. Daaihdī gó bá.
3. Bīn bún syù haih néih ga? /saidī/	3. Saidī gó bún.
4. Bīn gihn lāangsāam haih néih ga? /sa'ahsei houh/	4. Sa'ahsei houh gó gihn.

217

5. Bīn deui hàaih haih néih ga?   5. Baat houh gó deui.
   /baat houh/

6. Bīn tìuh fu haih néih ga?   6. Dyún gó tìuh.
   /dyún/

---

12. Substitution Drill: Repeat the first sentence, then substitute as
    directed.

1. Ngóh nóu jùngyi yám bējáu.   1. Ngóh nóu jùngyi yám bējáu.
   I like to drink beer. =
   I like beer.

2. /kéuih/   2. Kéuih hóu jùngyi yám bējáu.
                                           He likes to drink beer.

3. /séung/   3. Kéuih séung yám bējáu.
                                           He'd like some beer.

4. /mēyéh/   4. Kéuih séung yám mēyéh a?
                                           What would he like to
                                           drink?

5. /jùngyi/   5. Kéuih jùngyi yám mēyéh a?
                                           What does he like ...?
                                           or (Polite)
                                           What does he want ...?

6. /gafē/   6. Kéuih jùngyi yám gafē.
                                           He likes coffee.

7. /m̀hjùngyi/   7. Kéuih m̀hjùngyi yám gafē.
                                           He does not like coffee.

8. /m̀hséung/   8. Kéuih m̀hséung yám gafē.
                                           He does not want any
                                           coffee.

9. /séung m̀hséung/   9. Kéuih séung m̀hséung yám gafē
                                           a?
                                           Would he like some coffee?

10. /hóu séung/   10. Kéuih hóu séung yám gafē.
                                            He'd like very much to
                                            have some coffee.

11. /hóu jùngyi/   11. Kéuih hóu jùngyi yám gafē.
                                            He likes coffee.

IV. CONVERSATIONS FOR LISTENING

       (On tape. Listen to tape with book closed.)

V. SAY IT IN CANTONESE

A. On the telephone, you say:

1. Hello, who are you calling?

2. Mr. Chang is out--may I take a message [lit: What is your business?]

3. What did you say your name was? Please speak louder.

4. Mrs. Ma has gone to work.

5. May I speak to Mr. Lee?

6. Please ask Miss Ho to come to the phone.

7. My phone number is _____.

8. Hello, what number did you say?

9. When is Mr. Lau coming home?

10. When he comes back I'll tell him.

B. And the other person responds:

1. Please ask Mr. Chang to come to the phone.

2. My name is Wong. Please ask Mr. Chang to call me when he gets back.

3. My name is _____. My phone number is _____.

4. Will she be home for lunch?

5. He's gone home.

6. You have the wrong number.

7. Just a minute, let me get a pen.

8. _____.

9. I don't know. Do you have a message?

10. Thank you.

Vocabulary Checklist for Lesson 9

1. aan (var: ngaan)	bf:	noon, midday
2. chēut gāai	VO:	go out (from one's own house)
3. cho	n/v:	mistake, make a mistake
4. Daaihsèngdī	Ph:	Speak louder!
5. dáng yātján (also dáng yātjahn)	Ph:	wait awhile
6. Daap cho sin!	Ph:	Wrong number! [caught-mistake-line]
7. dá	v:	hit
8. dihnwá	VO:	make a telephone call
9. dáng	v:	wait
10. dáng Person Verb	v:	allow, let Person do something; wait while Person does something.
11. dihnwá	n:	telephone
12. dím bun	TW:	1:30 o'clock

13. fàan	v:	return (to/from a place you habitually go to)
14. fàan gùng	VO:	go [return] to work
15. fàan hohk	VO:	to to school
16. fàanlàih	v:	come back, return (here)
17. fàan (ng)ūkkéi	VO:	go [return] home
18. gamseuhnghá	Ph:	approximately
19. ge	bf:	mark of the possessive. joins with preceding personal noun (or pronoun) to form possessive.
20. géidō houh?	Ph:	what number?
21. géisi? or géisìh?	QW:	when?
22. giu	v:	instruct, tell, order, call
23. góng Person jī	Ph:	tell someone
24. góng Person tèng	Ph:	tell someone
25. gùngyàhn	n:	servant, laborer
26. heui gāai	VO:	go out (from one's own house)
27. -jó	Vsuf:	verb suf. indicating accomplishment of the action
28. joi dálàih	Ph:	call back (on the phone)
29. lèhng	nu:	'and a little bit' in a number phrase
30. lìhng	nu:	zero
31. ló	v:	fetch, to go get (something)
32. ngaan	bf:	noon, midday
33. ngūkkéi or ūkkéi	PW:	home
34. sih	v:	business, affair, matter
35. sihk (ng)aan	VO:	eat lunch
36. sīn	adv/ss:	first
37. sin	n:	line, thread
38. tèng	v:	hear, listen to
39. tèng dihnwá	VO:	talk [listen] on the telephone
40. ūkkéi or ngūkkéi	PW:	home
41. wah ngoh jī	Ph:	tell me
42. wah yàhn tèng	Ph:	tell someone
43. wah yàhn jī	Ph:	tell someone
44. wán	v:	look for, search
45. wán yàhn	VO:	look someone up

46. heui/làih wán yàhn   Ph: come/go see someone
47. Wéi!   ex: Hello! (Telephone greeting)
48. (Yáuh) mēyéh sih a?   Ph: What is it you want? (i.e.,(on the phone)
                                   May I take a message?)
49. yáuh sih   VO: have something to attend to; have errand,
                                   business
50. yiu   auxV: going to, intend to

I. BASIC CONVERSATION

A. Buildup:

yàuhhaak	tourist

<u>Yàuhhaak</u>

bÍndouh?	where?
hái	location verb, variously translated. 'is located.'
hái bÍndouh a?	where is (it)?
jáudim	hotel
Màhnwàh Jáudim	Mandarin Hotel
Màhnwàh Jáudim hái bÍndouh a?	Where is the Mandarin Hotel?
Chéng mahn ...?	May I ask ...? polite form used in asking questions, equivalent to English: Could you please tell me ...?
Chéng mahn, Màhnwàh Jáudim hái bÍndouh a?	Could you please tell me where the Mandarin Hotel is?

<u>Búndeihyàhn</u>

búndeihyàhn	a native, person belonging to a place by ancestry and upbringing.
-bihn	side
gó bihn	over there, on that side
hái gó bihn	(it) is over there
Nē!	there! an exclamation accompanying pointing out something to somebody.
Nē!-hái gó bihn.	There!--over there.

<u>Yàuhhaak</u>

táidóu	see [look successfully = see]
táimhdóu	look, but don't see; don't see.

Deuihàyjyuh, ngóh táimhdóu.   Excuse me, I don't see it. O.r
   Gó bihn bǐndouh a?   there where?

                 Bǔndeihyàhn

   deuimihn   opposite, facing
   màhtàuh   pier, wharf
   màhtàuh deuimihn   opposite the pier
   Tīnsīng Màhtàuh   Star Ferry Pier
Hái Tīnsīng Màhtàuh deuimihn.   It's opposite the Star Ferry
                                          Pier.

                 Yàuhhaak

   gūngsī   department store
   yáuh móuh gūngsī a?   is there a department store?
   nǐjógán, (var: jógán)   hereabouts, close by
Nǐjógán yáuh móuh gūngsī a?   Is there a department store
                                          near here?

                 Bǔndeihyàhn

Yáuh.   Yes, there is.
   gàan   measure for buildings
Nē - gó bihn yáuh gàan.   There's one over there.
   ngàhnhòhng   bank
   gó gàan ngàhnhòhng   that bank
   gaaklèih   next to, adjacent
Hái gó gàan ngàhnhòhng gaaklèih.   Next to the bank.

                 Yàuhhaak

A! Táidóu laak! Mhgòi.   Oh, I see it! Thanks.

_____

B. Recapitulation:

                 Yàuhhaak

Chéng mahn, Màhnwàh Jáudim   Could you please tell me where
   hái bǐndouh a?   the Mandarin Hotel is?

                 Bǔndeihyàhn

Nē!--hái gó bihn.   There!--over there.

                 Yàuhhaak

Deuimàhjyuh, ngóh táimhdóu.   Excuse me, I don't see it.
   Gó bihn bǐndouh a?   Over there where?

                        223

Búndeihyàhn

Hái Tīnsīng Màhtàuh deuimihn.	It's opposite the Star Ferry Pier.

Yàuhhaak

Nījógán yáuh móuh gūngsí a?	Is there a department store near here?

Búndeihyàhn

Yáuh. Nē - gó bihn yáuh gàan. Hái gó gàan ngàhnhòhng gaak-lèih.	Yes, there is. There's one over there. It's next to the bank.

Yàuhhaak

A! Táidóu laak! Mhgòi.	Oh, I see it! Thanks.

II. NOTES

A. Culture Notes: <u>Restaurants</u>:

In this lesson we introduce two of the many names for different types of restaurants: <u>chāansāt</u>, and <u>chàhlàuh</u>. <u>Chāansāt</u> is the generic term for a restaurant serving Western food. (Western in contrast to Chinese, that is.) <u>chàhlàuh</u> is the word for Cantonese teahouse, mentioned in the notes for Lesson 5. In the teahouse you select what you want to eat from trays of hot snacks that are circulated up and down the aisles of the restaurant by vendor-girls. You don't have to order, just point. Very convenient for beginning language students. Of other names for restaurants, <u>chāantēng</u> refers to restaurants serving Western food. (<u>chāansāt</u> is the generic term, <u>chāantēng</u> is more elegant, used more frequently in restaurant names. Ex: <u>Méih Sām Chāantēng haih gàan chāansāt</u>. 'Maxim's Restaurant is a restaurant serving Western food.)

Restaurants serving Chinese food are called <u>jáugā</u>, <u>jáulàuh</u>, <u>faahndim</u>, <u>choigwún</u>, and <u>faahngwún</u>.

B. Structure Notes

1. <u>Placewords</u>.

Placeword is a name given to expressions which can, as the final element in the sentence, follow the location verb <u>hái</u>. Placewords can occupy the positions of subject, object, and modifier.

There are several different kinds of placewords:

1. Geographic names:

    Hèunggóng = Hong Kong

    Kéuih yìhgā hái Hèunggóng. = He is in Hong Kong now.

Geographic names may also function as ordinary nouns, though this is not their most common use.

    Ex: Bīngo wah yáuh   Who says there are two Hong
        leuhng go   Kongs?
        Hèunggóng a?

2. Locatives

Locatives are pronouns of place, whose meanings derive from position in relation to another element:

    Ex: nīdouh = 'here' [near-place]

                    in relationship to the speaker =
                    near the speaker

        gódouh = 'there' [distant-place]

                    in relationship to the speaker =
                    distant from the speaker

        deuimihn = opposite, facing [facing-face]

                    in relationship to speaker or other
                    place element: facing the point of
                    reference.

    Kéuih hái nīdouh.   He is here.

    Kéuih hái gódouh.   He is there.

    Kéuih hái deuimihn.   He is facing (this way).

    (See BC and Drill _6_)

Locatives may be preceded by placeword nouns in modification-head structure.

    Ex: Kéuih hái gaaklèih.   He is next door.
                            [adjacent]

        Kéuih hái ngàhnhòhng He is next door to the
        gaaklèih.   bank.

    (See BC and Drill _7_)

3. Some ordinary nouns double as placewords.

    Ex: chàhlàuh = teahouse

      a. as an ordinary noun:

        Gó gàan chàhlàuh   That teahouse is very
        hóu gwai.   expensive.

225

b. as a placeword:

| Wòhng Sàang hái chàhlàuh. | Mr. Wong is at the tea-house. |

(See Drill _2_)

4. Nouns and pronouns which are not placewords (cannot follow hái as final element in sentence) form place-word phrases by suffixing a locative or the boundword -douh 'place.'

Ex: Bún syù hái ngóh (nī)douh.	The book is (here) by me.
Bún syù hái Léih Sàang douh.	The book is at Mr. Lee's.
Bún syù hái tói (gó)douh.	The book is (there) on the table.

2. -douh, -syu = placeword formants

-douh 'place,' is a boundform, left-bound to the verb hái, or to one of the specifiers nī/gó/bīn, or to a noun or pronoun to form a place phrase.

Ex: 1. Wòhng Táai hái mhhái douh a?	Is Mrs. Wong at home? or here? or there? [i.e., at the place where the listener is]
Hái douh.	(She) is here.
Mhhái douh.	She's not here.
2. Kéuih hái nīdouh.	She's at this place.
3. Kéuih hái ngóh douh.	She's at my place. (here by me.)

-syu, 'place,' is another boundword of place, which can be substituted for -douh everywhere. In Hong Kong -douh seems favored by most speakers, but -syu is occasionally heard also.

3. hái = location verb, requiring placeword object.

a. hái occurs: (1) as the only verb in the sentence, and
(2) as one verb in a series of verbal expressions.

(1) as the only verb in the sentence:

aff: Kéuih hái Méihgwok.	He's in America.
neg: Kéuih mhhái Méihgwok.	He isn't in America.
q: Kéuih hái mhhái Méihgwok a?	Is he in America?

(See BC and Drills 1, 2, 3, 4)

(2) as one verb in a series of verbal expressions:

aff: Kéuih hái ūkkéi dáng ngóh.	She's waiting (<u>or</u> waited) for me at home.
neg: Kéuih m̀hái ūkkéi dáng ngóh.	She's not waiting (<u>or</u> didn't wait) for me at home.
q: Kéuih haih m̀haih hái ūkkéi dáng néih a?	Is she waiting (<u>or</u> did she wait) for you at home?

(See Drill <u>9</u>)

b. Translation of <u>hái</u> into English

When hái is the only verb in the sentence, it translates into English as the appropriate tense and person of the verb 'be,' with in/on/at/ added as necessary, according to the requirements of English grammar.

Ex: 1. Kéuih hái mèihgwok.	He is/was in	America.
2. Kéuih hái ūkkéi.	He is/was (at)	home.
3. Kéuih hái sèjihlàuh.	He is/was at	the office.
4. Kéuih hái gódouh.	He is/was	there.

When hái is one verb in a series of verbs, it translates into English as a preposition-- 'at,' 'on,' or 'in.'

Ex: Kéuih hái Mèihgwok dáng ngóh.	He waited/is waiting for me in America.

4. <u>Placeword yáuh Noun</u> sentence type.

The <u>Placeword yáuh Noun</u> sentence is a form of SVO sentence, with <u>yáuh</u> as 'there is,' 'there are,' 'there exists.'

Ex: aff: 1. Gaakléih yáuh (gàan) ngàhnhòhng.	Next door there is a bank.
neg: 2. Gaakléih móuh ngàhnhòhng.	There's no bank next door.
q: 3. Gaakléih yáuh móuh ngàhnhòhng a?	Is there a bank next door?

(See BC and Drills <u>11, 12, 13</u>)

5. Pivotal constructions: <u>PW yáuh SVO</u>

The <u>PW yáuh N</u> sentence can be expanded to <u>PW yáuh SVO</u>, with the S of the SVO standing as the object of the first verb (yáuh) and the subject of the verb which follows it. Such a construction, in which the object of V_1 is the subject of V_2, we call a pivotal construction.

Ex: Gaakléih yáuh yàhn sihk faahn.	Next door there are people (<u>or</u> there is someone) eating dinner.

(See Drill <u>14</u>)

227

6. **-dóu** = verb suffix, indicating successful accomplishment of action
   of the verb.

   a. Verbs which take the suffix **-dóu** include the following:

Verb		V-dóu	
tái	look	táidóu	see [look successfully]
wán	search, look for	wándóu	find [search success-fully]
máaih	buy	máaihdóu	buy [i.e. after over-coming obstacles]

   b. Illustrative examples:

   A. Tái m̀táidóu gó gàan   A: Do you see that bank?
      ngàhnhòhng a?

   B. Táidóu.   B: Yes, I see it.

   C. Táim̀dóu.   C: No, I don't see it.

   A. Nē, hái gó gàan jáudim   A: There--next to the hotel.
      gaaklèih.

   C. A, yìhgā táidóu laak.   C: Oh, now I see it.

   c. Verb forms of **V-dóu**:

       aff: táidóu

       neg: táim̀dóu (<u>or</u> m̀táidóu)

        q: tái m̀táidóu? (<u>or</u> tái m̀táidākdóu?)

       Of the negative forms **V-m̀dóu** is more common, though
   m̀táidóu also is said. Both question forms are common.

                    (See BC and Drill _13_)

                    ─────────────────

II. DRILLS

1. Expansion Drill: Students point nearby for <u>nīdouh</u>, away for <u>gódouh</u>.

    Ex: T: /Ngóh/Néih/Kéuih/   T: I, you, he.
        + S: Ngóh hái <u>nīdouh</u>.   S: I'm <u>here</u>;
        +   Néih hái <u>gódouh</u>.   you're <u>there</u>;
             Kéuih hái bīndouh a?   where's she?

    1. /ngóhdeih/néihdeih/kéuihdeih/   1. Ngóhdeih hái nīdouh;
                                             néihdeih hái gódouh;
                                             kéuihdeih hái bīndouh a?

    2. /Chàhn Sàang/Chàhn Táai/Chàhn   2. Chàhn Sàang hái nīdouh;
       Síujé/   Chàhn Táai hái gódouh;
                                            Chàhn Síujé hái bīndouh a?

    3. /tiuh fu/gihn sēutsāam/   3. Tiuh fu hái nīdouh;
       deui hàaih/   gihn sēutsāam hái gódouh;
                                            deui hàaih hái bīndouh a?

    4. /jī yùhnbāt/jī yùhnjíbāt/   4. Jī yùhnbāt hái nīdouh;
       bún syù/   jī yùhnjíbāt hái gódouh;
                                            bún syù hái bīndouh a?

    5. /dī pìhnggwó/dī cháang/dī jíu/   5. Dī pìhnggwó hái nīdouh;
                                            dī cháang hái gódouh;
                                            dī jíu hái bīndouh a?

    ────────────────────────

2. Conversation Drill: Carry on the suggested conversations
   following the pattern of the example.

    Ex: T: /jáudim/   hotel
        S1: Kéuih hái bīndouh a?   Where is (<u>or</u> was) he? /hotel/
        S2: Kéuih hái jáudim.   He is (or was) at the hotel.

    1. /ngàhnhòhng/   1. S1: Kéuih hái bīndouh a?
                                            S2: Kéuih hái ngàhnhòhng.

    + 2. /<u>chāansāt</u>/   2. S1: Kéuih hái bīndouh a?
         (<u>Western restaurant</u>)   S2: Kéuih hái chāansāt.

    + 3. /<u>chàhlàuh</u>/   3. S1: Kéuih hái bīndouh a?
         (<u>teahouse</u>)   S2: Kéuih hái chàhlàuh.

    4. /jáudim/   4. S1: Kéuih hái bīndouh a?
                                            S2· Kéuih hái jáudim.

    + 5. /<u>séjihlàuh</u>/   5. S1: Kéuih hái bīndouh a?
         (<u>office</u>)   S2: Kéuih hái séjihlàuh.

229

6. /gūngsī/

6. S1: Kéuih hái bīndouh a?
   S2: Kéuih hái gūngsī.

+ 7. /tòuhsyùgwún/
     (library)

7. S1: Kéuih hái bīndouh a?
   S2: Kéuih hái tòuhsyùgwún.

---

3. Expansion Drill:

Ex: T: Chàhn Táai m̀hhái
       ngūkkéi.
       /chāansāt/

T: Mrs. Chan is not at home.

    S: Chàhn Táai m̀hhái
       ngūkkéi, hái
       chāansāt.

S: Mrs. Chan is not at home,
   she's at the restaurant.

1. Kéuih m̀hhái tòuhsyùgwún.
   /gūngsī/
   He's not at the library.
   /department store/

1. Kéuih m̀hhái tòuhsyùgwún,
   hái gūngsī.
   He's not at the library,
   he's at the department
   store.

2. Léih Sàang m̀hhái gūngsī.
   /jáudim/

2. Léih Sàang m̀hhái gūngsī,
   hái jáudim.

3. Léih Síujé m̀hhái chāansāt.
   /séjihlàuh/

3. Léih Síujé m̀hhái chāansāt,
   hái séjihlàuh.

4. Chàhn Sàang m̀hhái séjihlàuh.
   /chāansāt/

4. Chàhn Sàang m̀hhái séjihlàuh,
   hái chāansāt.

+ 5. Màhnwàh Jáudim m̀hhái Daaih
     Douh Jùng. /Tīnsīng Màhtàuh
     deuimihn/
     The Mandarin Hotel is not on
     Queen's Road Central.
     /opposite the Star Ferry/

5. Màhnwàh Jáudim m̀hhái Daaih
   Douh Jùng, hái Tīnsīng
   Màhtàuh deuimihn.

+ 6. Go chē jaahm m̀hhái deuimihn.
+   /nī bihn/
     The bus stop is not across
     the street. /this side/

6. Go chē jaahm m̀hhái deuimihn,
   hái nī bihn.
   The car stop is not across
   the street, it's on this
   side.

+ 7. Méihgwok Ngàhnhòhng m̀hhái nī
     bihn. /deuimihn/
     The Bank of America is not on
     this side.

7. Méihgwok Ngàhnhòhng m̀hhái
   nī bihn, hái deuimihn.
   The Bank of America is
   not on this side, it's in
   front.

+ 8. Kéuih gàan ngūk m̀hhái Hèunggóng
     nī bihn. /Gáulùhng gó bihn/
     His house is not here on the
     Hong Kong side. /there on the
     Kowloon side/

8. Kʻuih gàan ngūk m̀hhái Hèunggóng nī bihn, hái Gáulùhng
   gó bihn.

9. Hèunggóng chāansāt m̀hhái gó
   bihn. /nī bihn/

9. Hèunggóng chāansāt m̀hhái
   góbihn, hái nī bihn.

10. Tīnsīng Máhtàuh m̀hhái gaaklèih.
    /deuimihn/

10. Tīnsīng Máhtàuh m̀hhái
    gaaklèih, hái deuimihn.

+ 11. Méihgwok Jáudim m̀hhái (nī)
      jógán. (Jùngwàahn/
      The American Hotel is not
      hereabouts. /Central District/

11. Méihgwok Jáudim m̀hhái
    (nī) jógán, hái Jùngwàahn.

12. Gó gàan gūngsī m̀hhái nī jógán.
    /Daaih Douh Jùng/

12. Gó gàan gūngsī m̀hhái nī
    jógán, hái Daaih Douh
    Jùng.

Comments: (1) Méihgwok Jáudim, 'American Hotel' is the Hong Kong
              Hilton, also called 'Hèiyìhdeuhn Jáudim'

          (2) (ng)ūk 'house,' is not the one you live in.
              ngūkkéi, 'home,' 'house one lives in'

---

4. Alteration Drill

    Ex: T: Wòhng Sàang hái
           m̀hhái ūkkéi a?

        T: Is Mr. Wong at home?

        S: Wòhng Sàang haih
           m̀hhaih hái ūkkéi a?

        S: Is Mr. Wong at home?

   1. Kéuih hái m̀hhái séjihlàuh a?

   1. Kéuih haih m̀hhaih hái
      séjihlàuh a?

   2. Chàhn Síujé bá jē hái m̀hhái
      nīdouh a?
      Is Miss Chan's umbrella
      here?

   2. Chàhn Síujé bá jē haih
      m̀hhaih hái nīdouh a?

   3. Hòh Táai gihn lāangsāam hái
      m̀hhái néih ūkkéi a?
      Is Mrs. Ho's sweater at
      your house?

   3. Hòh Táai gihn lāangsāam
      haih m̀hhaih hái néih
      ūkkéi a?

   Comment: a location question of the choice type may be either
            hái m̀hhái Placeword? or haih m̀hhaih hái Placeword?

---

5. Substitution Drill: Repeat first sentence, then substitute as
   directed.

   1. Méihgwok Jáudim hái bīndouh a?
      Where is the American Hotel?

   1. Méihgwok Jáudim hái bīndouh
      a?

   2. /Màhnwàh Jáudim/

   2. Màhnwàh Jáudim hái bīndouh
      a?

3. /Méihgwok Ngàhnhòhng/	3. Méihgwok Ngàhnhòhng hái bĭndouh a?
4. /Daaih Douh Jùng/	4. Daaih Douh Jùng hái bĭndouh a?
5. /Néih ge séjihlàuh/	5. Néih ge séjihlàuh hái bĭndouh a?
+ 6. /Dākfuh Douh Jùng/ Des Voeux Road Central	6. Dākfuh Douh Jùng hái bĭndouh a?
7. /Tìnsìng Máhtàuh/	7. Tìnsìng Máhtàuh hái bĭndouh a?

---

6. Expansion Drill

Ex: T: Làuh Síujé hái nĭdouh. T: Miss Lau is (or was) here.

S: Wòhng Síujé wah ngóh ji Làuh Síujé hái nĭdouh. S: Miss Wong told me Miss Lau was here.

1. Làuh Síujé hái gódouh.

1. Wòhng Síujé wah ngóh ji Làuh Síujé hái gódouh.

2. Làuh Síujé hái nĭ bihn.

2. Wòhng Síujé wah ngóh ji Làuh Síujé hái nĭ bihn.

3. Làuh Síujé hái gó bihn.

3. Wòhng Síujé wah ngóh ji Làuh Síujé hái gó bihn.

4. Làuh Síujé hái deuimihn.

4. Wòhng Síujé wah ngóh ji Làuh Síujé hái deuimihn.

5. Làuh Síujé hái gaaklèih.

5. Wòhng Síujé wah ngóh ji Làuh Síujé hái gaaklèih.

6. Làuh Síujé hái nĭjógán.

6. Wòhng Síujé wah ngóh ji Làuh Síujé hái nĭ jógán.

+ 7. Làuh Síujé hái mùhnháu.
Miss Làuh is at the door.
(doorway)

7. Wòhng Síujé wah ngóh ji Làuh Síujé hái mùhnháu.

---

7. Expansion Drill

Ex: T: Gàan ngàhnhòhng hái deuimihn.
/chē jaahm/ T: The bank is on the opposite side. /bus stop/

S: Gàan ngàhnhòhng hái chē jaahm deuimihn. S: The bank is opposite the bus stop.

232

1. Gàan gūngsí hái deuimihn.
   /jáudim/
2. Gàan jáudim hái deuimihn.
   /gūngsí/
3. Gàan ngàhnhòhng hái nī jógán.
   /chē jaahm/
   The bank is near here.
4. Go chē jaahm hái nījógán.
   /ngàhnhòhng/
   The bus stop is nearby. /bank/
5. Gàan gūngsí hái gaaklèih.
   /chaansāt/
   The department store is next
   door. /restaurant/
6. Gàan chāansāt hái gaaklèih.
   /tòuhsyùgwún/
7. Ngóh ge séjihlàuh hái nībihn.
   /jáudim/
   My office is on this side
   of the street. /hotel/

1. Gàan gūngsí hái jáudim
   deuimihn.
2. Gàan jáudim hái gūngsí
   deuimihn.
3. Gàan ngàhnhòhng hái chē
   jaahm nī jógán.
   The bank is near the bus
   stop, here.
4. Go chē jaahm hái ngàhnhòhng
   nī jógán.
   The bus stop is near the
   bank.
5. Gàan gūngsí hái chāansāt
   gaaklèih.
   The department store is
   next the restaurant.
6. Gàan chāansāt hái tòusyùgwún
   gaaklèih.
7. Ngóh ge séjihlàuh hái jáudim
   nī bihn.
   My office is this side
   of the street, on the side
   where the hotel is.

Comment on #7:

chàh-làuh	gūng-sí

	jáu-dim	séjih-làuh	ngàhn-hòhng

Ngóh ge séjihlàuh hái jáudim nī bihn. Ngóh,
séjihlàuh, and jáudim are all on the same side
of the street. Above, in refering to the dept.
store, speaker would say: Gūngsí hái chàhlàuh
gó bihn. The dept. store is on that side (away
from me) where the teahouse is.

8. Response Drill

   Ex: T: Méihgwok Jáudim
          hái bindouh a?
          /Daaih Douh Jūng/

       S: Méihgwok Jáudim hái
          Daaih Douh Jūng.

   T: Where's the Hilton Hotel?

   S: The Hilton Hotel is on Queen's
      Road Central.

1. Néih ge séjihlàuh hái bīndouh
   a? /Dākfuh Douh Jùng/

2. Méihgwok Jáudim hái bīndouh a?
   /Daaih Douh Jùng/

3. Daaih Douh Jùng hái bīndouh a?
   /Hèunggóng nī bihn/
   on the Hongkong side

+ 4. Màhnwàh Jáudim hái bīnbihn a?
   /deuimihn/ (which side?)

5. Tīnsīng Máhtàuh hái bīndouh a?
   /gó bihn/

6. Go chē jaahm hái bīndouh a?
   /ngàhnhòhng deuimihn/

7. Tòuhsyùgwún hái bīndouh a?
   /gaaklèih/

1. Ngóh ge séjihlàuh hái Dākfuh
   Douh Jùng.

2. Méihgwok Jáudim hái Daaih
   Douh Jùng.

3. Daaih Douh Jùng hái
   Hèunggóng nī bihn.

4. Màhnwàh Jáudim hái deuimihn.

5. Tīnsīng Máhtàuh hái gó bihn.

6. Go chē jaahm hái ngàhnhòhng
   deuimihn.

7. Tòuhsyùgwún hái gaaklèih.

Comment: People in Hongkong identify places as being 'on the
Hongkong side' or 'on the Kowloon side'. Kowloon and Hongkong are on opposite sides of the Hongkong Harbour.
Hèunggóng nī bihn 'on the Hongkong side' [Hongkong this
side] is said from the standpoint of a person who is on
the Hongkong side. To him the Kowloon side would be
Gáulùhng gó bihn 'on the Kowloon side' [Kowloon that side].

---

9. Combining Drill

    Ex: T: Kéuih hái Méihgwok
         Jáudim.
         Kéuih dáng ngóh.

       S: Kéuih hái Méihgwok
          Jáudim dáng ngóh.

T: He is (or was) at the American
   Hotel.
   He is (or was) waiting
   (or He waited) for me.

S: He is (or was) waiting, (or
   He waited) for me at the
   American Hotel.

1. Kéuih hái mùhnháu.
   Kéuih dáng pàhngyáuh.

2. Kéuih hái Tīnsīng Máhtàuh.
   Kéuih dáng pàhngyáuh.

3. Jèung Sàang hái Yahtbún.
   Jèung Sàang gaau Yahtmàhn.

4. Ngóh hái Hèunggóng.
   Ngóh hohk Gwóngdùngwá.

+ 5. Kéuih hái Méihgwok Ngàhnhòhng.
   Kéuih ló chín.
   He withdraws money.

1. Kéuih hái mùhnháu dáng
   pàhngyáuh.

2. Kéuih hái Tīnsīng Máhtàuh
   dáng pàhngyáuh.

3. Jèung Sàang hái Yahtbún
   gaau Yahtmàhn.

4. Ngóh hái Hèunggóng hohk
   Gwóngdùngwá.

5. Kéuih hái Méihgwok Ngàhn-
   hòhng ló chín.
   He's at the Bank of
   America withdrawing money.

6. Chèuhn Táai hái chē jaahm.
+   Chèuhn Táai dáng chē.
    Mrs. Cheun is waiting for
    the bus. [vehicle]
7. Wòhng Síujé hái Jùnggwok
   Chàhlàuh.
   Wòhng Síujé sihk faahn.

6. Chèuhn Táai hái chē jaahm
   dáng chē.

7. Wòhng Síujé hái Jùnggwok
   Chàhlàuh sihk faahn.

---

10. Expansion Drill

Ex: T: Néih bá jē hái
       gódouh. /Làuh
       Táai/

T: Your umbrella is over there.
   /Mrs. Lau/

S: Néih bá jē hái Làuh
   Táai gódouh.

S: Your umbrella is there by Mrs.
   Lau.

1. Jí yùhnbāt hái nīdouh. /ngóh/

1. Jí yùhnbāt hái ngóh nīdouh.

2. Gihn yúhlāu hái gódouh.
   /Wòhng Táai/

2. Gihn yúhlāu hái Wòhng Táai
   gódouh.

3. Ngóh bāau yīnjái hái nīdouh.
   /Léih Sàang/

3. Ngóh bāau yīnjái hái Léih
   Sàang nīdouh.

4. Tìuh kwàhn hái nīdouh. /ngóh/

4. Tìuh kwàhn hái ngóh nīdouh.

5. Gihn sāam hái gódouh. /kéuih/

5. Gihn sāam hái kéuih gódouh.

Comment: Nouns and pronouns which do not in themselves have any
         reference to place, can function in placeword ex-
         pressions when joined to a following locative.

---

11. Conversation Exercise

Ex: A: Nīdouh jógàn yáuh
       móuh chāansāt a?

A: Is there a western restaurant
   around here?

   B: Yáuh. Deuimihn yáuh
      gàan.

B: Yes. There's one across the
   street.

1. A. ....?

1. A. Nīdouh jógán yáuh móuh
      chāansāt a?

   B. Yáuh. Gó bihn ......

   B. Yáuh. Gó bihn yáuh gàan.

2. A. ....?

2. A. Nīdouh jógán yáuh móuh
      chāansāt a?

   B. Yáuh. Gaaklèih ......

   B. Yáuh. Gaaklèih yáuh gàan.

3. A. ....?

3. A. Nīdouh jógán yáuh móuh
      chāansāt a?

B. Yáuh. Dāk Fuh Douh Jùng ...	B. Yáuh. Dāk Fuh Douh Jùng yáuh gàan.
4. A. ....?	4. A. Nǐdouh jógán yáuh móuh chāansāt a?
B. Yáuh. Daaih Douh Jùng ...	B. Yáuh. Daaih Douh Jùng yáuh gàan.
5. A. ....?	5. A. Nǐdouh jógán yáuh móuh chāansāt a?
B. Yáuh. Ngàhnhòhng gaaklèih.	B. Yáuh. Ngàhnhòhng gaaklèih yáuh gàan.
6. A. ....?	6. A. Nǐdouh jógán yáuh móuh chāansāt a?
B. Yáuh. Gó gàan gūngsī deuimihn ...	B. Yáuh. Gó gàan gūngsī deuimihn yáuh gàan.

---

12. Substitution Drill: Repeat the first sentence then substitute as directed.

1. Chéng mahn, nǐdouh jógán yáuh móuh gūngsī a? Could you please tell me, is there a department store around here?	1. Nǐdouh jógán yáuh móuh gūngsī a?
2. /chē jaahm/	2. Chéng mahn, nǐ jógán yáuh móuh chē jaahm a?
3. /jáudim/	3. Chéng mahn, nǐdouh jógán yáuh móuh jáudim a?
4. /chāansāt/	4. Chéng mahn, nǐ jógán yáuh móuh chāansāt a?
5. /ngàhnhòhng/	5. Chéng mahn, nǐdouh jógán yáuh móuh ngàhnhòhng a?

---

13. Conversation Drill

Ex: T: /deuimihn/	T: opposite
+ S1: Néih tái m̀htáidóu deuimihn yáuh mēyéh a?	S1: Can you see what there is opposite us?
T: /jáudim/	T: hotel
S2: Deuimihn yáuh gàan jáudim.	S2: Opposite us there's a hotel. or There's a hotel across the street.

236

1. /gaaklèih/   1. A. Néih tái mhtáidóu gaak-
                             lèih yáuh mēyéh a?

   /gūngsī/   B. Gaaklèih yáuh gàan
                             gūngsī.

2. /gódouh/   2. A. Néih tái mhtáidóu gódouh
                             yáuh mēyéh a?

   /chāansāt/   B. Gódouh yáuh gàan chāansāt.

3. /deuimihn/   3. A. Néih tái mhtáidóu deui-
                             mihn yáuh mēyéh a?

   /chē jaahm/   B. Deuimihn yáuh go chē
                             jaahm.

4. /gaaklèih/   4. A. Néih tái mhtáidóu gaak-
                             lèih yáuh mēyéh a?

   /ngàhnhòhng/   B. Gaaklèih yáuh gàan
                             ngàhnhòhng.

6. /nī bihn/   5. A. Néih tái mhtáidóu nībihn
                             yáuh mēyéh a?

   /jáudim/   B. Nī bihn yáuh gàan jáudim.

---

14. Alteration Drill

      Ex: T: Gó go yàhn dá dihn-   T: That man is making a phone
             wá. /gódouh/   call/there.

          S: Gódouh yáuh go   S: Over there there's a man
             yàhn dá dihnwá.   making a phone call.

   1. Gó go yàhn wán néih.   1. Mùhnháu gódouh yáuh go yàhn
      /mùhnháu gódouh/   wán néih.
                                        There's a man at the door
                                        looking for you.

   2. Gó wái sīnsàang dáng chē.   2. Chē jaahm gódouh yáuh wái
      /chē jaahm gódouh/   sīnsàang dáng chē.

   3. Gó go Yīnggwokyàhn sihk chāan. 3. Chāansāt gódouh yáuh go
      /chāansāt gódouh/   Yīnggwokyàhn sihk chāan.

 + 4. Gó go Méihgwokyàhn tái syù.   4. Séjihlàuh gódouh yáuh go
      /séjihlàuh gódouh/ ([read-   Méihgwokyàhn tái syù.
      book], read)
      That American is reading.

   5. Gó go yàhn maaih cháang.   5. Mùhnháu yáuh go yàhn maaih
      /mùhnháu/   cháang.

   6. Gó go yàhn dá dihnwá.   6. Gó bihn yáuh go yàhn dá
      /gó bihn/   dihnwá.

237

Comment: Note that in the left hand column sentences above, of
the structure: <u>Noun Phrase</u> <u>Verb Phrase</u>, the nouns are

góo go yàhn = <u>that</u> person.

In the right hand column sentences, of the structure:
<u>Placeword</u> <u>yáuh</u> <u>Noun Phrase</u> <u>Verb Phrase</u>, the nouns are
un-specific:

go yàhn = '<u>a</u> person'.

This is characteristic of the <u>Placeword</u> <u>yáuh</u> ......
structure.

Compare: (1) Góo go yàhn hái góo bihn
dá dihnwá.

That man is making a
phone call over there.

(2) Góo bihn yáuh go yàhn dá
dihnwá.

Over there, there's some-
one making a phone call.

IV. CONVERSATIONS FOR LISTENING

(On tape. Refer to wordlist below as you listen.)

Unfamiliar terms, in order of occurrence:

1) yātján = dángyātjahn = 'in a little while'
2) wán m̀hdóu = can't find it, search but not successful

V. SAY IT IN CANTONESE

A. You ask a pedestrian:

1. Could you please tell me
where the Star Ferry is?

2. Could you please tell me
where the Hilton Hotel is?

3. Is there a car stop around
here?

4. Where is the Bank of America?

B. And he responds:

1. There! (pointing) It's
over there.

2. There! It's across the
street.

3. Yes, there's one opposite
the library.

4. The Bank of America is in
Central District.

C. You ask a friend:

1. Where is your umbrella?

2. Where is your office?

3. Can you make out (see
successfully) what that is
across the street?

D. And he replies:

1. It's here.

2. It's on Des Voeux Road
Central.

3. Across the street there's
a tea-house.

238

4. Who is over there waiting   4. It's my wife.
   for you?

5. Where is Mr. Wong's office?   5. It's next to my office.

6. Is Mr. Wong in his office now?   6. No, he's at home.

7. There's a man over there   7. Yes, he's my student.
   making a phone call--
   do you know him?

Vocabulary Checklist for Lesson 10

1. bīnbihn?	PW:	which side?
2. -bihn	bf:	side
3. bīndouh?	QW:	where?
4. búndeihyàhn	n:	a native of the place under discussion
5. chāansāt	n/PW:	western style restaurant
6. chàhlàuh	n/PW:	Cantonese style tea-house
7. chē	n:	vehicle: car, bus, or tram
8. chē jaahm	n/PW:	car stop (bus or tram stop)
9. chéng mahn	Ph:	'May I ask...?'
10. Daaih Douh Jùng	PW:	Queen's Road Central
11. Dakfuh Douh Jùng	PW:	Des Veoux Road Central
12. deuimihn	PW:	opposite side
13. -dóu	vs:	verb suffix indicating successful accomplishment of the action of the verb.
14. gàan	m:	M. for buildings
15. gaaklèih	PW:	next door
16. gódouh	PW:	there
17. gó bihn	PW:	over there, on that side
18. gūngsī	n/PW:	department store; office (of a commercial company)
19. hái	v:	location verb, translated as: is in/at/on
20. Hèunggóng	PW:	Hong Kong
21. jaahm	n:	station, stop (as train station, bus stop)
22. jáudim	n/PW:	hotel
23. jógán	PW:	nearby, hereabouts
24. Jùngwàahn	PW:	Central District

25. ló chín	VO:	withdraw money (from bank)
26. máhtàuh	n/PW:	pier
27. Màhnwàh Jáudim	PW:	Mandarin Hotel
28. mahn	v:	ask
29. Méihgwok Jáudim	PW:	'American Hotel,' (in HK, the Hong Kong Hilton)
30. Méihgwok Ngàhnhòhng	PW:	Bank of America
31. mùhnháu	n/PW:	doorway
32. Nē!	ex:	'There!' an exclamation used when pointing out something to someone
33. nībihn	PW:	this side
34. nīdouh	PW:	here
35. nījógán	PW:	closeby, hereabouts
36. ngàhnhòhng	n/PW:	bank
37. ngūk (or ūk)	n/PW:	house
38. séjihlàuh	n/PW:	office
39. táimhdóu	VP:	can't see
40. táidóu	VP:	see [look successfully]
41. tái mhtáidóu?	VP:	can [you] see?
42. tái syù	VO:	read (a book)
43. Tīnsīng Máhtàuh	PW:	Star Ferry Pier
44. tòuhsyùgwún	n/PW:	library
45. ūk (var: ngūk)	n/PW:	house
46. yàhnhaak	n:	tourist

BASIC CONVERSATION

A. **Buildup:**

(A brother and sister are sharing a taxi to work)

saimúi   younger sister

Saimúi

mhgeidāk	forgot, forget
daai	carry, take or bring along
mhgeidāk daai chín	forgot to bring money
tìm	sentence suffix, indicating taken by surprise

Ngóh mhgeidāk daai chín   I forgot to bring my money!
   tìm!

Aiya! Ngóh mhgeidāk daai chín   Aiya! I forgot to bring my
   tìm!   money!

 agō   elder brother

Agō

Mhgányiu--ngóh yáuh.   Never mind--I have (some).

(He hands $3.00 to the driver)

jáaufàan	give back change (give change--return)
jáaufàan sàam hòuh	give back 30¢ change
dāk laak	that will be all right

Jáaufàan sàam hòuh dāk laak.   Give me 30¢ change, that'll
                                 be OK.

sìgēi   driver, cab driver,
                                 chauffeur

Sìgēi

mòuhdāk   not have available
Ngóh mòuhdāk jáau.   I don't have any change.
                                 [don't have (money) avail-
                                 able to give change]

sàan ngán   small coins
Néih yáuh móuh sàan ngán a?   Do you have any small coins?

Agō

Yáuh, yáuh.   Yes, I have.

m̀hginjó	lose/lost (something), 'nowhere to be seen' exclamation of distress
Yí!	
Yí! M̀hginjó gé?	Eh? Disappeared?
A--hái douh.	Oh--they're here.
nàh!	here!
Nàh, nǐdouh chāt hòuhjí.	Here, here's 70¢.

(The two get out of the taxi)

Agō

yuhng	use
Néih yiu chín yuhng.	You'll need some money to use.
je	lend
-jyuh	temporarily, for a short time
jejyuh béi néih	lend to you
Ngóh nǐdouh jejyuh béi néih sīn lā.	I'll lend you some (of what I have) here.
Yiu géidō a?	How much do you need?

Saimúi

Sahp mān gau laak.	Ten dollars will be enough.

Agō

baak	hundred
baak mān	hundred dollars
jí	paper. here, paper money, i.e. $ bill
baak mān jí	hundred dollar bill
jèung	measure for bank notes
jèung yāt baak mān jí	a one-hundred-dollar bill
dāk	have only, only have
ja	jē + a = ja
Ngóh dāk jèung yāt baak mān jí ja.	I only have a hundred dollar bill.
cheunghòi	break (a large note for ones of smaller denomination)

Dáng ngóh cheunghòi béi néih
lā.

I'll get it changed and give
you (the money).

(They stop in at a bank to change the $100
bill. The elder brother addresses a teller:)

Agō

cheunghoi jèung yāt baak mān jí
tùhng ngóh

split a hundred dollar bill
for me, on my behalf

Ìhgòi néih tùhng ngóh cheunghòi
jèung yāt baak mān jí lā.

Would you please change a
hundred dollar bill for me.

Síujé

dāk

OK, sure

Dāk. Sahp jèung sahp mān jí
hóu ìhhóu a?

Sure. Are 10 ten's OK?

Agō

Hóu aak.

Fine.

B. Recapitulation:

Saimúi

Aiya! Ngóh ìhgeidāk daai chín
tìm!

Aiya! I forgot to bring my
money!

Ìhgányiu--ngóh yáuh.

Never mind--I have some.

(He hands $3.00 to the driver)

Jáaufàan sàam hòuh dāk laak.

Give me 30¢ change, that'll
be OK.

Sīgēi

Ngóh móuhdāk jáau. Néih yáuh
móuh sáan ngán a?

I don't have any change. Do
you have any small coins?

Agō

Yáuh, yáuh. Yí! Ìhginjó gé?
A--hái douh. Nàh, nídouh
chāt hòuhjí.

Yes, I have. Eh? Disappeared?
Oh, they're here. Here,
here's 70¢.

(They get out of the taxi)

Agō

Néih yiu chín yuhng. Ngóh nídouh
jejyuh béi néih sīn lā. Yiu

You'll need some money to use.
I'll lend you some. How much

géidō a?	do you need?

<u>Saimúi</u>

Sahp mān gau laak.	Ten dollars will be enough.

<u>Agō</u>

Ngóh dāk jèung yāt baak mān jí ja. Dáng ngóh cheunghòi béi néih lā.	I only have a hundred dollar bill. I'll get it changed and give you (the money).

(They stop in at a bank to change the $100
bill. The elder brother addresses a teller:)

<u>Agō</u>

Mhgòi néih tùhng ngóh cheunghòi jèung yāt baak mān jí lā.	Would you please change a hundred dollar bill for me.

<u>Síujé</u>

Dāk. Sahp jèung sahp mān jí hóu mhhóu a?	Sure. Are ten 10's OK?

<u>Agō</u>

Hóu aak.	Fine.

II. NOTES

1. <u>sìn</u>, 'first,'

    <u>sìn</u>, 'first,' attaches to the end of a clause sentence, or a minor sentence consisting of a timeword, with the implication that something else is to follow.

Ex: 1. Dáng ngóh ló jí bāt sìn lā.	1. Let me get a pencil first-- (and then I can write down the number.)
2. Ngóh nīdouh jejyuh béi néih sìn lā.	2. I'll lend you (some money) first--(and then you can get through the day.)
3. A: Dāk meih a?	3. A: Ready yet?
B: Meih--dángjahn sìn lā.	B: Not yet--wait a minute first--(then I'll be ready.)

(See BC)

    Students of Mandarin will recall that the Mandarin equivalent of <u>sìn</u>, <u>syān</u>, occupies a different sentence position. In Mandarin <u>syān</u> comes before the verb, rather than coming at the end of the clause.

    Ex: Děng wǒ syān ná (yì) jř bǐ lái.   Let me first get a pen.

244

2. Dāk = OK, will do, all right

    a. Forms:

aff: dāk	That's OK, that'll do, all right, can do.
neg: m̀hdāk	That's not OK, that won't do, can't.
q: dāk m̀hdāk a?	Will that be all right?
Ex: 1. Ngóh séung yìhgā sihk faahn, dāk m̀hdāk a?	1. I'd like to eat now, OK?
2. M̀hdāk. Yiu dáng yāt- jahn sìn.	2. Not OK. We have to wait awhile.
3. Dāk. Sihk faahn lā.	3. Sure. Eat!

                    (See BC)

    b. Dāk joins with laak in the affirmative and meih in the negative and question forms to form fixed phrases:

aff: dāk laak.	It's OK now (change from before) It's ready.
neg: meih dāk	Not OK yet, it's not ready, it's not right yet.
q: dāk meih a?	Is it ready yet? Is it OK yet?
Ex: 1. Ngóh gihn chèuhng-sāam dāk meih a?	Is my dress ready yet?
2. Meih dāk.	Not OK yet.
3. Dāk laak. Néih sikháh sìn lā.	It's ready. Try it on!

3. Dāk + quantity phrase = have only, get only, obtain only:

    dāk in this sense has a quantity phrase as its object, with the implication that the quantity is insufficient. It contrasts with yáuh, 'have,' which does not have the connotation of insufficiency.

1. Ngóh dāk léuhng gihn sēutsāam.	I have only two shirts.
2. Ngóh yáuh léuhng gihn sēutsāam.	I have two shirts.

             (See BC and Drill 11)

    dāk, as 'have insufficient amount,' is a defective verb--that is, it does not have all three forms: affirmative, negative, and question. It is not used in the negative form, and does not form the choice question regularly:

Forms:

aff: Dāk jèung yāt baak   Have only a $100 bill.
     mān jí.

neg: -- --   -- --

q: Haih m̀haih dāk   Do you have only a $100 bill?
   jèung yāt baak
   mān jí a?

4. **yáuhdāk + verb** = 'have available to ..$\overset{V}{.}$.,' 'have available for .$\overset{V}{.}$ing,'

   dāk used between the verb **yáuh** (or its negative **móuh**) and a second verb, forms a verb phrase (VP) 'have (or not have) available for .$\overset{V}{.}$ing.'

   The basic meaning of **dāk** in a **yáuhdāk V** is 'can.'

   Ex: aff: yáuhdāk maaih   have-can-sell, have for sale
       neg: móuhdāk maaih   don't have-available for sale
       q: yáuh móuh dāk maaih   are there any available for
          a?   sale?

   (See BC and Drills 7, 8)

5. **tìm!** sentence suffix indicating that the speaker has been taken by surprise.

   tìm! adds the connotation that the situation expressed in the sentence is different from what the speaker expected.

   This **tìm!** perhaps is derived from **tìm**, 'more,' 'in addition,' which you encountered before in Lesson 4, but differs both in implication and in expressive intonation.

   tìm! expressing surprise is a stressed syllable in its sentence, but **tìm**, 'in addition' does not receive heavy sentence stress. Further, **tìm**, 'in addition' can be followed by another sentence suffix, but **tìm!**, expressing surprise, cannot.

   Ex: 1. Joi dáng ngóh géi   'Please wait for me a few
            fānjūng tìm lā.   minutes more.'
       2. M̀géidāk tìm!   I forgot it! (having just
                                    realized it)

   (See BC and Drill 3)

246

6. -dò and -síu phrases of indefinite amounts

a. -dò 'large amount' and -síu 'small amount' combine with preceding
   hóu- and others to form phrases of indefinite amounts.

   Ex: 1. hóudò   a lot, many, much
       2. géidò   quite a lot
       3. móuhgéidò   not very much
       4. hóusíu   very little, very few
       5. sèsíu   a little
       6. síusíu   just a little, just a few

b. These -dò/-síu phrases can be used as modifier to a following
   nominal construction or as head in a nominal construction.

   Ex:
       as modifier:
       Ngóh yáuh hóudò chín.   I have a lot of money.
       as head:
       Kéuih dōu yáuh hóudò.   He has a lot too.

c. sèsíu and síusíu modify mass nouns only, directly preceding the
   noun. As head structures they are used only in connection
   with mass nouns.

   Ex: 1. Béi sèsíu tòhng ngóh   Please give me a little sugar.
          lā.

       2. Béi síusíu tòhng   Please give me just a tiny
          ngóh lā.   bit of sugar.

       3. Sèsíu hóu lā.   A little bit is fine.
                                 (Someone asked how much sugar
                                 you want in your coffee.)

       4. Síusíu hóu lā.   Just a tiny bit is fine.

d. The following -dò/-síu phrases can modify individual and mass
   nouns directly:

-dò/-síu	Ind/Mass Noun	
1. hóudò	⎫ sēutsāam	1. many shirts; much sugar
2. géidò	⎬ tòhng	2. quite a few shirts; quite a bit of sugar
3. móuhgéidò	⎪	3. not many shirts; not much sugar
4. (QW) géidō	⎪ ....?	4. how many shirts?; how much sugar?
5. hóusíu	⎭	5. very few shirts; very little sugar

   (See Drills 11, 12)

247

e. The following can precede a Measure (+ Noun):

-dò	M	N	
hóudò	gihn	sēutsāam	many [M] shirts
móuhgéidò	"	"	not many [M] shirts
géidò (& géidõ?)	"	"	quite a few [M] shirts (how many [M] shirts?)

7. cheung and cheunghòi 'to change money into smaller denomination'

These both form VO phrases with a following money phrase.

cheung = change into (what you want) (followed by denomination wanted)

cheunghòi = change, i.e., break (a big bill) (followed by denomination held.)

Ex: cheung sahp mān jí   = change into $10 bills

cheunghòi jèung sahp mān jí = break a $10 bill

8. Sentence suffix gé

gé represents sentence suffix ge, 'that's the way it is' plus rising intonation for uncertainty and doubt.

Ex: Yí-m̀hgìnjó gé?   Eh? (They're) lost?

(See BC)

III. DRILLS

1. Alteration Drill

    Ex: 1. T: Nī go haih cháang   T: This is an orange.
            làih ge.

           S: Nàh--nīdouh yáuh   S: Here--here's an orange.
             go cháang.

1. Nī dī haih ngàuhyuhk làih ge.
                               1. Nàh--nīdouh yáuh dī ngàuh-
                                   yuhk.

2. Nī jī haih heiséui làih ge.
                               2. Nàh--nīdouh yáuh jī heiséui.

3. Nī dī haih tòhng làih ge.
                               3. Nàh--nīdouh yáuh dī tòhng.

4. Nī go haih pìhnggwó làih ge.
                               4. Nàh--nīdouh yáuh go pìhnggwó.

5. Nī jèung haih sahp mān jí
   làih ge.
                               5. Nàh--nīdouh yáuh jèung sahp
                                   mān jí.

+ 6. Nī go haih ńgh hòuhjí ngán
    làih ge. (ngán = coin)
                               6. Nàh--nīdouh yáuh go ńgh
                                   hòuhjí ngán.

7. Nī go haih yāt mān ngán
   làih ge.
                               7. Nàh--nīdouh yáuh go yāt mān
                                   ngán.

    a. Repeat, in **reverse**, teacher cueing with yáuh sentences,
       students responding with haih sentences.

---

2. Substitution Drill

    Ex: T: Béi ńgh hòuhjí   T: Give me 50¢. /give back change/
         ngóh. /jáaufàan/

       S: Jáaufàan ńgh hòuhjí   S: Give me back 50¢ change.
         ngóh.

1. Béi sahp mān ngóh. /je/
   Give me ten dollars.
                               1. Je sahp mān ngóh.
                               Lend me ten dollars.

2. Béi jī bāt ngóh. /ló/
                               2. Ló jī bāt ngóh.
                               Bring me a pen(cil).

3. Béi gihn sēutsāam ngóh. /máaih/
                          3. Máaih gihn sēutsāam ngóh.
                             Buy me a shirt. (Buy a
                             shirt to give me.)

4. Béi go dihnwá ngóh. /dá/
   Give me a phone call.
   (also: Give me a phone.)
                               4. Dá go dihnwá ngóh.

+ 5. Béi jèung sahp mān jí ngóh.
    /wuhn/
    Give me a ten-dollar bill.
    /Change (into)/
                             5. Wuhn jèung sahp mān jí ngóh.
                             Change (this) into a ten-
                             dollar bill for me. (The
                             speakers is holding small

> change and bills that
> he wants converted into a
> larger bill.)

Comment: <u>wuhn</u> 'exchange,' 'change (into)' in reference to
money, is usually used when you have small denominations that you want to change for larger. When you
have a large bill you want to break into smaller
denominations you use the verb <u>cheunghòi</u> 'break
(a bill into smaller denominations)', 'change.'
(See BC). <u>wuhn</u> also means to exchange one currency
for another, as exchange HK money for US money.

a. Repeat the above drill as expansion drill thus:

> T: Jáaufàan ǹgh hòuhjí ngóh.
>   Give me back 50¢ change.
>
> S: Ṁhgòi néih jáaufàan ǹgh hòuhjí ngóh lā.
>   Please give me back 50¢ change.

---

3. Substitution Drill

> Ex: T: Ṁhngāamjeuk bo.   It doesn't fit, that's for sure.
>
>   S: Ṁhngāamjeuk tìm!   It doesn't fit, shucks!
>   (<u>tìm</u> here carries the im-
>   plication that you are dis-
>   appointed. I like it, but
>   it doesn't fit - shucks.)

1. Maaihsaai bo.   1. Maaihsaai tìm!

+ 2. Ṁhhái douh bo.((He's) not here.)2. Ṁhhái douh tìm! (douh=place)

3. Chēutjó gāai bo.   3. Chēutjó gāai tìm!

4. Ṁhgau chín bo.   4. Ṁhgau chín tìm!

5. Tèng ṁhdóu bo.   5. Tèng ṁhdóu tìm!
   I can't hear it.

6. Wán ṁhdóu bo.   6. Wán ṁhdóu tìm!
   (I) can't find (it).

7. Dáṁhdóu bo.   7. Dáṁhdóu tìm!
   I can't reach him by phone.
   <u>or</u>
   He can't be reached by phone.
   (ambiguous as to whether
   he has no phone or his phone
   is busy.)

8. Ṁhgeidāk bo.   8. Ṁhgeidāk tìm!
   (I) forgot.

a. Reverse roles, teacher cueing with sentences in right hand
   column, students responding with those at the left.

---

4. Expansion Drill

Ex: T: Yāt baak mān jí.   T: This is a $100 bill.

    S: Mhgòi néih cheunghòi S: Please break this $100 bill
       jèung yāt baak   for me.
       mān jí ngóh lā!

1. /ńgh hòuhjí ngán/   1. Mhgòi néih cheunghòi go
                                  ńgh hòuhjí ngán ngóh lā!

2. /yāt mān ngán/   2. Mhgòi néih chèunghòi go
                                  yāt mān ngán ngóh lā!

3. /sahp mān jí/   3. Mhgòi néih chèunghòi jèung
                                  sahp mān jí ngóh lā!

4. /ńgh mān jí/   4. Mhgòi néih chèunghòi jèung
                                  ńgh mān jí ngóh lā!

5. /ńgh baak mān jí/   5. Mhgòi néih chèunghòi jèung
                                  ńgh baak mān jí ngóh lā!

6. /yāt baak mān jí/   6. Mhgòi néih chèunghòi jèung
                                  yāt baak mān jí ngóh lā!

a. Repeat, teacher writing visual cues ($100, 50¢, etc.)
   on the blackboard, students responding chèunghòi sentence.

   T: Write: $100
   S: Mhgòi néih chèunghòi jèung yāt baak mān jí ngóh lā!

---

5. Expansion Drill

Ex: T: Kéuih yámsaai dī   T: He drank up all the soft
       heiséui.   drinks.

    S: Kéuih yámsaai dī   S: He drank up all the soft
       heiséui. Gám,   drinks. So I don't have
       ngóh móuhdāk yám   any [available to drink],
       tìm.   blast it!

1. Kéuih yuhngsaai dī chín.   1. Kéuih yuhngsaai dī chín.
   He used up all the money.   Gám, ngóh móuhdāk yuhng
                                  tìm.

2. Kéuih sihksaai dī faahn.   2. Kéuih sihksaai dī faahn.
                                  Gám, ngóh móuhdāk sihk tìm.

251

3. Kéuih lósaai dī chín.   3. Kéuih lósaai dī chín.
                          Gám, ngóh móuhdāk ló tìm.

4. Kéuih yámsaai dī gafē.   4. Kéuih yámsaai dī gafē.
                          Gám, ngóh móuhdāk yám tìm.

---

6. Expansion Drill

    Ex· 1. T: Yìnggwok yáuh   T: In England there is Japanese
             Yahtbún bējáu   beer for sale. /nod/America/
             maaih. /nod/
             Méihgwok/

          S: Méihgwok dōu   S: In America also they have it
             yáuhdāk maaih.   for sale. [America also have-
                                 can-sell.]

         2. T: Yìnggwok yáuh   T: England has Japanese beer for
             Yahtbún bējáu   sale. /shake/America/
             maaih. /shake/
             Méihgwok/

          S: Yìnggwok yáuh   S: England has Japanese beer for
             Yahtbún bējáu   sale but in America they
             maaih, daahn-   don't have it for sale.
             haih Méihgwok   [America not have-can-sell.]
             móuhdāk maaih.

1. Ngóh yáuh chín yuhng.   1. Ngóh yáuh chín yuhng, ngóh
   /nod/ngóh pàhngyáuh/   pàhngyáuh dōu yauhdāk
                               yuhng.

2. Kéuih yáuh chàh yám.   2. Kéuih yáuh chàh yám, daahn-
   /shake/ngóh/   haih ngóh móuhdāk yám.

3. Chāansāt yáuh chàh yám.   3. Chāansāt yáuh chàh yám,
   /nod/chàhlàuh/   chàhlàuh dōu yáuhdāk yám.

4. Kéuih yáuh yúhlāu jeuk.   4. Kéuih yáuh yúhlāu jeuk,
   /shake/Léih Sàang/   daahnhaih Léih Sàang móuh-
                               dāk jeuk.

5. Hèunggóng yáuh Jùngmàhn syú   5. Hèunggóng yáuh Jùngmàhn syù
   maaih. /nod/Yahtbún/   maaih, Yahtbún dōu yáuh-
                               dāk maaih.

---

7. Follow Drill

Ex: T: Ngóh séung hohk   T: I'm thinking of studying
      Gwóngdùngwá.   Cantonese.

    S: Bīndouh yáuhdāk   S: Where can one study (it)?
      hohk a?   [Where have-can-study?]

1. Ngóh séung hohk Gwokyúh.   1. Bīndouh yáuhdāk hohk a?
2. Ngóh yiu dá dihnwá.   2. Bīndouh yáuhdāk dá a?
3. Ngóh séung sihk faahn.   3. Bīndouh yáuhdāk sihk a?
4. Ngóh séung yám gafē.   4. Bīndouh yáuhdāk yám a?
5. Ngóh séung máaih lāangsāam.   5. Bīndouh yáuhdāk maaih a?
   /maaih/
6. Ngóh séung máaih chē. /maaih/   6. Bīndouh yáuhdāk maaih a?

---

8. Alteration Drill

Ex: T: Gó júng chē, bīn-   T: That kind of car--where is it
      douh yáuhdāk   available for sale?
      maaih a?   /Hongkong/
      /Hèunggóng/

    S: Gó júng chē, Hèung-   S: That kind of car--is it for
      góng yáuh móuhdāk   sale in Hongkong? or
      maaih a?   Can you buy that kind of car
                                  in Hongkong?

1. Nī júng bīu, bīndouh yáuhdāk   1. Nī júng bīu, Yahtbún yáuh
   maaih a? /Yahtbún/   móuhdāk maaih a?
2. Nī júng pìhnggwó, bīndouh   2. Nī júng pìhnggwó, Jùnggwok
   yáuhdāk maaih a? /Jùnggwok/   yáuh móuhdāk maaih a?
3. Nī júng gafē, bīndouh yáuhdāk   3. Nī júng gafē, chāansāt
   yám a? /chāansāt/   yáuh móuhdāk yám a?
4. Nī júng béng, bīndouh yáuhdāk   4. Nī júng béng, Màhnwàh Jáudim
   sihk a?/Màhnwàh Jáudim/   yáuh móuhdāk sihk a?
5. Nī júng bāt, bīndouh yáuhdāk   5. Nī júng bāt, Hèunggóng yáuh
   maaih a? /Hèunggóng/   móuhdāk maaih a?

253

9. Expansion Drill

      Ex: T: Jáaufàan ngh hòuhjí   T: Give me back 50¢
              béi ngóh lā.

         S: Jáaufàan ngh hòuhjí   S: It'll be OK to give me back 50¢.
             béi ngóh dāk laak.   (You can keep the rest)
                                        [Give me back 50¢, then it
                                        will be OK.]

1. Mhgòi néih wah kéuih jí ngóh   1. Mhgòi néih wah kéuih jí ngóh
   mhfàanlàih sihk faahn la.   mhfàanlàih sihk faahn
                                    dāk laak. (i.e. you don't
                                    need to do anything fur-
                                    ther)

2. Mhgòi néih giu kéuih hái chē   2. Giu kéuih hái chē jaahm
   jaahm dáng ngóh lā.   dáng ngóh dāk laak.
                                    (i.e. doesn't need to come
                                    all the way to the house)

3. Giu kéuih hái jógán máaih lā.   3. Giu kéuih hái jógán máaih
                                    dāk laak. (i.e. doesn't
                                    have to go to town)

4. Daai yih baak mān lā.   4. Daai yih baak mān dāk laak.

5. Jejyuh baak lèhng mān béi   5. Jejyuh baak lèhng mān béi
   ngóh lā.   ngóh dāk laak.

6. Béi sáanjí ngóh lā.   6. Béi sáanjí ngóh dāk laak.

7. Ló béi kéuih lā.   7. Ló béi kéuih dāk laak.

8. Yuhng yùhnbāt sé lā.   8. Yuhng yùhnbāt sé dāk laak.

---

10. Response Drill

      Ex: 1. T: Néih gau mhgau chín máaih bējáu a? /nod/
           S: Gau. Ngóh ngāamngāam gau chín máaih.

         2. T: Néih gau mhgau chín máaih hàaih a? /shake/
           S: Mhgau. Ngóh mhgau chín máaih.

1. Néih gau mhgau chín máaih   1. Gau. Ngóh ngāamngāam gau
   yùhnbāt a? /nod/   chín máaih.

2. Néih gau mhgau chín máaih   2. Mhgau. Ngóh mhgau chín
   pìhnggwó a? /shake/   máaih.

3. Néih gau mhgau chín máaih   3. Gau. Ngóh ngāamngāam gau
   yīnjái a? /nod/   chín máaih.

4. Néih gau mhgau chín máaih   4. Gau. Ngóh ngāamngāam gau
   cháang a? /nod/   chín máaih.

5. Néih gau m̀hgau chín máaih   5. M̀hgau. Ngóh m̀hgau chín máaih.
   sēutsāam a? /shake/

6. Néih gau m̀hgau chín máaih   6. M̀hgau. Ngóh m̀hgau chín máaih.
   hàaih a? /shake/

---

11. Expansion & Substitution Drill

+ Ex: 1. T: Ngóh dāk hóusíu   T: I have very little money.
  +   chín. /houdò/   /a lot/
           (very little)

         S: Ngóh dāk hóusíu   S: I have very little money, but
            chín, daahnhaih   he has a lot.
            kéuih yáuh
            hóudò.

    2. T: Kéuih yáuh hóudò   T: He has a lot money. /very
          chín. /hóusíu   little/
          ja/

         S: Kéuih yáuh hóudò   S: He has a lot of money, but I
            chín, daahnhaih   have very little.
            ngóh dāk hóusíu
            ja.

  1. Kéuih yáuh hóudò chín.   1. Kéuih yáuh hóudò chín,
+   /móuhgéidò ja/   daahnhaih ngóh móuhgéidò
     /not much/   ja.
                                    He has a lot of money,
                                    but I don't have much.

  2. Ngóh móuhgéidò chín.   2. Ngóh móuhgéidò chín, daahn-
+   /géidò ga/   haih kéuih yáuh géidò ga.
     /quite a lot/   I don't have much money,
                                    but he has quite a lot.

  3. Kéuih yáuh géidò chín.   3. Kéuih yáuh géidò chín, daahn-
     /sèsíu ja/   haih ngóh dāk sèsíu ja.

  4. Ngóh yáuh sèsíu chín.   4. Ngóh yáuh sèsíu chín, daahn-
     /hóudò ga/   haih kéuih yáuh hóudò ga.
     /much, a lot/   I have a little money,
     I have a little money.   but he has a lot.

  5. Kéuih yáuh hóudò chín.   5. Kéuih yáuh hóudò chín, daahn-
     /hóusíu ja/   haih ngóh dāk hóusíu ja.

  6. Ngóh yáuh hóusíu chín.   6. Ngóh yáuh hóusíu chín, daahn-
     /géidò/   haih kéuih yáuh géidò ga.

7. Kéuih yáuh géidò chín.
/sèsiu ja/
/just a little/

7. Kéuih yáuh géidò chín, daahnhaih ngóh dāk sèsiu ja.

8. Ngóh yáuh sèsiu chín.
/hóudò ga/

8. Ngóh yáuh sèsiu chín, daahnhaih kéuih yáuh hóudò ga.

9. Kéuih yáuh géidò pàhngyáuh.
/móuhgéidò ja/
/not many/

9. Kéuih yáuh géidò pàhngyáuh,
daahnhaih ngóh dāk móuh-
géidò ja.
He has quite a few friends,
but I have not many.

10. Ngóh móuhgéidò pàhngyáuh.
/hóudò/
/many, a lot/

10. Ngóh móuhgéidò pàhngyáuh,
daahnhaih kéuih yáuh hóudò.

11. Kéuih yáuh hóudò pàhngyáuh.
/hóusiu ja/
/just a few/

11. Kéuih yáuh hóudò pàhngyáuh,
daahnhaih ngóh dāk hóusiu
ja.

Comment: 1) ja (pronounced [jə] is a fusion of jē and a, and
implies 'not much,' 'merely.'

2) ga is a fusion of final ge, indicating matter-of-
fact statement, and final a, the sentence softener.
Here ga is pronounced [gə].

12. Substitution Drill

Ex: T: Kéuih sihk hóudò
ngàuhyuhk ga.
/géidò ga/

T: He eats a lot of beef.
/quite a lot/

S: Kéuih sihk géidò
ngàuhyuhk ga.

S: He eats quite a lot of beef.

1. Kéuih sihk géidò ngàuhyuhk
ga. /faahn/

1. Kéuih sihk géidò faahn ga.

2. Kéuih sihk géidò faahn.
/jyùyuhk ga/

2. Kéuih sihk géidò jyùyuhk.

3. Kéuih sihk géidò jyùyuhk ga.
/yám chàh/

3. Kéuih yám géidò chàh.

4. Kéuih yám géidò chàh.
/hóusiu ge ja/

4. Kéuih yám hóusiu chàh ge ja.

5. Kéuih yám hóusiu chàh ge ja.
/bējáu/

5. Kéuih yám hóusiu bējáu.

6. Kéuih yám hóusiu bējáu.
/ngàuhnáaih/

6. Kéuih yám hóusiu ngàuhnáaih.

7. Kéuih yám hóusiu ngàuhnáaih
ge ja. /sihk faahn/

7. Kéuih sihk hóusiu faahn ge
ja.

8. Kéuih sihk hóusíu faahn ge ja.   8. Kéuih sihk móuhgéidò faahn.
   /móuhgéidò/

9. Kéuih sihk móuhgéidò faahn   9. Kéuih ló móuhgéidò chín ge
   ge ja. /ló chín/   ja.

---

13. Substitution Drill:

    Ex: T: Yí, ngóh jí bāt   S: Yí, ngóh jí yùhnbāt mhginjó gé.
        mhginjó gé.
        /yùhnbāt/

  1. Yí, ngóh go bíu mhginjó gé.   1. Yí, ngóh gihn sàam mhginjó
    /sàam/   gé.

  2. /dáifu/   2. Yí, ngóh tìuh dáifu mhginjó
                           gé.

  3. /kwàhn/   3. Yí, ngóh tìuh kwàhn mhginjó
                           gé.

  4. /jē/   4. Yí, ngóh bá jē mhginjó gé.

+ 5. /fu ngáhngéng/   5. Yí, ngóh fu ngáhngéng mhgin-
    (M. + eyeglasses)   jó gé.

+ 6. /go ngáhngéngdói/   6. Yí, ngóh go ngáhngéngdói
    (eyeglass case)   mhginjó gé.

+ 7. /go sáudói/   7. Yí, ngóh go sáudói mhginjó
    ((woman's) handbag)   gé.

  8. /gihn dáisāam/   8. Yí, ngóh gihn dáisāam
                           mhginjó gé.

---

14. Money Drill: For class practice: teacher writes on the blackboard.

    Ex: T: 2 (50¢)   T: 2 50¢ coins
        S: Béi léuhng go ńgh   S: Please give me 2 50¢ [5 dime]
           hóuhjí ngàn ngóh   coins.
           lā!

  1. 10   [$ 10]   1. Béi sahp jèung sahp mān jí
                  ngóh lā!

  2. 1   [$ 10]   2. Béi jèung sahp mān jí ngóh
                  lā!

  3. 1   [$ 100]   3. Béi jèung yāt baak mān jí
                  ngóh lā!

  4. 5   [$ 10]   4. Béi ńgh jèung sahp mān jí
                  ngóh lā!

5. 2 $ 500   5. Béi léuhng jèung ńgh baak
                                  mān jí ngóh lā!

6. 5   (50¢)   6. Béi ńgh go ńgh hòuhjí ngán
                                  ngóh lā!

7. 3   (10¢)   7. Béi sàam go yāt hòuhjí ngán
                                  ngóh lā!

8. 10   ($1⁰⁰)   8. Béi sahp go yāt mān ngán
                                  ngóh lā!

9. 2   (50¢)   9. Béi léuhng go ńgh hòuhjí
                                  ngán ngóh lā!

10. 10   (10¢)   10. Béi sahp go yāt hòuhjí ngán
                                  ngóh lā!

Comment: jí 'bill', and ngán 'coin', can be omitted from the
         sentences above without changing meaning or emphasis.

---

15. Money Exchange Drill: For class practice. Teacher writes on
    blackboard, or holds up actual or pretend money.

      Ex: T: 10 $ 10 →1 $ 100

          S1: Nīdouh yáuh sahp   S1: Here's ten $10 bills.
              jèung sahp mān
              (jí).

          S2: Mhgòi néih wuhn   S2: Please change into a $100
              jèung yāt baak   bill for me. [give me.]
              mān (jí) ngóh lā!

1. 5   ($1⁰⁰) → 1 $ 5⁰⁰   1. A. Nīdouh yáuh ńgh go yāt
                                        mān (ngán).
                                        Mhgòi néih wuhn jèung
                                        ńgh mān (jí) ngóh lā!

2. 10   ($1⁰⁰) → 1 $ 10   2. A. Nīdouh yáuh sahp go yāt
                                        mān (ngán).
                                        Mhgòi néih wuhn jèung
                                        sahp mān (jí) ngóh lā!

3. 5 $ 100 →1 $ 500   3. A. Nīdouh yáuh ńgh jèung yāt
                                        baak mān (jí).
                                        Mhgòi néih wuhn jèung
                                        ńgh baak mān (jí) ngóh
                                        lā!

4. 2 $ 5⁰⁰ →1 $ 10   4. A. Nīdouh yáuh léuhng jèung
                                        ńgh mān (jí).
                                        Mhgòi néih wuhn jèung
                                        sahp mān (jí) ngóh lā!

258

5.   10   (10¢) → 1   ($1⁰⁰)   5. A. Nīdouh yáuh sahp go yāt
                                         hòuhjí (ngán).
                                         Mhgòi néih wuhn go yāt
                                         mān (ngán) ngóh lā!

6.   2   (50¢) → 1   ($1⁰⁰)   6. A. Nīdouh yáuh léuhng go ńgh
                                         hòuhjí (ngán).
                                         Mhgòi néih wuhn go yāt
                                         mān (ngán) ngóh lā!

16. Money Change Drill: Teacher draws on board, or holds up real or
    pretend money.

            Ex: T: 1 $ 10   10 $ 1⁰⁰

            S1: Nīdouh yáuh jèung   S1: Here's a $10 bill.
                sahp mān (jí).

          + S2: Mhgòi néih cheung   S2: Please change (this) for me
                sahp go yāt mān   into 10 on-dollar coins.
                (ngán) (béi)
                ngóh lā!

1.   1 | $ 500 | → 5 | $ 100 | 1. A. Nīdouh yáuh jèung ńgh
                                            baak mān jí.

                                         B. Mhgòi néih cheung ńgh
                                            jèung yāt baak mān jí
                                            ngóh lā!

2.   1 | $ 100 | → 10 | $ 10 | 2. A. Nīdouh yáuh jèung yāt
                                            baak mān jí.

                                         B. Mhgòi néih cheung sahp
                                            jèung sahp mān jí ngóh
                                            lā!

3.   1 | $ 5⁰⁰ | → 10 (50¢)   3. A. Nīdouh yáuh jèung ńgh
                                            mān jí.

                                         B. Mhgòi néih cheung sahp
                                            go ńgh hòuhjí ngán
                                            ngóh lā!

4.   1 | $ 10 | → 10 ($1⁰⁰)   4. A. Nīdouh yáuh jèung sahp
                                            mān jí.

                                         B. Mhgòi néih cheung sahp
                                            go yāt mān ngán ngóh
                                            lā!

Comment: cheung 'change money into smaller denomination'
         (followed by denomination desired)

17. Number Drill I: Classroom practice.

A. Teacher writes examples on board, calls them out, students listen.

Example:

1. 10		1. sahp	
2. 100		2. yāt baak	
+ 3. 1000		3. yāt chīn (chīn = thousand)	
4. 20		4. yihsahp	
5. 200		5. yih baak	
6. 2000		6. yih chīn	

B. Teacher says number in Cantonese, students write it down. Teacher then writes figure on board. At end of section, teacher points to numbers on board at random, students say them.

1. 40	6. 700	11. 900
2. 80	7. 6000	12. 3000
3. 800	8. 500	13. 600
4. 9000	9. 4000	14. 5000
5. 300	10. 30	15. 100

(answers)

1. seisahp	6. chāt baak	11. gáu baak
2. baatsahp	7. luhk chīn	12. sàam chīn
3. baat baak	8. ńgh baak	13. luhk baak
4. gáu chīn	9. sei chīn	14. ńgh chīn
5. saam baak	10. sàamsahp	15. yāt baak

---

18. Number Drill II: Numbers with final zeroes.

A: Teacher writes example numbers on board, calls them out. Students listen.

Example:

1. 11	= sahpyāt
2. 110	= baak yāt or yāt baak yātsahp
3. 1100	= chīn yāt or yāt chīn yāt baak
4. 21	= yihsahpyāt or yahyāt
5. 210	= yih baak yāt or yih baak yāt sahp

6. 2100 = yih chīn yāt or yih chīn yāt baak

Comment: In numbers with a final zero (or zeroes), the Cantonese favor not calling the measure of the last number. It is of course predictable from the Measure preceding.

B. Teacher says number, students write it down (without looking at book). Teacher then writes figure on board. At end of section, teacher points to numbers on board at random, students say the numbers.

1. 340	9. 880	17. 38
2. 680	10. 480	18. 280
3. 7500	11. 170	19. 85
4. 9900	12. 990	20. 140
5. 440	13. 52	21. 14
6. 78	14. 540	22. 1400
7. 190	15. 180	23. 5900
8. 830	16. 710	24. 460

19. Number Drill III: Numbers with internal zeroes.

A. Teacher writes the numbers on the board and calls them out, pointing to them as he does so. Students listen.

Example:

1. 1   = yāt
2. 101   = yāt baak lìhng yāt
3. 1,001   = yāt chīn lìhng yāt
4. 1,010   = yāt chīn lìhng yātsahp
5. 4   = sei
6. 404   = sei baak lìhng sei
7. 4,004   = sei chīn lìhng sei
8. 4,040   = sei chīn lìhng seisahp

Comment: In saying a number, Cantonese marks the presence of an internal zero (or zeroes) by lìhng.

B. Teacher says number, students write it down; teacher then writes figure on blackboard. At end of section, teacher points to numbers on board at random, students say them.

1. 1018	3. 1101	5. 8008
2. 1029	4. 808	6. 8080

7. 209	12. 5008	17. 3303
8. 2029	13. 6708	18. 5804
9. 2008	14. 9009	19. 701
10. 2202	15. 307	20. 7406
11. 508	16. 708	21. 805
		22. 908

IV. CONVERSATIONS FOR LISTENING

(On tape. Refer to the wordlist below as you listen to the tape.)
Unfamiliar terms, in order of occurrence:

1) oi = here: to have in your possession

2) gàmyaht = today

3) yātján = dángyātjahn = 'in a little while'

V. SAY IT IN CANTONESE

A. You say to the person sitting next to you:

1. I forgot to bring money!

2. Do you have enough money to buy beer?

3. I don't have enough money to buy a dozen bottles.

4. What the...? I can't find my glasses.

5. Please break this $10 bill for me.

6. How much is US$10 in Hong Kong dollars?

7. How much is HK$100.00 in American money?

8. Does Hong Kong have that kind of car for sale?

9. You can't buy English beer in Japan--can you buy Japanese beer in England?

B. And he responds:

1. I'll lend you some--how much do you need?

2. I have just enough to buy six bottles, but I'd like to buy a dozen.

3. You want some money, huh?-- I'll lend you $20, OK?

4. They're here by me.

5. OK. One five and five ones, is that all right?

6. About $60.00.

7. About $16.60.

8. Sure, you can buy them in H.K. (Hongkong-available-sell)

9. I don't know, probably so.

10. I have very few sweaters,
but my younger sister has
a lot.

10. Not so! You have quite a
lot too!

11. Keep the change! (Don't need
to give back.)

11. Thanks.

Vocabulary Checklist for Lesson 11

1.	agō	n:	elder brother
2.	baak	nu:	hundred
3.	cheung	v:	change money into smaller denomination
4.	cheunghòi	v:	split, break up large banknote or coin to exchange for ones of lesser denomination.
5.	chĭn	nu:	thousand
6.	daai	v:	carry
7.	daai...heui	v:	take...along
8.	daai...làih	v:	bring...along
9.	dāk	v:	all right, OK, will do
10.	-dāk-	bf:	in yáuhdāk .$\overset{V}{.}$. = available, can
11.	dāk...	v:	only have ...
12.	fu	m:	M. for eyeglasses
13.	géidò	Ph:	quite a lot
14.	hái douh	Ph:	(he, she, it, etc.) is here; is at (this) place
15.	hóudò	Ph:	a lot
16.	hóusíu	Ph:	very little
17.	jáau	v:	give change
18.	jáaufàan	v:	give back change
19.	je	v:	lend, borrow
20.	jejyuh	v:	lend or borrow temporarily
21.	jèung	m:	M. for banknotes
22.	jí	n:	banknote; paper
23.	-jyuh	Vsuf:	temporarily, for a short time
24.	m̀hgeidāk	VP:	forget (not remember)
25.	m̀hginjó	VP:	lose, lost; 'nowhere to be seen'
26.	móuhdāk .$\overset{V}{.}$.	VP:	not have available for .$\overset{V}{.}$.ing
27.	móuhgéidò	Ph:	not much, not many

28. Nàh!	ex:	Here!
29. ngáhngéng	n:	eyeglasses
30. ngáhngéngdói	n:	eyeglasses case
31. ngán	n:	coin
32. sáanngán	n:	small coins
33. saimúi	n:	younger sister
34. sáudói	n:	(woman's) handbag
35. sīgēi	n:	taxi driver
36. tīm	ss:	sen. suf. indicating speaker has been taken by surprise.
37. tùhng	coV:	on behalf of, for
38. wuhn	v:	in ref. to money, change small denomination for larger one (followed by denomination desired); exchange one currency for another.
39. yáuhdāk	VP:	have available to .$\overset{V}{.}$., have available for .$\overset{V}{.}$.ing.
40. Yí!	ex:	exclamation of distress:'Oh-oh!'
41. yuhng	v:	use; spend (money)

. BASIC CONVERSATION

A. **Buildup:**

(Two friends meet at the bus stop)

Chàhn Táai

heui	go
heui bīndouh a?	where are you going?
A, Wòhng Táai, heui bīndouh a?	Ah, Mrs. Wong, where are you going?

Wòhng Táai

Ngóh heui ngàhnhòhng ló chín. Néih nē?	I'm going to the bank to get some money. And you?

Chàhn Táai

hohkhaauh	school
Ngóh heui hohkhaauh.	I'm going to school.

Wòhng Táai

Heui gódouh yáuh mēyéh sih a?	What is it you're going there to do?

Chàhn Táai

néui	daughter
ngóh gó néui	my daughter
jip	meet, fetch, pick up (a person)
heui jip ngóh go néui	go to get my daughter
Ngóh heui jip ngóh go néui.	I'm going to get my daughter.
Kéuih yìhgā hái hohkhaauh dáng ngóh.	She's at school now waiting for me.
màhmā	mother
ngóh màhmā	my mother
taam	visit
taam ngóh màhmā	visit my mother
daai kéuih	take/bring him along
Ngóh daai kéuih heui taam ngóh màhmā.	I'm taking her to visit my mother.

Wòhng Táai

jyuh	live
Néih màhmā hái bīndouh jyuh a?	Where does your mother live?

265

Chàhn Táai

Gáulùhng	Kowloon
Kéuih háí Gáulùhng jyuh.	She lives in Kowloon.

(Mrs. Wong looks down the street and sees a bus coming)

Wòhng Táai

làih	come
ga chē	a car
A, yáuh ga chē làih laak. Haih	Oh, there's a bus [car] coming.
m̀hhaih baat houh a?	Is it a Number 8?
táí m̀hchĭngchó	not see clearly
Ngóh táí m̀hchĭngchó.	I can't see clearly.

Chàhn Táai

M̀hhaih baat houh, haih sàam	It's not a Number 8, it's a
houh.	Number 3.
hauhbihn	in back, behind
Hauhbihn yáuh ga baat houh.	There's a Number 8 behind it.

Wòhng Táai

móuh cho	right! correct! [not have mistake]
A, móuh cho--	Ah, that's right--
sàam houh hauhbihn	behind the Number 3
gànjyuh	follow
Sàam houh hauhbihn gànjyuh	Behind the Number 3, following
yáuh ga baat hauh.	there is a Number 8.

B. **Recapitulation:**

Chàhn Táai

A, Wòhng Táai, heui bīndouh a?	Ah, Mrs. Wong, where are you going?

Wòhng Táai

Ngóh heui ngàhnhòhng ló chín.	I'm going to the bank to get
Néih nē?	some money. And you?

Chàhn Táai

Ngóh heui hohkhaauh.	I'm going to school.

266

Wòhng Táai

Heui gódouh yáuh mēyéh sih a?

What is it you're going there for?

Chàhn Táai

Ngóh heui jip ngóh go néui.
Kéuih yihgā hái hohkhaauh
dáng ngóh. Ngóh daai kéuih
heui taam ngóh māhmā.

I'm going to get my daughter.
She's at school now waiting
for me. I'm taking her to
visit my mother.

Wòhng Táai

Néih màhmā hái bīndouh jyuh a?

Where does your mother live?

Chàhn Táai

Kéuih hái Gáulùhng jyuh.

She lives in Kowloon.

Wòhng Táai

A, yáuh ga chē làih laak. Haih
m̀hhaih baat houh a? Ngóh tái
m̀hchīngchó.

Oh, there's a bus coming. Is
it a Number 8? I can't see
clearly.

Chàhn Táai

M̀hhaih baat houh, haih sàam
houh. Hauhbihn yáuh ga baat
houh.

It's not a Number 8, it's a
Number 3. There's a Number
8 behind it.

Wòhng Táai

A, móuh cho--
Sàam houh hauhbihn gànjyuh yáuh
ga baat houh.

At, that's right--
Behind the Number 3,
following there's a Number 8.

II. NOTES

A. Culture Notes

1. Greetings.

In Lesson 4 we touched on the matter of differences in the
way Americans and Cantonese greet each other. One very common
form of greeting between Cantonese who run into each other on the
street is Heui bīndouh a? or Heui bīn a? 'Where are you going?'
This isn't being nosey, it's just a greeting form, just as in
English 'How are you?' is a greeting form and doesn't call for a

detailed description of your health. To answer <u>Heui bīndouh a?</u>,
you say where you're going, or, if you don't want to tell, simply
say <u>Chēut gāai</u> or <u>Heui gāai</u> 'I'm going out' (said as you emerge
from your house) or <u>Chēutlàih hàahnghǎh</u> 'I've come out for a walk'
(if you're already out).

Other greetings are <u>Fàan gùng a?</u> (Going to work?' <u>Chēut gāai a</u>
'You're out?' <u>Fàan hohk a?</u> 'Going to school?' You can respond to
all of these by nodding you head, saying an <u>A</u> of assent, and
greeting the person by name: A, Hòh Tāai!

Around noontime or dinnertime if two acquaintances meet, a
common greeting form is <u>Sihk faahn meih a?</u> 'Have you eaten yet?'
Responses are: <u>Meih a, néih nē?</u> 'Not yet, and you?' and <u>Sihkjó</u>
<u>laak</u>, 'I've eaten.'

2. <u>Counting system of numbering the floors of a building.</u>

The Chinese system of numbering floors of a building is the
same as the American system, but different from the British system.
The floor above the ground floor is called <u>yih láu</u> [two-storey]
in Cantonese, 'the second floor' in American English, and 'the
first floor' in British English.

The British system of numbering floors is used in Hong Kong
when one speaks English. This, of course, means referring to the
floor above the ground floor as the first floor, the floor two
storeys up as the second floor, and so on.

Ex: Ngóh jyuh hái sàam   I live on the second floor.
    láu.   (British counting system)
                              I live on the third floor.
                              (American counting system)

(See Drill <u>2.8</u>)

B. Structure Notes

1. Sentence type: Subordinate clause-primary clause sentence.

In Cantonese sentences, subordinate clauses precede the
primary clause.

Ex: Kéuih fàanlàih, m̀hgòi When she comes back, please tell
    néih giu kéuih dá   her to phone Mrs. Cheung.
    dihnwá béi Jèung
    Tāai lā.

The order is fixed. This contrasts with the situation in the English counterpart, in which subordinate-primary clauses are reversible:

Ex: <u>Subordinate</u>   <u>Primary</u>

When she comes home   please tell her to call Mrs. Cheung.

or <u>Primary</u>   <u>Subordinate</u>

Please tell her to call Mrs. Cheung   when she comes home.

2. Sentence type: Multi-verb sentence.

The term multi-verb sentence refers to single-clause sentences containing a series of verb phrases. Whereas English typically expands a single clause sentence by retaining one principle verb and adding on such adjuncts as prepositional phrases (with me), participles (waiting for me), infinitive phrases (to fetch his girlfriend), adverbial nouns of place (home), Chinese typically expands a simple sentence into a series of verbal expressions, so that an expanded single clause sentence in Chinese has the shape: S + V(O) + V(O) (+ V(O)).

Ex: 1. Kéuih hái hohkhaauh dáng ngóh.
He's at school waiting for me [at-school+await-me]

2. Kéuih je chín béi ngóh.
He lent me money. [lend-money+give-me]

3. Mhgòi néih gàn ngóh làih.
Please come with me. Please follow me. [follow-me+come]

4. Kéuih heui ngàhn-hòhng ló chín.
He's going to the bank to get some money. [go-bank+get-money]

5. Kéuih sung ngóh fàan ngūkkéi.
He took me home. [deliver-me+return-home]

6. Kéuih séung maaih gihn sēutsāam.
He wants to buy a shirt. [wish+buy-shirt]

7. Kéuih heui tái hei.
He went to see a movie. [go+see-movie]

8. Kéuih heui Gáuluhng jip néuihpàhngyáuh.
He's going to Kowloon to fetch his girlfriend.

9. Kéuih jip kéuih go jái heui Gáuluhng tái hei.
He's fetching his son to take him to Kowloon to see a movie. [fetch-son+go-Kowloon+see-movie]

269

3. Auxiliary verbs.

    Auxiliary verbs cannot serve as the only verb in a sentence, but require another verb as their object. The negative and question forms attach to the auxiliary verb.

        Ex: séung = be of a mind to..., want to..., think (I'll)...

            aff: Ngóh séung sihk   I think I'll eat dinner.
               faahn.

            neg: Ngóh mhséung sihk   I don't think I'll eat.
               faahn.

            q: Séung mhséung sihk   Do you want to have dinner?
              faahn a?

4. Co-verbs.

    There is a category of verb in Cantonese which cannot serve as the only verb in a sentence, and which takes a noun as its object. This category is given the name co-verb (companion verb). A co-verb phrase precedes the verb it is companion to. Co-verbs ordinarily translate into English as prepositions, and the co-verb and its object as a prepositional phrase; but in Cantonese co-verbs are verbs, since they can occur in the three basic verb forms: affirmative, negative, and choice question.

      Ex: Co-V +   Noun object + Verb

        aff: Gàn   sīnsàang   góng. Repeat after the teache
                                       [Follow-teacher speak

        neg: Mhgàn   sīnsàang   góng. Don't repeat after the
                                       teacher.

          q: Gàn mhgàn sīnsàang   góng (Should we) repeat
                                   a?   after the teacher?

                (See Drills 11, 12)

5. Verb sequence: Aux V + Co-V + V

    Auxiliary verb precedes Co-Verb phrase in a sentence in which both occur:

        Ex: Ngóh séung gàn kéuih   I think I'll follow him.
           heui.

6. tùhng 'with' (Co-V) compared with tùhng 'and' (Cj)

    tùhng 'with' and tùhng 'and' both stand between two nouns (N tùhng N), but since otherwise they pattern differently in a sentence, they are classed as different parts of speech.

tùhng 'with' may take negative and question forms as well as
the affirmative, and may be preceded by an auxiliary verb. It is
therefore a verb. But as it cannot stand as the only verb in a
sentence, and requires another verb following its noun object, it
is classed as a Co-Verb.

    Ex: Ngóh mhséung tùhng   I don't want to go with Mrs.
        Léih Táai heui.   Lee.

    tùhng, 'and' does not take the negative and question forms,
therefore it cannot be called a verb. It cannot be preceded by an
auxiliary verb. It joins two nouns which then act as a compound
unit in subject or object position. tùhng, 'and' is classed as a
conjunction.

    Ex: Léih Táai tùhng ngóh   Mrs. Lee and I are going.
        heui. Máh Sàang   Mr. and Mrs. Ma aren't going.
        tùhng Máh Táai
        mhheui.

        Làuh Sàang tùhng Làuh   Mr. and Mrs. Lau don't wish
        Taaitáai mhséung   to go.
        heui.

        Ngóh mhsìk Làuh Síujé   I don't know Miss Lau and her
        tùhng kéuih màhmā.   mother.
                (See Drills 12.5 and 6)

7. gànjyuh, gàn, 'to follow'

    These two are alike in meaning, but different in use. gànjyuh
is a full verb, can serve as the only verb in a sentence. gàn is
a co-verb, cannot serve as the only verb in a sentence. It is
limited to multi-verb sentences in which it precedes another verb
phrase.

    Ex: Mhgòi néih gàn ngóh làih. Please follow me.

        Mhgòi néih gànjyuh ngóh   Please follow me.
        làih.

        Gànjyuh gó ga chē!   Follow that car!

    (-) Gàn gó ga chē!   (doesn't occur)

        Gàn (jyuh) gó ga chē   Follow that car!
        heui!

In the Basic Conversation of this lesson gànjyuh is used as
the subject of a clause, the clause itself being predicate in the
larger topic: comment sentence:

Subject (topic)	Predicate (Comment)	
	Subject	Predicate
Sàam houh hauhbihn	gànjyuh	yáuh ga baat houh.
[Three-number behind	following	there is [M] eight-number]

'Behind the Number 3 there's a Number 8 following.'

(See Drills 6, 7)

8. sung 'deliver (someone or something),' 'take (someone/something) to
   destination and leave him/it there.'

   sung, 'deliver,' can be the only verb in a sentence, or it can
be the verb of a VO expression which is followed by heui or some
other verb indicating movement.

Ex: Ngóh sung néih.	I'll see you to your destination.
Ngóh sung dī jáinéui heui taam pàhngyáuh.	I took the children to visit friends.
Gàan gūngsī sung dī yéh làih.	The department store delivered the goods (to speaker's place).

(See Drill 10)

9. daai, 'to bring, take along'

   daai, 'bring/take someone/something along' can serve as the
only verb in the sentence, usually with an impersonal object:

Ex: Kéuih daai chín.	He's brought money along.

   daai can also serve as the verb of a VO expression which is
followed by heui or some other verb indicating movement.

Ex: Ngóh daai ngóh go néui heui tái yīsāng.	I'm taking my daughter to see the doctor.

(See BC)

10. jip = 'fetch (someone),' 'meet (someone) and take him someplace else.'

Ex: Ngóh heui Gáuluhng jip ngóh go néui.	I'm going to Kowloon to get my daughter.
Ngóh jip ngóh go néui heui Gáuluhng.	I'm meeting my daughter to take her to Kowloon.

(See BC)

Ordinarily, the grammatical object of jip is a personal noun
(jip yàhn = go fetch someone), but the grammatical object can be
a vehicle (jip chē = meet the bus [car] and fetch someone away).
In such a case the vehicle is the grammatical object but a person
is the underlying object.

11. hái phrase in a multi-verb clause.

With most verbs a hái phrase precedes the other verb phrase,
but with verbs of thrust (put, place) it follows the other verb
phrase, and with verbs of station (live, sit, stand) it can precede
or follow the other verb phrase. In all cases hái has a placeword
object.

Ex: (before other V) Kéuih hái chāan-   He's eating (or he
                      sāt sihk faahn.   ate) at the re-
                                            staurant.

    (after other V) Jài dī chàh hái   Put the tea here.
                     nīdouh.

    (before or after)Kéuih hái Gēu-   He lives (or lived)
                     luhng jyuh.   in Kowloon.

                     Kéuih jyuh hái
                     Gáuluhng.

                  (See Drill 4)

12. Possessive modification with family names: ngóh màhmā, 'my mother'
    and others.

Some family names function irregularly with respect to possessive modification, not using either the general possessive ge or
the individual measures go and dī between modifier and head noun.
In such cases the modifier precedes the noun directly. With other
family names either ge or go/dī is required in modification
structure; with still other family names filling the ge/go
position is optional.

          (Examples are on following page)

Ex:

modifier	go/dĭ/ge or/--/	Noun		Eng. equivalents
ngóh	--	màhma	my your	mother
néih	--	bàhbā		father
Léih Táai	--	sīnsāang	Mrs. Lee's	husband
Léih Sàang	--	taaitáai	Mr. Lee's	wife
	/go/dĭ/ge/	jái		son(s)
	go/dĭ/ge/	néul		daughter(s)
	dĭ/ge/	jáinéui		children
	go/dĭ/ge	múi		younger sister
	/-/go/dĭ/ge	sáimúi		younger sister
	/-/go/dĭ/ge	gājē		elder sister
	/-/go/dĭ/ge/	sáilóu		younger brother
	/-/go/dĭ/ge/	agō		elder brother

(See Drill _3_)

13. Chinese response to questions negatively phrased.

(You're not going, are you? type):

Negatively phrased questions in Cantonese are tricky from the
English speaking student's point of view, because where the English
answer would be 'No,' the Cantonese answers seem to be 'yes,' and
where the English answer is 'yes,' the Cantonese answer sounds
like 'no.'

Ex: 1. A. Néih ūkkéi móuh
dihnwá àh.

B. Haih a. Móuh
dihnwá.

Your house doesn't have a
phone, does it.

That's right. There's no
phone.
(Idiomatic English answer:
No, it doesn't.)

2. A. Kéuih m̀hfàanlàih
sihk aan àh.

B. Móuh cho. M̀hfàan-
làih.

He's not coming home for
lunch, is he.

That's right. He's not coming
home.
(Idiomatic English answer:
No, he's not.)

3. A. Néih ūkkéi móuh
dihnwá àh.

B. M̀hhaih. Yáuh
dihnwá.

You don't have a phone at
your house, do you.

Not so! We do have one.
(Idiomatic English: Yes,
we do.)

274

4. A. Kéuih m̀hfàanlàih   He's not coming home for lunch,
      sihk aan àh.   is he.

   B. M̀hhaih. Kéuih   Not so. He is.
      fàanlàih.   (Idiomatic English: Yes,
                              he is.)

      (See Drill 14)

III. DRILLS

   1. Question & Answer Drill

        Ex: T: Hèunggóng.
           A: Néih hái bīndouh jyuh a?
           B: Ngóh hái Hèunggóng jyuh.

    1. Gáulùhng.
                             1. A. Néih hái bīndouh jyuh a?
                             B. Ngóh hái Gáulùhng jyuh.

    2. Méihgwok.
                             2. A. Néih hái bīndouh jyuh a?
                             B. Ngóh hái Méihgwok jyuh.

    3. Jùngwàahn.
                             3. A. Néih hái bīndouh jyuh a?
                             B. Ngóh hái Jùngwàahn jyuh.

    4. Hohkhaauh.
                             4. A. Néih hái bīndouh jyuh a?
                             B. Ngóh hái hohkhaauh jyuh.

    5. Hèunggóng.
                             5. A. Néih hái bīndouh jyuh a?
                             B. Ngóh hái Hèunggóng jyuh.

---

2. Expansion Drill: Repeat after the teacher.

+ 1. a. <u>jái</u>
     b. ngóh go jái
     c. Ngóh go jái heui
     d. Ngóh go jái heui Gáulùhng.

     e. Ngóh go jái yìhgā heui
        Gáulùhng.

+ 2. a. <u>jáinéui</u>

     b. dī jáinéui
     c. daai dī jáinéui
     d. daai dī jáinéui heui
     e. daai dī jáinéui heui Wòhng
        Táai douh.

 + f. Ngóh <u>sīnsàang</u> daai dī jáinéui
     heui Wòhng Táai douh.
     Note the new meaning for
     <u>sīnsàang</u>: 'husband.'

1. a. <u>son</u>
    b. my son
    c. My son is going
    d. My son is going to
       Kowloon.

    e. My son is going to
       Kowloon now.

2. a. <u>children</u> (of a family),
      <u>sons and daughters</u>
      (of a family)
    b. the children
    c. bring/take the children
    d. take the children.
    e. take the children to Mrs.
       Wong's.

    f. My <u>husband</u> is taking the
      children to Mrs. Wong's
      (Though <u>sīnsàang</u> may
      also mean 'teacher'

276

the context usually
makes the meaning
clear.)

+ 3. a. jouh

   b. jouh mēyéh

   c. heui Gáulùhng jouh mēyéh a?

   d. Kéuih heui Gáulùhng jouh
      mēyéh a?

   e. Kéuih heui Gáulùhng taam
      pàhngyáuh.

3. a. do

   b. do what?

   c. go to Kowloon to do what?

   d. What is he going to
      Kowloon to do?

   e. He's going to Kowloon
      to see a friend.

+ 4. a. yīsāng

   b. tái yīsāng

   c. heui tái yīsāng

   d. jip kéuih go néui heui tái
      yīsāng.

   e. Kéuih jip kéuih go néui heui
      tái yīsāng.

4. a. doctor

   b. see a doctor

   c. go to see a doctor

   d. meet her daughter and go
      to see the doctor.

   e. She's meeting her daughter
      to take her to the
      doctor.

+ 5. a. ngóh taaitáai

   b. tùhng ngóh taaitáai

   c. tùhng ngóh taaitáai heui

   d. m̀htùhng ngóh taaitáai heui

   e. Wòhng Táai m̀htùhng ngóh
      taaitáai heui.

5. a. my wife

   b. with my wife

   c. go with my wife

   d. not go with my wife

   e. Mrs. Wong isn't going
      with my wife.

+ 6. a. máaih yéh
        (yéh =
        things, stuff)

   b. heui máaih yéh

   c. bīngo heui máaih yéh a?

   d. tùhng bīngo heui máaih yéh a?

   e. Néih tùhng bīngo heui máaih
      yéh a?

6. a. buy things, do shopping

   b. go shopping

   c. who is going shopping?

   d. go shopping with whom?

   e. Who are you going shopping
      with?

7. a. sih

+ b. jouh sih

   c. hái bīndouh jouh sih a?

   d. Néih hái bīndouh jouh sih a?

   e. Ngóh hái Jùngwàahn jouh sih.

7. a. affairs, business

   b. work, have a job

   c. work where?

   d. Where do you work?

   e. I work in the Central
      District.

+ 8. a. douh

8. a. road

+   b. <u>Nèihdēun Douh</u>   b. <u>Nathan Road</u>

+   c. Nèihdēun Douh ńgh baak luhk-   c. Number 562 Nathan Road
       sahpyih <u>houh</u>
       (<u>houh</u> =
       <u>number</u>)

    d. Nèihdēun Douh ńgh baak luhk-   d. 562 Nathan Road 3rd
       sahpyih houh sàam láu   floor (2nd floor British
+   (<u>láu</u> =   counting system)
       <u>floor</u>, <u>story of a building</u>)

    e. Ngóh jyuh hái Nèihdēun Douh   e. I live at 562 Nathan
       ńgh baak luhksahpyih houh   Road, on the 3rd floor.
       sàam láu.

     Comment: In Hongkong, when speaking English, the British
              system of counting the floors of a building is
              used: ground floor, lst floor, 2d floor, etc.
              In speaking Cantonese, the Chinese (which is also
              the American) system is used: the ground floor
              is called lst floor the floor above the lst floor
              is called the 2d floor, etc.

---

3. Substitution Drill: Repeat the first sentence after the techer,
   then substitute as directed.

    1. Ngóh sīnsàang m̀hhái ngūkkéi.   1. Ngóh sīnsàang m̀hhái ngūkkéi.
       My husband is not at **home**.

    2. /ngóh go jái/   2. Ngóh go jái m̀hhái ūkkéi.

    3. /ngóh go néui/   3. Ngóh go néui m̀hhái ūkkéi.

    4. /ngóh ge jái/   4. Ngóh ge jái m̀hhái ūkkéi.

    5. /ngóh ge jáinéui/   5. Ngóh ge jáinéui m̀hhái ūkkéi.

    6. /ngóh ge néui/   6. Ngóh ge néui m̀hhái ūkkéi.

    7. /ngóh taaitáai/   7. Ngóh taaitáai m̀hhái ūkkéi.

+ 8. /ngóh <u>bàhbā</u>/   8. Ngóh bàhbā m̀hhái ūkkéi.
                                 My <u>father</u> is not at home.

+ 9. /ngóh ge <u>néuihpàhngyáuh</u>/   9. Ngóh ge néuihpàhngyáuh m̀hhái
                                 ūkkéi.
                                 My <u>girl friend</u> is not at
                                 home.

   10. /ngóh ge <u>nàahmpàhngyáuh</u>/   10. Ngóh ge nàahmpàhngyáuh
                                 m̀hhái ūkkéi.
                                 My <u>boy friend</u> is not at
                                 home.

---

4. Transformation Drill

    Ex: T: Ngóh hái Hèunggóng   T: I live in Hong Kong.
           jyuh.
        S: Ngóh jyuh hái Hèung-   S: I live in Hong Kong.
           góng.

    1. Ngóh màhmā hái Gáulùhng jyuh.   1. Ngóh màhmā jyuh hái Gáu-
                                          lùhng.
    2. Néih hái bīndouh jyuh a?   2. Néih jyuh hái bīndouh a?
    3. Ngóh néuihpàhngyáuh hái   3. Ngóh néuihpàhngyáuh jyuh
       Hèunggóng jyuh.   hái Hèunggóng.
    4. Kéuih bàhbā hái Yìnggwok jyuh. 4. Kéuih bàhbā jyuh hái
                                          Yìnggwok.
    5. Gó go yàhn hái douh jyuh.   5. Gó go yàhn jyuh hái douh.

_____

5. Expansion Drill

    Ex: T: Hòh Sàang heui   T: Mr. Ho is going to Kowloon.
           Gáulùhng.
        S: Hòh Sàang heui   S: What's Mr. Ho going to Kowloon
           Gáulùhng jouh māt-   to do? or
           yéh a?   What's Mr. Ho going to Kow-
                                        loon for?

    1. Ngóh heui hohkhaauh.   1. Néih heui hohkhaauh jouh
                                        mātyéh a?
    2. Ngóh sīnsàang heui gaaklèih. 2. Néih sīnsàang heui gaaklèih
                                        jouh mātyéh a?
    3. Kéuih nàahmpàhngyáuh heui Dāk 3. Kéuih nàahmpàhngyáuh heui
       Fu Douh Jùng.   Dāk Fu Douh Jùng jouh
                                        mātyéh a?
    4. Léih Sàang néuihpàhngyáuh heui 4. Léih Sàang néuihpàhngyáuh
       Jùngwàahn.   heui Jùngwàahn jouh
                                        mātyéh a?
    5. Ngóh màhmā heui ngàhnhòhng.   5. Néih màhmā heui ngàhnhòhng
                                        jouh mātyéh a?
    6. Ngóh bàhbā heui Hèunggóng   6. Néih bàhbā heui Hèunggóng
       Chāansāt.   Chāansāt jouh mātyéh a?

    Comment: Note that néuihpàhngyáuh and nàahmpàhngyáuh accept
             possessive modifiers with or without ge or go:

          Ex: Léih Síujé ⎱ - ⎰ nàahmpàhngyáuh   Miss Lee's boy-
                          ⎰ ge ⎰   friend
                          ⎰ go ⎰

_____

279

6. Transformation Drill

     Ex: T: M̀hgòi néih gànjyuh   T: Please follow me.
           ngóh làih lā.

        S: M̀hhóu gànjyuh ngóh   S: Don't follow me, please.
           làih lā.

1. M̀hgòi néih gànjyuh kéuih heui   1. M̀hhóu gànjyuh kéuih heui lā.
   lā.
   Please follow him.

2. M̀hgòi néih gànjyuh ngóh góng   2. M̀hhóu gànjyuh ngóh góng la.
   lā.
   Please repeat after me.

3. M̀hgòi néih gànjyuh gó ga hāak   3. M̀hhóu gànjyuh gó ga hāak
   chē heui lā.   chē heui lā.

4. M̀hgòi néih gànjyuh gó go yàhn   4. M̀hhóu gànjyuh gó go yàhn
   heui lā.   heui lā.

5. M̀hgòi néih gànjyuh ngóh làih lā. 5. M̀hhóu gànjyuh ngóh làih lā.

---

7. Response Drill

     Ex: T: M̀hgòi néih gànjyuh   T: Please follow me.
           ngóh heui lā.

   +   S: Sái m̀hsái <u>gàn</u> néih   S: Should I <u>follow</u> you?
           heui a?   [Should I following you, go?]

1. M̀hgòi néih gànjyuh kéuih   1. Sái m̀hsái gàn kéuih heui a?
   heui lā.

2. M̀hgòi néih gànjyuh Wòhng Táai 2. Sái m̀hsái gàn Wòhng Táai
   heui lā.   heui a?

3. M̀hgòi néih gànjyuh gó go Méih- 3. Sái m̀hsái gàn gó go Méihgwok-
   gwokyàhn heui lā.   yàhn heui a?

4. M̀hgòi néih gànjyuh ngóh màhmā 4. Sái m̀hsái gàn néih màhmā
   heui lā.   heui a?

5. M̀hgòi néih gànjyuh ngóh pàhng- 5. Sái m̀hsái gàn néih pàhngyáuh
   yáuh làih lā.   làih a?

   Comment: <u>gànjyuh</u> and <u>gàn</u> both mean 'follow' and in some cases
          may be used interchangeably; but <u>gàn</u> cannot be used
          as the only verb in a sentence, whereas <u>gànjyuh</u> can.

---

8. Substitution Drill: Repeat the first sentence after the teacher, then substitute as directed.

1. Ngóh heui Yìnggwok. I'm going to England.	1. Ngóh heui Yìnggwok.
2. /ngóh go jái/	2. Ngóh go jái heui Yìnggwok.
3. /tòuhsyùgwún/	3. Ngóh go jái heui tòuhsyù- gwún.
4. /kéuih taaitáai/	4. Kéuih taaitáai heui tòuhsyù- gwún.
5. /séjihlàuh/	5. Kéuih taaitáai heui séjih- làuh.
6. /kéuih sĭnsàang/	6. Kéuih sĭnsàang heui séjih- làuh.
7. /Méihgwok/	7. Kéuih sĭnsàang heui Méihgwok.
8. /ngóh màhmā/	8. Ngóh màhmā heui Méihgwok.

9. Conversation Exercise

Ex: A: Hòh Sàang heui bĭndouh a?

A: Where is Mr. Ho going?

B: Kéuih heui Gáulùhng.

B: He's going to Kowloon.

A: Heui Gáulùhng jouh mātyéh a?

A: What's he going to do there?

B: Heui máaih yéh.

B: He's going shopping.

A: A, heui máaih yéh.

A: Oh, he's going shopping.

1. A. Wòhng Síujé..........?

1. A. Wòhng Síujé heui bĭndouh a?

B. ....Hèunggóng.

B. Kéuih heui Hèunggóng.

A. ....?

A. Heui Hèunggóng jouh mēyéh a?

B. ....taam pàhngyáuh.

B. Heui taam pàhngyáuh.

A. ....

A. A, heui taam pàhngyáuh.

2. A. Néih taaitáai ....?

2. A. Néih taaitáai heui bĭndouh a?

B. ....ngàhnhòhng.

B. Kéuih heui ngàhnhòhng.

A. ....?

A. Heui ngàhnhòhng jouh mēyéh a?

B. ....ló chín.

B. Heui ló chín.

A. ....

A. A, heui ló chín.

281

3. A. Néih.............?   3. A. Néih heui bīndouh a?

   B. ....Tīnsīng Máhtàuh.   B. Ngóh heui Tīnsīng Máhtàuh.

   A. ....?   A. Heui Tīnsīng Máhtàuh
                                         jouh mēyéh a?

   B. ......jip ngóh ge jáinéui.   B. Heui jip ngóh ge jáinéui.

   A. ....   A. A, heui jip néih ge
                                         jáinéui.

Comment: To let the other person know you've been paying
         attention in English, we have such phrases as 'I see'
         and 'Is that so?'. On the telephone we signal we're
         still listening by such phrases as 'unhuh', 'yes',
         'I see,' during pauses in the flow of speech from
         the person at the other end of the phone. A favorite
         way to signal such information in Cantonese is for
         the listener to repeat the speaker's last sentence,
         or a portion of it.

---

10. Question and Answer Drill

    + Ex: T: Néih sung néih go   T: Where are you <u>taking</u> your
             néui heui bīndouh   daughter? /school/
             a? /hohkhaauh/
             (Sung = deliver)

         S: Ngóh sung ngóh go   S: I'm taking my daughter to
             néui heui hohkhaauh.   school.

1. Néih sung néih go néui heui   1. Ngóh sung ngóh go néui heui
   bīndouh a? /Tīnsīng Máhtàuh/   Tīnsīng Máhtàuh.

2. Néih sung néih go néui heui   2. Ngóh sung ngóh go néui heui
   bīndouh a? /Màhnwàh Jáudim/   Màhnwàh Jáudim.

3. Néih sung néih go jái heui   3. Ngóh sung ngóh go jái heui
   bīndouh a? /Chàhn Yīsāng   Chàhn Yīsāng douh.
   douh/   I'm taking my son to Dr.
                                        Chan's.

4. Néih sung néih go jái heui   4. Ngóh sung ngóh go jái heui
   bīndouh a? /hohkhaauh/   hohkhaauh.

5. Néih sung néih go jái heui   5. Ngóh sung ngóh go jái fàan
   bīndouh a? /fàan hohk/   hohk.

6. Néih sung néih ge néuihpàhng-   6. Ngóh sung ngóh ge néuih-
   yáuh heui bīndouh a?   pàhngyáuh fàan gùng.
   /fàan gùng/

7. Néih sung néih màhmā heui bīn-   7. Ngóh sung ngóh màhmā fàan
   douh a? /fàan ngūkkéi/   ngūkkéi.

    Comment: <u>sung</u> 'deliver,' is to accompany someone to a destination
             and leave him there, contrasts with <u>daai</u> 'take

282

along,'= take someone along with you and he stays
with you.

---

11. Response Drill

+ Ex: T: Néih <u>tùhng</u> bīngo   T: Who are you going shopping <u>with</u>?
        heui máaih yéh a?   /Miss Wong/
        /Wòhng Síujé/

     S: Ngóh tùhng Wòhng   S: I'm going with Miss Wong.
        Síujé heui.

1. Néih tùhng bīngo heui sihk   1. Ngóh tùhng ngóh taaitáai
   faahn a? /ngóh taaitáai/   heui.

2. Wòhng Sàang tùhng bīngo heui   2. Wòhng Sàang tùhng Wòhng Táai
   ngàhnhòhng a? /Wòhng Táai/   heui.

3. Kéuih tùhng bīngo heui tái   3. Kéuih tùhng kéuih sīnsàang
   yīsāng a? /kéuih sīnsàang/   heui.

4. Jèung Síujé tùhng bīngo heui   4. Jèung Síujé tùhng kéuih
   yám chàh a? /kéuih bàhbā/   bàhbā heui.

5. Néih tùhng bīngo làih a?   5. Ngóh tùhng ngóh màhmā làih.
   /ngóh màhmā/

Repeat, as Alteration Drill, thus:

    T: Néih tùhng bīngo heui máaih yéh a? /Wòhng Síujé/
       Who are you going shopping with? /Miss Wong/

    S: Néih tùhng m̀htùhng Wòhng Síujé heui maaih yéh a?
       Are you going shopping with Miss Wong?

---

12. Transformation Drill

    Ex: T: Ngóh tùhng kéuih   T: I'm going with him to the
           heui tái yīsāng.   doctor's.

        S: Ngóh m̀htùhng kéuih   S: I'm not going with him to the
           heui tái yīsāng.   doctor's.

1. Kéuih daai ngóh heui máaih   1. Kéuih m̀hdaai ngóh heui
   yéh.   máaih yéh.

2. Kéuih jip ngóh heui hohkhaauh.   2. Kéuih m̀hjip ngóh heui
                                        hohkhaauh.

3. Kéuih dáng ngóh sihk faahn.   3. Kéuih m̀hdáng ngóh sihk faahn.

4. Ngóh sung kéuih fàan ūkkéi.   4. Ngóh m̀hsung kéuih fàan ūkkéi.

5. Ngóh jùngyi tùhng kéuih heui   5. Ngóh m̀hjùngyi tùhng kéuih
   gāai.   heui gāai.

283

I like to go out with him.　　　　　I don't like to go out
　　　　　　　　　　　　　　　　with him.

6. Ngóh tùhng kéuih dōu jùngyi　　6. Ngóh tùhng kéuih dōu m̀hjùng-
   heui gāai.　　　　　　　　　　　yi heui gāai.
   We both like to go out.　　　　Neither one of us likes
   　　　　　　　　　　　　　　　to go out.

7. Ngóh gàn kéuih heui Méihgwok.　7. Ngóh m̀hgàn kéuih heui
   　　　　　　　　　　　　　　　Méihgwok.

8. Ngóh séung gàn kéuih heui　　　8. Ngóh m̀hséung gàn kéuih heui
   Yahtbún.　　　　　　　　　　　Yahtbún.

+ 9. Ngóh yiu daai kéuih heui <u>jouh</u>　9. Ngóh m̀hsái daai kéuih heui
   <u>sāam</u>.　　　　　　　　　　　jouh sāam.
   (<u>jouh sāam</u> =　　　　　　　I don't have to take her
   <u>make clothes</u>, have clothes　to have clothes made.
   made)
   I have to take her to <u>have</u>
   <u>clothes made</u>.

10. Kéuih tùhng ngóh heui máaih　　10. Kéuih m̀htùhng ngóh heui
    sáudói.　　　　　　　　　　　máaih sáudói.

---

13. Expansion Drill

    Ex: T: Kéuih heui hohkhaauh.　T: He's going to school.
        /baat dim bun/　　　　　/8:30/

        S: Kéuih baat dim bun　S: He's going to school at 8:30.
           heui hohkhaauh.

    1. Kéuih heui sihk faahn.　　　1. Kéuih tùhng ngóh heui sihk
       /tùhng ngóh/　　　　　　　faahn.

    2. Kéuih heui chàhlàuh. /yám chàh/　2. Kéuih heui chàhlàuh yám
       　　　　　　　　　　　　　chàh.

    3. Kéuih tùhng kéuih sīnsàang　3. Kéuih m̀htùhng kéuih sīnsàang
       heui Gáulùhng. /m̀htùhng/　　heui Gáulùhng.

    4. Kéuih daai kéuih go jái heui　4. Kéuih daai m̀hdaai kéuih go
       tái yīsāng. /daai m̀hdaai a?/　jái heui tái yīsāng a?

    5. Kéuih heui jip kéuih sīnsàang.　5. Kéuih heui séjihlàuh jip
       /séjihlàuh/　　　　　　　kéuih sīnsàang.

    6. Kéuih gàn màhmā heui chāansāt.　6. Kéuih gàn màhmā heui chāan-
       /yám chàh/　　　　　　　sāt yám chàh.

    7. Kéuih sung néuihpàhngyáuh fāan　7. Kéuih sung kéuih ge néuih-
       ūkkéi. /kéuih ge/　　　　pàhngyáuh fàan ūkkéi.

    8. Kéuih hái chāansāt dáng ngóh.　8. Kéuih yìhgā hái chāansāt
       /yìhgā/　　　　　　　　　dáng ngóh.

14. Response Drill

Ex: 1. T: Kéuih yám gafē àh.
       S: Haih a, yám gafē.

    2. T: Kéuih m̀hsīk góng
          Yìngmahn àh.
       S: Haih a, m̀hsīk góng.

T: He's drinking coffee. isn't he.
S: That's right--drinking coffee.

T: She doesn't know how to speak
   English, does she?
S: That's right; she doesn't.

1. Kéuih chēutjógāai àh.
   She's gone out, hasn't she.

2. Néih ūkkéi móuh dihnwá àh.

3. Hòh Sàang heui yám chàh àh.

4. Chàhn Síujé séung máaih hàaih àh.

5. Néih sīnsàang m̀hfàanlàih sihk
   faahn àh.

6. Gó go yàhn hái Méihgwok Ngàhnhòhng jouh sih àh.

7. Kéuihdeih heui Gáulùhng máaih
   yéh àh.

8. Néih m̀hjùngyi yám bējáu àh.

9. Kéuih taaitáai heui jip kéuih
   go néui àh?

1. Haih a, chēutjógāai.
   That's right, gone out.

2. Haih a, móuh dihnwá.

3. Haih a, heui yám chàh.

4. Haih a, séung máaih hàaih.

5. Haih a, m̀hfàanlàih sihk
   faahn.

6. Haih a, hái Méihgwok Ngàhnhòhng jouh sih.

7. Haih a, heui Gáulùhng máaih
   yéh.

8. Haih a, m̀hjùngyi yám bējáu.

9. Haih a, heui jip kéuih go
   néui.

---

15. Expansion Drill

1. Hauhbihn yáuh go chē jaahm.
   /Ngóh séjihlàuh/
   There's a car stop in back.

+ 2. Chìhnbihn yáuh gàan ngàhnhòhng.
   /Chàhn Síujé ūkkéi/
   (in front;
   front side)

3. Hauhbihn yáuh gàan jáudim.
   /Hèunggóng Ngàhnhòhng/

4. Hauhbihn yáuh gàan gūngsī.
   /Hèunggóng Chāansat/

5. Chihnbihn yáuh mēyéh a?
   /Jùnggwok Chàhlàuh/

1. Ngóh séjihlàuh hauhbihn
   yáuh go chē jaahm.
   Behind my office there's
   a car stop.

2. Chàhn Síujé ūkkéi chìhnbihn
   yáuh gàan ngàhnhòhng.
   In front of Miss Chan's
   house there's a bank.

3. Hèunggóng Ngàhnhòhng hauhbihn yáuh gàan jáudim.

4. Hèunggóng Chāansat hauhbihn
   yáuh gàan gūngsī.

5. Jùnggwok Chàhlàuh chìhnbihn
   yáuh mēyéh a?

Comment: chìhnbihn and hauhbihn literally mean 'front side' and
'back side' and are not specific as to whether the
positions designated are inside/outside the front/
back side. Only very rarely, though, is the meaning
unclear in context.

IV: CONVERSATIONS FOR LISTENING

(On tape. Refer to wordlist below as you listen.)

Unfamiliar terms, in order of occurrence:

1) bīn? = bīndouh?

2) Mēyéh sih a? = What's the matter?

3) lòh = sen. suf. expressing sympathy

4) ngāamngāam = just now, just on the point of, just

5) Yáuh mēyéh sih a? = What's going on?

6) Móuh mēyéh sih.= Nothing special.

7) ngāamngāam séung heui = just thinking of going

8) yātján = in a little while

V. SAY IT IN CANTONESE

A. You say to the person sitting next to you:

1. A, Mr. Lau, where are you going?

2. I'm going to Kowloon to buy something.

3. Where do you live?

4. I'm taking my daughter to see the doctor.

5. Who are you going shopping with?

6. You don't have a phone at home, do you. (confident that he doesn't)

7. She doesn't drink alcoholic beverages, does she. (confident that she doesn't.)

8. What are you going over to Kowloon to do?

9. Where is the Number 8 car stop?

10. I can't make out what bus that is over there.

11. Your office is behind the Mandarin Hotel, isn't it?

B. And he responds:

1. I'm going to work, how about you?

2. I'm going to Kowloon too.

3. I live in the Central District.

4. Which doctor are you going to?

5. I'm going with Miss Lee.

6. That's right, we don't have one.

7. Not so! She does drink alcoholic beverages.

8. I'm going to visit my father.

9. It's in front of the bank.

10. Over there where?

11. No, it's in the vicinity of the Central Market.

12. I take my son to school at eight.

12. What time does your daughter go?

13. Where are you going?

13. I'm going to my girl friend's house to meet her.

14. I'm going to Kowloon to go shopping.

14. Is your boy friend going with you?

15. My boy friend is not going shopping with me.

15. He told me he wanted to go with you.

16. Should I follow you?

16. Yes, please follow me.

Vocabulary Checklist for Lesson 12

1. bàhbā	n:	father
2. chìhnbihn	PW:	front (front side)
3. chìngchó	adj:	clear, vivid, clearly
4. daai	V/coV:	take/bring (someone/something) along
5. douh	bf:	road, restricted to use following named road
6. ga	m:	M. for vehicle
7. gàn	coV:	follow, come behind
8. gànjyuh	v:	follow, come behind
9. Gáulùhng	PW:	Kowloon
10. hauhbihn	PW:	back (back side); behind
11. heui	v:	go
12. hohkhaauh	n/PW:	school
13. houh	m:	number
14. jái	n:	son
15. jáinéui	n:	children (of a family), sons and daughters
16. jip	v:	meet, fetch, pick up (a person)
17. jouh	v:	do, work
18. jouh sāam	vo:	make clothes, have clothes made
19. jouh sih	vo:	to work, have a job
20. jyuh	v:	live
21. làih	v:	come
22. láu	m:	floor, storey of a building
23. màhmā	n:	mother
24. Móuh cho.	Ph:	That's right.

25. nàahmpàhngyáuh   n: boy-friend
26. Nèihdēun Douh   PW: Nathan Road
27. néui   n: daughter
28. néuihpàhngyáuh   n: girl-friend
29. sih   n: piece of business, affair, matter
30. sīnsàang   n: husband
31. sung   coV/V: deliver
32. taaitáai   n: wife; married woman
33. taam   v: to visit
34. tái yīsāng   vo: see the doctor
35. tùhng   coV: with
36. yéh   n: things, stuff
37. yīsāng   n: doctor

I. BASIC CONVERSATION

A. Buildup:

Sīgēi

Heui bīndouh a?	Where to?
daaphaak	passenger

Daaphaak

gāai	street
gó tiuh gāai	that street
méng	name
mēyéh méng	what name?
giujouh, or giu	called, be called
giujouh mēyéh méng a?	what's its name?
gó tiuh gāai giujouh mēyéh méng a?	what's the name of that street?
Ngóh mhgeidāk gó tiuh gāai giujouh mēyéh méng.	I don't remember the name of the street.
hàahng	go; walk; drive
yātjihk	straight
Néih yātjihk hàahng sīn.	Go straight first.
dou	arrive
wah néih tēng	tell you
Dou gamseuhnghá, ngóh wah néih tēng.	I'll tell you as we go along.
yauh	right
jyun	turn
jyun yauh	turn right
Hái nīdouh jyun yauh.	Turn right here.
jó	left
jyun jó	turn left
gwodī	a little farther on
Gwodī, jyun jó.	Just a little farther on, turn left.

Sīgēi

Haih mhhaih nīdouh a?	Is this the place?

Daaphaak

Mhhaih--gwodī tīm.	No--still farther.
gwo	pass, cross by
gwo géi gàan	pass a few buildings
jauh	clause connector: then; and
Gwo géi gàan, jauh haih laak.	Pass a few buildings (more) and that's it.
Dou laak!	Arrived! (i.e.: Here it is!)
jósáubihn or jóbihn	left hand side, left side
Hái jósáubihn gó gàan.	It's that building on the left.

Sīgēi

tìhng	stop
tìhng chè	stop the car
hóyíh	be permitted, can
Nīdouh mhhóyíh tìhng chè.	You can't stop here.

Daaphaak

(pointing to the driveway:)

yahp-	in
yahpheui	go in
Jyun yahpheui lā.	Turn in (the driveway).
wái	place; seat
paak	park
yáuh wái paak chè	there's a place to park
yahpbihn	inside
Yahpbihn yáuh wái paak chè.	Inside there's a place to park.

(The car goes into the driveway)

Daaphaak

Hóu laak. Hái nīdouh tìhng chè lā.	OK. Stop here.
Mhgòi néih dáng jahm--	Please wait--
jauh	immediately, soon
Ngóh jauh fàanlàih.	I'll be right back.

B. **Recapitulation:**

Sīgēi

Heui bīndouh a?   Where to?

Daaphaak

Ngóh mhgeidāk gó tiuh gāai   I don't remember the name of
  giujouh mēyéh méng.   the street.
Néih yātjihk hàahng sīn.   Go straight first.
Dou gamseuhnghá, ngóh wáh néih   I'll tell you as we go along.
  téng.
Hái nīdouh jyun yauh.   Turn right here.
Gwodī, jyun jó.   Just a little farther on, turn
                                          left.

Sīgēi

Haih mhhaih nīdouh a?   Is this the place?

Daaphaak

Mhhaih--gwodī tīm.   No--still farther.
Gwo géi gàan, jauh haih laak.   Pass a few buildings more and
                                          that's it.

Dou laak!   Here it is!

Sīgēi

Nīdouh mhhóyíh tìhng chè.   You aren't allowed to stop here.

Daaphaak
(pointing to the driveway:)

Jyun yahpheui lā.   Turn in (the driveway).
Yahpbihn yáuh wái paak chè.   Inside there's a place to
                                          park.

(The car goes into the driveway:)

Daaphaak

Hóu laak. Hái nīdouh tìhng chè lā.   OK--stop here.
Mhgòi néih dáng jahn--ngóh jauh   Please wait--I'll be right
  fàanlàih.   back.

291

II. NOTES

   1. (yāt)jihk 'straight,' 'straight-away'

      In combination with following heui, the portion yāt can be
omitted.

                (Yāt)jihk heui lā!   go straight.

      In combination with following hàahng, yātjihk is preferred:

                yātjihk hàahng: go (or walk) straight

                           (See BC)

         (yāt)jihk may have the meaning 'straight-away,' 'without being
interrupted or diverted'

            Ex: Nī ga chē jihk heui Jùng-   This bus goes straight to the
                waahn ga.   Central District.

   2. jauh = (1) ..., then....

         (2) immediately

   a. jauh in a two-clause sentence = ..., then ....

         jauh connects subordinate clause and main clause in a sentence
of sequential relationship:

               (When or After) _A_ , then _B_ .

         As clause connector jauh comes in the second clause (the
main clause), following the subject of the clause (if any) and
preceding the verb.

            Ex: 1. Gwo géi gàan, jauh   (After we) pass a few buildings,
                   haih laak.   then there it is.

                2. Gwo géi fānjūng, néih   After a few minutes pass, you
                   jauh hóyíh fàan-   can come back.
                   làih.

                  (See BC and Drill _10_)

   b. jauh in a single clause sentence = 'right away, immediately'

         In this jauh acts as an adverb, positioned immediately before
the verb it concerns:

            Ex: Ngóh jauh fàanlàih.   I'll be right back.

                Ngóh jauh tùhng kéuih   I'll be right back with him. or
                fàanlàih.   I'll bring him right back.

                Ngóh tùhng kéuih jauh   He and I will be right back.
                fàanlàih.

                Ngóh sàam dímjūng jauh   I'll be back at 3 o'clock.
                fàanlàih.   (an early hour from the
                                            speaker's point of view)

                        (See BC)

3. hóyíh = 'can,' in the sense of 1) 'permitted to'

                              2) 'willing and able,' 'can do a favor'

    hóyíh is an auxiliary verb, which takes another verb as its
object. The colloquial English equivalent is usually 'can,' but it
may have one of two different underlying meanings.

    a. 'can' in the sense of 'permitted to'

        Nīdouh m̀hhóyíh paak chē.   You can't park here.
                                    [Here it is not allowed to
                                    park]

            (See BC and Drills 1, 4)

    b. 'can' in the sense of 'can do a favor,' 'able and willing

       to...' In the negative = 'willing but unable'

        1. Ngóh hóyíh je yāt baak I can lend you $100.
           mān (béi) néih.

        2. Néih hó m̀hhóyíh je yāt Can you lend me $100?
           baak mān (béi) ngóh
           a?

        3. Deuìmhjyuh--ngóh m̀h-   I'm sorry, I can't come get
           hóyíh làih jip   you, I have some work (I
           néih--yáuh dī sih.   have to attend to.)

4. tìhng, 'stop' with hái phrases.

    tìhng, 'stop' is one of a group of verbs which a hái phrase
can either precede or follow. (See note on hái with verbs of station,p273.)

        Hái nīdouh tìhng chē lā.   Here stop. (i.e. Stop here.)

            (See BC)

        Tìhng hái bīndouh a?   Stop where?

            (See Drill 7)

    paak, 'park (a car)' also belongs to the group of verbs which
a hái phrase can either precede or follow. Abstracting a common
characteristic of this group of verbs, we say that they are 'standing
still' verbs, or verbs of station. The verbs for stand, sit, lie
down, stop, park and others are members of this group.

    As for which comes first, the hái phrase or the other verb, it
goes according to the Chinese language characteristic of making what
you're talking about the subject of the sentence and putting it at
the beginning of the sentence. If you're concerned about 'where' you
put the hái phrase first; if you're most concerned about stopping,

you put that part first.

(See BC and Drill <u> 7 </u>)

5. Sentence suffix <u>la</u> for friendly advice or persuasion.

An imperative sentence with sentence suffix <u>la</u> at mid pitch on the intonation scale adds the connotation of friendly advice or persuasion.

Ex: M̀hhóu fàanjyun tàuh la.   Don't turn and go back =
                                  Better not turn and go back.
                                  (Said as friendly advice
                                  rather than command)

(See Drill <u> 12 </u>)

6. <u>jó</u> and <u>yauh</u>, 'left' and 'right.'

<u>jó</u> and <u>yauh</u> are boundwords which may be bound to a preceding verb to form a VO phrase, or to a following boundword of place to become a PW, or to a following noun as a modifier.

Ex: VO: jyun jó   turn left
    PW: jóbihn   left side, left, to the left
    mod+N: jó sáu   left hand

(See BC)

294

II. DRILLS

1. Expansion Drill

+ 1. a. fàanjyuntàuh

1. a. <u>turn</u> (the car) <u>around</u>
      and go back the other
      way

   b. hái nĭdouh fàanjyuntàuh

   b. turn around here and go
      back

   c. hóyĭh hái nĭdouh fàanjyuntàuh

   c. you may turn around and
      go back here <u>or</u>
      it is permitted to turn
      around and go back from
      here

   d. m̀hhóyĭh hái nĭdouh fàanjyuntàuh

   d. it's not allowed to turn
      around and go back here

   e. Hó m̀hhóyĭh hái nĭdouh fàan-
      jyuntàuh a?

   e. May I turn around and go
      back here?

   Comment: fàanjyuntàuh [return-turn-head] is used when you
            have overshot the place you intend to go and want
            to direct the driver to turn the car around and
            go back.

+ 2. a. tanhauh

2. a. <u>back up</u>, <u>reverse</u> (a car)

   b. tanhauh lā

   b. back up please

   c. tanhauh lā, gódouh yáuh
      go wái

   c. back up, there's a place

   d. tanhauh lā, gódouh hauhbihn
      yáuh go wái

   d. back up, behind us
      there's a place

   e. Tanhauh lā, gódouh hauhbihn
      yáuh go wái paak chē.

   e. Back up, behind us there's
      a place to park.

+ 3. a. Wĭhng Ōn Gūngsĭ

3. a. <u>Wing On Company</u>. (a
      department store in
      Hong Kong)

   b. hái Wĭhng Ōn Gūngsĭ

   b. at Wing On

   c. hái Wĭhng Ōn Gūngsĭ tìhng chē

   c. stop the car at Wing On

   d. m̀hgòi néih hái Wĭhng Ōn
      Gūngsĭ tìhng chē lā

   d. please stop the car at
      Wing On

   e. M̀hgòi néih hái Wĭhng Ōn
      Gūngsĭ gwodĭ tìhng chē lā.

   e. Please stop the car a
      little beyond Wing On.

4. a. yahpheui

4. a. <u>enter</u>, go in.

   b. jyun yahpheui

   b. turn in (there)
      [turn, go in]

   c. gànjyuh jyun yahpheui.

   c. follow (that car) in

295

d. gànjyuh gó ga chē jyun
   yahpheui

d. follow that car in
   [follow that car, turn
   in]

e. gànjyuh gó ga hāak chē jyun
   yahpheui

e. follow that black car in
   [follow that black car
   there turn in]

f. Gànjyuh chìhnbihn gó ga hāak
   chē jyun yahpheui.

f. Follow that black car
   ahead in. or
   Turn where that black
   car up there is.
   [Follow that black car
   over there, turn in.]

5. a. yáuh wái

5. a. there is space

   b. yáuh go wái

   b. there is a space

   c. yáuh go wái paak chē

   c. there is a place to
      park cars

   d. hauhbihn yáuh go wái paak chē

   d. in the back there is a
      place to park cars

   e. ga hāak chē hauhbihn yáuh go
      wái paak chē

   e. behind the black car
      there is a parking
      place

   f. gó ga hāak chē hauhbihn yáuh
      go wái paak chē

   f. behind that black car
      there is a parking
      place

   g. Nē! Gó ga hāak chē hauhbihn
      yáuh go wái paak chē.

   g. There! Behind the black
      car there is a parking
      place.

---

2. **Substitution Drill: Repeat the first sentence, then substitute
   as directed.**

   1. Hàaih, Yìngmán giujouh mēyéh a?
      How do you say "shoes" in
      English?

   1. Hàaih, Yìngmán giujouh
      mēyéh a?

   2. /pìhnggwó/

   2. Pìhnggwó, Yìngmán giujouh
      mēyéh a?

   3. /tòhng/

   3. Tòhng, Yìngmán giujouh
      mēyéh a?

   4. /bīu/

   4. Bīu, Yìngmán giujouh mēyéh
      a?

   5. /jūng/

   5. Jūng, Yìngmán giujouh mēyéh
      a?

   6. /gāi/

   6. Gāi, Yìngmán giujouh mēyéh
      a?

7. /gāai/

7. Gāai, Yìngmán giujouh mēyéh
a?

Comment: giu may substitute for giujouh in all sentences above.

---

3. Response Drill

Ex: 1. T: Gó gàan gūngsī
giu mēyéh méng
a? /Wìhng Ōn
Gūngsī/

T: What's the name of that department store? /Wing On Company/

S: Giujouh Wìhng Ōn
Gūngsī.

S: It's called the Wing On Company.

2. T: Gó gàan gūngsī
giu mēyéh méng
a? /shake/

T: What's the name of that department store? /shake/

S: Deuimhjyuh, ngóh
mhjìdou giujouh
mēyéh méng.

S: Excuse me, I don't know what
it's called.

1. Gaaklèih gàan chàhlàuh giu
mēyéh méng a? /shake/

1. Deuimhjyuh, ngóh mhjìdou
giujouh mēyéh méng.

2. Jógán gó gàan ngàhnhòhng giu
mēyéh méng a? /Méihgwok
Ngàhnhòhng/

2. Giujouh Méihgwok Ngàhnhòhng.

3. Gó bihn gàan jáudim giu mēyéh
méng a? /Màhnwàh Jáudim/

3. Giujouh Màhnwàh Jáudim.

4. Daaih Douh Jùng gó gàan chāansāt giu mēyéh méng a?
/shake/

4. Deuimhjyuh, ngóh mhjìdou
giujouh mēyéh méng.

5. Deuimihn go máhtàuh giu mēyéh
méng a? /Tīnsīng Máhtàuh/

5. Giujouh Tīnsīng Máhtàuh.

6. Nī tiuh gāai giu mēyéh méng a?
/Daaih Douh Jùng/

6. Giujouh Daaih Douh Jùng.

7. Gó gàan gūngsī giu mēyéh méng
a? /shake/

7. Deuimhjyuh, ngóh mhjìdou
giujouh mēyéh méng.

a. Repeat: Omitting 'méng' in question and answer.

297

4. Alteration Drill

      Ex: T: Mhgòi néih hái nīdouh T: Please stop (the car) here.
            tìhng chē lā.

         S: Hó mhhóyih hái nīdouh S: May one stop here? or
            tìhng chē a?   Is it permitted to stop here?

1. Mhgòi néih gwodī jyun jó lā.   1. Hó mhhóyih gwodī jyun jó a?

2. Mhgòi néih jyun yahpheui lā.   2. Hó mhhóyih jyun yahpheui a?

+ 3. Mhgòi néih jyun yahp <u>yauhsáu-</u>   3. Hó mhhóyih jyun yahp
    <u>bihn</u> lā.   yauhsáubihn a?
    (<u>yauhsáubihn</u> =
    <u>right hand side</u>)
    Please turn in on the right
    hand side.

4. Mhgòi néih hái nīdouh jyun   4. Hó mhhóyih hái nīdouh jyun
    yahp heui lā.   yahp heui a?

5. Mhgòi néih tanhauh lā.   5. Hó mhhóyih tanhauh a?

---

5. Substitution Drill: Students gesture where appropriate. Repeat
first sentence, then substitute as directed.

1. Nīdouh mhhóyih jyun yauh.   1. Nīdouh mhhóyih jyun yauh.
    It's not allowed to turn
    to the right here.

+ 2. <u>diuhtàuh</u>   2. Nīdouh mhhóyih diuhtàuh.
    (<u>turn around</u> (a car))

3. jyun yahpheui   3. Nīdouh mhhóyih jyun yahpheui.

4. tanhauh   4. Nīdouh mhhóyih tanhauh.

5. yāt jihk heui   5. Nīdouh mhhóyih yāt jihk
                          heui.

6. jyun jó.   6. Nīdouh mhhóyih jyun jó.

    Comment: Compare word order of:

        1. <u>Nīdouh mhhóyih jyun jó.</u>   ⎫
        2. <u>Mhhóyih hái nīdouh jyun jó.</u> ⎬ You can't turn left
        3. <u>Hái nīdouh mhhóyih jyun jó.</u> ⎭ here.

    These are interchangeable. Note absence of <u>hái</u>
    before <u>nīdouh</u> in first sentence. Omission of <u>hái</u>
    before <u>PW</u> is permitted when <u>PW</u> begins the sentence.

---

6. Substitution Drill: Repeat the first sentence, then substitute as directed.

1. Yiu hái nídouh tanhauh.   1. Yiu hái nídouh tanhauh.
   (We) want to back up here. or
   Back up here.

2. mhsái   2. Mhsái hái nídouh tanhauh.

3. diuhtàuh   3. Mhsái hái nídouh diuhtàuh.

4. yiu   4. Yiu hái nídouh diuhtàuh.

5. jyun yahpheui   5. Yiu hái nídouh jyun yahpheui.

6. hóyíh   6. Hóyíh hái nídouh jyun yahp-
                                       heui.

7. jyun yauh   7. Hóyíh hái nídouh jyun yauh.

8. hóu mhhóu   8. Hóu mhhóu hái nídouh jyun
                                       yauh a?
                                       Is it OK to turn right
                                       here?

9. yātjihk heui   9. Hóu mhhóu hái nídouh yāt-
                                       jihk heui a?

10. fàanjyun tàuh   10. Hóu mhhóu hái nídouh fàan-
                                        jyuntàuh a?

---

7. Response Drill: Students gesture where appropriate.

   Ex: T: Tīnsīng Máhtàuh   T: Star Ferry
       S1: Tíhng hái bīndouh a? S1: Where should I stop?
       S2: Tíhng hái Tīnsīng   S2: Stop at the Star Ferry.
           Máhtàuh lā.

1. Tíhng hái bīndouh a?   1. Tíhng hái Màhnwàh Jáudim
   /Màhnwàh Jáudim mùhnháu/   mùhnháu lā.

2. Tíhng hái bīndouh a?   2. Tíhng hái Wìhng Ōn Gūngsī
   /Wìhng Ōn Gūngsī deuimihn/   deuimihn lā.

3. Tíhng hái bīndouh a?   3. Tíhng hái Méihgwok Ngàhn-
   /Méihgwok Ngàhnhòhng gaaklèih/   hòhng gaaklèih lā.

4. Tíhng hái bīndouh a?   4. Tíhng hái Jùnggwok Chàh-
   /Jùnggwok Chàhlàuh chìhnbihn/   làuh chìhnbihn lā.

5. Tíhng hái bīndouh a?   5. Tíhng hái tòuhsyùgwún
   /tòuhsyùgwún mùhnháu/   mùhnháu lā.

6. Tíhng hái bīndouh a?   6. Tíhng hái Tīnsīng Máhtàuh
   /Tīnsīng Máhtàuh gwodī/   gwodī lā.

7. Tìhng hái bīndouh a?
   /Mèihgwok Jáudim yauhsáubihn/

8. Tìhng hái bīndouh a?
 + /ngàhnhòhng yauhbihn/
   (right side)

7. Tìhng hái Mèihgwok Jáudim
   yauhsáubihn lā.

8. Tìhng hái ngàhnhòhng yauhbihn lā.

Comment: Tìhng, 'stop' is one of a group of verbs which accepts
a hái phrase in either pre-verb position or post-
verb position.

Ex: A: Tìhng hái bīndouh a? ⎫
       Hái bīndouh tìhng a? ⎬ Where should I stop?

    B: Tìhng hái Tīnsīng Máhtàuh lā. ⎫ Stop at the
       Hái Tīnsīng Máhtàuh tìhng lā. ⎬ Star Ferry.

---

8. Substitution Drill: Repeat the first sentence, then substitute
   as directed.

1. Jùnggwok Chàhlàuh gwodī, jyun
   yauh.
   A little beyond the China
   Teahouse, turn right.

1. Jùnggwok chàhlàuh gwodī,
   jyun yauh.

2. jyun jó

2. Jùnggwok Chàhlàuh gwodī,
   jyun jó.

3. chē jaahm

3. Chē jaahm gwodī, jyun jó.

4. jyun yauh

4. Chē jaahm gwodī, jyun yauh.

5. Hèunggóng Chāansāt

5. Hèunggóng Chāansāt gwodī,
   jyun yauh.

6. Màhnwàh Jáudim

6. Màhnwàh Jáudim gwodī,
   jyun yauh.

7. Dāk Fuh Douh

7. Dāk Fuh Douh gwodī, jyun
   yauh.

8. hohkhaauh

8. Hohkhaauh gwodī, jyun yauh.

9. Daaih Douh Jùng

9. Daaih Douh Jùng gwodī, jyun
   yauh.

10. jyun jó

10. Daaih Douh Jùng gwodī, jyun
    jó.

a. Do #1-4 as expansion drill, incorporating hàahngdou 'walk
   to, go to,' thus:

T: Jùnggwok Chàhlàuh
   gwodī, jyun yauh.

A little beyond the China
Teahouse, turn right.

S: Hàahngdou Jùnggwok
   Chàhlàuh gwodī,
   jyun yauh.

Go a little beyond the China
Teahouse, and turn right.

Note that hàahng is not limited to the meaning 'walk,' but
is used as a verb of locomotion for cars as well.

---

9. Expansion Drill: Students should gesture to indicate directions.

Ex: T: Wìhng Ōn Gūngsī   T: Turn left a little beyond Wing
        gwodī, jyun jó.   On Department Store.

    S: Wìhng Ōn Gūngsī   S: Turn left a little beyond Wing
        gwodī, jyun jó,   On Department Store; not
        m̀hhaih jyun yauh.   right.

1. Méihgwok Ngàhnhòhng gwodī,   1. Méihgwok Ngàhnhòhng gwodī,
   jyun jó.   jyun jó, m̀hhaih jyun yauh.

2. Chē jaahm gwodī, jyun yauh.   2. Chē jaahm gwodī, jyun yauh,
                                    m̀hhaih jyun jó.

3. Jùnggwok Chàhlàuh gwodī,   3. Jùnggwok Chàhlàuh gwodī,
   jyun yauh.   jyun yauh, m̀hhaih jyun jó.

4. Hèunggóng Chāansāt gwodī,   4. Hèunggóng Chāansāt gwodī,
   jyun jó.   jyun jo, m̀hhaih jyun yauh.

5. Màhnwàh Jáudim gwodī, jyun   5. Màhnwàh Jáudim gwodī, jyun
   yauh.   yauh, m̀hhaih jyun jó.

---

10. Substitution Drill: Repeat first sentence, then substitute as
    directed.

1. Gwo léuhng go chē jaahm, jauh   1. Gwo léuhng go chē jaahm,
   haih laak.   jauh haih laak.
   Pass two bus stops, and
   there you are.

2. yāt tìuh gāai   2. Gwo yāt tìuh gāai, jauh
                                       haih laak.

3. sàam go chē jaahm   3. Gwo sàam go chē jaahm, jauh
                                       haih laak.

4. léuhng gàan gūngsī   4. Gwo léuhng gàan gūngsī,
                                       jauh haih laak.

5. léuhng tìuh gāai   5. Gwo léuhng tìuh gāai, jauh
                                       haih laak.

6. yāt gàan   6. Gwo yāt gàan, jauh haih
                                       laak.

7. géi gàan   7. Gwo géi gàan, jauh haih laak.

---

11. Response Drill

    Ex: T: Kéuih hái bīn gàan   Which teahouse is he in?
           chàhlàuh a?   /next door, adjacent/
           /gaaklèih/

        S: Kéuih hái gaaklèih   He's in the one next door.
           gó gàan.

1. Kéuih hái bīn gàan ngàhnhòhng   1. Kéuih hái deuimihn gó gàan.
   a? /deuimihn/

2. Néih heui bīn gàan gūngsī a?   2. Ngóh heui chìhnbihn gó gàan.
   /chìhnbihn/

3. Néih màhmā hái bīn gàan séjih-   3. Ngóh màhmā hái yauhbihn gó
   làuh a? /yauhbihn/   gàan.

4. Néih séung heui bīn gàan   4. Ngóh séung heui nī bihn
   chāansāt a? /nī bihn/   gó gàan.

5. Kéuih hái bīn gàan hohkhaauh a?   5. Kéuih hái jósáubihn gó gàan.
   /jósáubihn/

    Comment: Compare the structure and meaning above with one you
             have studied previously:

             1. Kéuih hái gaaklèih gó gàan chàhlàuh.
                He's at the teahouse next door. [next-door teahouse]

             2. Kéuih hái gó gàan chàhlàuh gaaklèih.
                He's next door to the teahouse.

————————————

12. Transformation Drill: Affirmative to Negative.

    Ex: T: Kéuih heui Tīnsīng   T: He's going to the Star Ferry.
           Máhtàuh.

        S: Kéuih m̀hheui Tīnsīng   S: He's not going to the Star
           Máhtàuh.   Ferry.

1. Kéuih jip ngóh heui tái   1. Kéuih m̀hjip ngóh heui tái
   yīsāng.   yīsāng.

2. Hái nīdouh hóyíh tanhauh.   2. Hái nīdouh m̀hhóyíh tanhauh.

3. Ngóh yáuh sahp mān.   3. Ngóh móuh sahp mān.

4. Ngóh gau chín máaih bīu.   4. Ngóh m̀hgau chín máaih bīu.

5. Chàhn Táai deui hàaih géi leng. 5. Chàhn Táai deui hàaih
                                       m̀hhaih géi leng.

6. Wòhng Sàang jùngyi tùhng ngóh   6. Wòhng Sàang m̀hjùngyi tùhng
   bàhbā heui yám chàh.   ngóh bàhbā heui yám chàh.

+ 7. Sihk yīn lā!   7. M̀hhóu sihk yīn la!
                                       (friendly advice)

302

8. Wòhng Táai tùhng ngóh màhmā
   hóu jùngyi jouh sāam.

9. Ngóh táidóu Léih Síujé hái
   deuimihn gàan chàhlàuh.

10. Fàanjyun tàuh lā!

8. Wòhng Táai tùhng ngóh màhmā
   m̀hjùngyi jouh sāam.

9. Ngóh táim̀hdóu Léih Síujé
   hái deuimihn gàan chàhlàuh.

10. M̀hhóu fàanjyun tàuh la. or
    M̀hsái fàanjyun tàuh la.

Comment: in #7 and #10 above note that the sentence suffix
on the negative sentences is la and not lā. The mid-
pitched final la gives the imperative sentence a
connotation of friendly advice, contrasting to the high
pitch lā, polite but more urgent.

13. Transformation Drill: Change the sentence from a question-word
    question to a choice type question, following the pattern of
    the example.

Ex: T: Bīn tiuh haih Dāk
       Fuh Douh Jùng a?

    S: Nī tiuh haih m̀hhaih
       Dāk Fuh Douh Jùng
       a?

T: Which street is Des Voeux
   Central?

S: Is this Des Voeux Road Central?

1. Bīn gàan haih Jùnggwok
   Ngàhnhòhng a?

2. Bīn gàan haih Wìhng Ōn Gūngsī
   a?

3. Bīn gàan haih Méihgwok Jáudim
   a?

4. Bīn tiuh haih Daaih Douh Jùng
   a?

5. Bīn gàan haih Màhnwàh Jáudim
   a?

1. Nī gàan haih m̀hhaih Jùnggwok Ngàhnhòhng a?

2. Nī gàan haih m̀hhaih Wìhng
   Ōn Gūngsī a?

3. Nī gàan haih m̀hhaih Méihgwok Jáudim a?

4. Nī tiuh haih m̀hhaih Daaih
   Douh Jùng a?

5. Nī gàan haih m̀hhaih Màhnwàh
   Jáudim a?

14. Substitution Drill: Repeat the first sentence, then substitute as
    directed.

1. Chìhnbihn yáuh móuh wái paak
   chē a?
   Is there a place to park the
   car in front?

2. /yahpbihn/

3. /deuimihn/

1. Chìhnbihn yáuh móuh wái paak
   chē a?

2. Yahpbihn yáuh móuh wái
   paak chē a?

3. Deuimihn yáuh móuh wái
   paak chē a?

303

4. /mùhnháu/

4. Mùhnháu yáuh móuh wái paak chē a?

5. /gaaklèih/

5. Gaaklèih yáuh móuh wái paak chē a?

6. /nǐjógán/

6. Nǐjógán yáuh móuh wái paak chē a?

7. /jóbihn/

7. Jóbihn yáuh móuh wái paak chē a?

8. /yauhbihn/

8. Yauhbihn yáuh móuh wái paak chē a?

---

15. Response Drill:

+ Ex: T: Néih sīk m̀hsīk jà chē a? /m̀hsīk/

Do you know how to drive? [drive car] /not know how/

S: Ngóh m̀hsīk jà chē.

I don't know how to drive.

1. Bǐngo gaau néih jà chē ga? /Hòh Sàang/

1. Hòh Sàang gaau ngóh jà chē ge.

2. Hèunggóng yáuh móuh hohkhaauh gaau jà chē ga? /dāk géi gàan...ge ja/

2. Hèunggóng dāk géi gàan hohkhaauh gaau jà chē ge ja.

3. Néih hái bǐndouh hohk jà chē ga? /Gáulùhng/

3. Ngóh hái Gáulùhng hohk jà chē ge.

4. Nǐ tiuh gāai hó m̀hhóyíh hohk jà chē ga? /m̀hhóyíh bo/++ Is this a street that you can learn to drive on?

4. Nǐ tiuh gāai m̀hhóyíh hohk jà chē bo.

5. Néih jùngyi jà bīn gwok ge chē a? /Méihgwok chē/ Which country's cars do you like to drive?

5. Ngóh jùngyi jà Méihgwok chē.

6. Néih jùng m̀hjùngyi jà chē a? /m̀hhaih géi jùngyi ge ja/

6. Ngóh m̀hhaih géi jùngyi jà chē ge ja.

++ Access to some streets in Hong Kong is prohibited to learner drivers.

304

16. Expansion Drill

> Ex: T: Ṁhgòi néih, faaidī   T: Faster please. /drive/
>   lā! /jà/
>   S: Ṁhgòi néih jà faaidī S: Please drive faster.
>   lā!

1. Ṁhgòi néih, maahndī lā! /góng/   1. Ṁhgòi néih góng maahndī lā!

2. Ṁhgòi néih, faaidī lā! /hàahng/ 2. Ṁhgòi néih hàahng faaidī lā!

3. Ṁhgòi néih, chèuhngdī lā!   3. Ṁhgòi néih jouh chèuhngdī
   /jouh/   lā!
   Longer please. (said to a   Make it longer please.
   tailor)

4. Ṁhgòi néih, dyúndī lā! /jouh/   4. Ṁhgòi néih jouh dyúndī lā!

5. Ṁhgòi néih, pèhngdī lā! /maaih/ 5. Ṁhgòi néih maaih pèhngdī lā!
   Cheaper! (said to shopkeeper)   Sell it cheaper!

6. Ṁhgòi néih, daaihdī lā! /jouh/   6. Ṁhgòi néih jouh daaihdī lā!

7. Ṁhgòi néih, faaidī lā! /sé/   7. Ṁhgòi néih sé faaidī lā!

8. Ṁhgòi néih, saidī lā! /sé/   8. Ṁhgòi néih sé saidī lā!

9. Ṁhgòi néih, futdī lā. /jouh/   9. Ṁhgòi néih jouh futdī lā!
   Wider please. (said to a   Please make (it) a bit
   tailor)   wider.

10. Ṁhgòi néih, jaakdī lā. /jouh/ 10. Ṁhgòi néih jouh jaakdī lā!
    A bit narrower, please.   Please make (it) a bit
                                       narrower.

---

17. Classroom Conversation Drill: Teacher asks, students answer,
    giving their actual Cantonese names. Students should learn to
    react appropriately to the different questions.

1. Gwaising a? (polite)   1. Síu sing <u>Surname</u>. or
                                    Ngóh sing _____.

2. Sing mēyéh a? (ordinary)   2. Ngóh sing <u>Surname</u>.

+ 3. Gwaisingmìhng a? (polite)   3. <u>Surname Given name</u>.
   <u>Your family name and given
   name</u>?

4. Mēyéh méng a?   4. <u>Surname Given name</u>.

5. Néih giu mēyéh méng a?   5. <u>Surname Given name</u>.

6. Néih mēyéh méng a?   6. <u>Surname Given name</u>.

Comment: The response to #4 <u>mēyéh méng a</u>? may be simply the
         given name if the surname is not in question.

Comment: An expanded form of the responses to #3-6 is:

Ngóh sìng _____ giu(jouh) _____.

IV. CONVERSATIONS FOR LISTENING

(On tape. Refer to wordlist below as you listen.)

Unfamiliar terms, in order of occurrence:

1) yātján = in a little while

2) dīksí = taxi

3) gàaiháu = intersection [street-mouth]

4) hóu chíh = very likely ..., most likely ...

5) Ei! = mild exclamation

6) gwojó la = here: we've overshot it, we've passed it.
   gwo = pass by

7) sái = drive

V. SAY IT IN CANTONESE

A. Say to the classmate next to you:

1. Could you please tell me which building is the Wing On Company?

2. What's the name of this street?

3. Is this Nathan Road?

4. Here it is! Please stop here. (as if said to taxi-driver)

5. Is it OK to park here?

6. What street is your school on?

7. Can you drive a car?

8. Turn right just beyond the library.

B. And he responds:

1. It's that one on the right hand side.

2. This is Queens Road Central.

3. No--Nathan Road is on the Kowloon side.

4. It's not permitted to stop here--a little further down it's OK to stop.

5. No. Go in there to the right--there's a place inside to park.

6. I forget the name of the street--

7. Yes, I can--do you want me to teach you to drive?

8. You can't turn in to the right on that street. Should I stop here?

306

9. Is that the Mandarin Hotel
   there on the right?

9. No, that building is the
   Hilton Hotel.

---

ocabulary Checklist for Lesson 13

1.	daaphaak	n:	passenger
2.	diuhtàuh	vo:	turn (a car) around [reverse head]
3.	dou	v:	arrive
4.	fàanjyun tàuh	vp:	turn (the car) around and go back [return-turn head]
5.	gāai	n:	street
6.	giu(jouh)	v:	is called, is named
7.	gwaisingmìhng?	Ph:	what is your surname and given name? (polite)
8.	gwo	v:	pass by (a point); cross (a street); go over to (a place)
9.	gwodī	Ph:	beyond; a little farther on
10.	Gwodī tìm.	Ph:	Go further on; Keep going (said to taxi driver)
11.	hàahng	v:	go; walk; drive
12.	hóyíh	auxV:	can, as (1) be permitted, allowed to; (2) be willing to
13.	jà chē	vo:	to drive a car
14.	jauh	adv:	immediately, soon; as clause connector = then; and
15.	jihk	bf:	straight
16.	jó	bf:	left (direction)
17.	jóbihn	PW:	left side
18.	jósáubihn	PW:	lefthand side
19.	jyun	v:	turn
20.	la	ss:	as sen. suf. to imperative sentence, gives connotation of friendly advice
21.	méng	n:	name; given name
22.	paak (chē)	v(o):	park a car
23.	tanhauh	v:	back (a car) up, move back
24.	tìhng	v:	stop
25.	wái	n:	place, seat
26.	Wìhngōn Gūngsī	PW:	Wing On Department Store
27.	yahp	bf:	enter

307

28. yahpbihn	PW:	inside
29. yahpheui	v:	go in; enter
30. yātjihk	adv:	straight a) direction b) without being diverted: straight-away
31. yauh	bf:	right (direction)
32. yauhbihn	PW:	right side
33. yauhsáubihn	PW:	right hand side

I. BASIC CONVERSATION

A. Buildup:

(A Hong Kong native and a foreign friend
have lunch in a Chinese restaurant:)

Bûndeihyàhn

fôgei	waiter
A: Fôgei!	Waiter!
choipáai	menu, bill of fare
ning	carry
ninglàih; ningheui	bring; take
ning go choipáai làih lā	bring the food list please
ning go choipáai làih béi ngôh lā	please bring me a menu
táiháh	have a look
béi ngôh táiháh lā	please let me have a look
Mhgòi néih ning go choipáai làih béi ngôh táiháh lā.	Please bring me a menu to have a look at.

Fôgei

Hôu aak, jauh làih.	Yes sir; coming right away.
ngoihgwokyàhn	foreigner

Ngoihgwokyàhn

dím	order (food from a list)
choi	food, dishes
Ngôh mhsīk dím choi ga.	I don't know how to order food.
gaaisiuh	recommend, introduce
Mhgòi néih gaaisiuhháh lā.	Please make a recommendation.

Bûndeihyàhn

Gám, dáng ngôh dím lā.	Well then, I'll choose.
yùhjyū	suckling pig
gwo	verb-suffix: indicates experience; to have done something before.
meih	not yet
sihkgwo meih?	have (you) eaten (it) before?

	question formula: Verbed before, or not yet?
Néih sihkgwo yùhjyū meih a?	Have you ever eaten roast suckling pig?

Ngoihgwokyàhn

Meih a.	Not yet.
yāt chi dōu meih ...	not yet even one time
Yāt chi dōu meih sihkgwo.	I haven't eaten it even once.

Bùndeihyàhn

hóu ma?	OK?
ma?	sen. suf. which makes a question of the sentence it is attached to.
Sihāh lā, hóu ma?	Let's try it, OK?

Ngoihgwokyàhn

Hóu ā.	Fine.

Bùndeihyàhn

hā	shrimp
yìkwaahk?	... or ...?
Néih jùngyi sihk hā yìkwaahk sihk yú nē?	Do you like to eat shrimp, or eat fish?

Ngoihgwokyàhn

Sihdaahn lā.	As you wish. i.e., Either one.
jùngyi sihk hā	like to eat shrimp
dōuhaih jùngyi sihk hā	really like to eat shrimp
bātgwo	however, but, although
Bātgwo ngóh dōuhaih jùngyi sihk hā.	Although I really like shrimp. (i.e., I really like shrimp better.)
juhng	still, in addition, also (precedes verbal expression)
juhng oi dī mēyéh a?	also want some what?
juhng séung oi dī mēyéh a?	also want to have some what?

Ngóhdeih juhng séung oi dī   What else do we want to have?
   mēyéh a?

               Búndeihyàhn

   tòng   soup

Juhng séung oi go tòng tīm.   In addition let's have a soup
                              too.

  (Later the local resident calls the waiter again:)

               Búndeihyàhn

   -dò-   additional; another; more
                              (precedes Measure expres-
                              sion)

   bēi dò jī bējáu ngóh   give me another bottle of
                              beer

   -dò léuhng jī bējáu   two more bottles of beer

Fógei! Bēi dò léuhng jī bējáu   Waiter! Please give us two
   ngóhdeih tīm lā.   more bottles of beer.

               Ngoihgwokyàhn

   m̀hcho   good [not wrong]

Dī yùhjyù jànhaih m̀hcho.   The suckling pig is really good.

               Búndeihyàhn

   dōdī   more

Sihk dōdī lā!   Have some more!

               Ngoihgwokyàhn

   dòjeh   thank you (for the gift)

Gau laak. Dòjehsaai.   I've had plenty. Thanks a lot.

               Búndeihyàhn

   m̀aaihdāan   check please! [together-
                            list]

Fógei! Màaihdāan!   Waiter! The check please!

B. Recapitulation:

           (A Hong Kong native and a foreign friend
           have lunch in a Chinese restaurant:)

               Búndeihyàhn

A! Fógei!   Waiter!

Mhgòi néih nǐng go choipáai
láih béi ngóh táiháh lā.

Please bring me a menu to have
a look at.

Fógei

Hóu aak, jauh láih.

Yes sir, coming right away.

Ngoihgwokyàhn

Ngóh mhsǐk dǐm choi ga. Mhgòi
néih gaaisiuhháh lā.

I don't know how to order food.
Please make a recommendation.

Búndeihyàhn

Gám, dáng ngóh dǐm lā.
Néih sihkgwo yúhjyū meih a?

Well then, I'll choose.
Have you ever eaten roast
suckling pig?

Ngoihgwokyàhn

Meih a--yāt chi dōu meih
sihkgwo.

Not yet--I've not eaten it
even once.

Búndeihyàhn

Siháh lā, hóu ma?

Let's try it, OK?

Ngoihgwokyāhn

Hóu ā.

Fine.

Búndeihyàhn

Néih jùngyi sihk hā yīkwaahk
sihk yú nē?

Do you prefer shrimp, or fish?

Ngoihgwokyàhn

Sihdaahn lā.
Bātgwo ngóh dōuhaih jùngyi
sihk hā.

As you wish. i.e., Either one.
Although I really like shrimp.
(i.e., I really like shrimp
better.)

Ngóhdeih juhng séung oi dǐ
mēyéh a?

What else do we want to have?

Búndeihyàhn

Juhng séung oi go tòng tīm.

In addition, let's have a
soup, too.

(Later the Hong Kong native calls the waiter again:)

Fógei! Béi dò léuhng jī
bējáu ngóhdeih tīm lā.

Waiter! Please give us two
more bottles of beer.

312

Ngoihgwokyàhn
Dī yúhjyū jànhaih āhcho.   The suckling pig is really
                                            good!
Búndeihyàhn
Sihk dōdī lāi   Have some more!
Ngoihgwokyàhn
Gau laak. Dòjehsaai.   I've had plenty. Thanks a lot.
Búndeihyàhn
Fógei! Màaihdāan!   Waiter! The check please!

I. NOTES

A. Culture notes

1. Styles of cooking Chinese food.

Different areas of China have different styles of cooking and different specialties, making use of the foods particular to each area. For an interesting discussion of the hows and whats of Chinese food, see How to Cook and Eat in Chinese, by Buwei Yang Chao, (NY: John Day, 1949)

2. choi. 'a dish (of food),' 'food'.

The Chinese style of informal eating is for each person to have a bowl of rice (if it's in the South--in the North they eat bread more) for himself, and for there to be several dishes on the table which are communal property for everyone to eat from. The eater uses his chopsticks or a spoon to take food from the center dishes. The center dishes are called choi.

A choi can be a fish dish, a meat dish, or a vegetable dish. choi is also the general term for 'vegetable.' Finally, choi may mean 'cooking style,' or 'food,' as in Seuhnghói choi, 'Shanghai cooking,' 'Shanghai food'; Jùngchoi 'Chinese cooking,' 'Chinese food.'

(In this book we use the term Jùngchoi as the general term for Chinese food. There is another term sometimes used having the same meaning: Tòhngchoi = Chinese food.)

313

3. choipáai and choidāan, 'menu'

      choipáai, 'menu,' 'bill of fare,' is the list you choose from in a restaurant.

      choidāan, 'menu' is the written-down account of a particular meal.

B. Structure Notes:

  1. directional verb compounds. Ex: nìnglàih, 'bring (something) here; and nìngheui, 'take (something) there'

    a. Directional verbs use -làih and -heui as suffixes to indicate direction towards and away from the speaker (or other point of reference).

        Ex: nìng   carry

            nìnglàih carry towards the speaker--i.e., bring here

            nìngheui carry away from the speaker--i.e., take there

      We give the directional verb plus the heui/làih suffix the name directional verb compound.

    b. The noun object of a directional verb compound comes between the verb and the suffix. In the absence of a noun object, the verb and suffix come together, since a pronoun object is not stated:

        Ex: A: Nìng jì bējáu làih   Please bring a bottle of beer.
              là.

           B: Hóu, jauh nìnglàih.   Right--bringing it right away.

           (See BC and Drills 1,3, 10)

    c. Another way of forming sentences with directional verb compounds is to put the logical object of the verb into subject position.

        Ex: Dī bējá yìhgìng nìng-   The beer (I've) already
           làih laak.   brought.

  2. gwo 'pass,' used as verb suffix

      gwo, a verb with the basic meaning 'pass,' 'pass by,' 'pass through,' is used as a verb suffix indicating 'have passed through (experienced)' the action expressed by the verb.

        Ex: sihkgwo, 'pass through the experience of eating,' 'have eaten,' 'ate.'

        (See BC and Drills 7, 8, 9, 13)

3. __meih__ 'not yet.'

    The negative __meih__ 'not yet' precedes the verb in a negative
sentence. In a choice question, it follows the verb:

   Ex: 1. Meih sihkgwo.   (I) haven't had the experience
                of eating (it).

     2. Sihkgwo meih?   Have (you) had the experience
                of eating (this)?

     (See BC and Drills 3, 8, 9. 13)

  __meih__ 'not yet,' indicates that the action expressed by the
verb is one which the speaker contemplates doing--'I haven't eaten
it __yet__,' (but I'd like to.)

4. __mēyéh__, (__mātyéh__) as mass noun.

  __mēyéh__ functions as a mass noun, in taking the mass measure __dī__:

   Ex: dī mēyéh?   Some what?

     Sihk dī mēyéh a? What will you have to eat?
                [eat-a little-what?]

5. ...,__yīkwaahk__...... = '....., or .....?'

  __yīkwaahk__ 'or' can be called an interrogative conjunction. It
connects two verb phrases, indicating: .$\overset{A}{\cdot}$. or .$\overset{B}{\cdot}$., which one?

   Ex: Néih jùngyi sihk hā, Which do you prefer, to eat
     yīkwaahk sihk yú nē? shrimp, or to eat fish? __or__
              Do you want shrimp, or would
              you rather have fish?

     (See BC and Drills 2, 3)

  The English possibility of:

   A: Do you want coffee or tea?

   B: No thanks.

is not covered by __yīkwaahk__. In Chinese you would have to rephrase
the sentence to say something like 'Would you like something to
drink? We have coffee and tea.'

6. __dōuhaih__ 'really'

  In the following sentence taken from the Basic Conversation,

    Bātgwo ngóh dōuhaih Although I really like shrimp.
    jùngyi sihk hā.

  __dōuhaih__ is said with very light stress, and has very little
content meaning. It serves as an intonation marker, lightening an otherwise blunt statement. The same function is served by 'really' in
the English translation. The situation is: you'd rather have shrimp
than fish but you don't want to insist upon it.

7. sentence suffix <u>ma</u>?

      <u>ma</u>? is an interrogative sentence suffix which makes a question of the affirmative or negative sentence it attaches to. It is not used with a sentence which is already in question form--i.e., it is not used with choice-type and question-word questions.

                  (See BC)

8. sentence suffix <u>ā</u>

     In the Basic Conversation there is the following exchange:

          A: Siháh lā, hóu ma?   Let's try it, OK?
          B: Hóu ā.   Fine.

     The raised intonation on the final <u>ā</u> expresses liveliness.

                  (See BC)

9. <u>juhng</u> 'still,' 'in addition,' 'also'

     <u>juhng</u> is an adverb which positions before a verb.

        Ex: 1. Juhng séung oi dī   Also think you want some what?
              meyéh a?   i.e. What else would you
                               like to have?

           2. Juhng séung oi dī   We also think we want some soup
              tòng tìm.   too.

        (See BC and Drills <u>6,11</u>)

10. <u>dò</u> 'additional;' 'more'

     <u>dò</u> with the above meanings is bound to a following number-measure phrase. When the number is <u>yāt</u> 'one,' the number part may be omitted. Before mass nouns the measure <u>dī</u> follows <u>dò</u>, with the number <u>yāt</u> omitted.

        Ex: 1. dò (yāt)dī   another bottle, one more bottle,
                             an additional bottle

           2. dò léuhng go   two more, an additional two

           3. dò (yāt) dī tòng   more soup, additional soup
        (See BC and Drils <u>1.3, 1.4, 5, 10</u>)

11. <u>bātgwo</u> however, but, although

     <u>bātgwo</u> is a conjunction joining two clauses. Its sentence position is first word in the second clause.

        Ex: Yú tùhng hā dōu hóu   Fish and shrimp are both good--
            hóusihk, bātgwo   but I really prefer shrimp.
            ngóh dōuhaih
            jùngyi sihk hā.

II. DRILLS

1. Expansion Drill

+ 1. a.   Wún   a.   bowl

   b.   Wún tòng.   b.   bowl of soup

   c. Yám wún tòng.   c.   have a bowl of soup

   d. Yám wún tòng lā.   d. Please have a bowl of soup.

   e. Yám dò wún tòng lā.   e. Have another bowl of soup.

   f. Yám dōdī tòng lā.   f. Have some more soup.

Comment: In this group of sentences wún, 'bowl' is used as a
Measure. wún may also be used as a Noun, as in
sàam jek wún, '3 bowls.' (also sàam go wún, '3
bowls.')

+ 2. a.   Bùi   a.   cupful

   b.   Bùi chàh   b.   a cup of tea

   c.   Béi bùi chàh   c. Please give me a cup of tea.
      ngóh lā.

   d. Ñhgòi néih béi bùi chàh d. Please give me a cup of tea.
      ngóh lā.

+ 3. a.   Būi.   a.   cup

   b.   Jek būi.   b.   a cup

   c. Níng   jek būi làih.   c. Bring   a cup.

   d. Níng dò jek būi làih.   d. Bring another cup.

   e. Níng dò léuhng jek būi làih. e. Bring two more cups.

   f. Níng dò léuhng jek būi làih f. Bring two more cups too.
      tìm.

+ 4. a.   Baahk faahn.   a.   white rice.
                             (i.e. plain boiled or
                             steamed rice)

   b.   Wún baahk faahn.   b.   a bowl of rice.

   c. Béi wún baahk faahn ngóh. d. Give me   a bowl of rice.

   d. Béi dò wún baahk faahn ngóh. d. Give me another bowl of rice.

   e. Ñhgòi néih   e. Please
      béi dò wún baahk faahn ngóh lā. give me another bowl of rice.

+ 5. a.   Cháau mihn a.   fried noodles

   b.   Sihk cháau mihn b.   eat fried noodles

   c.   Jùngyi sihk cháau mihn c. like to eat fried noodles

   d.   Jùngyi sihk cháau mihn d. like to eat fried noodles or
+   yìkwaahk tòng mihn a?   soup noodles?

e. Néih jùngyi sihk cháau mihn   e. Would you like to eat fried
   yikwaahk tòng mihn a?   noodles or soup noodles?

---

2. Transformation Drill

Ex: T: Néih yám mātyéh a?   T: What will you have to drink?
       /chàh/gafē/   /tea/coffee/

    S: Néih yám chàh yīk-   S: Would you like tea, or coffee?
       waahk gafē nē?   (i.e., Which would you like,
                                   tea or coffee?)

1. Néih yám mātyéh a?   1. Néih yám heiséui yikwaahk
   /heiséui/bējáu/   bējáu a?

2. Néih oi mātyéh a?   2. Néih oi jyùyuhk yikwaahk
   /jyùyuhk/ngàuhyuhk/   ngàuhyuhk a?

3. Néih heui bīndouh a?   3. Néih heui Jùngwàahn yikwaahk
   /Jùngwàahn/Gáulùhng/   Gáulùhng a?

4. Néih wán bīngo a?   4. Néih wán Hòh Sàang yikwaahk
   /Hòh Sàang/Hòh Táai/   Hòh Táai a?

+ 5. Néih jùngyi bīndī a?   5. Néih jùngyi cháau faahn
     /cháau faahn/cháau mihn/   yikwaahk cháau mihn a?
     (cháau faahn =   Would you prefer fried
     fried rice)   rice, or fried noodles?

6. Néih jùngyi bīndī a?   6. Néih jùngyi Seuhnghói choi
+   /Seuhnghói choi/Gwóngdùng   yikwaahk Gwóngdùng choi nē?
     choi/   Would you prefer Shanghai
     (/Shanghai food/Cantonese   food or Cantonese food?
     food/)

7. Néih jùngyi bīndī a?   7. Néih jùngyi Jùng choi yik-
+   /Jùng choi/Sàichāan/   waahk Sàichāan nē?
     (/Chinese food/Western food/) Would you prefer Chinese
                                   food, or Western food?

318

3. Response Drill

Ex: T: /chaau faahn/ chaau mihn/

    T: /fried rice/fried noodles/

S1: Néih jùngyi sihk cháau faahn yìhwaahk sihk cháau mihn a?

    S1: Do you want to have fried rice, or fried noodles.

S2: <u>Sihdaahn lā.</u> Cháau faahn tùhng cháau mihn dōu dāk.

    S2: Either one. Fried rice and fried noodles are both fine.

1. /jyùyuhk/ngàuhyuhk/

    1. S1: Néih jùngyi sihk jyùyuhk yìkwaahk ngàuhyuhk a?

        S2: Sihdaahn lā. Jyùyuhk tùhng ngàuhyuhk dōu dāk.

2. /Jùngchoi/Sāichāan/

    2. S1: Néih jùngyi sihk Jùngchoi yìkwaahk Sāichāan a?

        S2: Sihdaahn lā. Jùngchoi tùhng Sāichāan dōu dāk.

3. /Seuhnghói choi/Gwóngdùng choi/

    3. S1: Néih jùngyi sihk Seuhnghói choi yìkwaahk Gwóngdùng choi a?

        S2: Sihdaahn lā. Seuhnghói choi tùhng Gwóngdùng choi dōu dāk.

4. /ngàuhnáaih/heiséui/

    4. S1: Néih jùngyi yám ngàuhnáaih yìkwaahk heiséui a?

        S2: Sihdaahn lā. Ngàuhnáaih tùhng heiséui dōu dāk.

5. /chàh/gafē/

    5. S1: Néih jùngyi yám chàh yìkwaahk gafē a?

        S2: Sihdaahn lā. Chàh tùhng gafē dōu dāk.

---

4. Expension Drill

Ex: T: /jī bējáu/

    T: /a bottle of beer/

S: Béi jī bējáu ngóh lā.

    S: Give me a bottle of beer.

1. /jī heiséui/

    1. Béi jī heiséui ngóh lā.

+ 2. /<u>jek gāng/</u>
   (a spoon)

    2. Béi jek gāng ngóh lā.
      Please give me a spoon.

3. /bùi chàh/

    3. Béi bùi chàh ngóh lā.

4. /bùi gafē/

    4. Béi bùi gafē ngóh lā.

5. /go cháau mihn/

    5. Béi go cháau mihn ngóh lā.

6. /go cháau faahn/

    6. Béi go cháau faahn ngóh lā.

7. /go tòng mihn/   7. Béi go tòng mihn ngóh lā.

8. /wún baahk faahn/   8. Béi wún baahk faahn ngóh lā.

9. /wún tòng mihn/   9. Béi wún tòng mihn ngóh lā.

10. /tìuh kwàhn/   10. Béi tìuh kwàhn ngóh lā.

11. /jek jīu/   11. Béi jek jīu ngóh lā.

    Comment: The sentences in the right hand column are appropriate
said by a diner in a restaurant to a waiter.

        Note that tòng mihn may be either go tòng mihn, 'an
order of soup noodles' (see #7) or wún tòng mihn,
'a bowl of soup noodles' (see #9).

---

5. Expansion Drill: Expand the sentences by adding dò.

    Ex: 1. T: Béi bàau yīnjái   T: Give me a pack of cigarettes.
          ngóh lā!

        S: Béi dò bàau yīn-   S: Give me another pack of
          jái ngóh lā!   cigarettes.

    2. T: Béi léuhng gihn   T: Give me two shirts.
          sēutsāam ngóh
          lā!

        S: Béi dò léuhng gihn   S: Give me two more shirts.
          sēutsāam ngóh lā!

+ 1. Béi deui faaijī ngóh lā!   1. Béi dò deui faaijī ngóh lā!
   (chopsticks)   Please give me another
                            pair of chopsticks.

2. Béi go tòng ngóh lā!   2. Béi dò go tòng ngóh lā!

3. Béi bá jē ngóh lā!   3. Béi dò bá jē ngóh lā!

4. Béi jek gāng ngóh lā!   4. Béi dò jek gāng ngóh lā!

5. Béi léuhng bàau yīnjái ngóh lā!   5. Béi dò léuhng bàau yīnjái
                                        ngóh lā!

---

6. Substitution Drill: Repeat the first sentence after the teacher,
then substitute as directed.

1. Juhng séung yiu dī mēyéh nē?   1. Juhng séung yiu dī mēyéh
   What else do you want?   nē?

2. /yám/   2. Juhng séung yám dī mēyéh nē?

3. /sihk/   3. Juhng séung sihk dī mēyéh
                        nē?

4. /oi/

5. /si/

6. /ló/

7. /máaih/

4. Juhng séung oi dĩ mēyéh nē?

5. Juhng séung si dĩ mēyéh nē?
   What else would you like
   to try? (in restaurant,
   ordering food)

6. Juhng séung ló dĩ mēyéh nē?
   What else do you want to
   get?

7. Juhng séung máaih dĩ mēyéh
   nē?

---

7. Response Drill

    Ex: T: Néih jeukgwo nĩ júng   T: Have you worn this kind of
           yúhlāu meih a?   raincoat before? /nod/
           /nod/

        S: Jeukgwo.   S: Yes.

        T: Néih jeukgwo gó deui   T: Have you worn that pair of
           hàaih meih a?   shoes yet?
           /shake/

        S: Meih.   S: No, not yet.

1. Néih sihkgwo hā meih a?   1. Meih.
   /shake/

2. Néih yámgwo nĩ júng bējáu   2. Yámgwo.
   meih a? /nod/

3. Néih làihgwo Hèunggóng meih   3. Meih.
   a? /shake/

4. Néih heuigwo Méihgwok meih   4. Heuigwo.
   a? /nod/

5. Néih jyuhgwo Gáulùhng meih a?   5. Meih.
   /shake/

6. Néih yuhnggwo faaijí meih a?   6. Meih.
   /shake/

7. Néih yámgwo nĩ dĩ tòng meih   7. Meih.
   a? /shake/

+ 8. Néih jouhgwo nĩ dĩ yéh meih a?   8. Jouhgwo.
   /nod/
   Have you done this kind of work
   before?
   (jouh yéh =
   do chores; have a job)

---

8. Transformation Drill

      Ex: T: Ngóh sihkgwo cháau   I've eaten fried noodles before.
            mihn.

         S: Ngóh meih sihkgwo cháau I've never eaten fried noodles
            mihn.   before.

1. Ngóh jàgwo chē.   1. Ngóh meih jàgwo chē.

2. Ngóh heuigwo Méihgwok.   2. Ngóh meih heuigwo Méihgwok.

3. Ngóh jyungwo Gáulùhng.   3. Ngóh meih jyuhgwo Gáulùhng.

4. Ngóh yámgwo nī júng bējáu.   4. Ngóh meih yámgwo nī júng
                          bējáu.

5. Ngóh yuhnggwo faaijí.   5. Ngóh meih yuhnggwo faaijí.

+ 6. Ngóh làihgwo nī gàan __jáugā__. 6. Ngóh meih làihgwo nī gàan
     (__Chinese style restaurant__)   jáugā.

---

9. Expansion Drill

      Ex: T: Ngóh meih sihkgwo hā.   I've never eaten prawns.

        S: Ngóh meih sihkgwo hā,   I've never eaten prawns; have
          néih sihkgwo meih a?   you?

1. Ngóh meih sihkgwo yúhjyū.   1. Ngóh meih sihkgwo yúhjyū.
                         Néih sihkgwo meih a?

2. Ngóh meih yámgwo nī júng tòng. 2. Ngóh meih yámgwo nī júng
                         tòng. Néih yámgwo meih a?

3. Ngóh meih sihkgwo gó júng   3. Ngóh meih sihkgwo gó júng
   yīnjái.   yīnjái. Néih sihkgwo
                         meih a?

4. Ngóh meih heuigwo gó gàan   4. Ngóh meih heuigwo gó gàan
   jáugā.   jáugā. Néih heuigwo
                         meih a?

5. Ngóh meih dímgwo nī júng choi. 5. Ngóh meih dímgwo nī júng
                         choi. Néih dímgwo meih a?

---

10. Expansion Drill

> Ex: T: M̀hgòi néih nǐng jǐ
> bējáu làih.

Please bring a bottle of beer.

> S: M̀hgòi néih nǐng dò jǐ
> bējáu làih.

Please bring another bottle of beer.

1. M̀hgòi néih nǐng deui faaijí làih.

1. M̀hgòi néih nǐng dò deui faaijí làih.

2. M̀hgòi néih nǐng jek gāng làih.

2. M̀hgòi néih nǐng dò jek gāng làih.

3. M̀hgòi néih nǐng jek būi làih.

3. M̀hgòi néih nǐng dò jek būi làih.

+ 4. M̀hgòi néih nǐng go <u>wúnjái</u> làih.
    /small bowl/

4. M̀hgòi néih nǐng dò go wúnjái làih.

+ 5. M̀hgòi néih nǐng jek <u>séui būi</u> làih. /<u>water glass</u>/

5. M̀hgòi néih nǐng dò jek séui būi làih.

> a. Repeat, teacher giving cue only, students responding with sentences in left hand column, thus:
>
> T: jǐ bējáu
>
> S: M̀hgòi néih nǐng jǐ bējáu làih.

---

11. Expansion Drill

> Ex: T: Néih sihksaai dǐ hā
> meih a?

Have you eaten up all the shrimp

> S: Sihksaai laak, ngóh
> juhng séung yiu dǐ
> tìm.

I've eaten (them all) up, and I still want some more. [in addition, want to have some more]

1. Néih sihksaai dǐ yú meih a?

1. Sihksaai laak, ngóh juhng séung yiu dǐ tìm.

2. Néih sihksaai dǐ cháau faahn meih a?

2. Sihksaai laak, ngóh juhng séung yiu dǐ tìm.

3. Néih yám saai dǐ chàh meih a?

3. Yám saai laak, ngóh juhng séung yiu dǐ tìm.

4. Néih yuhngsaai dǐ chìn meih a?

4. Yuhngsaai laak, ngóh juhng séung yiu dǐ tìm.

5. Néih sihksaai dǐ cháau mihn meih a?

5. Sihksaai laak, ngóh juhng séung yiu dǐ tìm.

6. Néih yámsaai dǐ tòng meih a?

6. Yámsaai laak, ngóh juhng séung yiu dǐ tìm.

323

12. Response Drill

> Ex: T: Yú tùhng hā, néih
> jùngyi bīn yeuhng
> a? (type, kind)
>
> S: Yú tùhng hā, ngóh
> léuhng yeuhng dōu
> jùngyi.

T: Which do you like better, fish
or prawns? [fish and prawns,
you like which kind more?]

S: Fish and prawns, I like both.

1. Jùngchoi tùhng Sāichāan, néih
   jùngyi bīn yeuhng a?

   1. Jùngchoi tùhng Sāichāan,
      ngóh léuhng yeuhng dōu
      jùngyi.

2. Gwóngdùng choi tùhng Seuhnghói
   choi, néih jùngyi bīn yeuhng
   a?

   2. Gwóngdùng choi tùhng Seuhng-
      hói choi, ngóh léuhng
      yeuhng dōu jùngyi.

3. Cháau mihn tùhng tòng mihn,
   néih jùngyi bīn yeuhng a?

   3. Cháau mihn tùhng tòng mihn,
      ngóh léuhng yeuhng dōu
      jùngyi.

4. Cháau faahn tùhng baahk faahn,
   néih jùngyi bīn yeuhng a?

   4. Cháau faahn tùhng baahk
      faahn, ngóh léuhng yeuhng
      dōu jùngyi.

+ 5. Jùnggwok choi tùhng Yahtbún
   choi, néih jùngyi bīn yeuhng a?
   (Chinese food)
   (Japanese food)

   5. Jùnggwok choi tùhng Yahtbún
      choi, ngóh léuhng yeuhng
      dōu jùngyi.

---

13. Response Drill

> Ex: T: Néih heuigwo géidō
> chi a?
>
> S: Yāt chi dōu meih
> heuigwo.

T: How many times have you been
there?

S: I've never been even once.

1. Néih làihgwo géidō chi a?
2. Néih yuhnggwo géidō chi a?
3. Néih heuigwo géidō chi a?
4. Néih sihkgwo géidō chi a?
5. Néih fàangwo Seuhnghói géidō
   chi a?

1. Yāt chi dōu meih làihgwo.
2. Yāt chi dōu meih yuhnggwo.
3. Yāt chi dōu meih heuigwo.
4. Yāt chi dōu meih sihkgwo.
5. Yāt chi dōu meih fàangwo.

324

14. Expansion Drill

     Ex: T: Kéuih yáuh léuhng   T: He has two cars.
          ga chē.

        S: Kéuih yáuh léuhng   S: He has two cars, but I don't
          ga chē, daahnhaih   even have one.
          ngóh yāt ga dōu
          móuh.

1. Gó go hohkwàang yáuh géi jí   1. Gó go hohksàang yáuh géi jí
   yùhnjíbāt.   yùhnjíbāt, daahnhaih ngóh
                            yāt jí dōu móuh.

2. Kéuih yáuh léuhng go taaitáai.   2. Kéuih yáuh léuhng go taai-
                             táai, daahnhaih ngóh yāt
                             go dōu móuh.

3. Kéuih yáuh léuhng go sáudói.   3. Kéuih yáuh léuhng go sáudói,
                             daahnhaih ngóh yāt go dōu
                             móuh.

4. Gó go sīgēi yáuh léuhng ga   4. Gó go sīgēi yáuh léuhng ga
   chē.   chē, daahnhaih ngóh yāt
                             ga dōu móuh.

5. Kéuih yáuh léuhng go jái.   5. Kéuih yáuh léuhng go jái,
                             daahnhaih ngóh yāt go
                             dōu móuh.

---

15. Transformation Drill

      Ex: T: Sihk dōdī lā.   T: Have some more.
        S: Mhhóu sihk gam dò a. S: Don't eat so much.

1. Jà maahndī lā!   1. Mhhóu jà gam maahn a.
2. Dím dōdī lā!   2. Mhhóu dím gam dò a.
3. Sihk dōdī lā!   3. Mhhóu sihk gam dò a.
4. Jà faaidī lā!   4. Mhhóu jà gam faai a.
5. Hàahng faaidī lā!   5. Mhhóu hàahng gam faai a.
6. Yám dōdī lā!   6. Mhhóu yám gam dò a.
7. Jouh chèuhngdī lā!   7. Mhhóu jouh gam chèuhng a.
8. Jouh dyúndī lā!   8. Mhhóu jouh gam dyún a.

IV. CONVERSATIONS FOR LISTENING

      (On tape. Refer to wordlist below as you listen.)

      Unfamiliar terms, in order of occurrence:

        1) ngāamngāam = just now

        2) fòng gùng = leave work, get off from work

        3) yìhm guhk gāi = salt-roasted chicken

        4) gaailáan cháau ngàuhyuhk = stir fried beef and broccoli

        5) taai - too, excessively

        6) sài yèuhng choi tòng = watercress soup

        7) giu = order, call for (without having to look at a listed menu)

        8) Yèuhngjàu cháau faahn = Yangchow fried rice

        9) Sàiyèuhngchoi tòng = watercress soup

        10) faai = soon, almost, approaching (preceding a time expression)

        11) yáuh méng = famous

        12) gù lòu yuhk = sweet & sour pork

        13) dōu yiu sai ge = want both to be small portions

V. SAY IT IN CANTONESE

A. Say to the classmate sitting next to you:

  1. Have you eaten fried noodles before?

  2. Which do you like better, fried noodles or fried rice?

  3. (deciding on a restaurant:) Which would you prefer-- Shanghai food or Cantonese food?

  4. I don't know how to order-- would you suggest something?

  5. What else shall we have?

  6. Waiter, would you please bring two bottles of beer?

  7. Waiter, please bring another glass.

B. And he answers:

  1. Yes, many times.

  2. Fried rice.

  3. Either one, I like both.

  4. Let's have fried noodles and a soup, OK?

  5. Shall we have some beer?

  6. Yes, sir, right away.

  7. All right--shall I bring another bottle of beer?

8. Can you use chopsticks?

9. The soup noodles are not bad!

10. Have some more!

11. Have you eaten in this
    (Western style) restaurant
    before?

12. Have you ever eaten roast
    suckling pig?

13. Have you drunk up all your
    beer?

14. Mr. Chan has 10 sons.

15. Don't eat so much!

8. No--please show me (introduce).

9. I think so too.

10. I've had enough, thanks.

11. No, I've never been here
    even once.

12. Yes, several times.

13. Yes, and I think I'd like
    some more.

14. Is that so! I don't even
    have one.

15. Don't drink so much!

Vocabulary Checklist for Lesson 14

1.	baahk faahn	n:	boiled or steamed rice [white rice]
2.	bātgwo	cj:	however; but; although
3.	būi	n:	cup, glass
4.	bùi	m:	M. for cup, glass
5.	cháau	v:	to toss-fry in small amt of oil, as in scrambling eggs.
6.	cháau faahn	n:	fried rice
7.	cháau mihn	n:	fried noodles
8.	choi	n:	food; a particular food, a dish
9.	choipáai	n:	menu, bill of fare
10.	dím	v:	to order (food)
11.	dò	bf:	additional, as modifier in Noun phrase
12.	dōdī	adv:	more (in addition) (follows V)
13.	Dòjeh.	Ph:	Thank you. (for a gift)
14.	Dòjehsaai.	Ph:	Thank you very much.
15.	dōuhaih	adv:	always, really
16.	faaijí	n:	chopsticks
17.	fógei	n:	waiter in restaurant
18.	gaaisiuh	v:	recommend; introduce
19.	gāng	n:	spoon

327

20. -gwo	Vsuf:	indicates experience; to have done something before
21. Gwóngdùng choi	n:	Cantonese food
22. hā	n:	shrimp
23. Hóu ma?	Ph:	Is that OK?
24. jáugā	n/PW:	Chinese style restaurant
25. jek	m:	M. for spoon
26. jouh yéh	vo:	do chores; have a job
27. juhng	adv:	still, in addition, also (+ verb)
28. Jùngchoi	n:	Chinese food
29. Jùnggwok choi	n:	Chinese food
30. ma?	ss:	sen. suf. making a question of the sentence it attaches to
31. Màaihdāan!	Ph:	The check please!
32. meih	adv:	negative, 'not yet'
33. m̀hcho	Ph:	good [not-wrong], 'not bad!'
34. ngoihgwokyàhn	n:	foreigner(s)
35. níng	v:	carry (something)
36. níng...heui	v:	take, carry off (something)
37. níng...làih	v:	bring (something)...here
38. Sāichāan	n:	Western meal
39. Seuhnghói choi	n:	Shanghai food
40. séui būi	n:	water glass
41. Sihdaahn lā.	Ph:	Either one. No preference. As you wish. (when offered a choice)
42. táiháh	VP:	have a look
43. tòng	n:	soup
44. tòng mihn	n:	soup noodles
45. wún	m:	M. a bowl of...
46. wún	n:	bowl
47. wúnjái	n:	small bowl
48. Yahtbún choi	n:	Japanese food
49. yāt chi dōu meih...	VP:	not even once...
50. yāt..M..dōu .Neg..V.	Ph:	Not even one...; can't V. even one <u>M</u>.
51. yéh	n:	work (as in <u>jouh yéh</u>) (with restricted use)
52. yeuhng	m:	kind, type

328

53. yĭkwaahk...?   cj: or?
54. yúhjyū   n: roast suckling pig

I. BASIC CONVERSATION

  A. **Buildup:**

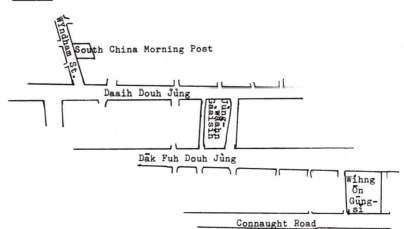

South China Morning Post

Daaih Douh Jùng

Dāk Fuh Douh Jùng

Wihng Ōn Gūngsī

Connaught Road

(Mr. Wong approaches another pedestrian
on the street in front of the South China
Morning Post building on Wyndham Street)

Wòhng Sàang

dím heui?	how go?, how (do you) go (to)?
dím heui Wihng Ōn Gūngsī a?	how do you go to the Wing On Company?
yàuh	from
yàuh nīdouh	from here
yàuh nīdouh dím heui Wihng Ōn Gūngsī a?	how do you get to the Wing On Company from here?
Chéng mahn néih, yàuh nīdouh dím heui Wihng Ōn Gūngsī a?	Could you please tell me how to get to the Wing On Company from here?
louhyàhn	pedestrian

Louhyàhn

lohk	down

lohkheui	go down [down go]
hàahng lohkheui	walk down (to)
hàahng lohkheui Daaih Douh Jūng	go down to Queen's Road Central
hàahng lohkheui Daaih Douh Jūng sìn	first go down to Queen's Road Central
yìhn(jì)hauh	then, after that
Hàahng lohkheui Daaih Douh Jūng sìn, yìhnhauh jyun jó.	First go down to Queen's Road Central, then turn left.

<u>Wòhng Sàang</u>

Jyun jó.	Turn left.

<u>Louhyàhn</u>

gàaisíh	food market
Jùngwàahn Gàaisíh	Central Market
hàahngdou Jùngwàahn Gàaisíh	walk to Central Market
-dou	verb suf. to verbs of action indicates arrival at goal.
Gám, yātjihk hàahngdou Jùngwàahn Gàaisíh, jyun yauh.	Then, go straight till you get to Central Market, and turn right.
gwojó gàaisíh	get past the market
Gwojó gàaisíh, jauh haih Dāk Fuh Douh Jùng laak.	When you get past the market, you are on Des Voeux Road Central.
mahn yàhn lā	ask someone
Heuidou gódouh, joi mahn yàhn lā.	When you get there, ask again.

(Mr. Wong arrives at Wing On and approaches a salesclerk:)

<u>Wòhng Sàang</u>

bouhfahn	department (in a store)
gó go bouhfahn	that department
maaih lāangsāam gó go bouhfahn	the sweater department [the department that sells sweaters]

331

| Maaih lāangsāam gó go bouh-
fahn hái bĭndouh a? | Where is the sweater
department? |

Sauhfoyùhn

séuhng	go up
séuhng sàam láu	go up to the third floor (Chinese and American style of counting; 2nd floor British style of counting)
chéng	invite; please
Chéng séuhng sàam láu lā.	Please go up to the second (or third) floor.

B. **Recapitulation:**

Wòhng Sàang

| Chéng mahn néih, yàuh nĭdouh
dĭm heui Wíhng Ŏn Gūngsĭ a? | Could you please tell me how
to get to the Wing On
Company from here? |

Louhyàhn

| Hàahng lohkheui Daaih Douh
Jùng sìn, yìhnhauh jyun jó. | First go down to Queen's Road
Central, then turn left. |

Wòhng Sàang

| Jyun jó. | Turn left. |

Louhyàhn

| Gám, yātjihk hàahngdou
Jùngwàahn Gàaisĭh, jyun yauh. | Then go straight till you get
to Central Market, and turn
right. |

| Gwojó gàaisĭh, jauh haih Dāk
Fuh Douh Jùng laak. | When you get past the market,
you are at Des Voeux Road
Central. |

| Heuidou gódouh, joi mahn yàhn
lā. | When you get there, ask again. |

(Mr. Wong gets to the store and asks a clerk:)

Wòhng Sàang

| Maaih lāangsāam gó go bouhfahn
hái bĭndouh a? | Where is the sweater
department? |

Sauhfoyùhn

Chéng séuhng sàam láu là!   Please go up to the second
                                     floor.

I. NOTES

1. Paired conjunctions:

   ...sìn, yìhnhauh (or yìhnjìhauh).... = 'first..., then....'

   This set of paired conjunctions connects two primary clauses in
   a sentence of sequential relationship.

   Ex: Hàahng lohkheui Daaih Douh   Go down to Queen's Road
       Jùng sìn, yìhnhauh   Central first, then turn left.
       jyun jó.

              (See BC and Drills 10, 11)

2. Directional verbs.

   a. Examples of directional verbs are:

       1. séuhng = up
       2. lohk   = down
       3. yahp   = in
       4. chēut = out
       5. gwo   = over, across

   b. In Cantonese these words pattern as verbs. They can be preceded by
      m̀h, and form a question on the Vm̀hV pattern.

       Ex: A: Néih lohk m̀hlohk a?   Are you going down? (Said at
                                         top of escalator)

           B: M̀hlohk.   No, I'm not going down.

   c. These directional verbs can be followed by either a placeword
      object, or one of the two directional suffixes, -làih and -heui,
      or both.

       Ex: 1. Kéuih séuhng sàam láu.   He went up to the 2nd floor.

           2. Ngóh dōu séuhngheui.   I went up too.

           3. Kéuih séuhng(làih)   He came up to the 2nd floor.
              sàam láu.

           4. Kéuih chēutheui Daaih   He went out to Queen's Road
              Douh Jùng.   Central.

                 (See Drills 13, 14)

333

  d. The directional verbs may combine with a preceding verb of movement,
    such as <u>hàahng</u> 'walk,' <u>jyun</u> 'turn,' <u>nǐng</u> 'carry.'

          Ex: 1. Kéuih hàahng lohk-   He walked down to the second
                 (heui) sàam láu.   floor.

              2. Kéuih jyun yahp(heui)   He turned into Des Voeux Road
                 Dāk Fuh Douh Jùng.   Central.

              3. Mhgòi néih nǐng   Please bring it out.
                 chēutlaih.

                        (See Drill _12_)

3. <u>deihhá</u>, <u>làuhhah</u>, <u>hahbihn</u> differentiated.

  1. <u>deihhá</u> simply means 'ground floor.'

  2. <u>làuhhah</u> [floor-below] is a pronoun of place whose meaning derives
     from position in relationship to another location. If you are on
     the 3d floor <u>làuhhah</u> is a floor below the 3d floor. If you are
     on the ground floor <u>làuhhah</u> is the basement.

  3. <u>hahbihn</u> [below-side] is also a locative whose meaning derives from
     position in relationship to another position. It can mean
     'downstairs' in relation to upstairs, 'under' something, 'below'
     something.

4. Two-part Verb forms: performance and achievement. Chinese verbs are
   often in two parts, with the first part telling of the performance
   and the second part telling of the achievement. For example:

          tái + dóu   = look + successful = see
          wán + dóu   = search + successful = find
          heui + dou = go + arrive = reach (a place)
          gwo + jó   = pass + accomplish = get past (a place)
          chéng + dóu = invite + successful = invite (someone) and have
                                             him accept

   The second part of these two-part verbs we regard as suffix to the
   first part.

5. <u>-dou</u> as verb suffix, indicates reaching the destination or goal.

          Ex: 1. heuidou = arrive [go-arrive]

                 Kéuih heuidou gódouh,...   When he got there,.... <u>or</u>
                                            When he gets there,....

              2. duhkdou = read to [read-arrive]

                 Kéuih duhkdou sa'ahsei   He read to page 34.
                 yihp.

                        (See BC and Drills <u>3,4</u>)

6. -jó verb suffix = accomplish the performance: 'get/got it done'

        Ex: Gwojó Jùngwàahn Gàaihsih,   When you get past the Central
             jyun jó.   Market, turn left.

    The -jó indicates that the action of the verb to which it is
attached is viewed from the standpoint of its being accomplished.

        Ex: gwojó X = 'accomplish going past X'

                (See BC and Drill _9_)

7. daih- = ordinal prefix.

    a. daih- prefixed to a number makes it an ordinal number:

        Ex: sàam fo = 3 lessons

           daih sàam fo = the 3d lesson

               (See Drill _3_)

    b. daihyih- is ambiguous.

        daihyih-, bound to a following measure, may mean 'the second';
'the next'; or 'another, some others   Only rarely is there any
mixup in an actual situation.

        Ex: 1. daihyih ga chē   the second car

           2. daihyih tìuh gāai   the next street, the second
                                street. (i.e. the first one
                                after the place you're
                                talking about)

           3. daihyih go gùngyàhn   another servant

           4. daihyih dī gùngyàhn   other servants

        In this lesson we practice only the first two meanings.

    daihyih as 'other' you will meet in Lesson 16.

8. yàuh (and hái) as 'from ..PW..'

        yàuh (or alternately, hái) serves as 'from' in the PW phrase:

        yàuh ..PW.. + .Verb.of.movement. = go/come/etc. from ..PW..

Though similar to co-verbs in having an object, yàuh differs from
co-verbs in not normally being preceded by m̀h, but using the verb
haih between m̀h and itself.

        Ex: M̀hhaih yàuh nīdouh chēut- Don't exit from here.
           heui.

Occasionally you may hear someone say M̀hyàuh nīdouh chēutheui or some
other phrase with m̀hyàuh, but it is not common usage. Therefore we
class yàuh (and hái used in this position) not as a co-verb but as a
preposition.

            (See BC and Drill _6_)

9. yihp 'page' and fo 'lesson' classed as measures.

Note that in the grammatical sense yihp and fo are measures, inasmuch as they can follow numbers directly. From the point of view of having substantive meaning, they are like nouns.

(See Drills 3,4)

10. chéng... = invite (someone to do something); Please .V.

chéng basically means 'invite.' chéng + Verb is used as a polite imperative:

   Ex: Chéng séuhng sàam láu. Please go up to the 3d floor
               [invite you to go up]

(See BC)

As polite imperative it is only used affirmatively. To say 'Please don't.V.' with chéng, the negative attaches to the following verb.

   Ex: Chéng m̀hséuhng sàam láu. Please don't go up to the 3d
               floor.

II. DRILLS

1. Substitution Drill: Repeat the first sentence after the teacher,
   then substitute as directed.

1. Kéuih hái douh dáng néih. He's waiting for you here.	1. Kéuih hái douh dáng néih.
2. /hauhbihn/	2. Kéuih hái hauhbihn dáng néih.
+ 3. /<u>yahpbihn</u>/	3. Kéuih hái yahpbihn dáng néih. He's waiting for you <u>inside</u>.
+ 4. /<u>deihhá</u>/ <u>ground floor</u>	4. Kéuih hái deihhá dáng néih. He's waiting for you on the ground floor.
+ 5. /<u>seuhngbihn</u>/ <u>above; upstairs</u>; <u>on top</u> [up-side]	5. Kéuih hái seuhngbihn dáng néih. He's waiting for you upstairs.
+ 6. /<u>hahbihn</u>/ <u>downstairs</u>; <u>below</u>; <u>under</u> [down-side]	6. Kéuih hái hahbihn dáng néih. He's waiting for you downstairs.
+ 7. /<u>làuhseuhng</u>/ <u>upstairs</u> [floor-above]	7. Kéuih hái làuhseuhng dáng néih. He's waiting for you upstairs.
+ 8. /<u>làuhhah</u>/ <u>downstairs</u> [floor[below]	8. Kéuih hái làuhhah dáng néih. He's waiting for you down- stairs.
9. /sei láu/	9. Kéuih hái sei láu dáng néih.
+ 10. /<u>chēutbihn</u>/ <u>outside</u>	10. Kéuih hái chēutbihn dáng néih.

---

2. Response Drill: Students gesture the directions.

Ex: 1. T: Màhnwàh Jáudim hái chìhnbihn, haih m̀hhaih a? /hauhbihn/	T: The Mandarin Hotel is in front, isn't it? /behind, in the back/
S: M̀hhaih, hái hauh- bihn.	S: No, it's in the back.
2. T: Màhnwàh Jáudim hái chìhnbihn, haih m̀hhaih a? /chìhnbihn/	T: The Mandarin Hotel is in front, isn't it? /in front, ahead/

337

S: Haih. Hái chìhn-   S: That's right, it's in front.
   bihn.

1. Méihgwok Ngàhnhòhng hái jósáu-   1. M̀hhaih, hái yauhsáubihn.
   bihn, haih m̀hhaih a?
   /yauhsáubihn/

2. Néih sīnsàang (ge) séjihlàuh   2. M̀hhaih, hái hauhbihn.
   hái chìhnbihn, haih m̀hhaih
   a? /hauhbihn/

3. Wòhng Sàang hái chēutbihn, haih   3. Haih, hái chēutbihn.
   m̀hhaih a? /chēutbihn/

4. Léih Táai hái yahpbihn, haih   4. M̀hhaih, hái chìhnbihn.
   m̀hhaih a? /chìhnbihn/

5. Tīnsīng Máhtàuh hái yauhsáubihn,   5. Haih, hái yauhsáubihn.
   haih m̀hhaih a? /yauhsáubihn/

6. Maaih hàaih gó go bouhfahn hái   6. M̀hhaih, hái deihhá.
   yih láu, haih m̀hhaih a?
   /deihhá/

7. Maaih syù gó go bouhfahn hái   7. M̀hhaih, hái làuhhah.
   làuhseuhng, haih m̀hhaih a?
   /làuhhah/

Comment: Note (#2 above) that ge can be omitted in everyday
       speech in modification structure before séjihlàuh.

      a. Repeat, students taking both parts, teacher
         cueing thus:

         1. /Màhnwàh Jáudim/chìhnbihn/hauhbihn/

     or 2. /Màhnwàh Jáudim/chìhnbihn/

---

3. Expansion Drill

+ 1. a. yihp   1. a. page

    b. sei'ah yihp.   b. 40 pages

+   c. duhk sei'ah yihp   c. read 40 pages

+   d. duhkdou sei'ah yihp   d. read to page 40

+   e. seuhngchi duhkdou sei'ah yihp   e. last time read to page
                              40

+   f. seuhngchi duhkdou daih sei'ah   f. last time read to the
      yihp   40th page.
      (ordinal number marker,
      -st, -nd, -rd, etc.)

    g. Ngóhdeih seuhngchi duhkdou   g. Last time we read to
      daih sei'ah yihp.   the 40th page.

338

+ 2. a. <u>fo</u>
    b. géi fo a?
    c. daih géi fo a?
    d. duhk daih géi fo a?
    e. seuhngchi duhk daih géi fo a?

    f. Ngóhdeih seuhngchi duhk daih géi fo a?

3. a. daih sahp yihp
+   b. dáhòi bún syù daih sahp yihp
    c. dáhòi bún syù daih sei'ah sàam yihp
    d. Dáhòi bún syù daih sàam baak sei'ah sàam yihp.

2. a. <u>lesson</u>
    b. how many lessons?
    c. which[th] lesson?
    d. read which lesson?
    e. last time read which lesson?

    f. What lesson did we do last time?

3. a. the 10th page
    b. open your book to page 10
    c. open your books to the 43rd page (page 43)
    d. Open your books to page 343.

4. Response Drill

    Ex: 1. T: Ngóhdeih seuhng-   T: What page did we get to last
            chi duhkdou daih   time?
            géi yihp a? /43/

          S: Duhkdou daih   S: We got to page 43.
            sei'ahsàam yihp.

      2. T: Ngóhdeih seuhng-   T: What lesson did we do last
            chi duhk daih   time?
            géi fo a? /3/

          S: Daih sàam fo.   S: We did lesson 3.

1. Ngóhdeih seuhngchi duhkdou daih géi yihp a? /86/

2. Ngóhdeih seuhngchi duhk daih géi fo a? /7/

3. Ngóhdeih seuhngchi duhk daih géi fo a? /15/

4. Ngóhdeih seuhngchi duhkdou daih géi yihp a? /254/

5. Ngóhdeih seuhngchi duhk daih géi fo a? /26/

1. Duhkdou daih baatsahpluhk yihp.

2. Daih chāt fo.

3. Daih sahpńgh fo.

4. Duhkdou daih yih baak ńgh-sahpsei yihp.

5. Daih yahluhk fo.

5. Substitution Drill: Repeat the first sentence after the teacher, then substitute as directed.

1. Sàam láu yáuh dī mēyéh maaih
   a?
   What's for sale on the 2nd
   floor? What do they have
   (for sale) on the 2nd floor?

1. Sàam láu yáuh dī mēyéh
   maaih a?

2. /sei láu/

2. Sei láu yáuh dī mēyéh
   maaih a?

3. /làuhhah/

3. Làuhhah yáuh dī mēyéh maaih
   a?

4. /làuhseuhng/

4. Làuhseuhng yáuh dī mēyéh
   maaih a?

5. /yahpbihn/

5. Yahpbihn yáuh dī mēyéh
   maaih a?

6. /seuhngbihn/

6. Seuhngbihn yáuh dī mēyéh
   maaih a?

7. /hahbihn/

7. Hahbihn yáuh dī mēyéh
   maaih a?

Comment: Note in #1 and #2 above the absence of ordinalizing
         prefix daih in connection with láu, 'floor, story'.

Compare: sàam láu = the third floor.
            daih sàam fo = the third lesson.

            daih is not used before numbers when modifying
            láu.

---

6. Substitution Drill: Repeat the first sentence after the teacher, then substitute as directed.

1. Yàuh nīdouh, dím heui Tīn-
   sīng Màhtàuh a?
   How do you get to the Star
   Ferry from here?

1. Yàuh nīdouh, dím heui Tīnsīng Màhtàuh a?

2. /Màhnwàh Jáudim/

2. Yàuh nīdouh, dím heui
   Màhnwàh Jáudim a?

3. /Méihgwok Ngàhnhòhng/

3. Yàuh nīdouh, dím heui
   Méihgwok Ngàhnhòhng a?

4. /Jùngwàahn Gàaisíh/

4. Yàuh nīdouh, dím heui
   Jùngwàahn Gàaisíh a?

5. /Hèunggóng Chāansāt/

5. Yàuh nīdouh, dím heui
   Hèunggóng Chāansāt a?

340

Comment: <u>hái</u> is used in place of <u>yàuh</u> by some speakers, with
no difference in meaning.

Ex: Hái nīdouh, dím heui   How do you get to the
Tīnsīng Máhtàuh a?   Star Ferry from here?
<u>or</u> Yàuh nīdouh, dím
heui Tīnsīng Máhtàuh
a?

---

7. Expansion Drill

Ex: T: /Wìhngōn Gūngsī/   T: The WingŌn Company

S: Chéng mahn néih, dím   S: Can you please tell me how to
heui Wìhngōn Gūng-   get to the WingŌn Company?
sī a?

1. /Jùnggwok Jáugā/   1. Chéng mahn néih, dím heui
Jùnggwok Jáugā a?

2. /Jùngwàahn Gàaisíh/   2. Chéng mahn néih, dím heui
Jùngwàahn Gàaisíh a?

3. /Tīnsīng Máhtàuh/   3. Chéng mahn néih, dím heui
Tīnsīng Máhtàuh a?

4. /Gáulùhng Wìhngōn Gūngsī/   4. Chéng mahn néih, dím heui
Gáulùhng Wìhng Ōn Gūngsī
a?

5. /Nèihdēun Douh/   5. Chéng mahn néih, dím heui
Nèihdēun Douh a?

---

8. Alteration Drill

Ex: T: Gwo sàam gàan,   T: Pass three buildings, then
jauh dou laak.   (you) arrive. (i.e., It's
just 3 buildings away.)

S: Gwojó daih sàam gàan,   S: When you've passed the third
jauh dou laak.   building, then you're there.

+ 1. Gwo sàam go gàaiháu, jauh   1. Gwojó daih sàam go gàaiháu,
dou laak.   jauh dou laak.
Pass three <u>intersections</u>   When you've passed the
[street-mouth], and there   third intersection, it's
it is.   right there.

2. Gwo yāt gàan, jauh haih laak.   2. Gwojó daih yāt gàan, jauh
haih laak.

3. Gwo sàam gàan, jauh jyun jó.   3. Gwojó daih sàam gàan, jauh
jyun jó.

341

4. Gwo sei go gàaiháu, jauh
   jyun yauh.

4. Gwojó daih sei go gàaiháu,
   jauh jyun yauh.

5. Gwo léuhng gàan, jauh táidóu
   laak.

5. Gwojó daih yih gàan, jauh
   táidóu laak.

6. Gwo sàam go gàaiháu, jauh tìhng
   lā.

6. Gwojó daih sàam go gàaiháu,
   jauh tìhng lā.

Comment: -jó may be added to gwo in left hand column, but not
subtracted from right hand. Instead of gwojó on
right, hàahngdou is permissable.

---

9. Alteration Drill

Ex: T: Gwojó Méihgwok Jáu-   T: After you pass the Hilton,
       dim, jauh jyun yauh.   turn right.

    S: Méihgwok Jáudim   S: Beyond the Hilton, turn right.
       gwodī, jyun yauh.

1. Gwojó Jùngwàahn Gàaisíh, jauh
   jyun yauh.

1. Jùngwàahn Gàaisíh gwodī,
   jyun yauh.

2. Gwojó Wìhngōn Gūngsī, jauh
   haih laak.

2. Wìhngōn Gūngsī gwodī, jauh
   haih laak.

3. Gwojó Màhnwàh Jáudim, jauh
   jyun jó.

3. Màhnwàh Jáudim gwodī, jyun
   jó.

4. Gwojó Nèihdēun Douh, jauh
   haih laak.

4. Nèihdēun Douh gwodī, jauh
   haih laak.

5. Gwojó daih sàam go gàaiháu,
   jauh jyun yauh.

5. Daih sàam go gàaiháu gwodī,
   jyun yauh.

---

10. Substitution Drill: Repeat the first sentence after the teacher,
    then substitute as directed.

1. Ṁhgòi néih heui Jùngwàahn sìn,
   yìhnhauh heui Gáulùhng.
   Please go to the Central
   District first, and after
   that go to Kowloon.

1. Ṁhgòi néih heui Jùngwàahn
   sìn, yìhnhauh heui Gáulùhng.

2. /Méihgwok Ngàhnhòhng/
   /Jùngwàahn Gàaisíh/

2. Ṁhgòi néih heui Méihgwok
   Ngàhnhòhng sìn, yìhnhauh
   heui Jùngwàahn Gàaisíh.

3. /Màhnwàh Jáudim/
   /Wìhngōn Gūngsī/

3. Ṁhgòi néih heui Màhnwàh
   Jáudim sìn, yìhnhauh heui
   Wìhngōn Gūngsī.

4. /Jùnggwok Jáugā/
   /Tīnsīng Màhtàuh/

4. Mhgòi néih heui Jùnggwok
   Jáugā sīn, yìhnhauh heui
   Tīnsīng Màhtàuh.

5. /séjihlàuh/fàan ūkkéi/

5. Mhgòi néih heui séjihlàuh
   sīn, yìhnhauh fàan ūkkéi.

---

11. Expansion Drill

   1. /heui máaih yéh/
      /fàan hohk/

   1. Ngóh séung heui máaih yéh
      sīn, yìhnhauh fàan hohk.
      I think I'll go shopping
      first, and after that go
      to school.

   2. /heui yám chàh/fàan gùng/

   2. Ngóh séung heui yám chàh
      sīn, yìhnhauh fàan gùng.

   3. /heui taam Wòhng Táai/
      /heui wán Léih Síujé/

   3. Ngóh séung heui taam Wòhng
      Táai sīn, yìhnhauh heui
      wán Léih Síujé.

   4. /heui Jùngwàahn Gàaisíh/
      /fàan ūkkéi/

   4. Ngóh séung heui Jùngwàahn
      Gàaisíh sīn, yìhnhauh
      fàan ūkkéi.

   5. /yám būi chàh/
      /chēutheui mùhnháu dáng kéuih/

   5. Ngóh séung yám būi chàh sīn,
      yìhnhauh chēutheui mùhnháu
      dáng kéuih.

++ 6. /wuhn sāam/dá dihnwá giu chē/
      /change clothes/phone for
      a cab/

   6. Ngóh séung wuhn sāam sīn,
      yìhnhauh dá dihnwá giu
      chē.
      I'll change clothes first,
      and after that call for
      a cab.

---

12. Expansion Drill

   Ex: 1. T: /deihhá/yih láu/   T: /ground floor/1st floor/

       S: Ngóh yàuh deihhá   S: I walked from the ground floor
          hàahng séuhng   up to the 1st floor.
          (heui) yih láu.

       2. T: /sàam láu/yih láu/ T: /2nd floor/1st floor/

       S: Ngóh yàuh sàam   S: I walked from the 2nd floor
          láu hàahng lohk   down to the 1st floor.
          (heui) yih láu.

   1. /yih láu/deihhá/

   1. Ngóh yàuh yih láu hàahng
      lohk (heui) deihhá.

2. /sàam láu/ńgh láu/

2. Ngóh yàuh sàam láu hàahng séuhng (heui) ńgh láu.

3. /luhk láu/sei láu/

3. Ngóh yàuh luhk láu hàahng lohk (heui) sei láu.

4. /chāt láu/baat láu/

4. Ngóh yàuh chāt láu hàahng séuhng (heui) baat láu.

5. /baat láu/luhk láu/

5. Ngóh yàuh baat láu hàahng lohk (heui) luhk láu.

---

13. **Expansion Drill: Students should gesture the directions.**

    Ex: T: Ngóh hái sàam láu.   I am on the 2nd floor.
        /sei láu/   /3rd floor/

        S: Ngóh hái sàam láu,   I am on the 2nd floor, now
           yìhgā séuhng sei láu. I'm going up to the 3rd
                                 floor.

1. Ngóh hái yih láu. /sàam láu/

1. Ngóh hái yih láu, yìhgā séuhng sàam láu.

2. Ngóh hái sàam láu. /yih láu/

2. Ngóh hái sàam láu, yìhgā lohk yih láu.

3. Ngóh hái deihhá. /yih láu/

3. Ngóh hái deihhá, yìhgā séuhng yih láu.

4. Ngóh hái yih láu. /deihhá/

4. Ngóh hái yih láu, yìhgā lohk deihhá.

5. Ngóh hái deihhá. /sei láu/

5. Ngóh hái deihhá, yìhgā séuhng sei láu.

---

14. **Expansion Drill**

    Ex: T: Ngóh hái Dākfuh   T: I am at Des Voeux Road
           Douh Jùng.   Central. /Wing On Company/
           /Wìhng Ōn Gūngsī/

        S: Ngóh hái Dākfuh Douh S: I'm at Des Voeux Road Central,
           Jùng, yìhgā ngóh   now I'm going into Wing On
           yahpheui Wìhng Ōn   Company to wait for you.
           Gūngsī dáng néih.

1. Ngóh hái Dākfuh Douh Jùng.
   /Jùngwàahn Gàaisíh/

1. Ngóh hái Dākfuh Douh Jùng, yìhgā ngóh yahpheui Jùngwàahn Gàaisíh dáng néih.

2. Ngóh hái Wìhng Ōn Gūngsī.
   /Dākfuh Douh Jùng/

2. Ngóh hái Wìhng Ōn Gūngsī,
   yìhgā ngóh chēuthēui
   Dākfuh Douh Jùng dáng néih.

3. Ngóh hái Méihgwok Ngàhnhòhng.
   /Daaih Douh Jùng/

3. Ngóh hái Méihgwok Ngàhnhòhng,
   yìhgā ngóh chēuthēui Daaih
   Douh Jùng dáng néih.

4. Ngóh hái Daaih Douh Jùng.
   /Méihgwok Ngàhnhòhng/

4. Ngóh hái Daaih Douh Jùng,
   yìhgā ngóh yahphēui Méihgwok Ngàhnhòhng dáng néih

---

15. Response Drill: Do the right hand column of this drill first as a
    Listen & Repeat drill, teacher writing picture on blackboard &
    pointing to appropriate section as he speaks, students repeating
    after him.

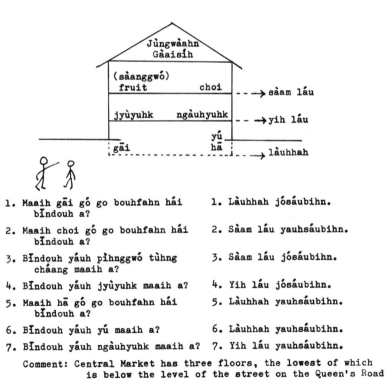

1. Maaih gāi gó go bouhfahn hái
   bīndouh a?

1. Làuhhah jósáubihn.

2. Maaih choi gó go bouhfahn hái
   bīndouh a?

2. Sàam láu yauhsáubihn.

3. Bīndouh yáuh pìhnggwó tùhng
   cháang maaih a?

3. Sàam láu jósáubihn.

4. Bīndouh yáuh jyùyuhk maaih a?

4. Yih láu jósáubihn.

5. Maaih hā gó go bouhfahn hái
   bīndouh a?

5. Làuhhah yauhsáubihn.

6. Bīndouh yáuh yú maaih a?

6. Làuhhah yauhsáubihn.

7. Bīndouh yáuh ngàuhyuhk maaih a?

7. Yih láu yauhsáubihn.

Comment: Central Market has three floors, the lowest of which
         is below the level of the street on the Queen's Road

Central side. Thus <u>làuhhah</u> instead of <u>deihhá</u>.

---

16. Response Drill

Ex: 1. T: Máaih hàaih   T: What floor do I go up to
          séuhng géi   buy shoes?
          láu a?

       S: Séuhng sei láu   S: Go up to the 3rd floor.
          lā.

    2. T: Máaih jē hái géi   T: What floor do you buy umbrellas
          láu a?   on?

       S: Hái deihhá.   S: On the ground floor.

1. Máaih lāangsāam séuhng géi   1. Séuhng sei láu lā!
   láu a?

2. Máaih bāt séuhng géi láu a?   2. Séuhng sàam láu lā!

3. Máaih jē hái géi láu a?   3. Hái deihhá.

4. Máaih syù hái géi láu a?   4. Hái sàam láu.

5. Máaih hàaih séuhng géi láu a?   5. Séuhng sei láu lā!

6. Máaih bīu séuhng géi láu a?   6. Séuhng sàam láu lā!

7. Máaih sēutsāam hái géi láu a?   7. Hái deihhá.

8. Máaih bou hái géi láu a?   8. Hái sei láu.

9. Máaih būi hái géi láu a?   9. Hái yih láu.

10. Máaih fu séuhng géi láu a?   10. Séuhng sei láu lā!

11. Máaih maht hái géi láu a?	11. Hái deihhá.
12. Máaih gāng séuhng géi láu a?	12. Séuhng yih láu lā!
13. Máaih wún séuhng géi láu a?	13. Séuhng yih láu lā!
14. Máaih yúhlāu hái géi láu a?	14. Hái deihhá.
15. Máaih jūng séuhng géi láu a?	15. Séuhng sàam láu lā!

IV. CONVERSATIONS FOR LISTENING

(On tape. Refer to wordlist below as you listen.)

Unfamiliar terms, in order of occurrence:

1) yáuh yuhng = useful

V. SAY IT IN CANTONESE

A. Say to the classmate sitting next to you:

B. And he responds:

1. Where did we read to last time?

1. We read to page 300.

2. What lesson did we read last time?

2. Lesson 14.

3. Could you please tell me how to get to the Mandarin Hotel?

ᵡ Go straight, and when you get to the 3d intersection, turn left. Go two blocks and you'll be there.

4. How do you get to the Central Market from here?

4. Turn left at the next intersection and it's two blocks down.

5. (in a dept store:) Where is the umbrella department?

5. On the ground floor.

6. Where is the shoe department?

6. Go up to the 1st floor.

7. I'm going down to the ground floor to buy a raincoat I'll wait for you there, OK?

7. Wait just a sec, and I'll go with you.

8. Turn left just beyond the library.

8. You can't turn in there-- I'll stop at the intersection, OK?

9. What's for sale on the 4th floor?

9. Sweaters and shoes and fabrics.

10. Go up to the 3d floor first, then go down to the 1st floor.

10. OK, want to come with me?

347

11. Could you please tell me how
    to get to the Wing On Company
    from here?

11. From here you go straight,
    after you pass the 2d
    intersection, it's the
    1st building on the right.

12. When you get to Queens Road
    Central, turn left.

12. Thanks a lot.

13. Your father is waiting for
    you upstairs.

13. What does he want, do you
    know?

14. My glasses are downstairs--
    would you go down and get
    them for me?

14. OK. Downstairs where?

15. Your boy friend is outside
    waiting for you.

15. Please ask him to come in.

Vocabulary Checklist for Lesson 15

1.	bouhfahn	n:	department (in a store)
2.	chéng...	v:	please (+ verb); invite
3.	chēut	v:	out
4.	chēutheui	v:	go out
5.	chēutlàih	v:	come out
6.	chēutbihn	PW:	outside, exterior
7.	dá dihnwá giu chē	VP:	phone for a cab
8.	dáhòi	v:	open (as of a book)
9.	daih-	bf:	ordinal number marker: -st, -nd, -rd, -th.
10.	daihyāt	Ph:	the first
11.	deihhá	PW:	ground, ground floor
12.	-dou	Vsuf:	suffix to verbs of motion, indicating arrival at goal
13.	duhk	v:	read
14.	duhkdou...	v:	read to...
15.	fo	m:	lesson
16.	gàaiháu	n/PW:	street opening, i.e. intersection
17.	gàaisíh	n/PW:	food market
18.	hàahng	v:	walk; go
19.	hahbihn	PW:	below; under
20.	hái	prep:	from

21.	-heui	Vsuf:	attaches to verbs of motion, indicating direction away from speaker
22.	-jó	Vsuf:	verb suf. indicating 'accomplish the performance'
23.	Jùngwàahn Gàaisíh	PW:	Central Market
24.	-làih	Vsuf:	attaches to verbs of motion, indicating direction towards the speaker
25.	làuhhah	PW:	[floor-below] downstairs
26.	làuhseuhng	PW:	[floor-above] upstairs
27.	lohk	v:	descend
28.	lohkheui	v:	go down
29.	louhyàhn	n:	pedestrian
30.	séuhng	v:	ascend
31.	seuhngbihn	PW:	above; on top
32.	seuhngchi	TW:	last time
33.	...sìn, yìhnhauh...	FCj:	...first, then...
34.	wuhn sāam	VO:	change clothes
35.	yàhn	n:	someone
36.	yàuh	prep:	from
37.	yìhn(jì)hauh	Cj:	afterwards, then
38.	yihp	m:	page

349

IV. CONVERSATIONS FOR LISTENING

Lesson Two

1. At a party:

    Man   : Síujé gwaising a?

    Woman: Ngóh sing Chàhn. Sīnsàang gwaising a?

    Man   : Síusing Hòh. Chàhn síujé haih m̀hhaih Gwóngdùngyàhn a?

    Woman: M̀hhaih a. Ngóh haih Seuhnghóiyàhn. Néih nē? Néih haih m̀hhaih
             Méihgwokyàhn a?

    Man   : Haih a. Ngóh haih Méihgwokyàhn.

2. At the first day of school, students are getting acquainted:

    First student: Néih sing mēyéh a?

    Second student: Ngóh sing Wòhng.

    First student: Néih pàhngyáuh nē?

    Second student: Kéuih dōu haih sing Wòhng ge.

    First student: Néih haih m̀hhaih Gwóngdùngyàhn a?

    Second student: Haih.

    First student: Néih pàhngyáuh haih m̀hhaih dōu haih Gwóngdùngyàhn a?

    Second student: M̀hhaih a. Kéuih haih Seuhnghóiyàhn.

Lesson Three

            The following conversations take place among
            some university students between classes.

1. A: Léih Sàang sīk m̀hsīk góng Yahtbúnwá a?

    B: Sīk sèsíu.

    A: Gám, kéuih sīk m̀hsīk góng Yìngmán nē?

    B: Dōu sīk sèsíu.

    A: Bīngo gaau kéuih góng Yìngmán ge nē?

    B: Haih Wòhng Sàang gaau kéuih ge.

2. A: Néih sīk m̀hsīk góng Gwokyúh a?

    B: Deuim̀hjyuh. Ngóh tèng m̀hchìngchó - m̀hgòi néih joi góng yātchi.

    A: Néih sīk m̀hsīk góng Gwokyúh a?

    B: Sīk sèsíu jē.

    A: Gám, néih sīk m̀hsīk Yìngmàhn nē?

    B: Sīk góng, m̀hsīk sé. Néih nē?

    A: Ngóh dōu m̀hsīk. 'Yāt yih sàam' dōu m̀hsīk góng.

350

3. A: Néih gaau bīngo Gwóngdùngwá a?

    B: Ngóh gaau Wòhng Táai.

    A: Kéuih haih m̀hhaih Méihgwokyàhn a?

    B: M̀hhaih. Kéuih haih Yìnggwokyàhn.

    A: Kéuih sīk m̀hsīk sé Jùngmàhn nē?

    B: M̀hsīk. Kéuih hohk góng, daahnhaih m̀hhohk sé.

    A: Kéuih hohk m̀hhohk Gwokyúh a?

    B: Ngóh m̀hjīdou a.

Lesson Four

1. Man   : Ngóh go bīu maahn sèsíu. Néih go haih m̀hhaih a?

    Woman: M̀hhaih. Ngóh go haih jéun ge.

    Man   : Gám, yìhgā géidímjūng a?

    Woman: Yìhgā ngāamngāam sahpyih dím.

    Man   : Ngóh go bīu yìhgā haih sahpyāt dím daahp sahp.

    Woman: Gám, néih go maahn léuhnggojih.

2. Woman: Yìhgā haih m̀hhaih baat dím sāamgogwāt a?

    Man   : M̀hhaih. Ngóh go bīu yìhgā haih baat dím daahp baat jē.

    Woman: Néih go bīu jéun m̀hjéun a?

    Man   : Jéun. M̀hfaai m̀hmaahn.

    Woman: Gám, ngóh go faai yāt go jih.

    Man   : Waahkjé haih.

3. Woman: Jóusàhn, Wòhng Sàang. Néih jī m̀hjī yìhgā géidímjūng a?

    Man   : A, jóusàhn, Chàhn Síujé. Ngóh go bīu yìhgā haih gáu dím
            daahp yāt.

    Woman: Néih go bīu haih m̀hhaih faai sèsíu a?

    Man   : Waahkjé haih. Ngóh m̀hjī.

    Woman: Néih jī m̀hjī Léih Táai géidímjūng hohk Gwóngdùngwá a?

    Man   : Ngóh jīdou. Haih sahp dím bun.

Lesson Five

1. Two friends in a coffee shop deciding what to have for a mid-after-
   noon tea:

    A: Néih yám mēyéh a?

    B: Ngóh yám gafē. Néih nē?

A: Ngóh yám chàh. Sihk m̀hsihk béng a?

B: Hóu aak.

A: Néih géidímjūng yiu jáu a?

B: Sei dím.

A: Jànhaih gam faai yiu jáu mē?

B: Haih a, jànhaih.

2. A hostess is entertaining a new acquaintance at tea:

Hostess: Yám chàh lā.

Guest: Hóu, m̀hgòi.

Hostess: Sihk béng lā.

Guest: Hóu aak, m̀hgòi.

Hostess: Sihk yín lā.

Guest: Síu sihk. M̀hsái haakhei.

Hostess: Néih haakhei jē.

3. At lunchtime Mrs. Wong instructs her servant about the work for the rest of the day:

Mrs. Wong: Ngóh tùhng Wòhng Sàang sàam dím bun yiu yám chàh.

Servant : Sihk m̀hsihk béng a?

Mrs. Wong: Sèsíu lā.

Servant : Gám, géidímjūng sihk faahn a?

Mrs. Wong: Baat dím lā.

Servant : Hóu aak.

Lesson Six

1. In a department store:

Clerk: Jóusàhn, séung máaih mēyéh a?

Customer: Ngóh séung máaih tìuh fu. Nī léuhng tìuh yiu géidò chín a?

Clerk: Nī tìuh sahpbaat mān, gó tìuh yahyih mān.

Customer: Gám, ngóh máaih nī tìuh lā.

2. In a department store:

Customer: Nī gihn sēutsāam haih m̀hhaih yahsei mān a?

Clerk   : M̀hhaih. Haih yahgáu mān.

Customer: Gó gihn dōu haih yahgáu mān, haih m̀hhaih nē?

Clerk   : Haih. Néih haih m̀hhaih léuhng gihn dōu máaih nē?

Customer: M̀hhaih. Ngóh máaih nī gihn, m̀hmáaih gó gihn.

3. In a department store:

   Clerk   : Máaih mēyéh a?
   Customer: Ngóh séung máaih sēutsāam. Nī gihn géidò chín a?
   Clerk   : Nī gihn sahpyih mān jē. Máaih géidò gihn nē?
   Customer: Béi yāt gihn ngóh lā.

Lesson Seven

                     The following conversations take
                     place between clerk and customer:

1. Clerk   : Máaih mēyéh a?
   Customer: Ngóh séung máaih bējáu. Géidō chín jī a?
   Clerk   : Go baat ngàhnchín. Oi géidō jī a?
   Customer: Oi léuhng jī.
   Clerk   : Sái m̀hsái máaih yīnjái a?
   Customer: Hóu, béi bāau ngóh lā!

2. Customer: Nī dī bou géidō chín máh a?
   Clerk   : Yahsàam go bun. Néih yiu géido máh a?
   Customer: Ngóh m̀hyiu laak. Gó dī nē? Géidō chín máh a?
   Clerk   : Gó dī sahpsàam go bun ngàhnchín máh. Néih máaih m̀hmáaih a?
   Customer: Hóu. Ngóh oi léuhng máh.
   Clerk   : Yahchāt mān léuhng máh lā.

3. Clerk   : Máaih mēyéh a?
   Customer: Ngóh séuhng máaih dī ngàuhyuhk. Dím maaih nē?
   Clerk   : Nī dī sei go baat ngàhnchín gàn. Gó dī chāt go bun
             ngàhnchín gàn.
   Customer: Béi sàam gàn gó dī ngóh lā.
   Clerk   : Sàam gàn yahyih go bun.
   Customer: Ngóh dōu séung oi léuhng gàn nī dī.
   Clerk   : Hóu aak, gàn go luhk ngàhn chín lā.

Lesson Eight

1. In a department store:
   Clerk   : Jóusàhn. Séung máaih mēyéh a?
   Customer: Yáuh móuh baahk sēutsāam a?
   Clerk   : Haih m̀hhaih néih jeuk ga?

Customer: Haih.

Clerk   : Néih jeuk géidō houh a?

Customer: Sàamsahp luhk, waahkjé sàamsahp baat.

Clerk   : Nī gihn haih sàamsahpluhk.

Customer: Nī gihn m̀hgau daaih. Yáuh móuh sàamsahpbaat ge nē?

Clerk   : Deuim̀hjyuh - sàamsahpbaat ge maaihsaai laak.

2. In a department store:

Customer: Yáuh móuh baahk hàaih maaih a?

Clerk   : Yáuh. Néih jùng m̀hjùngyi nī deui nē?

Customer: Géi leng. Géi(dō) chín deui a?

Clerk   : Nī deui haih Méihgwok hàaih. Chāt'ahgáu mān deui.

Customer: Yáuh móuh pèhngdī ge nē?

Clerk   : Yáuh. Gó deui haih Yahtbún hàaih. Yahng̀h mān deui jē.

Customer: M̀hgòi néih béi deui Yahtbún ge ngóh lā.

Clerk   : Hóu aak.

3. In a department store:

Customer: Yáuh móuh maht a?

Clerk   : Yáuh. Nī dī néih jùng m̀hjùngyi nē?

Customer: Géi jùngyi. Dím maaih a?

Clerk   : Luhk go bun ngàhnchín deui. Néih jeuk géi houh a?

Customer: M̀hjī - Ngóh jeuk luhk houh ge Méihgwok hàaih.

Clerk   : Gám, gáu houh lā. Néih séung máaih géidō deui a?

Customer: Béi sàam deui ngóh lā.

Clerk   : Hóu aak. Oi m̀hoi hàaih nē?

Customer: M̀hoi laak. M̀hgòi.

4. At a grocery store:

Customer: Yáuh móuh tòhng maaih a?

Clerk   : Yáuh. Máaih géidō bohng nē? Ǹgh bohng gau m̀hgau a?

Customer: M̀hsái gam dò. Léuhng bohng gau laak. A! Ngóh séung oi dī
          ngàuhyuhk, dím maaih a?

Clerk   : Sei go baat ngàhnchín gàn.

Customer: Béi yāt gàn ngóh lā.

Clerk   : Hóu.

Lesson Nine

1. Mr. Wong phones Mrs. Ho:

Amah   : Wéi.

Caller : Haih m̀hhaih chāt-sàam-lìhng-sei-ńgh-lìhng a?

Amah   : M̀hgòi néih daaihsēngdī. Ngóh tēng m̀hchīngchó.

Caller : Chāt-sàam-lìhng-sei-ńgh-lìhng, haih m̀hhaih a?

Amah   : Haih. Wán bīngo a?

Caller : M̀hgòi néih giu Hòh Táai tēng dihnwá lā.

Amah   : Hóu. Dáng (yāt)ján.

Mrs. Ho: Wéi.

Caller : Hòh Táai, jóusàhn.

Mrs. Ho: Jóusàhn.

Caller : Ngóh haih Wòhng Sàang a. Néih jī m̀hjī Chàhn Sīnsàang ge dihnwá géidō houh a?

Mrs. Ho: A! Jī. Kéuih ge dihnwá haih ńgh sei sàam yih yāt lìhng.

Caller : Hóu, m̀hgòi.

Mrs. Ho: M̀hsái m̀hgòi.

2. Mr. Wong calls a businessman at his office:

Secretary: Wái.

Caller   : Wái. Haih m̀hhaih sàam baat luhk lìhng ńgh gáu a?

Secretary: Haih. Wán bīnwái nē?

Caller   : Ngóh séung wán Léih Sàang tēng dihnwá.

Secretary: Deuim̀hjyuh laak. Kéuih chēutjó gāai bo.

Caller   : Gám, kéuih géidímjūng fàanlàih nē?

Secretary: Léuhng dím lèhng jūng gamseuhnghā lā.

Caller   : Hóu. M̀hgòi néih.

Secretary: M̀hsái m̀hgòi.

3. Mr. Ho telephones Mr. Chan:

Amah   : Wéi. Wán bīngo a?

Caller: Wái. M̀hgòi néih giu Chàhn Sīnsàang tēng dihnwá lā.

Amah   : Kéuih fàanjó gūng bo. Gwaising wán kéuih a?

Caller: Sing Hòh ge. Kéuih géisìh fàanlàih nē?

Amah   : M̀hjī bo.

Caller: Dáng kéuih fàanlàih m̀hgòi néih giu kéuih dá dihnwá béi ngóh lā. Ngóh ge dihnwá haih....

Amah   : Ṁhgòi néih dáng yātján; ngóh ló jī bāt sīn. Wéi, néih ge
dihnwá haih....

Caller: Chāt-yāt-yāt-yih-lìhng-chāt.

Amah   : Hóu lā. Kéuih fàanlàih, ngóh giu kéuih dá béi néih lā.

Lesson Ten

1. Asking directions:

   A: Chéng mahn Tīnsīng Màhtàuh hái bīndouh a?

   B: Hái Màhnwàh Jáudim deuimihn.

   A: Ngóh m̀hjī Màhnwàh Jáudim hái bīndouh bo.

   B: Nē -- hái gó bihn gó gàan - néih tái m̀htáidóu a?

   A: A, táidóu. Ṁhgòisaai.

   B: Ṁhsái m̀hgòi.

2. Two friends discuss restaurants:

   A: Néih séjihlàuh hái m̀hhái Hèunggóng nī bihn a?

   B: Hái. Hái Daaih Douh Jūng.

   A: Gódouh jógán yáuh móuh hóu ge chàhlàuh a?

   B: Yáuh. Ngóh séjihlàuh gaaklèih yáuh gàan hóu hóu ga. Ngóh hóu
jungyi hái gódouh yám chàh ga.

   A: Ngóh séjihlàuh jógán ge chàhlàuh dōu m̀hhaih géi hóu, daahnhaih
yáuh gàan géi hóu ge chāansāt. Ngóh jùngyi hái gódouh sihk
ngaan.

3. Mrs. Ho compliments Miss Wong on her sweater:

   Mrs. Ho : Néih gihn lāangsāam hóu leng. Hái bīndouh máaih ga?

   Miss Wong: Hái Jùngwàahn yāt gàan gūngsī máaih ge.

   Mrs. Ho : Bīn gàan nē?

   Miss Wong: Hái ngóh séjihlàuh gaaklèih gó gàan.

   Mrs. Ho : Haih m̀hhaih hái chējaahm deuimihn a?

   Miss Wong: Haih. Haih gó gàan.

4. Mr. Ho calls Mr. Lee on the phone:

   Léih Sàang: Wéi.

   Hòh Sàang : Léih Sàang àh.

   Léih Sàang: Haih a, bīn wái a?

   Hòh Sàang : Ngóh haih Hòh Yaht-sīn a. Néih jī m̀hjī Méihgwok Jáudim

hái bĭndouh a? Yáuh go pàhngyáuh <u>yātján</u> sàam dĭm hái
gódouh dáng ngóh. Kéuih wáh ngóh jì Mĕihgwok Jáudĭm
hái Seuhnghói Ngàhnhòhng gàakléih, daahnhaih ngóh
<u>wán ṁhdóu</u>.

Léih Sàang: Mĕihgwok Jáudĭm ṁhhaih hái Seuhnghói Ngàhnhòhng gaakléih.
Hái Jùnggwok Ngàhnhòhng deuimihn. Néih jì ṁhjì Jùnggwok
Ngàhnhòhng hái bĭndouh a?

Hòh Sàang : O. Gám, ngóh jì laak. Ṁhgòisaai. Joigin.

1) yātján = dángyātjahn = 'in a little while'

2) wán ṁhdóu = can't find it, search but not successful

ˌesson Eleven

1. A clerk totals the bill for a customer at a grocery store:

Clerk   : Sei jì bējáu, luhk jì heiséui, sahp go cháang...sahpsàam
go yih lā.

Customer: Nàh, nĭdouh yāt baak mān.

Clerk   : Hóu, dáng ngóh jáaufàan béi néih lā. Aiya, deuiṁhjyuh,
ṁhgau sáanjí tìm. Néih yáuh móuh sáanjí a?

Customer: Ngóh dōu móuh bo.

Clerk   : Gám, ṁhgòi néih dáng jahn, ngóh wán yàhn cheunghòi kéuih
lā.

Customer: Hóu lā.

Clerk   : Nĭdouh jáaufàan baatsahpluhk go baat béi néih.

Customer: Néih yáuh móuh yāt mān ngán a?

Clerk   : Yáuh, néih séung yiu géidō nē?

Customer: Ṁhgòi néih cheung sahp mān ngóh lā.

Clerk   : Hóu.

Customer: Ṁhgòisaai.

2. At the teller's window in the bank Mr. Wong puts down a $500 bill
and says:

Mr. Wòhng: Ṁhgòi néih tùhng ngóh cheunghòi kéuih lā!

Teller   : Cheung géidō a? Haih ṁhhaih ngoisaai sahp mān jì a?

Mr. Wòhng: Ṁhhaih. Oi sei jèung yāt baak mān jí, sahp jèung sahp
mān.

Teller   : Ṁhgau sahp mān jì bo. Oi gáu jèung sahp mān jì, sahp go
yāt mān ngán, hóu ṁhhóu a?

Mr. Wòhng: Hóu, <u>oi</u> dĭ sáangán dōu hóu.

1) oi = here: to have in your possession

357

3. Talking about a borrowed book:

A: Néih gàmyaht mhgeidāk daai gó bún syù fàanlàih béi ngóh a?

B: Aiya! Mhgeidāk tìm! Jànhaih deuimhjyuh laak! Néih géisìh (géisí) yiu yuhng a?

A: Ngóh dáng jahn yiu ga. Yātján ngóh hohk Yingmán móuh syù tái, mhdāk ge bo!

B: Gám, ngóh yìhgā fàan ūkkéi ló béi néih lā.

A: Yiu fàan ūkkéi ló àh. Mhhóu laak. Néih jī mhjī nídouh bīngo yáuh nī bún syù hóyíh jejyuh béi ngóh sīn ga?

B: A! Chàhn Sàang dōu yuhng gó bún syù hohk Yingmán, dáng ngóh giu kéuih je béi néih lā.

A: Hóu aak! Mhgòisaai.

1) gàmyaht = today

2) yātján = dángyātjahn = 'in a little while'

Lesson Twelve

1. Two women meet in the elevator of their apartment building. One woman has her daughter with her:

Wòhng Táai: A, Léih Táai, tùhng gó néui heui bīn a?

Léih Táai : Ngóh daai kéuih heui tái yīsāng a.

Wòhng Táai: Mēyéh sih a?

Léih Táai : Kéuih mhséung sihk faahn lòh.

Wòhng Táai: Néih daai kéuih heui tái bīn go yīsāng a?

Léih Táai : Ngóh sīnsàang giu ngóh daai kéuih tái Jèung Yīsāng. Kéuih haih ngóhdeih gè pàhngyáuh.

Wòhng Táai: Bīn go Jèung Yīsāng a? Haih mhhaih Seuhnghói Ngàhnhòhng gó go a?

Léih Táai : Móuh cho, haih kéuih laak.

Wòhng Táai: Gám, ngóh sung néihdeih heui lā. Ngóh ngāamngāam yiu heui ngàhnhòhng ló chín.

Léih Táai : Hóu aak. Mhgòisaai bo.

1) bīn = bīndouh?

2) Mēyéh sih a? = What's the matter?

3) lòh = sen. suf. expressing sympathy

4) ngāamngāam = just now, just on the point of, just

2. Two men on their way to the bus stop. They have just finished work:

A: Néih haih mhhaih fàan ūkkéi a?

B: Mhhaih, ngóh yìhgā yiu heui ngóh néuipàhngyáuh ūkkéi taam kéuih màhma.

A: Kéuih màhmā yáuh mēyéh sih a?

B: Móuh mēyéh sih. Kéuih giu ngóh heui kéuihdeih douh sihk faahn jē.

A: O--kéuihdeih jyuh hái bīn a?

B: Kéuihdeih ngāamngāam jyuh hái néih hauhbihn.

A: Haih mē? Gám, ngóh sung néih heui lā.

B: Ṁhgòisaai.

    1) Yáuh mēyéh sih a? = What's going on?

    2) Móuh mēyéh sih = Nothing special.

3. Mr. and Mrs. Lee at home:

Léih Táai : Ngóh yātján yiu heui gūngsī máaih yéh. Néih yáuh móuh chín a?

Léih Sàang: Ngóh dāk sèsíu ja. Ngóh ngāamngāam séung heui ngàhnhòhng ló chín. Néih géidímjūng cheutgaai a?

Léih Táai : Hmmm...Ngóh yiu dáng Hòh Táai dihnwá bo.

Léih Sàang: Gám...Ngóh yìhgā heui ngàhnhòhng ló chín sīn. Néih yātján làih ngóh séjihlàuh ló chín, hóu ṁhhóu a?

Léih Táai : Hóu! ...A, ...néih yáuh móuh yéh yiu máaih a?

Léih Sàang: Móuh laak.

    1) ngāamngāam séung heui = just thinking of going

    2) yātján = in a little while

Lesson Thirteen

1. Two girls driving in a car talk about a young man they see:

A: Hái hāak sīk gó ga chē hauhbihn gó go yàhn haih ṁhhaih néih pàhngyáuh a?

B: Haih bo! Ṁhgòi néih fàanjyuntàuh lā. Ngóh yáuh dī yéh séung wah kéuih jī ge.

A: Hóu aak. Kéuih haih ṁhhaih sing Jèung ga?

B: Ṁhhaih, kéuih sing Chàhn ge.

A: Kéuih giujouh mēyéh méng a?

B: Kéuih giujouh Gwok-wàh.

A: Chàhn Gwok-wàh...Hmm...Gám, ṁhhaih laak.

B: Ṁhhaih mēyéh a?

A: Kéuih ṁhhaih Léih Síujé ge nàahmpàhngyáuh laak.

2. A young girl calls home:

Wòhng Táai: Wéi!

Síu-Yīng   : Wéi, màhmā àh? Ngóh haih Síu-Yīng a. Ngóh yihgā hái
              Màhnwàh Jáudim yám chàh. Néih làih m̀hlàih a?

Wòhng Táai: Néih tùhng bīngo yám chàh a?

Síu-Yīng   : Ngóh tùhng Hòh Méi-Wàh. Nīdouh dī béng hóu leng ga.
              Néih làih lā.

Wòhng Táai: Néih yáuh pàhngyáuh hái douh, ngóh m̀hlàih la.

Síu-Yīng   : Làih lā, màhmā, ngóh séung néih <u>yātján</u> tùhng ngóh heui
              máaih yéh a.

Wòhng Táai: Gám àh, sái m̀hsái ngóh jà chē làih ā?

Síu-Yīng   : Nī jógán hóu síu wái paak chē ge bo. Néih giu <u>dīksí</u> làih
              lā.

Wòhng Táai: Hóu lā, ngóh jauh làih laak.

        1) yātján = in a little while

        2) dīksí = taxi

3. **Asking directions:**

A: Chéng mahn nī tiuh haih m̀hhaih Daaih Douh Jùng a?

B: M̀hhaih, néih hái nīdouh yātjihk heui, haahng dou daih sàam go
   <u>gàaiháu</u> gó tiuh jauh haih laak.

A: O, m̀hgòi.

                      (He goes on...)

A: Chéng mahn, Daaih Douh Jūng ńgh baak lìhng sei houh hái m̀hhái
   nī jógán a?

C: Ńgh baak lìhng sei houh àh. Nē, chìhnbihn yauhsáubihn daih sàam
   gàan jauh haih laak.

A: Gó douh yáuh móuh wái paak chē ga?

C: Hóu chíh móuh bo.

A: Hóu. M̀hgòisaai.

        1) gàaiháu = intersection [street-mouth]

        2) hóu chíh = very likely..., most likely...

4. **Passenger and taxi driver:**

A: M̀hgòi Néih Dèun Douh, ńgh baak yihsahp sei houh.

B: Hóu.

                 (They ride for awhile)

A: Gwojó daih yih go gàaiháu yauhbihn, tìhng chē lā.
   <u>Ei!</u> <u>Gwojó la</u>, m̀hgòi néih tanhauh sèsíu lā.

B: O, m̀hdāk bo, hauhbihn yáuh chē làih, m̀hhóyíh tanhauh.

        1) Ei! = mild exclamation

        2) gwojó la = here: we've overshot it, we've passed it. gwo =
   pass by

A: Gám, joi **sái** gwodí, fàanjyuntàuh lā.

B: Dāk.

> The driver makes a U-turn at the
> intersection and goes back)

A: Hóu. Hái douh tìhng.

> (He pays the driver $3 for the $2.70 ride)

   Ṁhsái jáau la.

B: Dòjeh.

    1) sái = drive

esson Fourteen

1. Lunchtime:

Wòhng Sàang: A, Léih Síujé. Heui bīndouh a?

Léih Síujé : O, Wòhng Sàang. Ngóh **ngāamngāam fòng gùng**. Néih nē?

Wòhng Sàang: Ngóh ngāamngāam hái ngàhnhòhng ló chín fàanlàih. Sihk
            faahn meih a?

Léih Síujé : Meih a! Néih nē?

Wòhng Sàang: Ngóh dōu meih a, ngóh chéng néih heui sihk faahn lā,
            hóu ṁhhóu a?

Léih Síujé : Hóu aak, heui bīn gàan nē?

Wòhng Sàang: Gwóngjàu Jáugā dī **yihm guhk gāi** hóu leng ga, néih
            sihkgwo meih a?

Léih Síujé : Meih sihkgwo.

Wòhng Sàang: Gám, ngóhdeih heui siháh lā.

> (They arrive at the restaurant)

Wòhng Sàang: Fógei! Ngóhdeih séung yiu jek yihm guhk gāi, mm...Léih
            Síujé, juhng yiu mēyéh choi tìm ne?

Léih Síujé : **Gaailáan cháau ngàuhyuhk** lā, mm...yāt jek gāi **taai** dò,
            ngóhdeih sihk ṁhsaai, yiu bun jek jauh gau la, joi
            dím go **sài yèuhng choi tòng**, hóu ṁhhóu a?

Wòhng Sàang: A. Hóu, Léih Síujé jànhaih sīk dím choi ge laak. Fógei
            ṁhgòi néih faai dī bo.

      1) ngāamgnāam = just now

      2) fòng gùng = leave work, get off from work

      3) yìhm guhk gāi = salt-roasted chicken

      4) gaailáan cháau ngàuhyuhk = stir fried beef and
                               broccoli

      5) taai = too

      6) sài yèuhng choi tòng = watercress soup

Léih Síujé : Nídouh dí choi jànhaih m̀hcho, ngóh dōu yiu daai ngóh
      māhmā làih sìháh.

       (They finish eating)

Wòhng Sàang: Fógei, màaihdāan.

Fógei   : Sīnsàang, yahsàam mān lā!

Wòhng Sàang: Nídouh yah ńgh mān, m̀hsái jáau laak.

Léih Síujé : Wòhng sīnsàang, dòjehsaai bo.

Wòhng Sàang: M̀hsái haakhei.

2. Miss Lee takes her foreign friend to a restaurant for lunch:

  A: Nī gàan jáugā m̀hcho ga. Dī yéh yauh pèhng yauh leng.

  B: O. Haih mē?

  A: Wai, fógei! M̀hgòi néih nǐng go choipáai làih táiháh lā.

  W: Hóu. Jauh làih.

  A: Nídouh yáuh Gwóngdùng choi, Seuhnghói choi. Néih séung sihk bīn
    yeuhng nē?

  B: Ngóh séung sìháh Gwóngdùng choi. M̀hgòi néih gaaisiuhháh lā.

  A: Gám, dím go yùhjyù, joi yiu go daaih hā. Hóu m̀hhóu a?

  B: Hóu aak. <u>Giu go Yèuhngjàu cháau faahn</u> sìháh lā.

  A: Mmm...Néih séung oi go mēyéh tòng tìm nē?

  B: <u>Sàiyèuhngchoi tòng</u> lā.

  A: A, fógei, m̀hgòi lǒ dò léuhng jì heiséui làih lā.

  B: Mmm, dī cháau faahn tùhng daaih hā jànhaih m̀hcho laak.

  A: Sihk dōdī tìm lā! M̀hhóu haakhei a.

  B: Gau la! Dòjehsaai.

  A: Fógei! Màaihdāan!

    1) giu = order, call for (without having to look at a listed
          menu)

    2) Yèuhngjàu cháau faahn = Yangchow fried rice

    3) Sàiyèuhngchoi tòng = watercress soup

3. Deciding where to eat:

  A: Néih jùngyi sihk mēyéh nē?

  B: Néih wah lā, ngóh mēyéh dōu sihk gé.

  A: Gám, néih séung sihk Jùngchoi yǐkwaahk sāichāan nē?

  B: Dōu dāk; néih wah lā.

  A: Gam, ngóhdeih heui sihk Gwóngdùng choi, hóu m̀hhóu a?

  B: Hóu! Néih jì m̀hjì bīndouh ge Gwóngdùng choi hóusihk a?

A: Jùnggwok Chàhlàuh ge géi hóu. Heui gódouh, hóu mhhóu a?

B: Hóu aak. Jà mhjà chē heui nē?

A: Mhsái la. Jùnggwok Chàhlàuh hái deuimihn jē. Ngóhdeih hàahng heui lā.

4. Time for lunch. Two women friends:

A: A! Yìhgā jauh _faai_ sahp-yih dím la. Ngóhdeih heui sihk aan sin, hóu mhhóu a?

B: Hóu aak!

A: Nīdouh jógán yáuh gàan hóu _yáuh méng_ ge Gwóngdùng jáugā. Ngóh daai néih heui siháh lā.

B: Hóu a.

> (In the restaurant a waiter
> gives them a menu card:)

Waiter: Léuhng wái séung dím dī méyéh choi nē?

A   : Wòhng Táai, néih jùngyi sihk dī méyéh a?

B   : Ngóh mhsīk dím ga. Néih gaaisiuh géi yeuhng jauh dāk la.

A   : Gám, ngóh dím géi yeuhng nīdouh yáuh méng ge béi néih siháh lā. Fógei, yiu go _gùlòu yuhk_, yāt go daaih hā, _dōu yiu sai ge_.

B   : Joi yiu yāt go jyùhhk tòng, hóu mhhóu a?

A   : Hóu aak! Fógei, juhng yiu yāt go jyùyuhk tòng tìm. Faaidī bo.

Waiter: Hóu.

A   : Wòhng Táai, sihk dōdī lā.

B   : Gau la--nīdouh dī choi jànhaih mhcho bo!

A   : Haih a. A! Yìhgā jauh faai yāt dím bun la, ngóhdeih jáu la, hóu ma?

B   : Hóu aak.

A   : Fógei! Màaihdāan. (She pays the check, leaving a tip.)

Waiter: Dòjehsaai.

> 1) faai = soon, almost, approaching (preceding a time expression)
>
> 2) yáuh méng = famous
>
> 3) gùlòu yuhk = sweet & sour pork
>
> 4) dōu yiu sai ge = want both to be small portions

Lesson Fifteen

1. Asking directions:

   A: Chéng mahn néih, Méihgwok Gūngsī hái bĩndouh a?

   B: Hái Dāk Fuh Douh Jùng.

   A: Yàuh nĩdouh dím heui a?

   B: Hái nĩdouh yātjihk hàahng, gwojó daih yih go gàaiháu, yìhnhauh jyun yauh.

   A: Jyun yauh jíhauh nē?

   B: Joi yātjihk hàahng, gwojó gàaisíh, jauh haih Dāk Fuh Douh Jùng. Heuidou gódouh, néih jauh táidóu ga laak.

   A: Hóu, mhgòi.

   B: Mhsái mhgòi.

2. At a department store, looking for a friend who works there:

   A: Chéng mahn, Léih Síu-lìhng Síujé hái bĩndouh a?

   B: Léih Síu-lìhng, kéuih hái bĩn go bouhfahn jouh sih ga?

   A: Hái maaih lāangsāam gó go bouhfahn.

   B: O, haih laak. Kéuih wah ngóh jī yáuh wái sīnsàang yiu wán kéuih, yìhgā kéuih hái yahpbihn dáng néih.

   A: Gám, ngóh hái bĩndouh yahpheui a?

   B: Hmm...Néih hái nĩdouh yātjihk hàahng, yìhnhauh jyunchēut jósáubihn, Léih Síujé jáuh hái gódouh laak.

   A: Mhgòisaai.

   B: Mhsái mhgòi.

3. Mr. Cheung has rung the bell of apt. 12-A. A servant answers the door, and Mr. Cheung says:

   A: Chéng mahn néih, Wòhng Sīnsàang hái mhhái douh a?

   B: Bĩn wái Wòhng Sīnsàang a?

   A: Wòhng Wíhng-yihp Sīnsàang.

   B: Mhhái nĩdouh bo. Chéng néih séuhngheui sei láu mahnháh lā.

   (Goes up)

   A: Chéng mahn, Wòhng Wíhng-yihp Sīnsàang hái mhhái douh a?

   C: Néih wán bĩngo a? Ngóhdeih nĩdouh móuh sing Wòhng ge bo.

   A: Haih mē? Deuimhjyuh bo. Daahnhaih ngóh ngāamngāam mahngwo yih láu yāt go yàhn, kéuih wah Wòhng Wíhng-yihp jyuh hái sei láu ge bo.

   C: Oh! Wòhng Wíhng-yihp! Kéuih haih mhhaih gaau Gwóngdùngwá ga?

   A: Móuh cho, haih kéuih laak.

C: Kéuih jyuh hái sàam láu, néih hàahng fàan lohk heui lā.

A: Hóu, mhgòisaai.

4. Discussing Cantonese lessons:

A: Yìhgā bīngo gaau néih góng Gwóngdùngwá a?

B: Dōu haih Jèung Sàang.

A: Hohkdou daih géi fo a?

B: Daih sahpńgh fo ge la.

A: Daih sahpńgh fo góng mēyéh ga?

B: Haih góng heui gūngsī máaih yéh gé, nī fo jànhaih hóu yáuh yuhng.
   Hohkjó nī fo ngóh jauh hóyíh tùhng gūngsī ge fógei góng Gwóngdùngwá laak.

A: Haih àh.

B: Haih a! Go fógei juhng wah ngóh ge Gwóngdùngwá hóu hóu tìm.

A: Haih ā. Néih ge Gwóngdùngwá haih mhcho aak.

B: Néih gám góng, ngóh jauh jànhaih mhhóu yisi la.

   1) yáuh yuhng = useful

GRAMMATICAL INDEX

Numbers to the left of the period refer to
lesson numbers, and those to the right, to
page numbers.

<u>yáuhdāk</u> <u>V</u> , 'have available for <u>V-ing,</u>
     11.246

<u>yih</u>, '2,' compared with <u>léuhng</u>, 4.93

<u>yìkwaahk</u>, '...., or...?, 14.315

<u>yihp</u>, 'page,' 15.336

<u>yiu</u>, 'must,' 5.115; relationship with
     <u>ḿhsái</u>, 5.115, 6.136; with follow-
     ing money expression 'wants,'
     'costs,' 6.140; 'intends to,'
     9.209; contrasted with <u>séung</u>,
     9.209

CUMULATIVE VOCABULARY LIST

LESSONS 1-15

Entries are arranged in alphabetical order by syllable, with **h** indicating lower register disregarded alphabetically. When words having the same syllable but different tones are listed, the sequence of tone listing is: high level, mid level, low level, high falling, low falling, high rising, low rising. Numbers in the right hand column refer to the lesson in which the item first appears, thus:

$$12 \quad = \text{Lesson 12 Basic Conversation}$$

12.1 = Lesson 12, Drill 1

1CP = Lesson 1, Classroom Phrases

1N = Lesson 1, Notes

Items which appear for the first time in the Classroom Phrases and Notes are listed again when appearing for the first time in the main body of the text. Measures for the nouns follow the noun entries in brackets.

ā	啊呀	sen. suf. **a** (QV) + raised intonation for liveliness	14
A	呀	oh, ah. (a mild exclamation)	1
a	呀	sen. suf., to soften abruptness	2
agō [go]	阿哥	elder brother	11
àh	呀	sen. suf. with force of 'I suppose.'	8
aak	呃	sen. suf. **a** (QV) + **-k** (QV)	5.7
āam (var: ngāam)	啱	fitting, proper, right	2CP
āamāam (var: ngāamngāam)	啱啱	exactly	4.5
āamjeuk (var: ngāamjeuk)	啱着	well-fitting (for clothes), fits well	8.2
aan (var: ngaan)	晏	noon, midday	9
Aiya!	哎吔	exclamation of consternation	5
bá	把	Measure for things with handles, such as umbrellas	6.1
baak	百	hundred	11
baahk	白	white	8
baahk faahn [wún] [dī]	白飯	boiled or steamed rice	14.1
baat	八	eight	4.0
bàau	包	package, Measure for cigarette pack	7.1
bàhbā [go]	爸爸	father	12.3
bāt [jī]	筆	writing implement, either pen or pencil	6.1
bātgwo	不過	however; but; although	14

béi	俾	give	6
béi	俾	let, allow	7CP
bējáu [jī] [bùi] [jèun]	啤酒	beer	5.2
béng [go] [dī] [faai]	餅	cake	5
bīn-?	邊	which?	8
bīnbihn?	邊便	which side?	10.8
bīndouh?	邊度	where? [which place?]	4CP;10
bīngo	邊個	whomever, whoever, whichever	3CP
bīngo?	邊個	who?; which person?	3.12
-bihn	便(邊)	side	10
bīu [go]	錶(個)	watch, wristwatch	4
bo	嘓	sen. suf. expressing certainty	4
bohng	磅	pound (weight)	7
bou [fàai] [fāt]	布	cloth	7.1
bouhfahn [go]	部分(個)	department (in a store)	15
būi [jek] [go]	杯隻(個)	a cup, glass	14.1
bùi	杯	cupful, glass-full (measure of volume)	14.1
bun	半	half	4.3
bún	本	Measure for book	1CP;7.1
búndeihyàhn [go]	本地人(個)	a native of the place under discussion [this-place-person]	10
chàmhdō	差唔多	approximately	2CP;4
chàh [bùi] [wùh]	茶(杯)(壺)	tea	5
chàhlàuh [gàan]	茶樓(間)	Cantonese style tea-house	10.2
chāansāt [gàan]	餐室(間)	Western style restaurant	10.2
cháang [go]	橙(個)	orange (fruit)	5.1
cháau	炒	to toss-fry in a small amount of oil, as in scrambling eggs	14.2
cháau faahn [wún] [dihp]	炒飯(碗)(碟)	fried rice	14.2
cháau mihn [wún] [dihp]	炒麵(碗)(碟)	fried noodles	14.1
Chàhn	陳	Chan (sur.)	1
chāt	七	seven	4.0
chē [ga]	車(架)	vehicle: car, bus, or tram	10.9
chē jaahm [go]	車站(個)	car stop (bus or tram stop)	10.3
chéng...	請	please (+ Verb). polite preface to imperative sentence.	15

chéng mahn	請問	'May I ask...?' Polite form used to preface a question equivalent to English 'Could you please tell me...?'	10
chèuihbín	隨便	As you wish. At your convenience.	5
chèuihbín chóh lā.	隨便生嗱	'Sit anywhere you like.' Polite phrase used by host to guest.	5
cheung	暢(唱)	change money into smaller denomination (followed by denomination desired)	11.16
cheunghòi	暢(唱)開	split, break up a large banknote or coin for ones of lesser denomination (followed by denomination held)	11
chèuhng	長	long (in length)	8.1
chèuhng sāam [gihn]	長衫(件)	cheongsaam. Chinese style dress for women, with high collar and slit skirt	8.7
chēut	出	out, emerge	15
chēutheui	出去	go out	
chēutlàih	出嚟	come out	
chēutbihn	出便(邊)	outside, exterior	15.1
chēut gāai	出街	to go out (from one's own house)	9.3
chi	次	time, occasion	1CP;3
chīn	千	thousand	11.17
chìhnbihn	前便(邊)	front side, in front, at the front	12.15
chín [dī]	錢[啲]	money	6
chīngchó	清楚	clear	3
chìhngyìhng	情形	circumstances, conditions	7CP
cho	錯	mistake (v/n)	9
chóh	坐	sit	5
choi [dihp] [go]	菜(蝶)(個)	food; a particular food, a dish	14
choidāan [jèung]	菜單(張)	menu of a specific dinner	14N
choipáai [go]	菜牌(個)	menu, bill of fare	14
dā	打	dozen	8
dá	打	hit	9
dá dihnwá	打電話	make a telephone call	9
dá dihnwá giu chē	打電話叫車	phone for a cab	15.11
dáhòi	打開	open (as of book)	1CP;15.3
daai	帶	carry; bring/take something along; bring/take someone along	11;12

-dóu	到	verb suf., indicating successful accomplishment of what is attempted	10
duhk	讀	read aloud; recite; read	3CP;15.3
duhkdou	讀到	read to...	15.3
duhk syù	讀書	to study	18
dyún	短	short	8
faahn [wún] [túng]	飯(碗)(桶)	rice (cooked)	5.1
fàan	返	return (to/from a place you habitually go to)	9.3
fàan gùng	返工	go [return] to work	9.3
fàanheui	返去	go back, return	17
fàan hohk	返學	go to school	9.3
fàanjyuntàuh	返轉頭	turn (the car) around and go back in the direction you had been coming. [return-turn-head]	13.1
fàanlàih	返嚟	come back, return (here)	9
fàan (ng)ūkkéi	返屋企	go [return] home	9.3
faai	快	fast	4
faaijí [deui] [jek] [sēung]	筷子(對)(隻)(雙)	chopstick(s)	14.5
fānjūng 分鐘		minute(s)	4
fànbiht	分別	difference	7CP
fo	課	lesson	4CP;15.3
fógei [go]	伙記(個)	clerk in a grocery store	6
fógei [go]	伙記(個)	waiter in a restaurant	14
fu [tìuh]	褲(條)	trousers, slacks, long pants	6.1
fu	副	pair; M. for eyeglasses	11.13
fut	闊	wide	8.3
ga	㗎	sen. suf: a fusion of noun-forming boundword ge and sen.suf. a (QV)	2.9
ga (var: ge, [gə])	㗎	sen. suf. for matter of fact assertion: 'that's a fact'	3
ga	架	M. for vehicles	12
gāai [tìuh]	街(條)	street	13
gaaisiuh	介紹	recommend; introduce	14
gàaiháu [go]	街口(個)	street opening; i.e., intersection	15.8
gàaisìh [go]	街市(個)	food market	15
gáai(sīk)	解(釋)	explain	7CP

aaih	大	large	8
aaih Douh Jùng	大道中	Queen's Road Central	10.3
aaihsēng	大聲	loud (voice)	2CP
aaihsēngdī!	大聲的	Speak louder!	9
aahnhaih	但係	but	3
aap	答	to answer	2CP
aap cho sin.	搭錯線	Wrong number. [connected the wrong line] (said over the phone)	9.3
aaphaak [dī]	搭客(的)	passenger	13
aahp	搭	tread on. in time expression daahp combines with the numbers on the clock face to indicate the 5-minute subdivisions of the hour. Thus, daahp yāt = 5 after, daahp yih = 10 after, etc.	4
aahp bun	搭半	half past (the hour)	4.4
aahp géi?	搭幾	how many five minutes past the hour? [tread on-which number?]	4.4
aih	第	ordinal number marker: -st, -nd, -rd, -th, etc.	3CP;15.3
aihyāt	第一	the first	15
aifu [tiuh]	底褲(條)	underpants, undershorts	6.3
aikwàhn [tiuh]	底裙(條)	slip, petticoat	6.1
aisāam [gihn]	底衫(件)	underwear	8.13
āk	得	OK, all right	7CP;11
āk...	得....	have only..., only have .X.quantity. (dāk with a quantity phrase as object implies that the quantity is insufficient.)	11
auh -dāk-	有-得-	available, can. (used between the verb yáuh (or its negative móuh) and a second verb, forms a phrase: 'have (or not have) available for .V.-ing'; 'can .V.'	11
ākfuh Douh Jùng	德輔道中	Des Veoux Road Central	10.5
āk meih?	得未	Are you (Is he, etc.) ready?	4
áng	等	wait (for)	4
áng Person.Verb	等	allow, let Person do something; wait while Person does something	9
áng (yāt)ján or dáng yātjahn	等(一)陣 等一陣	wait awhile; in a little while	9.3

deihhá	地下	ground, ground floor	15.1
deui	對	pair; group measure for shoes, socks, chopsticks, things that come in two's	6.1
Deuimhjyuh.	對唔住	Excuse me; I beg your pardon; I'm sorry.	1
deuimihn	對面	opposite side, facing; across the street	10
dī	的	the; some. (plural M for individual nouns)	1CP;7
dī	的	a little, some; the. (general M for mass nouns)	3;7
-dī	的	suffixed to Adj. to mean: a little Adj, somewhat Adj, Adj-er. Attached to predicate Adj. means: a little too Adj.	2CP;8
dihnwá [go]	電話[個]	telephone	9
dím	點	to order (food, by pointing out your choice from a list.)	14
dím?	點	how?	3
dím bun	點半	1:30 o'clock	9.7
dím(jūng)	點(鐘)	o'clock. (represents the hour place in a time phrase)	4
diuhtàuh	掉頭	turn (a car) around [turn-head]	13.4
dōdī	多的	more (in addition). (follows Verb)	14
dò	多	much, many	8
dò	多	additional, another, more. (precedes Number + M phrase)	14
Dòjeh.	多謝	Thank you (for gift)	14
Dòjehsaai.	多謝晒	Thank you very much.	14
dōu	都	also	2
dōu	都	both; and	3
dōuhaih	都係	really	14
dōu + neg.:.V.	都	not even ..V.	3.16
dou	到	arrive	13
-dou	到	verb suf. to verbs of motion, indicating arrival at goal	15
Douh	道	Road (restricted to use following named road)	12.2
-douh	度	place. also see: hái douh	11

gaaklèih	隔離	next door, adjacent	10
gàan	間	M. for buildings	10
gaau	教	teach	3.3
gaaudou	教到	teach to...	4CP
gafē [būi] [wùh]	喋啡杯[壺]	coffee	5.2
gāi [jek]	雞[隻]	chicken	7.1
gaijuhk	繼續	continue	2CP
gam	咁	so (+ Adj.)	5
gamseuhnghá	咁上下	approximately	9.7
gám	咁	that way, this way, thus, such a way	2CP;3CP
gám,...	咁	'Well then,...' 'Say,...' (Sen. preface, resuming the thread of previous discussion)	3
gàn	斤	catty. unit of weight equalling 600 gms., ca. 1 lb 5 oz.	7
gàn	跟	follow, come behind	12.7
gànjyuh	跟住	follow, come after	1CP; 3CP 12.7
gāng [jek]	羹[隻]	spoon	14.4
gau	夠	enough	6
gauh	舊	old (not new)	8.1
gáu	九	nine	4.0
gáulùhng	九龍	Kowloon	12
-ge	嘅	noun-forming boundword. added to Verb Phrase makes it a Noun Phrase	2
-ge	嘅	as noun substitute	8.8
ge	嘅	possessive marker, joins with preceding personal noun or pronoun to form possessive.	9.10
gēibún	基本	basic; foundation	4CP
géi	幾	several	4
géi_?	幾	which number?; how many?	4; 6
géi	幾	rather, quite	8
géidím? (var: géidímjūng?)	幾點 (幾點鐘)	what time is it? [which number - o'clock?]	4
géidō?	幾多	how much?, how many?	6
géidò	幾多	quite a lot	11.11

géidō houh?	幾多號	what number?	9
géisí? (var: géisìh?)	幾時	when?	9
geui	句	sentence	3CP;3.14
géui	舉	give (an example)	7CP
gihn	件	M. for clothes, such as shirt, dress, raincoat	6
giu	叫	instruct, tell (someone to do something); order; call	9
giu chē	叫車	call a cab	15.11
giu(jouh)	叫(做)	is called, is named	13
go	個	general M. for many nouns	1CP;4
go	個	M. for dollar; represents the dollar place in a money phrase	7
gó-	嗰	that; those	6
gó bihn	嗰便(邊)	over there, on that side	10
gódī	嗰啲	those (in reference to unit nouns); that (in reference to mass nouns)	7
gódouh	嗰度	there [that-place]	10.1
góng	講	speak	1CP;2CP; 3
góng Person jī	講……知	tell Person	9.8
góng Person tèng	講……聽	tell Person	9.8
guhaak [dī]	顧客	customers	6
gūngsī [gàan]	公司[間]	department store; office (of a commercial company)	10
gùngyàhn [go]	工人[個]	servant, laborer	9
gwai	貴	expensive	8.3
gwaising?	貴姓	what is (your) surname? (polite)	2
gwaisingmìhng?	貴姓名	what is your surname and given name? (polite)	13.17
gwāt	骨	quarter (hour)	4
gwo	過	pass by (a point); cross (a street); go over (to a place)	13
-gwo	過	V. suf. indicating experience; to have done something before.	14
gwodī	過啲	beyond; a little farther on	13
Gwodī tīm.	過啲添	Go further on; i.e. Keep going. (said to taxi driver)	13
Gwokyúh	國語	Mandarin spoken language [National-language]	3

...ôngdùng	廣東	Kwangtung, province in SE China	2
...ôngdùng choi	廣東菜	Cantonese food	14.2
...ôngdùngwá	廣東話	Cantonese spoken language	3.1
...ôngdùngyàhn [go]	廣東人[個]	Cantonese person, person from Kwangtung province	2
... [jek]	蝦[隻]	shrimp	14
...hbihn	下便(邊)	below, downstairs	15.1
...âh	吓	verb suf. giving casual effect to the verb it is joined to.	5
...aih [deui] [jek]	鞋[對][隻]	shoes	6.2;7.1
...ak	黑	black	8
...akhei	客氣	polite	5
...ahng	行	go; walk; drive	13
...ih	係	am, is, are, was, were, etc.	1
...ih...làih ge	係...嚟嘅	is...; grammatical structure emphasizing enclosed noun	7
...i PW	喺	from PW	15.6
...i PW	喺	location verb, translated as '(is) in/on/at' (requires PW following)	7CP;10
...í douh	喺度	(he, she, it) is here; is at (this) place	11
...uhbihn	後便(邊)	back side; behind, in the back, at the back	12
汽水[支][樽][杯]			
...iséui [jì] [jèun] [bùi]		soft drink	5.2
...ui	去	go	12
...eui	去	attaches to verbs of motion, indicating direction away from the speaker	15
...ui gāai	去街	go out (from one's own house)	9.3
...unggóng	香港	Hong Kong	10.3
...óh	何	Ho (sur.)	1
...óyíh	可以	be permitted, allowed to	13
...ohk	學	study, learn	3
...ohkhaauh [gàan]	學校[間]	school	12
...ohksāang [go]	學生[個]	student	1
...ouh	號	number; 'size' (for some articles of clothing)	8
...ouh	號	number (for street number in giving an address)	12.2

hòuh(jí)	毫子	dime (represents the dime place in a money expression when the figure is less than a dollar)	7
hóu	好	very, quite	2CP;8
hóu	好	well, good	2CP;8
Hóu	好	OK, All right, Fine, Agreed. (Response phrase indicating agreement.)	4
Hóu aak.	好呃	OK. Agreed. (Lively response phrase indicating agreement.)	5.7
hóudò	好多	a lot	11.11
Hóu ma?	好嗎	Is that OK?	14
hóu m̀hhóu a?	好唔好呀	OK?, is (that) all right?	8
hóusihk	好食	good to eat; tasty	8.2
hóusíu	好少	very little	11.11
hóuyám	好飲	good to drink; tasty	8.2
ja	喳	sen. suf: a fusion of sen. suffixes jē and a, implying not much, merely	11.11
jà	揸	to clutch in the hand(s), grab	13.15
jà chē	揸車	to drive a car	13.15
jaak	窄	narrow	8.3
jaahm	站	stop, station, as in 'bus stop,' 'train station'	10.3
jáau	找	give change	11
jáaufàan	找翻	give back change [change-return]	11
jái [go]	仔[個]	son	12.2
jáinéui [dī]	仔女[的]	children of a family, sons and daughters of a family	12.2
jànhaih	真係	really, indeed	5
jauh	就	then; and; immediately; soon	3CP;13
jáu	走	leave, depart	5
jáu [jèun] [bùi]	酒[樽][杯]	alcoholic beverage	5.2
jáudim [gàan]	酒店[間]	hotel	10
jáugā [gàan]	酒家[間]	Chinese style restaurant	14.8
jē	嗜	sen. suf: only, merely; that's all	3
jē [bá]	遮	umbrella	6.1
je	借	lend, borrow	11
je jyuh	借住	lend or borrow temporarily	11

jek	隻	M. for shoe, sock, ship, cup, spoon, chicken and others.	7.1
jeuk	著	wear; put on (clothes)	8
jéun	準	accurate, right	2CP;4
Jèung	張	Cheung (sur.)	1.1
jèung	張	M. for banknote, table, chair, newspaper, and other sheet-snaped objects	11
jih [go]	字[個]	written figure; word; used in telling time, indicates the 5-minute divisions of the hour, thus: yāt go jih = 5 minutes; 5 min. past the hour.	4;7CP
jihgéi	自己	my-, your-, nim-self; our-, your-, them-selves	2CP
jí	支	M. for pens, pencils, bottles, and other things that are small thin and striplike in size	6.1
jí(dou)	知	to know (something)	3
jí [jèung]	紙[張]	banknote; paper	11
jídou	知道	point to	3CP
jip	接	meet, fetch, pick up (a person)	12
jíu [jek] [sō]	蕉[隻][梳]	banana	5.1
-jó	咗	verb suf. indicating accomplish-ment of performance undertaken	**9**
jó	左	left (direction)	13
jóbihn	左便(邊)	left side	13
-jógán	左近	nearby,(t)hereabouts	10
jósáubihn	左手便(邊)	lefthand side	13
joi	再	again	1CP;3
joi dá làih	再打嚟	call back (on the phone)	9.3
Joigin.	再見	Goodbye.	1
joi góng yātchi	再講一次	say it again	3
jouh	做	do; work; act as	2CP;3CP;12.2
jouh sāam	做衫	make clothes, have clothes made	12.12
jouh sih	做事	to work, have a job	12.2
jouh yéh	做嘢	do chores, have a job	14.7
Jóusàhn.	早晨	Good morning.	1
jūng [go]	鐘[個]	clock	6.1

juhng	重	still, in addition, also (+ verb)	14
Jùngchoi	中菜	Chinese food	14.2
Jùnggwok choi	中國菜	Chinese food	14.13
Jùnggwokyàhn	中國人	Chinese person	2.1
Jùngmàhn	中文	Chinese (written) language	3.3
Jùngwàahn	中環	Central District (in Hong Kong)	10.3
Jùngwàahn Gàaihsíh	中環街市	Central Market (in Hong Kong)	15
jùngyi	鍾意	like; prefer; like to	8
júng	種	type, kind	8
jyuh	住	live, reside	12
-jyuh	住	V. suf. indicating temporarily, for a short time	11
jyùyuhk [gàn] [bohng] [dì]	豬肉[斤][磅][的]	pork	7
jyúyàhn [wái] [go]	主人[位][個]	host, hostess	5
jyun	轉	turn	13
-k		glottal stop ending to certain sen. suffixes, giving sentence a lively air	5
kàhmyaht	琴日	yesterday	4CP
kámmàaih	冚埋	to close, shut (as of books)	1CP
kéuih	佢	he/him, she/her, it	2
kéuihdeih	佢地	they, them, their	2.1
kwàhn [tìuh]	裙[條]	skirt	6.1
lā	啦	sen. suf. for polite imperative, polite suggestion.	4
lā	啦	sen. suf. la for change + raised intonation for casualness	4
la	啦 (嘑)	sen. suf. indicating change-- (that change has occurred, or is about to occur, or may occur)	4CP;4; 5
la	啦 (嘑)	sen. suf. to imperative sentence, giving connotation of friendly advice	13.12
laak	嘞	sen. suf. la indicating change or potential change + suffix -k indicating lively mood (la + -k = laak)	2CP;5
làangsāam [gihn]	冷杉[件]	sweater	8.1
laih	例	example	7CP
laihgeui	例句	example, example sentence	3CP

làih	嗒	for the purpose of	7CP
làih	嚟 (來)	come	12
-làih	嚟	attaches to verbs of motion, indicating direction towards the speaker	15
...làih ge	嚟 嘅	see: haih...làih ge	7
Làuh	劉	Lau (sur.)	1.1
làuhhah	樓下	downstairs [floor-below]	15.1
làuhseuhng	樓上	upstairs [floor-above]	15.1
láu	樓	floor, story of a building	12.2
léh	咧	sen. suf. for definiteness	5
Léih	李	Lee (sur.)	1
leng	靚	pretty, good-looking; good, nice (for edibles)	8
lèhng	零	'-and a little bit' in a time phrase following dím, thus: -dím lèhng jūng = a little after the hour	9
léuhng	兩	two	4.1
lihnjaahp [go]	練習 [個]	exercise, drill	3CP
lìhng	零	zero	9
ló	攞	fetch, go get (something)	9
ló chín	攞錢	withdraw money (from bank)	10.9
lohk	落	descend	15
lohkheui	落去	go down	15
louhyàhn [go]	路人 [個]	pedestrian	15
luhk	六	six	4.0
ma?	嗎	sen. suf. making a question of the sentence it attaches to	14
màhmā	媽媽	mother	12
Máh	馬	Ma (sur.)	1.1
máh	碼	yard (in length)	7.1
máhtàuh [go]	碼頭 [個]	pier	10
maaih	賣	sell	7
Maaihsaai laak.	賣晒嘞	All sold out.	8
-màaih	埋	V. suf. meaning together, close	1CP
Màaihdāan!	埋單	The check please! (said to a waiter in restaurant)	14

máaih	買	buy	6
maahn	慢	slow	4.8
mān	蚊	dollar	6
mahn	問	ask	2CP;10
mahntàih [go] [dī]	問題個的	question	3CP
Màhnwàh Jáudim	文華酒店	Mandarin Hotel	10
mātyéh?	乜野	what?	2
maht [deui] [jek]	襪對隻	socks	6.1;7.1
mē?	咩	interrogative sen. suf. indicating surprise	3
mēyéh?	咩野	what?	2
meih	未	neg: not yet	4
Méihgwok Jáudim	美國酒店	American Hotel (in HK, another name for the Hong Kong Hilton)	10.3
Méihgwok Ngàhnhòhng	美國銀行	Bank of America	10.3
Méihgwokyàhn	美國人	American person	2.1
méng [go]	名個	name; for persons = given name (in contrast to surname)	13
m̀h-	唔	not	1
m̀hcho	唔錯	good, 'not bad' [not-mistake] (said in commenting favorably about something)	14
M̀hgányiu.	唔緊要	That's all right; It doesn't matter; Never mind.	1
m̀hgeidāk	唔記得	forget (not remember)	11
m̀hginjó	唔見咗	lose, lost; 'nowhere to be seen'	11
m̀hgòi	唔該	Thank you (for a service)	5
M̀hgòi néih...	唔該你	Please..., Would you please... (sen. preface preceding a request)	3
m̀hhaih géi Adj	唔係幾...	not very Adj, not Adj	8.1
m̀hhaih hóu Adj	唔係好...	not very Adj	8.4
m̀hhóu .V.	唔好...	don't .V. (as a command) [not good to .V.]	1CP;3CP;5
V.dāk m̀hhóu	得唔好	badly, not well	2CP
M̀hhóu haakhei.	唔好客氣	'Don't be polite.' Polite phrase used by host to urge guest to have something that he has just politely declined.	5

Mhhóu yisi.	唔好意思	I'm sorry; It's embarrassing. (used in apologizing for social gaffe)	4
Mhjì(dou)...a?	唔知(道)..呀	I wonder...?	6.1
Mhsái	唔使	no need to, not necessary	5
Mhsái haakhei.	唔使客氣	[don't need to be polite.] 'No thanks!' (to an offer) 'You're welcome.' (when someone thanks you)	5
Mhsái la.	唔使啦	[Not necessary] No thanks. polite phrase used in declining a courtesy or a gift.	5
Mhsái mhgòi.	唔使唔該	[Not necessary to (say) thanks] Polite response when someone thanks you for something you have done for him.	5
mīyéh?	乜嘢	what?	
móuh	有	not have, there isn't (aren't)	3CP;8
Móuh cho.	有錯	That's right.	
móuhdāk ...V	有得...	not have available for V-ing, there's none to ...V.., not have available to ... (used in combination with following verb)	11
móuhgéidò	有幾多	not much, not many	11.11
mùhnháu [go]	門口〔個〕	doorway	10.6
nàahmpàhngyáuh [go]	男朋友〔個〕	boyfriend	12.3
Nàh!	嗱	Here! (expression accompanying giving something to someone)	11
nē?	呢	interrogative sen. suf.	2
Nē!	呢	There! (expression accompanying pointing out something to someone)	10
Nèihdēun Douh	彌敦道	Nathan Road	12.2
néih	你	you, your	2
néihdeih	你哋	you (plu.)	1CP;2
néui [go]	女〔個〕	daughter	12
néuihpàhngyáuh [go] [wái]	女朋友〔個〕〔位〕	girlfriend	12.3
ńgh	五	five	3
ngāam	啱	fitting, proper, right	2CP
ngāamjeuk	啱著	well-fitting (for clothes), fits well	8.2

ngāamngāam(var:āamāam)	啱啱	exactly, just	4.5
ngaan (var:aan)	晏	noon, midday	9
ngàhnchín [go]	銀錢[個]	money [silver-money]	7
ngàhnhòhng [gàan]	銀行[間]	bank	10
ngán	銀	coin	11.1
ngáhngéng [fu]	眼鏡[副]	eyeglasses	11.13
ngáhngéngdói [go]	眼鏡袋[個]	eyeglasses case	11.13
ngahp táu	頷頭	nod the head	3CP
ngàuhnáaih [dī]	牛奶[的]	milk [cow-milk]	5.2
ngàuhyuhk [gàn] [bohng] 　[dī]	牛肉 [斤][磅][的]	beef	7
ngóh	我	I, me, my	1
ngóhdeih	我哋	we, our, us	2.1
ngoi (var: oi)	愛	want, want to have, want to possess	7
ngoihgwokyàhn [go]	外國人[個]	foreigner [outside-country-person] (in practice, this word refers 　to Caucasians only)	14
ngūk (var: ūk) [gàan]	屋[間]	house	10.3
ngūkkéi (var: ūkkéi)	屋企	home	9.3
nī	呢	this	6
nī bihn	呢便	this side	10.3
nī dī	呢的	these (in reference to individual 　nouns), this (in reference to 　mass nouns)	7
nīdouh	度	here [this-place]	10.1
nī jógán	左近	close by, hereabouts	10.3
nihng táu	擰頭	shake the head	3CP
níng	拎	carry (something)	14
níngheui, níng...heui	拎去拎去	take, carry something away	14
nínglàih, níng...làih	拎嚟拎嚟	bring something here	14
oi (var: ngoi)	愛	want, want to have, want to possess	7
paak	泊	park (a car)	13
paak chē	泊車	to park a car	13
pàhngyáuh [go]	朋友[個]	friend	2
pèhng	平	cheap	8
pìhnggwó [go]	蘋果[個]	apple	5.1
-saai	晒	completely	8

sàam	三	three	3
sàam go gwat	三個骨	three quarters after the hour	4.6
sáanngán [dī]	散銀(的)	small coins, small change	11
Sàang	生	Mr.	1
Sāichāan [go]	西餐(個)	Western meal	14.2
sai	細	small	8.2
saimúi [go]	細妹(個)	younger sister	11
sàn	新	new	8.1
sahp	十	ten	4.0
sahpyāt	十一	eleven	4.1
sahpyih	十二	twelve	4.1
sauhfoyùhn [go]	售貨員(個)	salesclerk [sell-goods-personnel]	6
sáudói [go]	手袋(個)	(woman's) handbag	11.13
sèsíu	些少	a little	3
sé	寫	write	3
séjihlàuh [gàan]	寫字樓(間)	office [write-words-building]	10.2
sei	四	four	3
seuhngbihn	上便(邊)	above, upstairs	15.1
seuhngchi	上次	last time, the previous time	4CP;15.3
Seuhnghói	上海	Shanghai	2
Seuhnghói choi	上海菜	Shanghai food	14.2
Seuhnghóiwá	上海話	Shanghai dialect (spoken language)	3
Seuhnghóiyàhn [go]	上海人(個)	person from Shanghai	2
séung	想	be of a mind to, wish to, would like to, want to, considering. (always followed by Verb)	3
séuhng	上	ascend	15
séui [bùi] [dī]	水(杯)(的)	water	5.2
séui būi [jek]	水杯(隻)	water glass	14.10
sēutsāam [gihn]	恤衫(件)	shirt	6
sīgēi [go]	司機(個)	taxi driver; chauffeur	11
si	試	try	5
siháh	試吓	give it a try	5
sih	事	business, affair, matter	9
Sihdaahn lā.	是但啦	Phrase used when offered a choice, meaning: As you wish; Either one; Both equally preferable.	14

387

sìhhauh	時候	time	7CP
sīk	識	know how (to do something)	3
sīk	識	know someone	3.11
sīk	色	color (n.)	8
sihk	食	eat	5
sihk (ng)aan	食晏	eat lunch	2.1
sihk yīn	食烟	to smoke [eat-tobacco]	5
sīnsàang [go]	先生[個]	husband	12.2
sīnsàang [go] [wái]	先生[個][位]	man, gentleman	1N;2
Sīnsàang	先生	Mr.	1N
sīnsàang	先生	'Sir,' polite term of direct address	2
sīnsàang [go]	先生[個]	teacher	1
sin	線	line, thread (n.)	9
sìn	先	first	3CP;9
...sìn, yìhnhauh...	...先,然後...	...first, then...	15
sìnji	先至	then	7CP
sing	姓	be surnamed, have the surname; surname	1
síujé [wái] [go]	小姐[位][個]	unmarried woman; woman, lady	1N;2
Síujé	小姐	Miss (polite term of direct address; also, title following surname)	1
Síu sihk.	少食	Thanks, I don't smoke. [seldom-smoke] (response by non-smoker when offered a cigarette.)	5.8
Síusing...	小姓	My surname is... (polite)	2
suhk	熟	ripe (in regard to speech = smoothly and with understanding of the content)	2CP
sung	送	deliver	12.10
-syu	處	place (PW boundword)	10N
syù [bún]	書[本]	book	1CP;3CP; 7.1
tāai [tìuh]	呔[條]	tie	6.2
Taaitáai	太太	Mrs.	1N;1
taaitáai [go] [wái]	太太[個][位]	married woman; wife	1N;12.2
Taai	太	Mrs. (title to surname)	1
taam	探	to visit	12
tái	睇	look, look at	1CP;3CP; 10

táidóu	睇倒	see (look-successfully)	10
táiháh	睇吓	have a look	14
tái syù	睇書	read (a book)	10.14
tái yīsāng	睇醫生	see a doctor	12.2
tanhauh	踉後	back (a car) up, move back, reverse [move-back]	13.1
táu = tàuh	頭	head	3CP
tèng	聽	hear, listen (to)	1CP;3CP;3
tèng dihnwá	聽電話	talk [listen] on the telephone	9
tìm	添	sen. suf. indicating speaker is taken by surprise by a situation contrary to his expectation	11
tìm	添	in addition, also, more	4
Tīnsīng Máhtàuh	天星碼頭	Star Ferry Pier	10
tìhng	停	to stop	13
tìuh	條	M. for trousers, ties, and certain other objects long and narrow in shape	6.1
Tòihsāan	台山	Taishan, a county in Southern Kwangtung about 100 mi. west of Hong Kong	2.1
Tòihsāanwá	台山話	Taishan dialect	3.7
Tòihsāanyàhn	台山人	person from Taishan	2.1
tòng [go] [wún]	湯[個][碗]	soup	14
tòng mihn [go] [wún]	湯麵[個][碗]	soup noodles	14.1
tòhng	糖	sugar	7
Tòhngchoi	唐菜	Chinese food	14N
tòuhsyùgwún [gàan]	圖書館[間]	library	10.2
tùhng	同	and (connects nouns)	3
tùhng	同	on behalf of, for	11
tùhng	同	with	12.11
ūk (var: ngūk) [gàan]	屋[間]	house	10.3
ūkkéi (var: ngūkkéi)	屋呢	home	9.3
wá	話	spoken language; dialect	3
wá?	話	interrogative sen. suf. calling for repeat of the preceding sentence	4
waahkjé	或者	maybe	4

wah	話	say; opine	8.3
wah yàhn jì	話人知	tell someone (any personal noun or pronoun can fill yàhn position)	9
wah yàhn tèng	話人聽	tell someone	9.8
wái	位	polite M. for persons	6.1
wái [go]	位[個]	a place, seat	13
wānjaahp	溫習	to review	4CP
wán	搵	look for, search	9
Wán bīnwái a?	搵邊位呀	(on telephone:) Who do you wish to speak to?	9
wán yàhn	搵人	look someone up	9.9
làih wán person	嚟搵....	come/go see someone	9.9
heui wán person	去搵....		
Wéi!	喂	Hello! (telephone greeting)	9
Wíhngōn Gūngsī	永安公司	Wing On Department Store	13.1
Wòhng	黃(王)	Wong (sur.)	1.1
wuihwá	會話	conversation	4CP
wuhn	換	to change. re money, to change into... (followed by denomination of money desired); to exchange one national currency for another (followed by currency desired)	11
wuhn sāam	換衫	change clothes	15.11
wún [go] [jek]	碗[個][隻]	bowl (n.)	14.1
wún	碗	a bowl of... (m)	14.1
wúnjái [go] [jek]	碗仔[個][隻]	small bowl	14.10
yám	飲	to drink	5
yàhn [go]	人[個]	person	2,6
yàhn [go]	人[個]	someone	15
yàhnhaak [wái]	人客[位]	guest	5
yahp	入	enter	13
yahpbihn	入便(邊)	inside	13
yahpheui	入去	go in; enter	13
yāt	一	one	1CP;3
yātchàih	一齊	together	1CP
yātchi	一次	once, one time	3
yāt chi dōu meih...	一次都未...	not even once	14

āt ... M̱. dōu Neg̱. V̱. ...	一...都...	not even one...	14
āt go gwāt	一個骨	a quarter after the hour	4.6
āt go jih	一個字	five minutes; five minutes after the hour	4.7
āt go yāt go	一個一個	one by one	1CP
ātjihk	一直	straight a) in a straight direction b) without being interrupted or diverted.	13
ātyeuhng	一樣	same	7
ahtbún choi	日本菜	Japanese food	14.12
ahtbúnwá	日本話	Japanese (spoken) language	3.1
ahtbúnyàhn	日本人	Japanese person	2.1
ahtmán	日文	Japanese (written) language	3.6
ahtmàhn	日文	Japanese (written) language	3.6
auh	右	right (direction)	13
auh	又	also (connects Verb Phrases)	3.9
auh .V̱.yauh.V̱.	又...又...	both..., and....	3.9
auhbihn	右便(邊)	right side	13.7
auhsáubihn	右手便(邊)	right hand side	13.4
àuh.....PW	由...	from .....PW	15
àuhhaak [go]	遊客(個)	tourist	10
áuh	有	has/have; there is/are	3CP;8
áuhdāk.V̱.	有得	to have available to .V̱., have available for .V̱-ing. (used in combination with following verb)	11.7
Yáuh) mēyéh sih a?	(有)咩野事呀	What is it you want? (on the phone: May I take a message?)	9
áuh sih	有事	have something to attend to; have errand, business	9
éh	嘢	work; chores	14.7
éh	嘢	things, stuff	12.2
euhng	樣	kind, type	14.12
īsāng [go]	醫生(個)	doctor	12.2
ih	二	two	3
ihgā	而家	now, at this moment	1CP;2CP; 3CP;4
i!	噫	Exclamation of distress	11

...yīkwaahk...?	...抑或...	..., or...? (connects two verbal expressions)	14
yīn [bāau] [dī]	烟(包)(啲)	tobacco	5
yīnjái [jī]	烟仔(支)	a cigarette	7.1
yìhn(jī)hauh	然(之)後	then; immediately afterwards	15
Yìngmán	英文	English language	3
Yìngmàhn	英文	English language	3
Yìnggwokyàhn [go]	英國人(個)	Englishman, person from England	2.1
yihp	頁	page	4CP;15.?
yiu	要	want, require	2CP
yiu	要	must; need; have to	5
yiu + money expression	要	want X amount, costs X amount. (i.e., the asking price is X amount)	6.1
yiu	要	going to, intend to	9
yú	魚	fish	7.1
yúhjyū [jek]	乳豬(隻)	roast suckling pig	14
yúhlāu [gihn]	雨褸(件)	raincoat	6.1
yùhnbāt [jī]	鉛筆(支)	pencil	6.1
yùhnjíbāt [jī] [dī]	原子筆(支)(啲)	ballpoint pen	6.2
yuhng 用	(支)(啲)	use	7CP;11

CHINESE DICTIONARIES FROM HIPPOCRENE

**CLASSIFIED AND ILLUSTRATED
CHINESE-ENGLISH DICTIONARY (revised)**
Guangzhou Institute of Foreign Languages
Contains 35,000 entries and 2,000 illustrations. Includes terms used in popular science, finance, agriculture and technology.
897 pages, 5 1/4 x 7 1/2
ISBN 0-87052-714-2
(27) $19.95

CHINESE-ENGLISH HANDBOOK OF IDIOMS
Edited by Chen Zhiyuan
Contains over 4,000 entries transcribed in Hanyu Pinyin.
603 pages, 4 x 5 3/4
ISBN 0-87052-454-2
(270) $12.95

CHINESE HANDY DICTIONARY
A combination dictionary-phrasebook for the Mandarin dialect. Includes pronunciation, a grammar reference section and appendices of numbers and measures.
120 pages, 5 x 7 3/4
ISBN 0-87052-050-4
(347) $8.95

BASIC COURSE SERIES

These guides include dialogues, response drills, glossaries and intensive instruction. Each guide is a reprint of a course used by the U.S. Foreign Service Institute.

Greek Basic Course
327 pages, 5 1/2 x 8 1/2
ISBN 0-7818-0167-2
(461) $14.95pb

Twi Basic Course
225 pages, 6 1/2 x 8 1/2
ISBN 0-7818-0394-2
(65) $16.95pb

Hungarian Basic Course
266 pages, 5 1/2 x 8 1/2
ISBN 0-87052-817-3
(131) $14.95pb

Lao Basic Course
350 pages, 5 1/2 x 8 1/2
ISBN 0-7818-0410-8
(248) $19.95pb

Saudi Arabic Basic Course
288 pages, 5 1/2 x 8 1/2
ISBN 0-7818-0257-1
(171) $14.95pb

(All prices subject to change.)

TO PURCHASE HIPPOCRENE BOOKS contact your local bookstore, or write to: HIPPOCRENE BOOKS, 171 Madison Avenue, New York, NY 10016. Please enclose check or money order, adding $5.00 shipping (UPS) for the first book and $.50 for each additional book.

HIPPOCRENE HANDY DICTIONARIES

For the traveler of independent spirit and curious mind, this practical series will help you to communicate, not just to get by. Common phrases are conveniently listed through key words. Pronunciation follows each entry and a reference section reviews all major grammar points. *Handy Extras* are extra helpful—offering even more words and phrases for students and travelers.

ARABIC
$8.95 • 0-87052-960-9

CHINESE
$8.95 • 0-87052-050-4

CZECH EXTRA
$8.95 • 0-7818-0138-9

DUTCH
$8.95 • 0-87052-049-0

FRENCH
$8.95 • 0-7818-0010-2

GERMAN
$8.95 • 0-7818-0014-5

GREEK
$8.95 • 0-87052-961-7

HUNGARIAN EXTRA
$8.95 • 0-7818-0164-8

ITALIAN
$8.95 • 0-7818-0011-0

JAPANESE
$8.95 • 0-87052-962-5

KOREAN
$8.95 • 0-7818-0082-X

PORTUGUESE
$8.95 • 0-87052-053-9

RUSSIAN
$8.95 • 0-7818-0013-7

SERBO-CROATIAN
$8.95 • 0-87052-051-2

SLOVAK EXTRA
$8.95 • 0-7818-0101-X

SPANISH
$8.95 • 0-7818-0012-9

SWEDISH
$8.95 • 0-87052-054-7

THAI
$8.95 • 0-87052-963-3

TURKISH
$8.95 • 0-87052-982-X

THE HIPPOCRENE MASTERING SERIES

MASTERING ARABIC
Jane Wightwick and Mahmoud Gaafar
320 pages, 5 1/2 x 8 1/2
0-87052-922-6 $14.95pb
2 Cassettes
 0-87052-984-6 $12.95
Book and Cassettes Package
0-87052-140-3 $27.90

MASTERING FINNISH
Börje Vähämäki
278 pages, 5 1/2 x 8 1/2
0-7818-0233-4 $14.95pb
2 Cassettes
0-7818-0265-2 $12.95
Book and Cassettes Package
0-7818-0266-0 $27.90

MASTERING FRENCH
E.J. Neather
288 pages, 5 1/2 x 8 1/2
0-87052-055-5 $11.95pb
2 Cassettes
0-87052-060-1 $12.95
Book and Cassettes Package
0-87052-136-5 $24.90

MASTERING GERMAN
A.J. Peck
340 pages, 5 1/2 x 8 1/2
0-87052-056-3 $11.95pb
2 Cassettes
0-87052-061-X $12.95
Book and Cassettes Package
0-87052-137-3 $24.90

MASTERING ADVANCED GERMAN
278 pages, 5 1/2 x 8 1/2
0-7818-0331-4 $14.95pb
2 Casettes
0-7818-0332-2 $12.95
Book and Cassettes Package
0-7818-0348-9 $27.90

MASTERING ITALIAN
N. Messora
360 pages, 5 1/2 x 8 1/2
0-87052-057-1 $11.95pb
2 Cassettes
0-87052-066-0 $12.95
Book and Cassettes Package
0-87052-138-1 $24.90

MASTERING ADVANCED ITALIAN
278 pages, 5 1/2 x 8 1/2
0-7818-0333-0 $14.95
2 Cassettes
0-7818-0334-9 $12.95
Book and Cassettes Package
0-7818-0349-7 $27.90

MASTERING JAPANESE
Harry Guest
368 pages, 5 1/2 x 8 1/2
0-87052-923-4 $14.95pb
2 Cassettes
0-87052-938-8 $12.95
Book and Cassettes Package
0-87052-141-1 $27.90

MASTERING POLISH
Albert Juszczak
288 pages, 5 1/2 x 8 1/2
0-7818-0015-3 $14.95pb
2 Cassettes
0-7818-0016-3 $12.95
Book and Cassettes Package
0-7818-0017-X $27.90

MASTERING RUSSIAN
Erika Haber
278 pages, 5 1/2 x 8 1/2
0-7818-0270-9 $14.95
2 Cassettes
0-7818-0270-9 $12.95
Book and Cassettes Package
0-7818-0272-5 $27.90

MASTERING SPANISH

Robert Clarke

338 pages, 5 1/2 x 8 1/2

0-87052-059-8 $11.95pb

2 Cassettes

0-87052-067-9 $12.95

Book and Cassettes Package

0-87052-139-X $24.90

MASTERING ADVANCED SPANISH

Robert Clarke

300 pages, 5 1/2 x 8 1/2

30 b/w photos

0-7818-0081-1   14.95pb

2 Cassettes

0-7818-0089-7 $12.95

Book and Cassettes Package

0-7818-0090-0 $27.90

In praise of the Mastering Series:

• "Truly the best book of its kind."

• "Your book is truly remarkable, and you are to be congratulated."
  —a field editor for college textbooks.

All prices subject to change.

TO PURCHASE HIPPOCRENE BOOKS contact your local bookstore, or write to: HIPPOCRENE BOOKS, 171 Madison Avenue, New York, NY 10016. Please enclose check or money order, adding $5.00 shipping (UPS) for the first book and $.50 for each additional book.

HIPPOCRENE BEGINNER'S SERIES

Do you know what it takes to make a phone call in Russia? To get through customs in Japan? How about inviting a Czech friend to dinner while visiting Prague? This new language instruction series shows how to handle typical, day-to-day situations by introducing the business person or traveler not only to the common vocabulary, but also to the history and customs.

The Beginner's Series consists of basic language instruction, which includes vocabulary, grammar, and common phrases and review questions; along with cultural insights, interesting historical background, the country's basic facts, and hints about everyday living.

Beginner's Romanian
This is a guide designed by **Eurolingua**, the company established in 1990 to meet the growing demand for Eastern European language and cultural instruction. The institute is developing books for business and leisure travelers to all Eastern European countries. This Romanian learner's guide is a one-of-a-kind for those seeking instant communication in this newly independent country.
0-7818-0208-3 • $7.95 paper

Beginner's Hungarian
For the businessperson traveling to Budapest, the traveler searching for the perfect spa, or the Hungarian-American extending his or her roots, this guide by **Eurolingua** aids anyone searching for the words to express basic needs.
0-7818-0209-1 • $7.95 paper

Beginner's Czech
The city of Prague has become a major tour destination for Americans who are now often choosing to stay. Here is a guide to the complex language spoken by the natives in an easy to learn format with a guide to phonetics. Also, important Czech history is outlined with cultural notes. This is another guide designed by Eurolingua.
0-7818-0231-8 • $9.95

Beginner's Russian
Eurolingua authors **Nonna Karr** and **Ludmila Rodionova** ease English speakers in the Cyrillic alphabet, then introduce enough language and grammar to get a traveler or businessperson anywhere in the new Russian Republic. This book is a perfect stepping-stone to more complex language.
0-7818-0232-6 • $9.95

Beginner's Japanese

Author **Joanne Claypoole** runs a consulting business for Japanese people working in America. She has developed her Beginner's Guide for American businesspeople who work for or with Japanese companies in the U.S. or abroad.

Her book is designed to equip the learner with a solid foundation of Japanese conversation. Also included in the text are introductions to Hiragana, Katakana, and Kanji, the three Japanese writing systems.
0-7818-0234-2 • $11.95

Beginner's Esperanto

As a teacher of foreign languages for over 25 years, **Joseph Conroy** knows the need for people of different languages to communicate on a common ground. Though Esperanto has no parent country or land, it is developing an international society all its own. *Beginner's Esperanto* is an introduction to the basic grammar and vocabulary students will need to express their thoughts in the language.

At the end of each lesson, a set of readings gives the student further practice in Esperanto, a culture section presents information about the language and its speakers, a vocabulary lesson groups together all the words which occur in the text, and English translations for conversations allow students to check comprehension. As well, the author lists Esperanto contacts with various organizations throughout the world.
0-7818-0230-X • $14.95 (400 pages)

In addition to the above titles in the Beginner's Series, Hippocrene offers the following:

Beginner's Bulgarian
0-7818-0034-4 • $ 9.95 (200 pages)

Two volumes in the series have companion cassettes to aid in the language learning process:

Beginner's Polish	**Beginner's Swahili**
0-7818-0299-7 • $ 9.95 (200 pages)	0-7818-0335-7 • $ 9.95 (200 pages)
0-7818-0330-6 • $12.95 (cassettes)	0-7818-0336-5 • $12.95 (cassettes)

Available soon:
Beginner's Brazilian-Portuguese
0-7818-0338-1 • $ 9.95 (200 pages)

HIPPOCRENE LANGUAGE AND TRAVEL GUIDES

These guides provide an excellent introduction to a foreign country for the traveler who wants to meet and communicate with people as well as sightsee. Each book is also an ideal refresher course for anyone wishing to brush up on their language skills.

LANGUAGE AND TRAVEL GUIDE TO AUSTRALIA, by Helen Jonsen
Travel with or without your family through the land of "OZ" on your own terms; this guide describes climates, seasons, different cities, coasts, countrysides, rainforests, and the Outback with a special consideration to culture and language.
250 pages • $14.95 • 0-7818-0166-4 (0086)

LANGUAGE AND TRAVEL GUIDE TO FRANCE, by Elaine Klein
Specifically tailored to the language and travel needs of Americans visiting France, this book also serves as an introduction to the culture. Learn the etiquette of ordering in a restaurant, going through customs, and asking for directions.
320 pages • $14.95 • 0-7818-0080-3 (0386)

LANGUAGE AND TRAVEL GUIDE TO INDONESIA (Coming soon)
350 pages • $14.95 • 0-7818-0328-4 (0111)

LANGUAGE AND TRAVEL GUIDE TO MEXICO, by Ila Warner
Explaining exactly what to expect of hotels, transportation, shopping, and food, this guide provides the essential Spanish phrases, as well as describing appropriate gestures, and offering cultural comments.
224 pages • $14.95 • 0-87052-622-7 (503)

LANGUAGE AND TRAVEL GUIDE TO RUSSIA, by Victorya Andreyeva and Margarita Zubkus
Allow Russian natives to introduce you to the system they know so well. You'll be properly advised on such topics as food, transportation, the infamous Russian bath house, socializing, and sightseeing. Then, use the guide's handy language sections to be both independent and knowledgeable.
293 pages • $14.95 • 0-7818-0047-1 (0321)

LANGUAGE AND TRAVEL GUIDE TO UKRAINE, by Linda Hodges and George Chumak
Written jointly by a native Ukrainian and an American journalist, this guide details the culture, the people, and the highlights of the Ukrainian experience, with a convenient (romanized) guide to the essentials of Ukrainian.
266 pages • $14.95 • 0-7818-0135-4 (0057)